CW01676779

National Food Strategy

Independent Review

THE PLAN.

Contents

Introduction 6

Executive summary 12

1. Why it matters 16

The Health of the Planet 18

Our Health 27

2. Systems thinking 32

3. How did we get here? 40

4. Escaping the Junk Food Cycle 46

5. Inequality 60

6. Exposing the invisibility of nature 68

7. Food and climate 76

8. The complexities of meat 84

9. A nature-positive, carbon-negative food system 90

10. A Three Compartment Model 100

11. Can we have it all? 110

12. At what price? 116

13. The protein transition 124

14. Food security 134

15. Trade 142

16. The Plan 148

Chapter references 175

Appendices 203

Appendix 1 – Recommendation 1 204
Introduce a sugar and salt reformulation tax. Use some of the revenue to help get fresh fruit and vegetables to low income families.

Appendix 2 – Recommendation 2 213
Introduce mandatory reporting for large food companies.

Appendix 3 – Recommendation 3 216
Launch a new "Eat and Learn" initiative for schools.

Appendix 4 – Recommendation 4 222
Extend eligibility for free school meals.

Appendix 5 – Recommendation 5 226
Fund the Holiday Activities and Food programme for the next three years.

Appendix 6 – Recommendation 6 229
Expand the Healthy Start scheme.

Appendix 7 – Recommendation 7 233
Trial a "Community Eatwell" programme, supporting those on low incomes to improve their diets.

Appendix 8 – Recommendation 8 237
Guarantee the budget for agricultural payments until at least 2029 to help farmers transition to more sustainable land use.

Appendix 9 – Recommendation 9 244
Create a rural land use framework based on the Three Compartment Model.

Appendix 10 – Recommendation 10 249
Define minimum standards for trade, and a mechanism for protecting them.

Appendix 11 – Recommendation 11 252
Invest £1 billion in innovation to create a better food system.

Appendix 12 – Recommendation 12 260
Create a National Food System Data programme.

Appendix 13 – Recommendation 13 264
Strengthen government procurement rules to ensure that taxpayer money is spent on healthy and sustainable food.

Appendix 14 – Recommendation 14 271
Set clear targets and bring in legislation for long-term change.

Appendix 15 – Acknowledgments 276

Appendix 16 – Who we have met 280

Appendix 17 – Additional reading list 288

Appendix 18 – Terms of Reference 290

Appendix 19 – The problems of BMI measurement in children 292

Appendix 20 – Call for Evidence 294

Glossary 296

Acronyms 300

In July of last year, I published Part One of the National Food Strategy, a Government-commissioned independent review into the food system. This had originally been intended as a broad analysis of the strengths and flaws of the entire food system from farm to fork, with Part Two following on behind with recommendations. But COVID-19 intervened, and Part One became instead an urgent response to the issues of hunger and ill health raised by the pandemic, as well as the trade and food standards issues created by the end of the EU Exit transition period.

Part One contained seven specific recommendations, intended to help the most disadvantaged families eat well, protect the UK's high food standards and ensure proper scrutiny of any trade deals. The Government has already agreed to implement four of those. I will be returning to the other three in this report. (Please see the box on page 5 for details.)

For Part Two, I have returned to the original brief. In these pages, we will take a close look at how the food system really works, the damage it is doing to our bodies and our ecosystem, and the interventions we could make to prevent these harms. We will consider the characteristics of complex systems and the mechanisms that cause system failures. And we will set out a strategy for the future, based not just on rigorous science but on the needs and wishes of ordinary citizens.

In writing this strategy, I have been able to call upon the research, commitment, energy and insight of academics, farmers, scientists, business leaders, charity workers, politicians and experts from many fields, some of whom are on our Advisory Panel (see Acknowledgements, p. 264). Above all, I have been lucky enough to work with a dedicated and extraordinary group of civil servants and consultants, led by the indefatigable Tamsin Cooper. Together, we have spent the past two years travelling the country, holding Zoom meetings, talking to people from all over the food system, crunching numbers, digging into research, questioning received wisdoms, running mathematic models and inspecting policy ideas for hidden bear traps. I usually refer to "us" and "we" in this report because it has been such a collaborative effort.

In the course of researching this strategy, we – the National Food Strategy team – conducted extensive interviews with people at the sharp end of the food system. We also held "deliberative dialogues" with citizens across the country to establish what changes the public is willing to embrace. The recommendations we have put together are intended to create the kind of food system the people of this country say they want – and need.

The food system we have now has evolved over many years. It won't be easy to reshape it. But time is not on our side. The effects of climate change are already becoming apparent around the world. Diet-related disease is putting an intolerable strain on our nation's health and finances – and COVID-19 has only increased the pressure. For our own health, and that of our planet, we must act now.

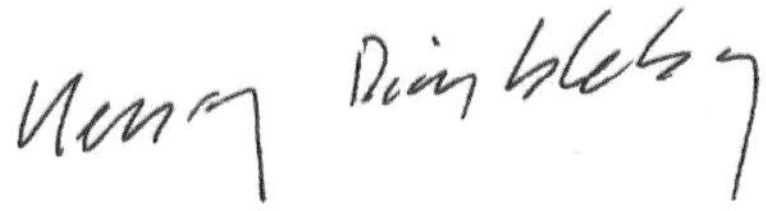

Government's response to Part One

The Government has already acted on four of the seven recommendations in Part One of the National Food Strategy:

- The Government **extended the Holiday Activities and Food programme (HAF)** to all areas in England for the duration of 2021. These holiday clubs will run four days a week for four weeks over the summer, and again this Christmas. They provide hot food, cooking lessons, sports and fun activities for children, as well as advice for families and carers on how to source, prepare and cook nutritious, low-cost food. They are free to all children in receipt of free school meals (FSM). The majority of local authorities are also making these clubs available to children who aren't eligible for FSM, for a small fee. The Government has made a total of £220 million available to fund HAF programmes in 2021.[1]
- The Government **increased the value of Healthy Start vouchers** from £3.10 to £4.25 per week.[2] Parents or carers of babies under 12 months now receive two Healthy Start vouchers per week to spend on vitamins, fruit, vegetables and milk. Several national supermarket chains have also stepped forward to supplement the value of the vouchers. For example, Sainsbury's agreed to top up the vouchers by a further £2, Waitrose by £1.50 and Tesco, Iceland and Co-op by £1.[3]
- The Government agreed to continue collecting, assessing, and monitoring **data on the number of people suffering from food insecurity.** The Department for Work and Pensions has established a Cost of Living Roundtable, where food vulnerability is discussed (alongside other issues affecting those living in poverty) across government. The UK Food Security Assessment and DWP's Family Resource Survey has also been updated to cover the issue of household food security.
- The Government adopted the recommendation that it **should commission an independent report on any proposed trade agreement**, assessing its impact on economic productivity, food safety and public health, the environment and climate change, society and labour, human rights and animal welfare; and that this report should be presented alongside a Government response when any final trade treaty is laid before Parliament.

The Government has not implemented two of the other recommendations on trade. It has not committed to **giving preferential tariffs to food products which meet our core standards**, nor **to giving Parliament the time and opportunity to properly scrutinise any new trade deal**. The first of these is particularly concerning, and we return to it in Chapter 15. The Government appears to be heading in a direction on trade that not only means it will break its own manifesto commitments, it will undermine the huge efforts it is making domestically to mitigate climate change, restore nature and improve animal welfare.

The Government has not implemented the recommendation to **expand the eligibility for the free school meal** scheme to include every child (up to the age of 16) from a household where a parent or guardian is in receipt of Universal Credit, or equivalent benefits. We return to this in Chapter 16.

Our scope

England and the United Kingdom

The Terms of Reference for this report set its geographic scope as England but ask us also to consider our "relationship with the devolved administrations, the European Union and our other trading partners". Policy responsibility for food and health is largely devolved to Scotland, Wales and Northern Ireland. The notable exceptions are trade, taxation and welfare.

However, our food systems are so tightly interwoven as to be in places inextricable: for example, almost 600 farms straddle England's borders with Scotland or Wales. So we have worked closely with, and learned much from, the food strategy teams of the devolved authorities. I hope they might in turn find some useful ideas in this document.

Food vs Drink

The strategy covers the production, marketing, processing, sale and purchase of food and non-alcoholic drinks for consumption in the home and out of it.

The Oceans

In this report we have concentrated our energies on the two most urgent problems embedded in the food system: what we have termed the Junk Food Cycle and the Invisibility of Nature. Addressing the harms caused just by these destructive feedback loops, particularly against our most deprived communities, is a daunting task.

We have deliberately narrowed our focus onto the land, but there is a parallel story to be told about the seas.

Between 1970 and 2012, global marine biodiversity is estimated to have fallen by 49%. That means that nearly half of all our marine mammals, birds, reptiles and fish species have experienced a substantial loss in a relatively short space of time.[4]

No form of fishing has caused more harm than bottom trawling. Since the 1890s, when fossil-fuel powered bottom trawling began, there has been a staggering decline in overall fish abundance. Cod landings have declined by 87%, hake by 95%. For halibut, the decline is a catastrophic 99.8%.[5] To put this in perspective, in the 1830s small sailing vessels around the Dogger Bank could catch a tonne of halibut per day. Today, all fishing across the entire Dogger Bank lands less than two tonnes of halibut a year.[6]

Recent research suggests that, as well as causing biodiversity collapse, stirring up the seabed releases large quantities of so-called "blue carbon" from marine sediments, which would otherwise remain locked away in the seabed.[7]

The UK is already proposing to establish Marine Protected Areas (MPAs) covering nearly half of the UK's territorial waters.[8] Similar preservation areas in Scotland and South Africa have seen fish stocks recover fast.[9] But they are not without their opponents. According to the National Federation of Fishermen's Organisations, the MPAs are being implemented as part of an "insanely rushed" policy[10] – a "blitzkrieg approach" – run by "a cohort of environmental zealots".[11]

Inevitably, both camps have some pertinent insights. Changing the way we use our oceans will be a huge transition. It will require a similarly nuanced, and diverse, approach to the one we are proposing for the land.

Allergens

One of the less-discussed symptoms of our flawed food system is the extraordinary rise in food allergies.

There has been a 338% increase in children's A&E admissions caused by food allergies since

1998.[12] There are now two million people in the UK suffering from food allergies (1–2% of adults, and up to 5–8% of children).[13]

The reasons for this rise are still unclear – environment, genetics and the gut microbiome might all play a part. Clearly, we need more and better scientific research to help us understand what causes food allergies, and how to treat them.

In the meantime, the Government has introduced new legislation to improve allergy labelling – known as Natasha's Law after Natasha Ednan-Laperouse, who died in 2016 after eating unlabelled sesame seed flour in a sandwich. This law will come into force in October 2021 and requires businesses to label all packaged food with full ingredients.

Production vs Consumption

The Government has committed to reducing the UK's carbon production to 78% below 1990 levels by 2035, and to Net Zero by 2050.[14] This is one of the most ambitious targets in the world, and has been justly praised. But it contains an accounting error. This target only measures the carbon produced within the UK; it ignores the carbon generated by goods that are produced or manufactured abroad and then imported into this country.

Logically, in fact, the quickest way for this country to reach Net Zero would be simply to shut down all domestic agriculture and manufacturing, and import everything we need from abroad – shrugging off our carbon responsibilities altogether. This is clearly an absurd notion, but following the logic of an idea to its absurd conclusion can help us grasp its unintended consequences.

The danger of outsourcing environmental damage is especially acute for the food system, which is the predominant cause of biodiversity loss and rainforest destruction, and the second-largest emitter of greenhouse gases in the global economy.[15] It makes no sense for politicians, farmers and manufacturers in this country to put in all the work necessary to create a sustainable domestic food system only to find the market flooded with food imports produced in ways that cause environmental devastation abroad.

Measuring the emissions created by domestic production remains vitally important (not least because of the Government's legal commitment to reaching net zero). In this report, however, we consider consumption, as well as production, when measuring the environmental damage caused by our food system. This enables us to assess more honestly the effect our consumption of food has on the environment, both here and abroad.

Where we have been and who we have met

Over the course of developing this report, our team has travelled all over the UK, and to parts of Europe, to experience first-hand some of the moving parts of the food system. We have watched drones whizzing around food distribution centres, visited soilless fruit farms, walked across newly restored peat fields, spongy underfoot, eaten in community kitchens and holiday food clubs, and toured abattoirs, agro-forests and processing plants. We also witnessed at close quarters how the food system responded and adapted to its biggest disruption in recent history: the COVID-19 pandemic.

On top of the 300-plus organisations we consulted for ideas, advice and data (see full list on page 268), our team engaged with just under 180 citizens in a series of "deliberative dialogues" in five locations (Grimsby, Bristol, Lewisham, Kendal and Norwich). Fifty of these people joined us at a Citizen Summit in April 2021, where they got a chance to discuss their insights and experiences of the food system with senior civil servants, MPs and the heads of food businesses and NGOs.

We also held three town hall events in York, Manchester and Birmingham, where over 100 people, local businesses, community groups, healthcare professionals and elected members came together to explore food issues.

The Food Foundation carried out consultations with young people on our behalf. Over 400 young people came together in 24 workshops at 15 secondary schools and 9 youth groups to discuss food in relation to their health, the environment and affordability.

The food industry provides employment to nearly one in every seven people in this country, in both town and country. And absolutely everyone participates in it as a consumer. We wanted this strategy to be informed by the broadest possible range of experiences. The map below (Figure 1) shows the locations we have visited.

Figure 1

Locations we visited

- Conferences and roundtables
- Farm or food chain visit
- Research organisation
- Public dialogues and youth workshops
- Food banks and social enterprises
- Schools and hospitals

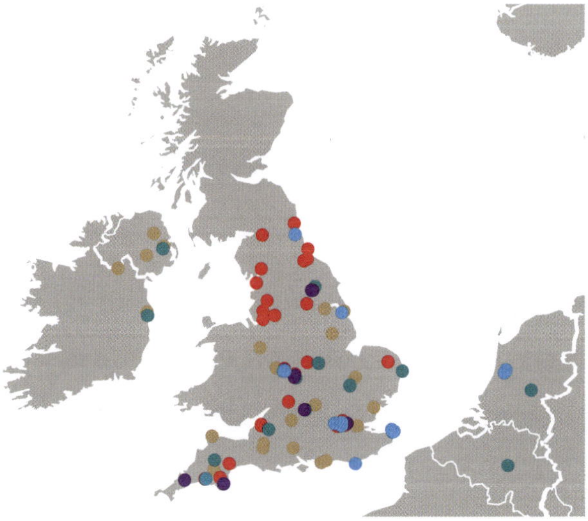

Executive summary

THE food system we have today is both a miracle and a disaster. Defying Malthusian predictions of mass famine, modern intensive agriculture produces more than enough calories (albeit unevenly distributed) to feed 7.8 billion of us: the biggest global population in human history.[1]

But the food we eat – and the way we produce it – is doing terrible damage to our planet and to our health. The global food system is the single biggest contributor to biodiversity loss, deforestation, drought, freshwater pollution and the collapse of aquatic wildlife. It is the second-biggest contributor to climate change, after the energy industry.

Our eating habits are destroying the environment. And this in turn threatens our food security. The next big shock to our food supply will almost certainly be caused by climate change in the form of extreme weather events and catastrophic harvest failures. Agriculture alone produces 10% of UK greenhouse gas emissions, despite constituting less than 1% of our GDP.[2]

Cheap, highly processed food is also taking a toll on our bodies. Eighty per cent of processed food sold in the UK is unhealthy.[3] There is a sound commercial reason for this: unhealthy food is more popular. The human appetite evolved in a world where calories were hard to come by. We are predisposed to pounce on any food that is high in fat and sugar. And once we start eating this kind of food, we are programmed to keep going: our hormones take longer to send out satiety signals (the feeling of fullness) than they do with lower-calorie foods.

Because there is a bigger market for unhealthy food, companies invest more into developing and marketing it. This in turn expands the market further still. The bigger the market, the greater the economies of scale. Highly processed foods – high in salt, refined carbohydrates, sugar and fats, and low in fibre – are on average three times cheaper per calorie than healthier foods. This is one reason why bad diet is a particularly acute problem among the least affluent.[4]

We have become trapped in a vicious circle – the Junk Food Cycle. The consequences for our health are devastating. The UK is now the third-fattest country in the G7, with almost three in ten of our adult population obese.[5] The Institute for Health Metrics and Evaluation (IHME) does an annual estimate of how many years of healthy life have been lost to avoidable illness, disability and death. Four out of the top five risk factors are diet related.[6]

This plague of dietary ill health crept up on us slowly, without generating much public uproar. But the COVID-19 pandemic has provided a painful reality check. Our obesity problem has been a major factor in the UK's tragically high death rate.

The UK now has a once-in-a-lifetime opportunity to reshape the food system. The pandemic has created a momentum for change – in Government and in industry, as well as among the public. There is widespread recognition that we need to change our national diet as a matter of urgency.

The CEOs of several major food companies have told us that the pandemic has shocked them into wanting to do things better. As one put it: "You wouldn't believe it if you look at our collective record in the past, but it is without doubt true. Something has changed fundamentally." They also told us, however, that some changes will require legislation to ensure a level playing field. If food companies are to start making their products healthier, they must be confident that the competition won't simply move in and undercut them.

The environmental damage caused by intensive agriculture must also be addressed. Our exit from the European Union has already required the government to draw up a new system of agricultural subsidies. The proposed Environmental Land Management scheme (ELMs) will – if properly implemented – reward those farmers who manage their land sustainably and work to restore biodiversity. But it won't be enough on its own.

The Government has made a legal commitment to reduce the UK's carbon emissions to net zero by 2050 and pledged to ensure that 30% of our land is protected for nature by 2030. In order to meet these commitments, we will have to ask a lot from our land – and from those who tend it.

The farming sector itself will have to become carbon neutral, something the National Farmers' Union has already committed to. But some areas of farmland will also have to be repurposed or adapted so that they actively sequester carbon, mopping up the emissions from those industries (such as air travel and heavy industry) that will still largely depend on fossil fuels for the foreseeable future; all this, while maintaining a steady supply of affordable food. We will have to produce more food from the remaining land without resorting to the kind of intensive farming practices that have already done so much damage.

This feat of acrobatics is achievable – but only with a concerted effort of will. We will need to draw on diverse methods of agriculture, including regenerative farming practices that work with nature instead of against it. We must invest in the latest science – AI, robots and new breeding techniques – to increase yields without polluting the land. We must unleash the potential of soilless farming, develop new proteins, and tap the plant-farming potential of the oceans instead of just pillaging them for fish.

Some farmers are introducing livestock back into traditional rotations, to improve the soil and reduce the need for fertilisers. Careful livestock farming can be a boon to the environment, but our current appetite for meat is unsustainable: 85% of total land that produces UK food is used to graze livestock or produce crops to feed to animals.[7] We need some of that land back.

The Government's Climate Change Committee has said we must reduce the amount of meat we eat by 20–50% in order for the UK to reach net zero by 2050.[8] In this strategy, we have set a goal of a 30% reduction over ten years. This is significant, and it won't be easy to achieve.

One idea that has been proposed is the imposition of a "meat tax". We quickly realised this would be politically impossible. It was – by a long way – the least popular of any measure we discussed with citizens in our "deliberative dialogues". It would also have the consequence of penalising poorer households, because the tax would have to be imposed by weight. The price hike on cheap cuts or mince would be proportionally much bigger than on, say, steak.

For now, at least, we believe the Government would be better off nudging consumers into changing their habits while investing in methane-reduction projects and the development of alternative proteins. In much the same way that multiple state interventions have made renewable energy cheaper than fossil fuels, this would create a shift in behaviour without the need for an unpopular and regressive tax.

Farmers must be at the centre of this transition in our food system. They are the custodians of the land. They know better than anyone how depleted the soil is and how reduced wildlife numbers are. Many farmers are already trialling new ways to manage their land for the benefit of nature.

But farms are businesses, not philanthropic hobbies. They need to make a profit. They cannot be expected to develop and adopt more sustainable practices – including some that will deliberately lower their yields, and some that return the land entirely to nature – if it destroys their balance sheet. We are asking farmers to change the way they work for the public good. We must ensure they are properly recompensed. And we must protect them from unfair competition.

This will be impossible if we don't get our trade deals right. There is no point making UK farmers do all the hard work necessary to reduce carbon emissions and restore biodiversity only to open up the market to cheap food produced to lower standards abroad. This would mean exporting all the environmental harms we wish to avoid, while undercutting – and potentially bankrupting – our own farmers.

The Government needs a trade policy that supports its environmental ambitions. Otherwise we will end up transferring damaging practices from one part of the planet to another and driving thousands of our own farmers to the wall.

The National Food Strategy contains recommendations to address the major issues facing the food system: climate change, biodiversity loss, land use, diet-related disease, health inequality, food security and trade. We have grouped them under four main National Food Strategy objectives (see box on following page):

Strategic Objectives

1. **Escape the junk food cycle to protect the NHS.**
2. **Reduce diet-related inequality.**
3. **Make the best use of our land.**
4. **Create a long-term shift in our food culture.**

Some of our recommendations will be met with protests from those industries whose business models are shaped to fit the current food system. Change is never easy. But we cannot build a sustainable, healthy and fair food system by doing business as usual.

This is an interventionist strategy. Even without the exacerbating effect of COVID-19, the damage being done to our health and our planet by the food system demands urgent action.

However, state intervention is rarely, if ever, sufficient by itself. You can't send in the army to improve the cooking in schools, or imprison people for serving bad hospital meals. Every delicious and nourishing plate of food that has ever been set before a hungry person tasted good because of the skill, effort and care of the individual who made it. Every school that serves its pupils appetising, nutritious lunches instead of fodder that is bland, boring, beige and bad for you does so because of a head teacher, school cook or business manager who aspired to something better. Change starts at a local level, with talented and dedicated people.

Some of our recommendations are designed to encourage and harness this individual energy, by making connections within neighbourhoods, communities and professions, investing in skills, and challenging unspoken assumptions about how things work and what is possible.

Transforming the food system will require change at all levels: structural, cultural, local and individual. But it is work that must be done. If we seize this opportunity, we can improve our health, protect our environment and build a better future for our children and grandchildren.

Please see Chapter 16 for our recommendations

1

Why it matters

The Health of the Planet

Worried about biodiversity loss?	Focus on food.
Worried about freshwater supply and quality?	Focus on food.
Worried about deforestation?	Focus on food.
Worried about overfishing?	Focus on food.
Worried about climate change?	Focus on energy, and food.

Richard Waite, World Resources Institute, April 2021[1]

BEFORE we get into the faulty mechanics of the food system, let us take a moment to consider its extraordinary achievement. It feeds us. Billions of us. More humans than ever before in history.

The two graphics on page 16 illustrate how successfully humans have thrived since we first began to farm our own food. The first shows the estimated biomass of humans and wild land-dwelling vertebrates (mammals and birds) on the planet in 10,000 BC. This was the start of the Holocene era, when global temperatures entered an unprecedented era of stability, and agriculture became possible. At this point, there were 2.5 million humans on Earth – a population dwarfed by the multitude of wild animals.

Figure 1.2 shows the situation today. The population of humans has swollen to 7.8 billion. The biomass of wild animals has withered, in part thanks to our enthusiastic hunting of megafauna (the first big extinction event caused by humans), destruction of habitats, pollution and environmental damage. The animals we keep, as pets and for leisure (green circle), now weigh almost as much as all the wild mammals and birds on the planet put together.[2]

Success breeds its own problems. We have a lot of mouths to feed. Around 50% of Earth's habitable land is now used for agriculture. Our appetite for meat and dairy products puts a particular strain on the Earth's resources: 77% of the world's farmland[3] is used to graze animals or to produce crops to feed to animals (see Figure 1.3). The combined weight of animals bred for food is now ten times the combined weight of all wild mammals and birds put together.

Figure 1.1

12,000 years ago humans were a tiny proportion of biomass compared to wild animals[4]

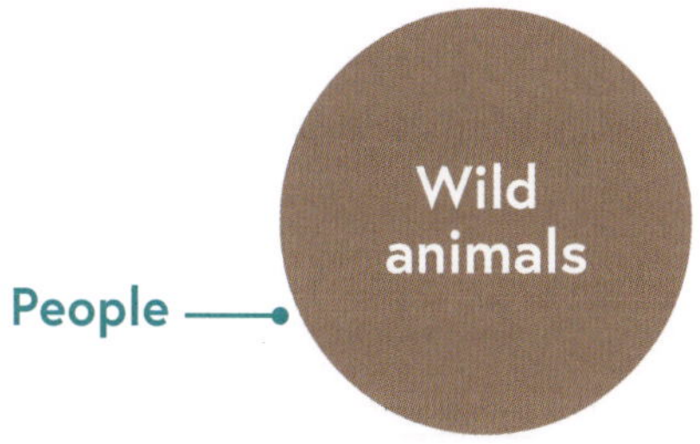

Figure 1.2

Today, the combined weight of animals bred for food dwarfs that of the combined weight of all wild mammals and birds put together[5]

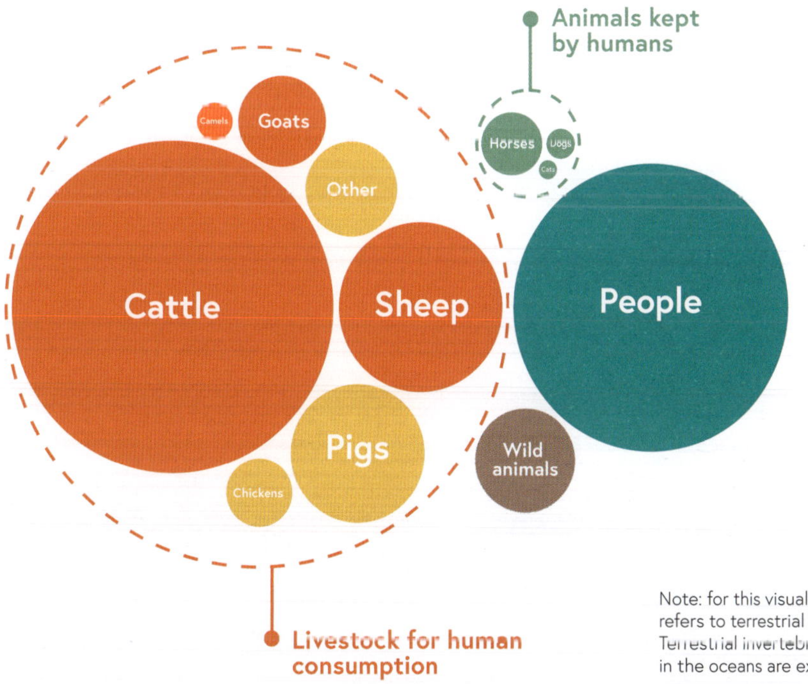

Note: for this visualisation "animals" refers to terrestrial vertebrates. Terrestrial invertebrates and all life in the oceans are excluded.

Figure 1.3

More than 77% of the world's farmland is used to graze animals or to produce crops to feed to animals[6]

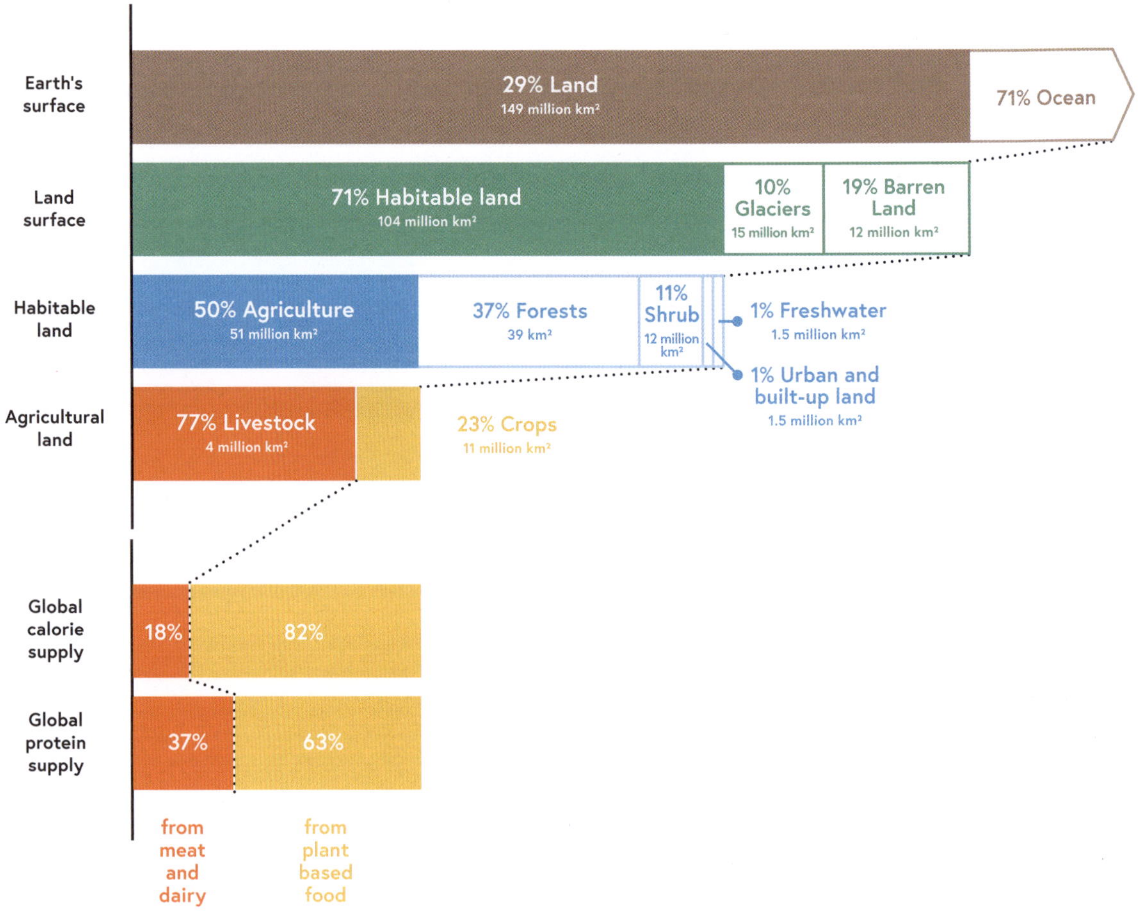

Biodiversity

The ingenuity with which the human race has used the Earth to feed itself has been disastrous for the global ecosystem. As Homo sapiens have thrived, almost all other forms of wildlife have declined. The wild biomass of mammals has fallen by 85% since the rise of human civilisation.[7] A quarter of all remaining mammal species are currently threatened with extinction as their natural habitats are converted to food production.[8]

The state of our oceans is no better. The Food and Agriculture Organisation of the UN estimates that 35% of stocks globally are being fished at unsustainable levels, up from 10% in 1974 (see Figure 1.4).

It might seem an odd question, but why does this collapse in natural abundance matter? The American biologist Edward O. Wilson sets out the answer in his seminal work, *The Diversity of Life*.

He starts from a utilitarian standpoint. It is impossible to put a true value on genetic diversity, he points out, because we cannot know its worth to future generations. He takes as an example the rosy periwinkle (Catharanthus Roseus) of Madagascar. In the fifties, this pretty herbaceous flower was found to produce two alkaloids[†] that cure most victims of two deadly cancers – Hodgkin's disease, which mostly afflicts young adults, and acute lymphocytic leukaemia, which used to be a death sentence for children. By the early nineties, the income from the manufacture and sale of these two substances exceeded $180 million.Over 40% of today's medicines are extracted from plants, microorganisms or animals.[9] Yet, as Wilson notes, 99% of all of the species that ever lived are now extinct. Who knows what medicinal potential has vanished with them?

[†] Vinblastine and vincristine.

Figure 1.4

Globally, 35% of stocks are being fished at unsustainable levels[10]

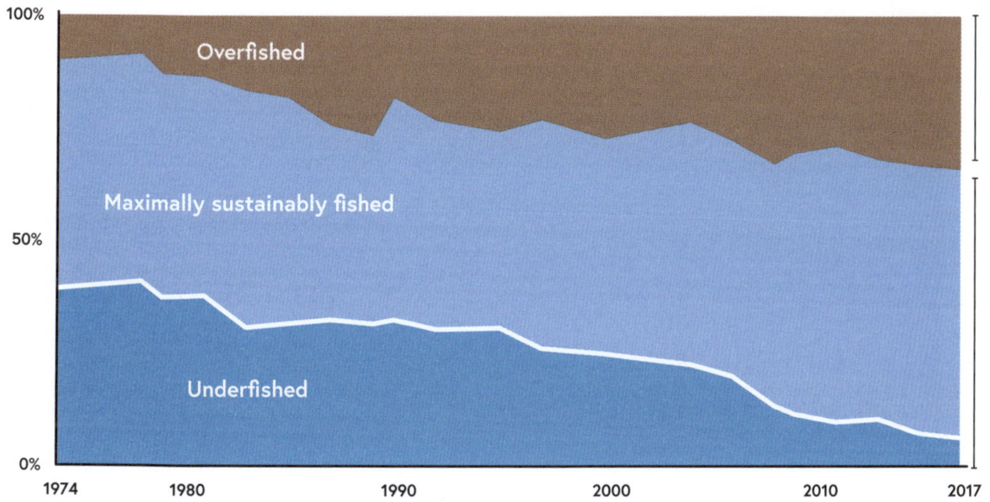

Another utilitarian argument for genetic diversity is that it could help future-proof the food system. Currently, while 300,000 species of plant have edible parts, just 20 species account for 90% of the world's food, and three – wheat, maize and rice – supply more than half.[11] To be so heavily reliant on a tiny handful of crops puts humanity in a precarious position. "This thin cushion of diversity," writes Wilson, "is biased toward cooler climates, and in most parts of the world is sown in monocultures sensitive to disease and attacks from insects and nematode worms. Modern agriculture is only a sliver of what it could be. Waiting in the wings are tens of thousands of unused plants." These alternative crops could be farmed as they are, or their traits bred into other plants to increase the resilience of the food system as our climate changes.

Only 20 species make up 90% of the world's food

Beyond the utilitarian arguments, there is the intrinsic – to some even sacred – value of nature. "Wilderness settles peace on the soul because it needs no help; it is beyond human contrivance," writes Wilson. Being in nature, having access to wild spaces, enriches the human spirit. It raises the quality of human life. And leaving humans out of the equation altogether, the natural world is precious in and of itself.

The precise motive doesn't matter as much as the shared imperative: to halt the destruction of nature, and to restore it to abundance. "The stewardship of environment," Wilson concludes, "is a domain on the nearside of metaphysics where all reflective persons can surely find common ground".

Abiotic systems

Biodiversity is not the only element of the natural world that has been radically disrupted by our food system. Its effect on nature's abiotic systems has also been dire. An abiotic system is a cycle in which nature recycles non-living things. The three most important of these are the water, nitrogen and carbon cycles, all of which are vital to maintaining the delicate balance of life on Earth.

The water cycle sees water enter our atmosphere, largely through the evaporation of sea water. When warm air hits cold air, it condenses and falls out of the sky as rain, snow or hail. Fresh water makes up only 3% of the world's water and yet is essential to life for almost all land-based creatures.[12] Farming uses 70% of all the fresh water on Earth.[13] The impacts of this – ranging from water shortages to drought, harvest failure, famine and even war – are more apparent abroad than in the wet, temperate climate of the UK, although we contribute to the problem by importing foods from drier regions (see Figure 1.5). But even in this country, the pumping of ground water to irrigate fields is a key contributor to droughts during hot summers.

The second major abiotic cycle is the nitrogen cycle. Plants need certain forms of nitrogen – chiefly nitrates and nitrites – to perform many of their critical functions. Bacteria in the soil, and attached to the roots of some plants, convert nitrogen from the atmosphere and turn it into nitrates and nitrites, which are then absorbed by plants. When the plant dies (or is eaten) and eventually returns to the soil, a different set of "denitrifying" bacteria convert these chemicals back into nitrogen gas and release it into the atmosphere.

Figure 1.5

The UK is relatively water secure, but not in every region[14]

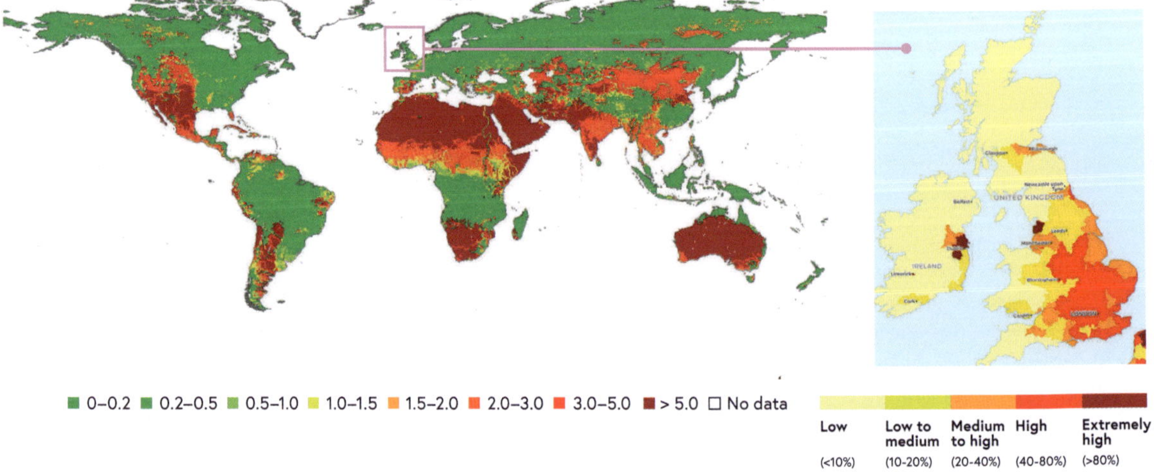

Note: this global map measures the ratio of blue water footprint in grid cells of 30 x 30 arc min to total blue water availability in the cell. The inset map measures the ratio of total annual water withdrawals to total available annual renewable supply, accounting for upstream consumptive use. Higher values indicate less water availability and more competition among users.

Figure 1.6

The UK has some of the most polluted waters in Europe[15]

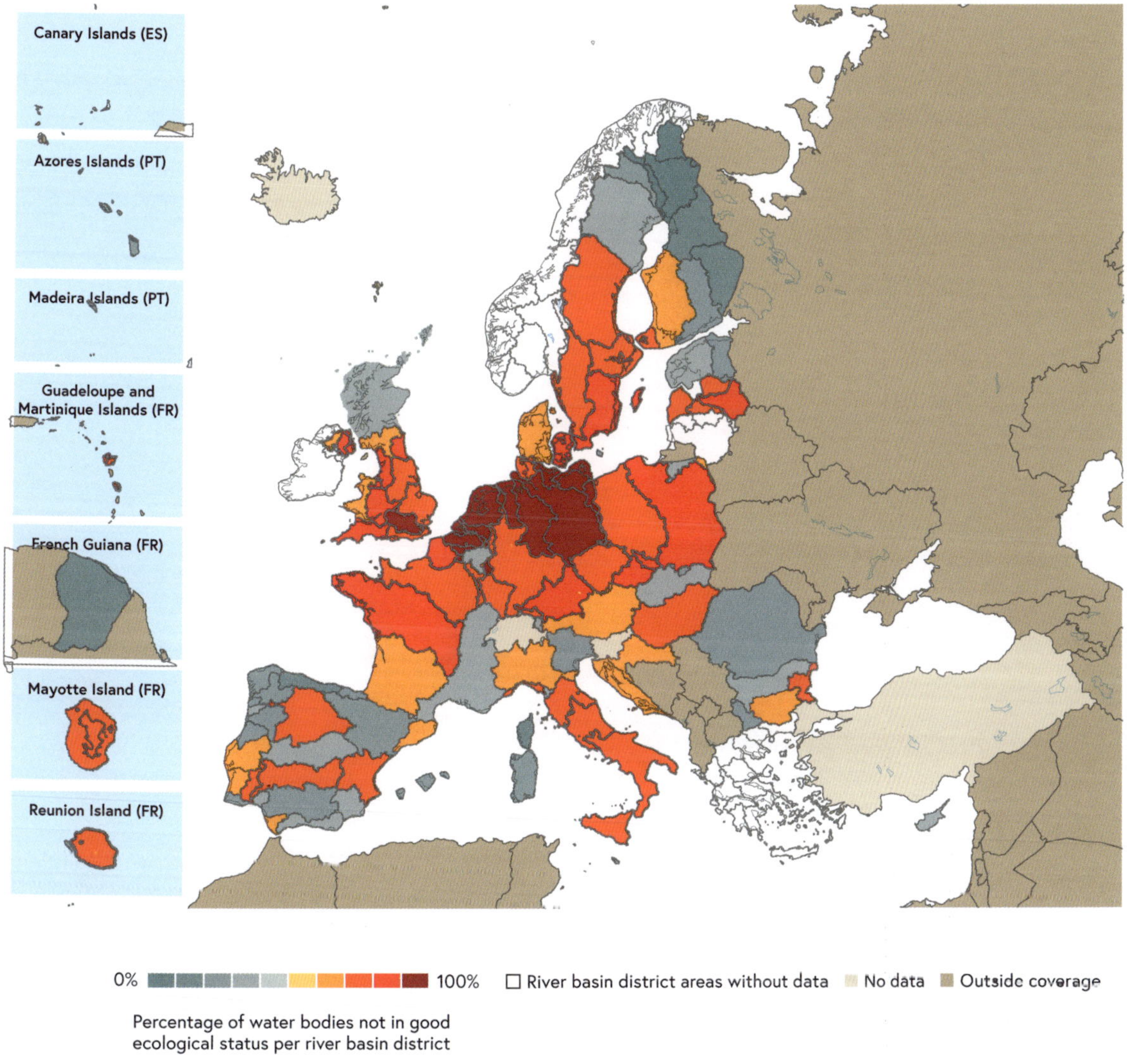

Intensive farming has played havoc with this cycle. The invention of the Haber–Bosch process at the start of the 20th century allowed scientists to use intense heat and pressure to combine nitrogen from the atmosphere with hydrogen to create ammonia, from which all industrial fertilisers are made. This process releases a huge amount of carbon in itself: 1% of global greenhouse gas emissions.[16] Once on the soil, man-made fertiliser – together with the vast quantity of slurry produced by our livestock – often leaches into our watercourses, with disastrous results.

Nitrogen run-off from farms is leading to high levels of eutrophication: excessive plant and algal blooms in both fresh and sea water. These blooms stop light penetrating the water, plunging entire ecosystems into darkness. Other plants can't grow. Fish and other animals cannot see to hunt, so they starve. Eutrophication can also raise the pH of water, making it uninhabitable for many species. When the algal blooms eventually die, their decomposing cells suck oxygen out of the water, creating hypoxic or anoxic dead zones in lakes and oceans. Run-off from farmland causes more than three-quarters of global eutrophication. In England, just 16% of our surface and ground waters meet the criteria for "good ecological status", and none of our lakes or rivers meet the criteria for "good chemical status". We have some of the most polluted waters in Europe (see Figure 1.6).

Finally, there's the carbon cycle – which we will be returning to again and again in this strategy. For now, suffice to say that the food system produces a huge amount of greenhouse gases. (This catch-all term is used to cover several different gases – primarily carbon dioxide, methane and nitrous oxide – all of which contribute to climate change in different ways.) Globally, the food system is responsible for up to one-third of all greenhouse gases (GHG), a figure that dwarfs the 3.5% caused by air travel.[17] In the UK, our domestic food system alone (ignoring the GHGs from the food we import) accounts for around 20% of our greenhouse gas emissions.[†18] The UK's food system has decarbonised at half the pace of the wider economy, and agriculture hasn't decarbonised at all in over a decade (Figure 1.7).

Figure 1.7

Since 2008, the food system has decarbonised at less than half the pace of the wider economy[19]

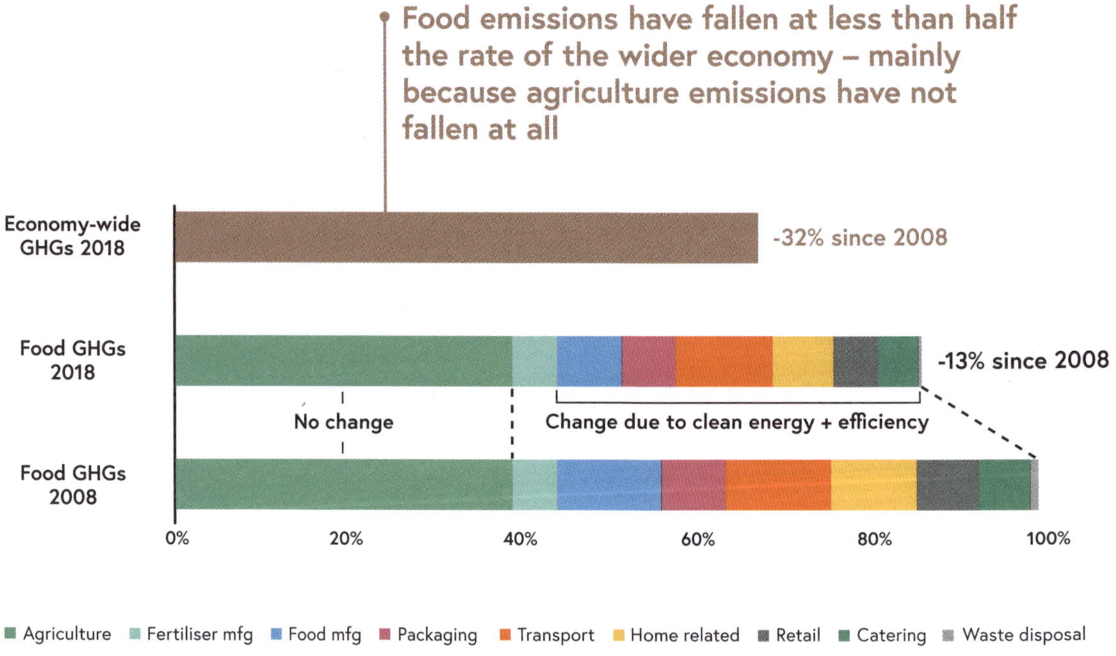

Antimicrobial resistance and zoonotic diseases

The history of infectious disease goes hand in hand with that of farming. It wasn't until early humans started to keep livestock that infectious diseases such as smallpox, malaria and yellow fever began to jump the species barrier and spread through human populations.[20]

The closer we live to animals – and the closer animals live to each other – the bigger the threat of zoonotic diseases. Unfortunately, cramming livestock together in intensive systems is one of the simplest ways to reduce the price of meat. On a purely commercial front, it has proved successful: the cost of chicken, for example, is nearly three times cheaper today than in the 1960s in real terms. (This accounts for its simultaneous rise in popularity, from 10% to 40% of UK meat consumption over the same period.)[21]

....

† The relationship between the rearing of ruminant livestock and climate change is complicated and we will go into it in much more detail in Chapter 7.

When chickens, pigs or cows are forced to live in crowded conditions – sometimes by the tens of thousands (see Figure 1.8) – disease is inevitable. This has led to the widespread use, and overuse, of antimicrobial drugs in farming. In some countries, antibiotics are routinely added to livestock feed, regardless of the health of the animals (see Figure 1.9), because it can make them grow faster: immune systems that aren't fighting off infections use less energy, leaving more for growth.

But the microbes have fought back, becoming resistant to many antibiotics – including some that are used to treat humans. Intensive farming of pigs and chickens is responsible for the majority of antimicrobial resistance worldwide. In some parts of the world, microbes have already evolved to resist 80% of the antibiotics used on animals.[22] Drug resistant infections could eventually make some surgeries, including caesarean sections, and cancer treatments too dangerous to perform.[23]

Figure 1.8

An intensive 12-storey pig production unit near Guigang in Southern China

Alongside the threat of antibiotic resistance, we must contend with the emergence of new zoonotic diseases – those that jump between species.

When forests and wild areas are cleared to make way for livestock farming, the animals that manage to survive the clearance tend to be rats and bats. These also happen to be the animals most likely to carry viruses that can infect other species.

Once such a virus passes into a livestock population, it can incubate and mutate until it is capable of infecting people.[24] Intensively reared animals, which are selectively bred to have nearly identical genomes, act as vast replication vessels for some viruses. Research shows that eight in ten of the animals that host viruses that cross into human populations are domesticated, with livestock in the lead.[25]

Over the past year we have seen how a new infectious disease – even one with a relatively low mortality rate – can devastate our health, economies and wellbeing.

Figure 1.9

In OECD countries, agricultural antibiotic use is highest in pig meat[26]

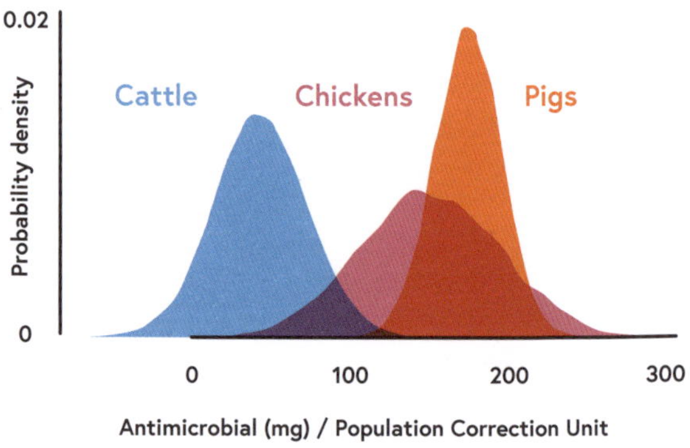

Figure 1.10

Globally, land use change has been the predominant cause of emerging infectious disease (EID)[†27]

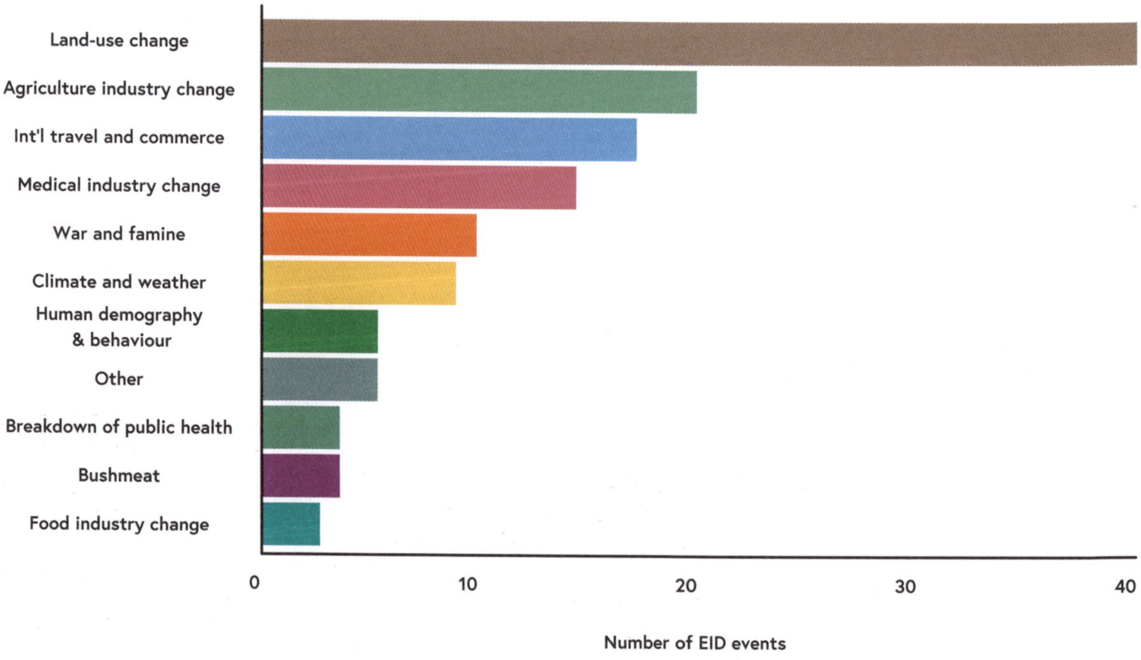

[†] Emerging infectious diseases are those that are either newly recognised or which existed but are rapidly increasing in incidence or geographic range.

Our Health

ALMOST one in three people over 45 in England is clinically obese.[28] This can be a tiring, depressing condition in itself. And it brings with it all sorts of attendant health problems. Being obese is like carrying around an enormous rucksack all day long: it takes a toll on your bones and joints.[29]

It also massively increases your risk of developing a chronic, life-changing illness, and of dying young.[30] There is a strong association between obesity and the likelihood of becoming severely ill or dying from COVID-19.[31] You are 1.5 times more likely to die from COVID-19 if you are obese, and this rises to 2.25 times more likely if you are severely obese.[32]

But you don't have to be fat to be made ill by bad diet. In England, one in three people over the age of 45 has diabetes or a heart condition – both conditions strongly associated with dietary ill health.[33] Some of these people register as obese; some are not even overweight. People with Type 2 diabetes (both controlled and uncontrolled) are 81% more likely to die from COVID-19.[34]

Figure 1.11 shows the number of years lost to ill health or death in the UK as a result of avoidable causes. All the circles in pink represent conditions that are caused or exacerbated by poor diet. Even smoking doesn't come close to doing the same amount of damage.

Figure 1.11

Proportion of years lost to avoidable ill health and death by cause[35]

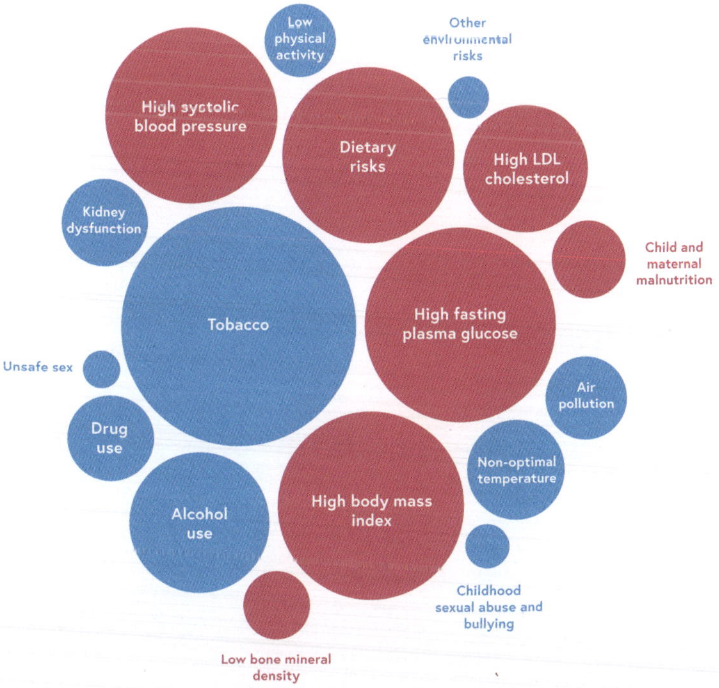

"Even before COVID-19 we had pressure on the NHS, and I think that is going to have a big impact in terms of making us think about food, because of the amount of sugar we're eating, red meat and all that kind of stuff."

"Deliberative dialogue" participant, London & the South East

It's extraordinary, really, that there isn't public uproar about this. Imagine if a novel virus suddenly started killing and disabling people on such a scale, and with no end in sight. You don't have to imagine it: we now know the lengths that politicians and the public would go to combat such a plague.

The trouble is, this disaster has crept up on us so slowly that we have forgotten to be shocked by it. This is a classic "systems trap", as described in Chapter 4. In this particular trap, sometimes called "boiling the frog", a system drifts downhill slowly enough that no-one panics about the decline until it's too late. Everyone is gently lulled into lower and lower expectations.

The average Brit now consumes five times the volume of crisps that we did in 1972 (see Figure 1.12). We eat 1.5 times the amount of breakfast cereal that we did in 1970 (and breakfast cereals have become much more sugary over the same period).[36] Similar shifts in behaviour have been repeated across the whole spectrum of our national diet. In 1980, on average, 57% of a household's grocery budget was spent on ingredients for home-cooked food. By 2000, this had fallen to 35%, while the share of processed foods which required little preparation rose from 26% to 45%.[37]

The cost of bad diet is astronomical, both in terms of human misery and actual money. The government spends an estimated £18 billion – 8% of all government healthcare expenditure – on conditions related to high BMI every year.[38] (This is before you account for diet-related disease not linked to weight.) In 2019/20, there were just over 1 million hospital admissions where obesity was recorded as the primary or secondary diagnosis – a 17% increase on 2018/19.[39] If we don't get diet-related disease under control, we risk overwhelming the NHS – or having to cut other public services to pay for it. Currently it is projected that by 2035/36 type 2 diabetes alone will cost the NHS 1.5 times the amount currently spent on treating all cancers.[40]

Ill people are also less able to work. The Organisation of Economic Co-operation and Development (OECD) estimates that the combined cost of conditions related to high BMI, in lost workforce productivity, reduction in life expectancy and NHS funds, is £74 billion every year. This is equivalent to cutting the UK's GDP by 3.4%.[41] To cover these costs, each person in the United Kingdom pays an additional £409 in taxes per year.[42]

Figure 1.12

Purchasing of crisps and sweetened breakfast cereals has risen sharply since the 1970s[43]

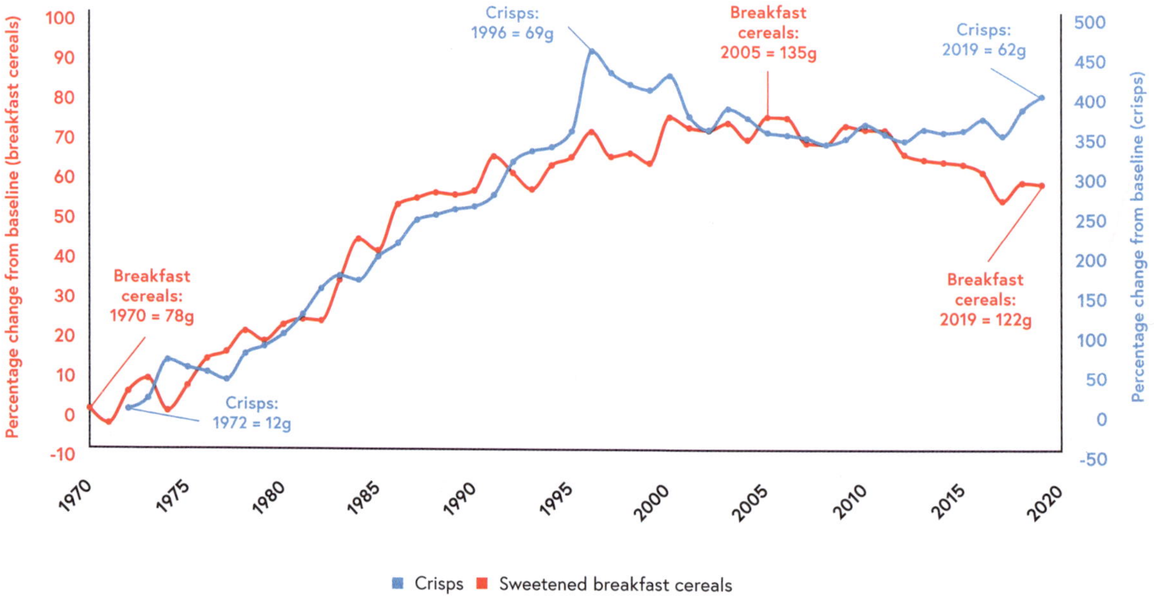

But perhaps the heaviest toll is on us as individuals: all those good years lost to sickness and early death. It is estimated that 1.5 million years of healthy life are lost to diet-related illness, disease and premature death each year.[44] Bringing everyone into the healthy BMI range alone could increase life expectancy by 2.7 years.[45] That could be the difference between getting to know your grandchildren or dying before they are born. For people in the poorest areas – who are more likely to suffer from diet related illness – the added years would be even greater.[46]

Changing the food system isn't just about averting disaster. It is also an opportunity to create something wonderful for ourselves. We can increase the beauty of our countryside, create more woodland, clearer waters and abundant wildlife. We can leave the Earth in better shape for our children – and ensure they have longer, healthier lives to enjoy it.

Figure 1.13

High BMI is strongly correlated with the chances of hospital admission[47]

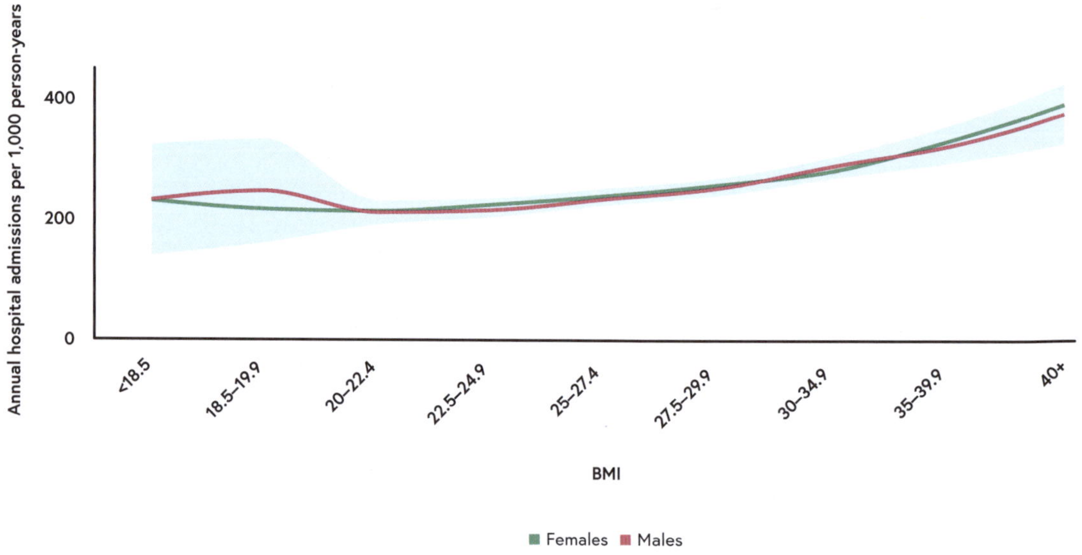

Figure 1.14

There is a link between excess NHS costs and BMI upon admission[48]

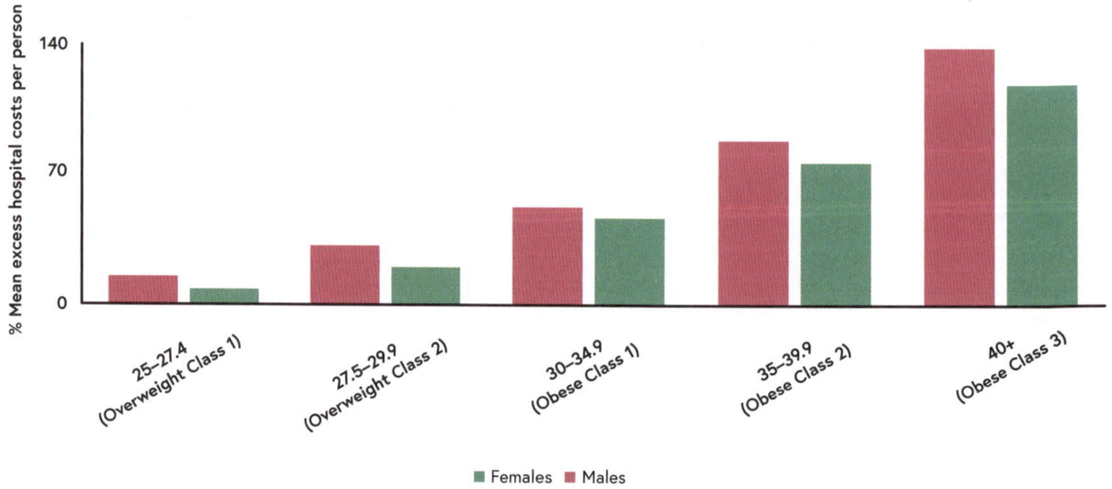

Note: Excess costs relative to healthy weight cohort.

Figure 1.15

Obesity is projected to keep rising[49]

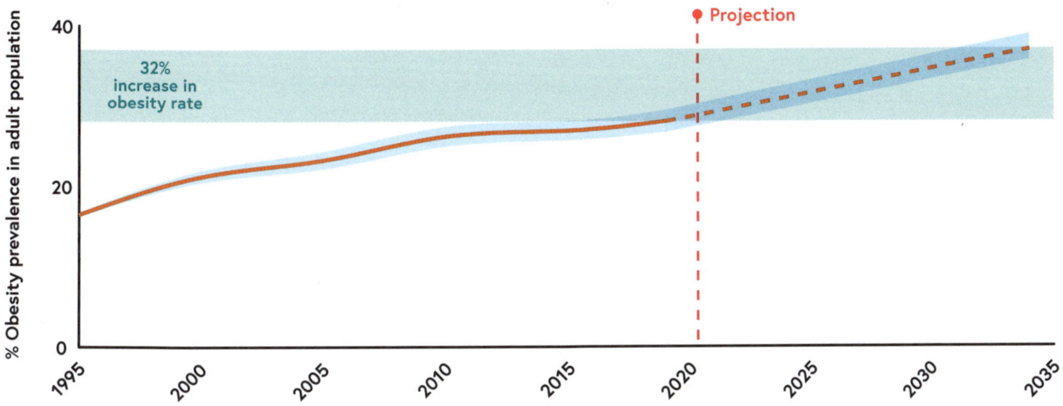

2

Systems thinking

FIRST things first. What do we actually mean by the "food system"? The dictionary definition of a system is any set of things working together as a larger whole, towards some purpose or end. The railway system, for example, is made up of tracks, trains, stations, train drivers and so on, all combining to get us about.

The food system is the combination of all of the elements – natural and man-made – that combine to produce, process, market and sell the food we eat and the connections between them. It can be said to include everything from the sun and the soil to the till at the corner shop.

When we started this report, we were urged by many experts in the field to take a "systems" approach. But when we asked what that approach would look like, we got several different responses. Some pointed to the Foresight Obesity Map, now famous in the field, which was produced in work commissioned by Government to tackle obesity in 2007 (see Figure 2.1). This intricate spider's web of a chart does a great job of illustrating the multifactorial nature of obesity, but it is of limited help in devising policy. In fact, the "it's complicated" approach to changing systems can be so demoralising that it actually stops us making progress. If change is this hard, is it even worth trying?

Figure 2.1

The Foresight Obesity System Map is mind-bogglingly complicated[1]

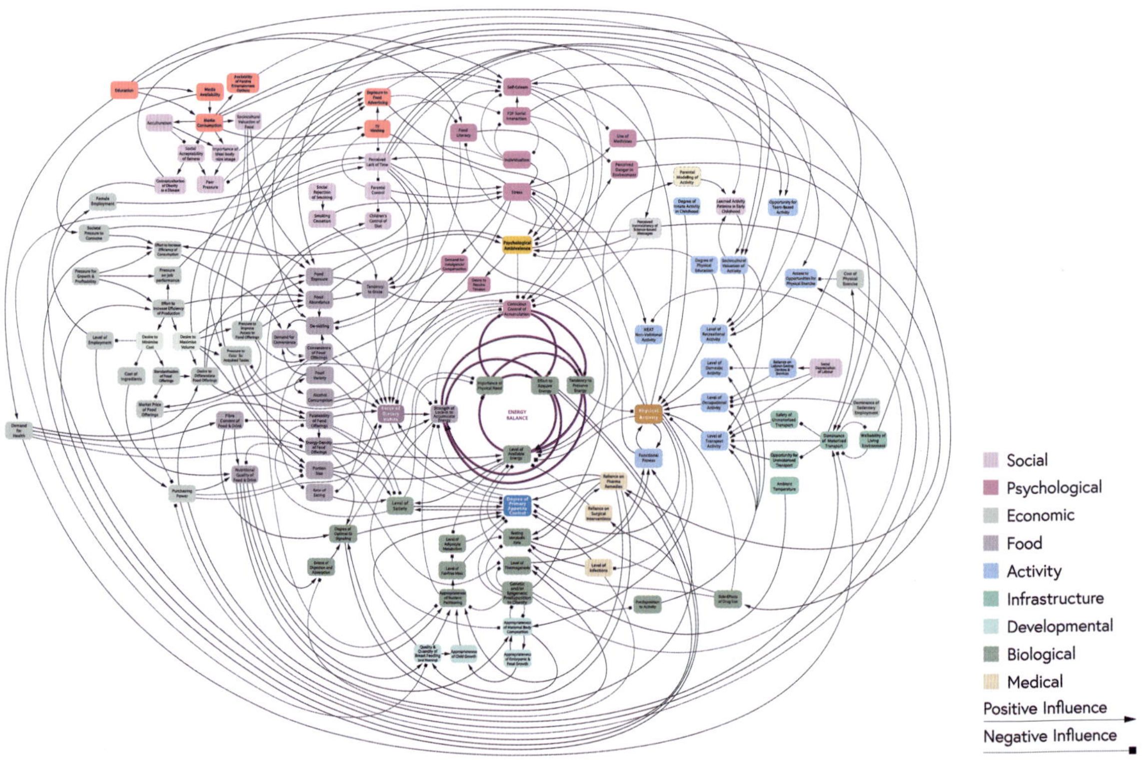

Another chart that was regularly pressed on us shows how responsibility for decision making on food policy is spread, like a thin layer of jam on toast, across government (Figure 2.2). There is no single department with responsibility for food, goes the argument: instead, every department gets a shout, and so chaos ensues. There is much to learn from this excellent chart, which was produced by Kelly Parsons for the Centre For Food Policy at City University, London.[2] We shall see how a lack of joined-up thinking between government departments has led to particular incoherence in the areas of trade and health policy.

But the food system is not unique in being regulated by multiple arms of government. An understanding of these relationships is important in policy making but not fundamental to understanding the system itself.

Another form of systems thinking which inevitably arises when considering food policy is the need to consider trade-offs. We want food to be more sustainable, but will that make it more expensive? Is there enough land to grow food sustainably and still feed the world? These are important questions, and we will address them explicitly.

Figure 2.2

Responsibility for food policy in England is highly dispersed[3]

Source: Adapted from Parsons, K. (2020). Who makes food policy in England? A map of governance actors and activities. Rethinking Food Governance Report 1. London: Food Research Collaboration

What has been most helpful to us in understanding the food system as a whole is the study of "system dynamics". This was developed in the early 1950s to enable scientists to create mathematical models to understand complex system behaviour.[4] It breaks all systems down into four component parts, each of which may be repeated many times: a "stock" (which is a quantity of something); a "flow" (the movement of that something from one place to another); "feedback loops" (which control the flow); and the "purpose" or "output" of the system.

Let us examine one tiny example: one of the countless smaller systems contained within the food system. Every leaf of every wheat plant is peppered with tiny holes called stomata: thousands of them per square centimetre.[5] Each stoma (the singular of the noun) is formed by two long, thin guard cells, connected to each other at both ends. These cells are banana shaped when full of water, bending outwards to create an oval hole in the middle. When empty, they lie straight alongside one another, sealing off the interior of the leaf.

The purpose of the stoma is to allow carbon dioxide (CO_2) into the leaf, where it is combined with water to produce glucose using the energy of the sun: photosynthesis. But while the hole is open, the plant loses precious water vapour through it. So the stomata must stay open long enough to let in sufficient CO_2, but not so long as to desiccate the plant. To perform this balancing act, the plant employs a series of feedback mechanisms.

As the sun rises, specialised proteins in the guard cells absorb photons. This changes their chemical structure, which in turn causes the plant to pump salt into the guard cells. The salt causes the cells to suck in water. They become banana shaped, and the stomata open. At night – when photosynthesis cannot take place – they close.

In the language of systems dynamics, these feedback mechanisms control the flow of stocks (CO_2 and water) so that the system can fulfil its purpose of enabling photosynthesis.

It is one of innumerable feedback systems in nature – in the plant, in the soil, in the atmosphere – that must all function properly for a single wheat plant to grow. And wheat, although providing 20% of our total calories, is only a small part of the food system we rely on to keep us nourished.[6] That system is made up of billions of interlinked smaller systems such as this one – some created by nature and some by man.

Stocks within a system do not need to be homogeneous physical substances – they could be more complex physical entities, such as biodiversity levels within a given area of land. They don't even need to be physical things. It is possible to model what happens in a system when the "stock" of trust in a regulator declines, for example, or when the stock of skill in a workforce increases.

Feedback loops also take many forms. A feedback loop could be an automatic prompt (telling a supermarket manager to restock a product), or a piece of information (the speedometer on a car showing the driver she is going too fast), or a chemical signal (the hormone prolactin telling a mother's body to produce more milk).

Figure 2.3

Stomata

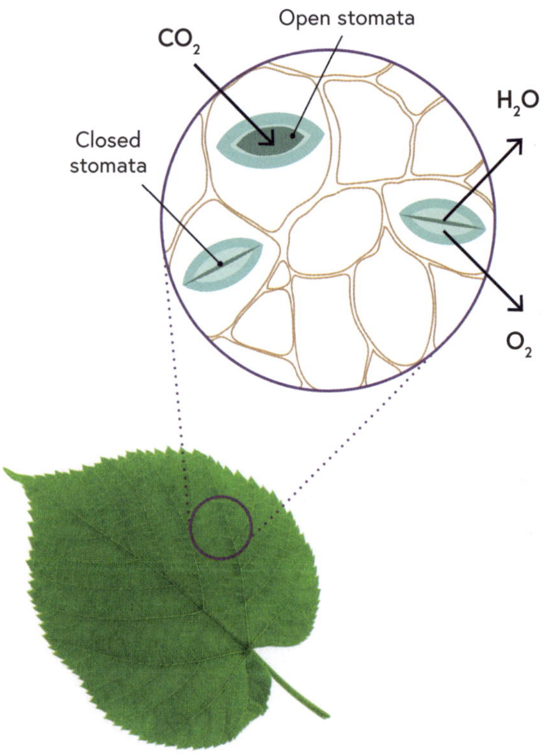

There are two kinds of feedback loop: "balancing" and "reinforcing". Balancing feedback loops (also known as negative feedback loops, although their effects can be positive) serve to maintain the stocks at certain levels. They limit, or reverse, whatever direction of change is imposed on the system. Our appetite, for example, responds to the levels of a suite of chemicals in our blood and gut to regulate how much we eat. If we eat too much, we feel full, and that stops us eating more. If we eat too little, we get hungry and go in search of more food. (Quite clearly, this feedback mechanism doesn't always work as well as it should. We will examine why in Chapter 4.)

Reinforcing feedback loops amplify the direction of change. They are also known as positive feedback loops, although they can have negative effects. They create both virtuous circles (more people buy free range eggs, there is more investment in free range egg production, the cost of free-range eggs comes down, more people buy free range eggs) and vicious circles (an over reliance on chemical inputs reduces soil quality, necessitating yet more chemical inputs). These reinforcing feedback loops can create runaway systems that are very hard to stop, such as nuclear fission or melting polar ice caps.

Mathematical modelling shows that complex systems are hard to predict, even across small timescales. Miniscule changes in starting conditions can, over time, lead to huge differences in outcomes. Systems can appear stable and then collapse without warning (as we witnessed in the 2008 financial crash). Attempting to control them (even loosely) is extremely difficult, and many well-intentioned endeavours fail.

But this is not a counsel of despair. Systems science also shows that different systems from very different fields – the stomata of a leaf, the stock ordering system of a supermarket, the entire carbon cycle – exhibit similar and predictable behaviours, which depend on the nature of the feedback loops that connect their stocks. There is a common set of identifiable patterns in system failures (see the box below on systems traps). And, depending on the structure of the system, some interventions are more likely than others to create sustained positive change.

The key to employing a systems approach is not simply to recognise that everything is connected, that there are trade-offs, that life is complex – it is to follow an established process that will give us the best chance of successful intervention.

First we need to be clear on what the purpose of the system is and to ensure that every actor in the system is united in pursuit of this purpose. Since the Second World War, the chief purpose of our food system has been to maximise the production of cheap food above all other objectives. As we shall see in the next chapter, this purpose needs to change.

Once we are clear on our purpose, we need to identify the feedback loops within the food system that are most destructive or dysfunctional, and propose policy responses designed to break or mend those loops. We will identify two which we call the Junk Food Cycle and the Invisibility of Nature.

Finally, we need to gather the best possible data. Measuring the impact of any intervention means you can see whether it is working, and how well; it also makes it much easier to adjust your course if unintended consequences arise.

Systems traps

The field of system dynamics – the study of complex systems using mathematical modelling – was created by Jay Forrester at the Massachusetts Institute of Technology in the mid-fifties.[7] To begin with, Forrester did his calculations by hand on paper, painstakingly modelling the workings of various systems (predominantly within businesses). As computer power increased exponentially, so did the complexity and number of the systems that could be studied.

Donella Meadows was one of the early members of Forrester's group. In *Thinking in Systems*, she drew on thousands of such studies to identify archetypal ways in which systems can go wrong – some of which we describe here.[8] She called these systems traps.

"The destruction [system traps] cause is often blamed on particular actors or events," she wrote, "although it is actually a consequence of system structure." Depending on the structure of the system, promising-sounding remedies might prove bafflingly ineffective. "Blaming, disciplining, firing, twisting policy levers harder, hoping for a more favourable sequence of events, tinkering at the margins – these standard responses will not fix structural problems … But system traps can be escaped – by recognizing them in advance and not getting caught in them, or by altering the structure – by reformulating goals, by weakening, strengthening, or altering feedback loops, [or] by adding new feedback loops."

As we will see in the following chapters, many of the structural traps described by Meadows exist in our current food system.

Seeking the wrong goal

If the goals of the system are defined inaccurately or incompletely, the system may work obediently to produce a result that is not really intended.

We have a system of national accounting, for example, that – as Partha Dasgupta points out in his groundbreaking review on the value of biodiversity – bears no real relation to our national wealth or wellbeing. Even on its own terms it doesn't work. GDP is not the record of our material wealth but the fever chart of our consumption. It is a measure of the gross addition to stocks – the flows of stuff made and purchased in a year – rather than the stocks themselves: the houses, cars, and computers that are in themselves sources of pleasure and indications of wealth.

We do not even attempt to measure the other stocks that are critical for our long-term survival and happiness: those of natural and human capital. Because they are not written into the system, the system does not value them. We describe this in more detail in Chapter 6.

Policy resistance

This trap occurs when balancing feedback loops keep bringing the system back to the same spot, no matter how hard you try to shift it. Take traditional drug prevention policies. No matter how many wars on drugs are fought, drug dealing remains a problem. This is because if enforcement is successful, it reduces the stock (drugs) within the system, which increases its value and incentivises drug smugglers to circumvent the system. Together, these countermoves produce a standoff, and the stock remains unchanged. Everyone makes a huge effort to achieve their own objectives, but the system is unmoved.

The tragedy of the commons

This phrase was coined by the American ecologist Garrett Hardin in a 1968 article of the same name, although the problem was first identified by 19th-century English economist William Forster Lloyd.[9]

It occurs when an erodible resource is accessible to everyone. Rather than preserve the resource, each actor in the system is incentivised to take as much of it for themselves as they can before it runs out.

A recent example is the collapse of the cod populations on Newfoundland's Grand Banks. When Europeans first became aware of these thriving shoals, in the twilight of the 15th century, they were "so thicke by the shoare that we heardlie have been able to row a Boate through them".[10]

As long as there was a technological limit on how much each fishing boat could catch, the cod provided an abundant source of food and livelihoods. But technology moved fast in the 20th century, with the invention of bottom trawling, on-board freezing and larger boats. Fearing to be outdone by their competitors, each fishing boat became better equipped and increased its catch until, in 1992, the cod population collapsed almost completely, signalling not just an end to the cod but to the entire ecosystem of the local coast. Despite a fishing moratorium, the cod population has still not recovered.[11]

"Ruin is the destination toward which all men rush," wrote Hardin in his essay, "each pursuing his own best interest in a society that believes in the freedom of the commons."

Drift to low performance

Also known as "boiled frog syndrome", "eroding goals" or "shifting baselines", this trap occurs when a system drifts downhill slowly enough for the actors in the system to forget how much better things used to be. Everyone is lulled into lower and lower expectations, lower effort, lower performance. The system requires a balancing feedback mechanism, a burst of energy to raise standards to where they once were. But instead, a reinforcing feedback loop is created as low expectations lead to less corrective action, which leads to continuous degradation of the system.

In the School Food Plan, which I co-authored in 2013, we argued that this is what had happened to the food served in schools, until Jamie Oliver intervened and made everyone realise how bad things had become. Standards are now increasing, slowly, as expectations in the system have been raised.[12]

Escalation

This happens when the goal of a system is not absolute but is related to another variable in the system. I raise my voice to be heard over you, you yell a bit louder and soon we are both shouting at the top of our voices. A reinforcing feedback loop carries us into escalating loudness, escalating violence, an arms race, a wealth race.

We can see this in the food system. Humans have evolved to like calorie-dense food. Food companies respond to this innate desire by putting more effort into the development and marketing of calorie-dense food, which increases the consumption of that food, which in turn increases the incentive for companies to make and market it. Increasing sales increases marketing spend which increases sales. We describe this problem in greater depth in Chapter 4.

Shifting the burden to the intervenor

Colloquially this phenomenon is known as addiction or dependence. "Addiction is finding a quick and dirty solution to the symptom of the problem," wrote Meadows, "which prevents or distracts one from the harder and longer-term task of solving the real problem."

We can see this in intensive agriculture, where an over-reliance on fertilisers and pesticides has damaged the ecosystem and depleted the soil. This in turn results in increased reliance on fertilisers and pesticides, to make crops grow in such unfertile conditions.

Rule beating

This is a trap that anyone attempting to change a system must be particularly alert to. Wherever there are rules, there is likely to be rule beating. Rule beating means evasive action to get around the intent of a system's rules – abiding by the letter, but not the spirit, of the law. Rule beating becomes a problem when it leads a system into large distortions or unnatural behaviours that would make no sense at all in the absence of the rules.

We saw this in the food system when European countries restricted imported feed grains in the 1960s to support local farmers. Cassava – a good animal feed – was not restricted. So corn imports from the USA were replaced by cassava imports from Asia. European farmers did not benefit. Regardless of whether you agree with the policy in the first place, it did not achieve its objective.

3

How did we get here?

HOW did we end up with a food system that can feed the world but makes us so ill? One that destroys wildlife, pollutes our rivers and air, and produces almost a third of our greenhouse gases?

Norman Borlaug, Green Revolution pioneer

How did we get into this strange predicament?

The story of how the modern world feeds itself is a triumph of human ingenuity – but also of devastating unintended consequences. It can be told using three lines on a chart.

Three lines on a chart: a story of unintended consequences.

In 1945, as the Second World War ground to a close, humanity faced an even greater existential threat.

Despite all the bloodshed, the global population had more than doubled over the last 150 years – from one billion to two-and-a-half billion people.[1] And thanks to huge advances in medicine and hygiene, scientists were anticipating an even bigger surge to come. Within the next 100 years, they predicted (probably correctly) there would be nine billion people on the planet.[2] How on earth were we to feed them all?

At one time, the answer would have been simple: dig up more land to produce more food. This is what our farmers did during the Second World War. Before the war, the UK produced just over 30% of the food it consumed.[3] Our dependence on food imports, brought in from the empire and beyond, put us in constant peril. German U-Boats attempted to starve the country into submission by sinking the ships carrying our food imports. In every month of the war before May 1943, more merchant ships were destroyed by U-boats in the North Atlantic than could be built.[4] The vital supply lines between Britain and the US were almost severed. Churchill later said "the U-boat peril" was the thing that frightened him most during the War.[5]

It was farmers who saved the day, with a mass conversion of scrubland to farmland. They grubbed up heather and tore down hedges in order to farm every precious inch of land. By the end of the war, British food production had increased from 30% to 75% of demand.[6]

It seemed obvious back then that in order to produce more food, you had to cultivate more land. Indeed, this correlation between the number of mouths to feed, the quantity of food produced and the

Figure 3.1

The same amount of land now produces much more food, for more people[7]

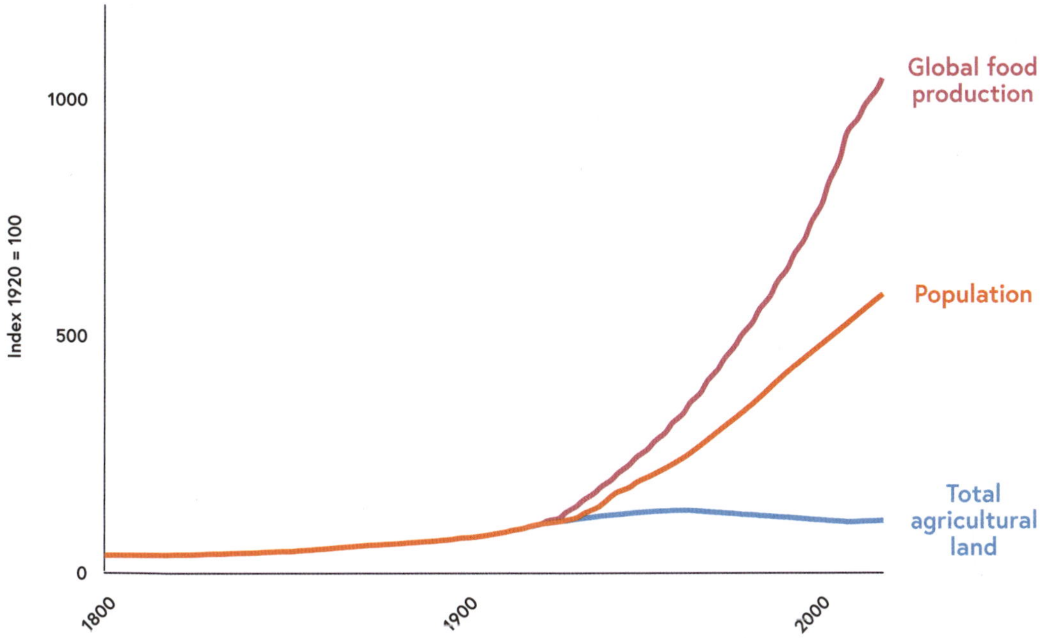

proportion of land in cultivation had stayed true for centuries. Figure 3.1 shows three lines representing how those three variables changed over time with the increase in global population. You can see that from the start of the 19th century to the early 20th century they rise together gradually at an almost identical rate.

By the end of the war, however, most of the world's decent farming land was already taken. With the population explosion already under way, it seemed there simply wouldn't be enough land to cultivate the extra food needed. Mass starvation looked inevitable.

But no one had reckoned on Norman Borlaug. The botanist had grown up on a small farm in Iowa during the Great Depression. He had seen starving people begging on the streets and rioting over food. It set him on a mission to fight hunger.

Borlaug moved to Mexico in 1944, hoping to develop more productive strains of wheat. The living conditions of the half-starved local population were even worse than the things he had seen in his youth.

"These places I've seen have clubbed my mind," he wrote to his wife Margaret. "The earth is so lacking in life force; the plants just cling to existence. They don't really grow; they just fight to stay alive. The levels of nourishment in the soil are so low that wheat plants produce only a few grains ... I don't know what we can do to help, but we've got to do something."[8]

Borlaug spent his days in the heat-blasted fields, painstakingly crossbreeding wheat plants. He tweezered off stamen, placed tiny hoods over hundreds of thousands of individual heads of wheat, snipped florets and mingled pollens by hand. Completely absorbed in his work, he often slept on the dirt floor of his research hut. The Mexican farm workers thought he was crazy.

But he pressed on, and his efforts paid off. When Borlaug first arrived in Mexico, it imported 60% of the wheat it consumed. By 1956† – thanks to the high-yielding, short-stemmed, rust-resistant wheat he developed – Mexico was self-sufficient.[9]

This miracle was repeated in India and Pakistan and then across the world. New breeds of wheat, rice and corn, combined with modern irrigation techniques and industrial fertilisers and pesticides, created a new era of high-yield, high-input, intensive farming.

As expected, the global population soared. (In 1950, the average global life expectancy was 46; today, it is 73.[10]) There are almost eight billion humans alive on Earth – more than ever before – and yet the threat of mass starvation has receded.[11]

....

† Borlaug saw the genetically superior plants as part of a three-part system that also included irrigation infrastructure and chemical fertiliser.

For the first time in agricultural history, the increase in food production, and in calories harvested per person, has massively outstripped the additional land being farmed. We now need just a third of the land to produce the same amount of food as in the sixties.[12] Population has risen, but the world produces 1.7 times more food per person than it did in 1960.[13] This is what has become known as the Green Revolution. By adopting Borlaug's methods, farmers saved billions of people from starvation.[†]

But as so often happens, the solution to one problem created others.

As the amount of food available per person increased – and as companies found increasingly innovative ways to process, package and market this surplus – we became heavier.

Humans evolved in a world where food was scarce. We are programmed to seek out calorie-rich foods. We have a palate that finds fat and sugar almost irresistible and when they are within arm's reach, we tend to eat more of them than is good for us. The Green Revolution made calorie-dense foods – refined wheat, sugar, vegetable fats – abundant and cheap.

It is bizarre, but not really surprising, that in the UK you can buy 28 different kinds of KitKat.[14] Chocolate snacks are an easier sell than runner beans, and therefore a more interesting commercial proposition. Eighteen of the largest food and drink companies rely on product portfolios of which 85% are so unhealthy as to be considered unsuitable for marketing to children under World Health Organization guidelines.[15]

This isn't a corporate conspiracy, dreamed up by an evil genius bent on making us ill. It is the economics of supply and demand. (We shall examine the causes and effects of this "Junk Food Cycle" in more detail in the next chapter.)

The side effects of the Green Revolution are not limited to our health.[††] As the amount of food being produced from a given area of land has increased, the amount of other life occupying that same area of land has decreased. In the UK, where 70% of our landmass is occupied by farmland, intensive agriculture has devastated the habitats of many wild animals and insects.[16] Since 1930, we have lost 97% of our wildflower meadows, half our ancient woodland, 56% of our heathland, and 90% of our lowland ponds.[17] As wheat yields in the UK doubled from 1970 to today, the number of farmland birds decreased by 54%.[18] The UK now sits in last place on the European farmland bird index.[19] More broadly, as Figure 3.2 shows, there has been a 60% decline in priority UK species since 1970, with a 22% decline since 2011.[20]

Figue 3.2

As agricultural production has intensified, biodiversity has declined[21]

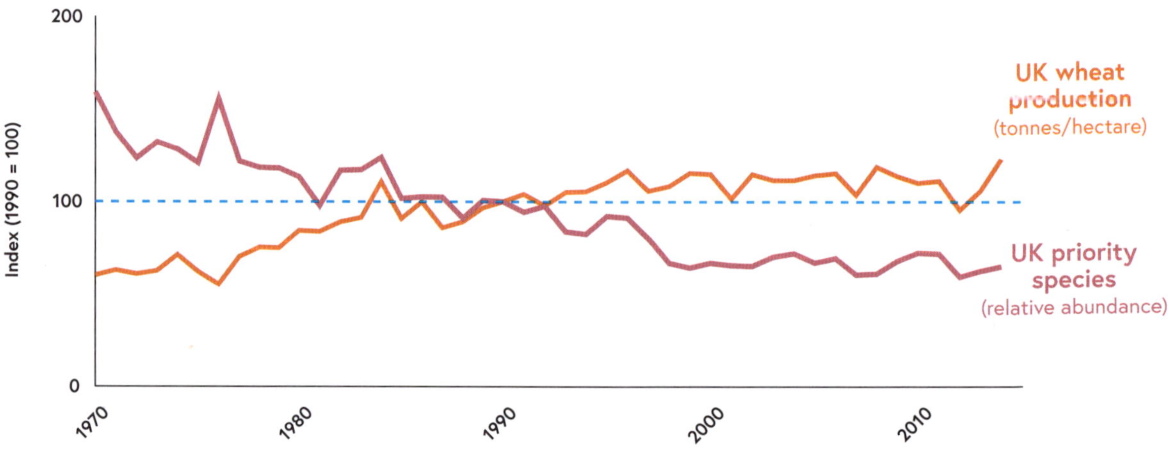

....

[†] The Food and Agricultural Organization of the UN (FAO) estimates that 50% of the world's population were undernourished in 1945 versus 11% in 2018 (Ritchie, H and Roser, M. (2019). Hunger and Undernourishment. OurWorldInData.org. [online]. Available at https://ourworldindata.org/hunger-and-undernourishment). To point out that the world is a better place than it once was does not mean that, for many, existence is not still cruel and brutish: the FOA also estimates that 820 million people today face chronic food deprivation, leaving 150 million children stunted, while the United States government's Centers for Disease Control and Prevention estimates that 2 billion people, including half of the world's children aged six months to five years, suffer from one or more micronutrient deficiency.

[††] Our diagnosis features health and environment impacts. There were other consequences of the green revolution that shape today's food system. Impact on peasant farmers, agrarian tradition (some of the points the Landworker's Alliance made to us).

On top of all this, we now know something that Borlaug couldn't have. Every stage of food production exacerbates the carbon crisis: the forests cleared to plant crops; the energy-intensive manufacture of fertiliser; the release of carbon from degrading soils; the methane produced by rice paddies and livestock; the energy used by manufacturing plants and retail outlets; and the fuel used to power the vehicles in the supply chain. In total the food system is responsible for an estimated 20–30% of global greenhouse gas emissions.[22] In the UK the food sector's emissions represent just under 20% of everything we produce, but that rises to close to the global average if you factor in the carbon from the imported food that we consume (see Figure 3.3).[23]

This, then, is the story of how we reached this point. We concentrated on an existential risk – growing enough food to avoid mass starvation – and we largely solved that problem. But the food system we ended up with prioritises quantity over nutritional quality. We have changed our diets to match what the system is now producing, and this diet is now making both us and our planet ill.

But we can draw hope from this story. It shows us that humans are capable of solving enormous, existential threats. We must now muster our ingenuity and determination once more.

Figure 3.3

In 2008, a fifth of all UK emissions were from the food system[24]

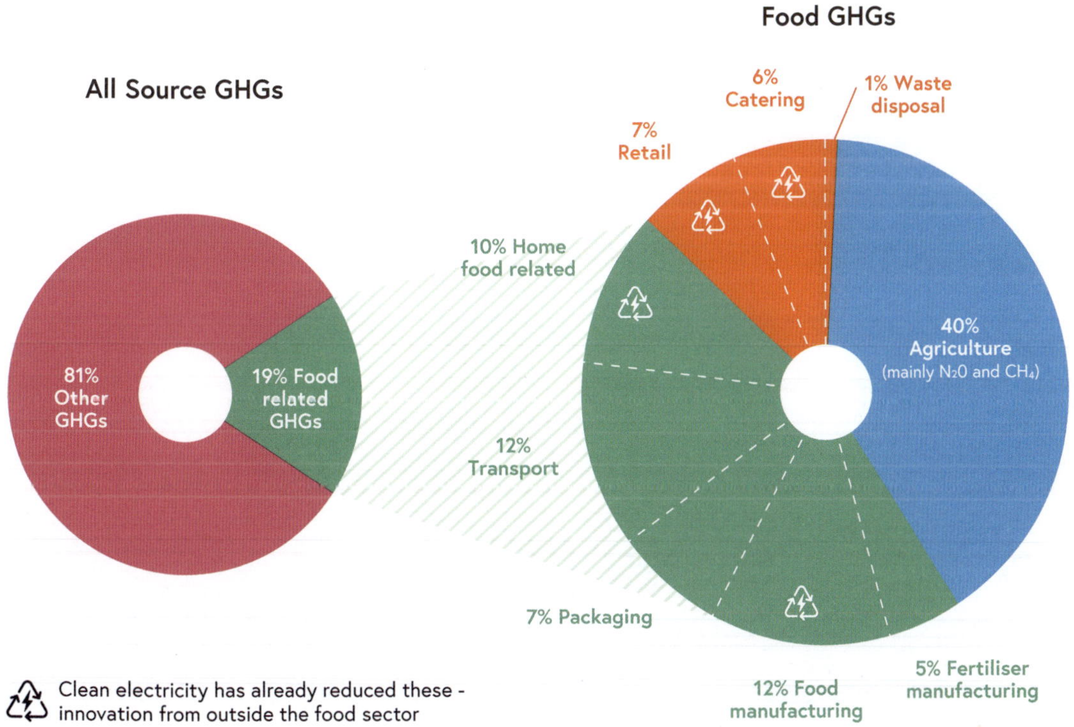

4

Escaping the Junk Food Cycle

MOST people in this country believe there is a simple formula for tackling dietary ill health: education, exercise, food labelling and willpower. Provide information through schools and public health campaigns, encourage people to move more, and leave the rest to individual willpower.

One tabloid newspaper made this argument with typical vigour in a recent editorial attacking proposals to ban junk food adverts before 9pm. Citing flawed data suggesting that such a ban would only trim two calories off a child's daily intake, the newspaper poured scorn on other "nanny state" interventions such as the (actually quite successful) Soft Drinks Industry Levy. The Government, it said, should abandon such "ludicrous" measures in favour of the "common sense" solution: "Better education on diet – and exercise."[1]

The underlying belief here is that we are getting fat and ill because we are too lazy to take exercise, and too ignorant to eat well. If only we were better informed about healthy eating, and more conscientious about getting up off our enormous bottoms, the obesity crisis would melt away. (The unspoken corollary, incidentally, is that if you do know how to eat healthily but still resort to processed foods, you deserve to be miserable and ill.)

Opinion polls show that this is a majority opinion even among those most likely to suffer from diet-related ill health.[2] The idea of free will is precious to us. We want to believe we have control over our own appetites and behaviours; and to some extent, of course, we do. But humans are part of the food system too, and our behaviour has been radically affected by the malfunctioning of its feedback loops.

Why is our appetite failing us?

The human appetite is one of the miracles of evolution. Our bodies deploy a series of delicately interwoven feedback loops involving numerous hormones to ensure that we eat the nutrients we need without even having to think about it. This isn't just a case of feeling hungry or full. Our appetite prompts us to seek out specific nutrients if we are short of them. Some people, when short of iron, will even eat soil. (This is known as geophagia.[3]) The appetite is a miraculous mechanism, and hard to resist.

But not all appetites are the same. Our genes create differences in how our appetites are regulated.[4] For social animals like humans, there is an evolutionary benefit to this diversity. It makes sense to have some people with bigger fat reserves, who will be better able to survive a famine. Others are predisposed to stay lean, meaning they can move fast against predators and other sudden threats.

This does not mean that some people are doomed to get fat. It just means that, in an environment where calories are easy to come by, some of us need to work much harder than others to maintain a healthy weight. You have to swim against the powerful current of your appetite.

The variation in levels of appetite produces a distribution of weight in the population that follows a classic bell curve. Figure 4.1 shows what this looked like in 1950, when calorie-dense food was still in relatively modest supply.[5]

The solid vertical line on this chart represents a BMI of 25: defined today as overweight. The dotted vertical line represents a BMI of 30: defined today as obese. You can see that the average BMI in 1950 was about 20: in today's terms, somewhere between the ideal weight and a little underweight.

Evenly distributed either side of that, some people were underweight, some overweight. But very few were obese.

Let's roll the clock forward slowly to the eighties (see Figure 4.2).

Figure 4.1

In 1950, weight distribution in the UK followed a classic bell curve[6]

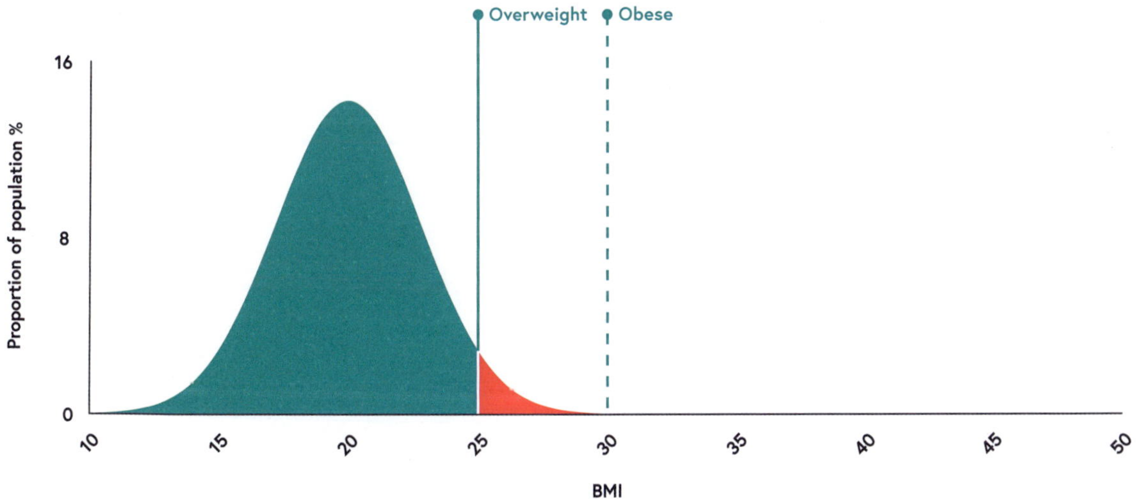

Figure 4.2

By the 1980s, people in the UK had become on average heavier, meaning the bell curve moved to the right[7]

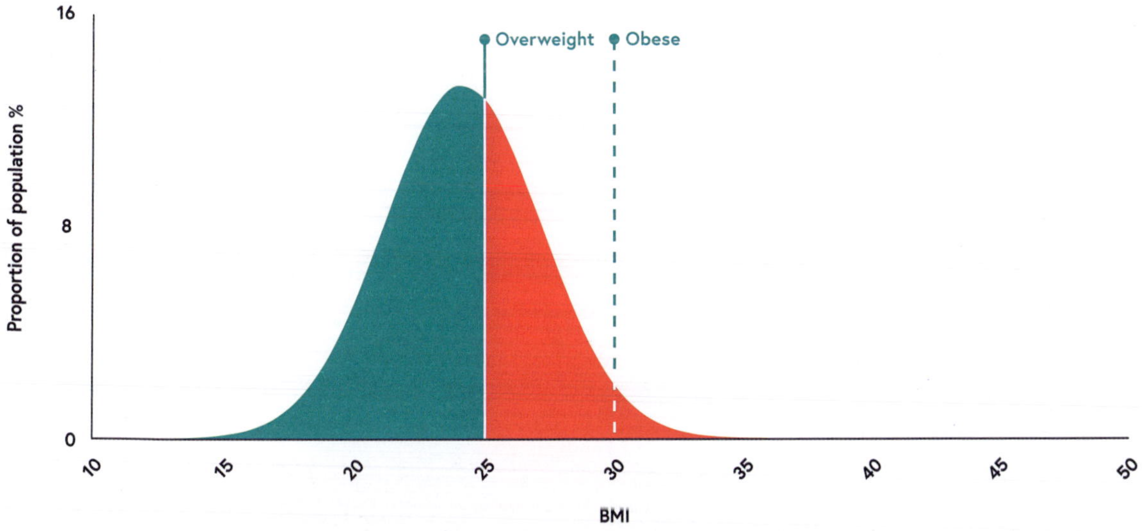

During this time, calorie-dense food became much cheaper and more available. As we consumed more, we became heavier. Everyone – even the naturally slender – put on some weight, but those with a genetic predisposition to lay down fat began to tip over into obesity. These people are represented by the red slope on the right of the bell curve, where it crosses the 30 BMI marker.

Now let's roll the clock forward again to the current day. Figure 4.3 shows the red slope growing much longer and thicker, and crossing the line that marks a BMI of 40: defined today as severely obese. A significant chunk of the population is now severely obese.

Taken together, these charts illustrate the momentum of our so-called obesity epidemic. It hasn't been a sudden disaster, but more like a slow-moving landslide.

It's not just an abundance of food that has caused this landslide. It is also the particular nature of the food.

The appetite is a classic complex system, controlled by multiple feedback loops. Sophisticated nutrient sensors in our cells and hormones feed information to the hypothalamus in the brain.[9] These hormones include ghrelin, adiponectin, insulin and glucagon. The release of appetite-inducing or -supressing hormones can be triggered by the level of sugar in your blood, the amount of fat you are already carrying, even how full different parts of your stomach or intestines are.[10] Our responses to flavour, and the pleasure we get from eating, are also part of the appetite system.[11]

Numerous studies have shown that most people already know what a healthy diet looks like. More than 90% of us know we should restrict our intake of foods that are high in fat, sugar and salt (HFSS), and 99% know eating fruit and vegetables is important for a healthy lifestyle.[12] The problem is not information, but implementation. We find it incredibly hard to resist sugary, fatty foods because our appetites keep overriding our good intentions.[13] (There is, as we shall discuss later on, important work to be done on food education, but this is more about imparting kitchen skills and expanding palates than preaching about diet.)

Our appetite steers us towards calorie-dense foods because these are rare and precious in the wild. We find these kinds of foods particularly delicious. Research has found that if they are also low in water content and insoluble fibre – as is the case with many processed foods – they interfere with the feedback mechanisms of our appetite.[14] Our hormones take longer to convey satiety signals (the feeling of fullness) when we eat processed foods.[15] And because these products are high in calories, eating just a few extra mouthfuls means consuming a lot more calories.[16]

There are hormonal reward mechanisms built into our appetite, which is where poor diet and mental health problems sometimes overlap.[17] You can give yourself a temporary dopamine rush by eating a chocolate bar or a burger.[18] People who are stressed, tired and anxious often respond by overeating.[19]

Figure 4.3

Today, many more people in the UK are obese and severely obese[0]

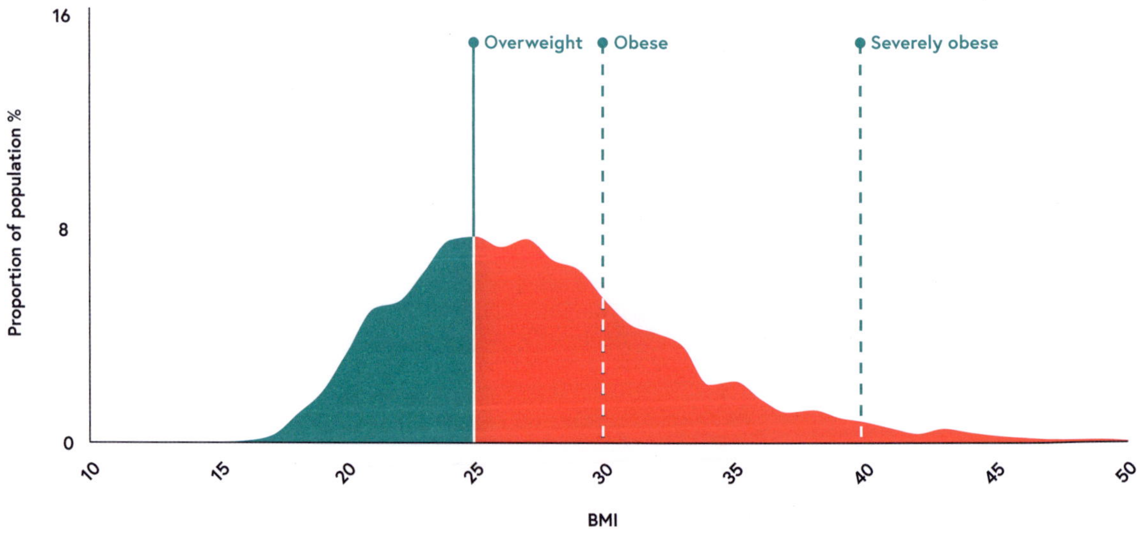

It's a cheap and modest high: one that, unlike drugs or alcohol, doesn't cause immediate incapacitation or interfere with your ability to get stuff done.

The way appetite malfunctions in the modern world creates a huge market for unhealthy foods. Not only are they easier to sell, they are also cheaper to make

Figure 4.4

Healthy food tends to cost more per calorie[†20]

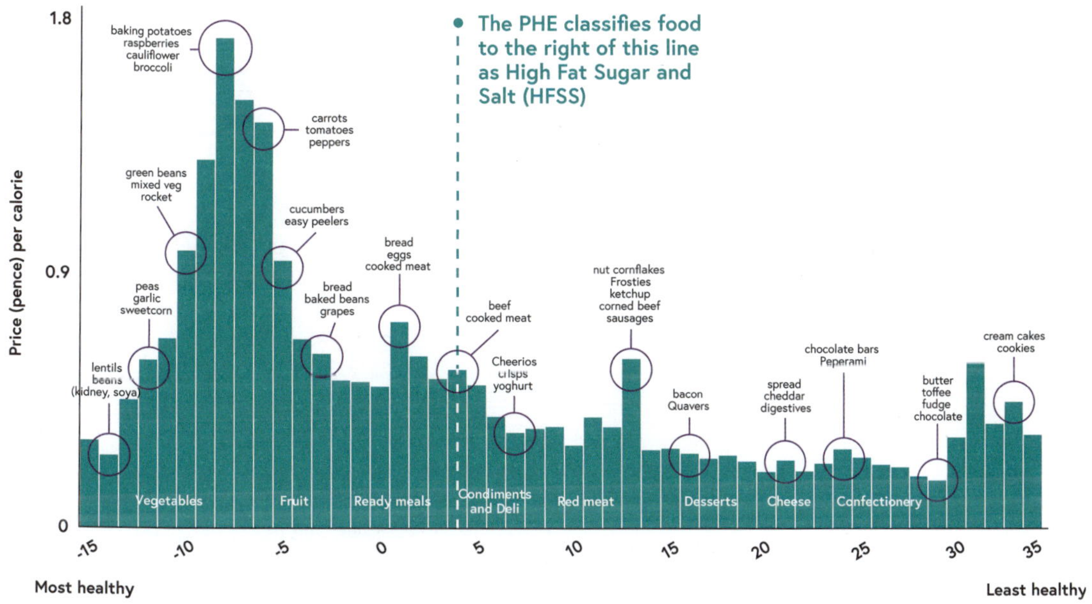

because they use ingredients that have been made abundant by the Green Revolution, such as refined sugar, flour and vegetable oil.[21] This has led to a situation where healthier food tends to be much more expensive, per calorie, than HFSS food (see Figure 4.4).

For sound commercial reasons, then, companies invest more money into researching, developing and marketing unhealthy foods (see Figure 4.5). This investment is intended not just to help capture a bigger slice of the market, but to grow the market itself.

Young marketeers are taught about the "consumption effect" – meaning that consumers who have more food in their house will eat more of it. In-store promotions such as the classic BOGOF deal (buy-one-get-one-free) are explicitly designed to persuade shoppers to buy and take home more than they actually need, as are attempts to create "new eating occasions" outside of classic mealtimes. Research by Public Health England found that volume promotions such as BOGOFs increase purchases of a product by an average of 15%.[22]

Marketeers pore over academic papers with equations showing which promotions are most likely to lead to increased consumption.

"I tried to eat healthy, but I found that more expensive as time went on, trying to feed a family of six. I've given up."

East of England participant, "deliberative dialogue"

"If you're going to keep chucking cheap beer and two tubs of Celebrations for £7 ... I'm lucky, I don't put a lot of weight on me but in four years' time, I'll be a right heifer, won't I? I just think we've got it all wrong, haven't we?"

North East England participant, "deliberative dialogue"

....

† The scale on this chart ranges from most to least healthy based on PHE's nutrient profile scoring. The Nutrient Profile Model scores food and drink according to their overall nutritional composition rather than just calories. Points are awarded for unhealthy qualities (e.g. energy density, saturated fat, sugar and salt) and for healthy qualities (e.g. fruit, vegetables and nut content, fibre and protein). A score is calculated by subtracting the healthy points from the unhealthy points. Foods which score over 4 points (shown by the geen dashed line) and drinks which score over 1 are defined as HFSS.

Figure 4.5

Most marketing money is spent promoting unhealthy products[23]

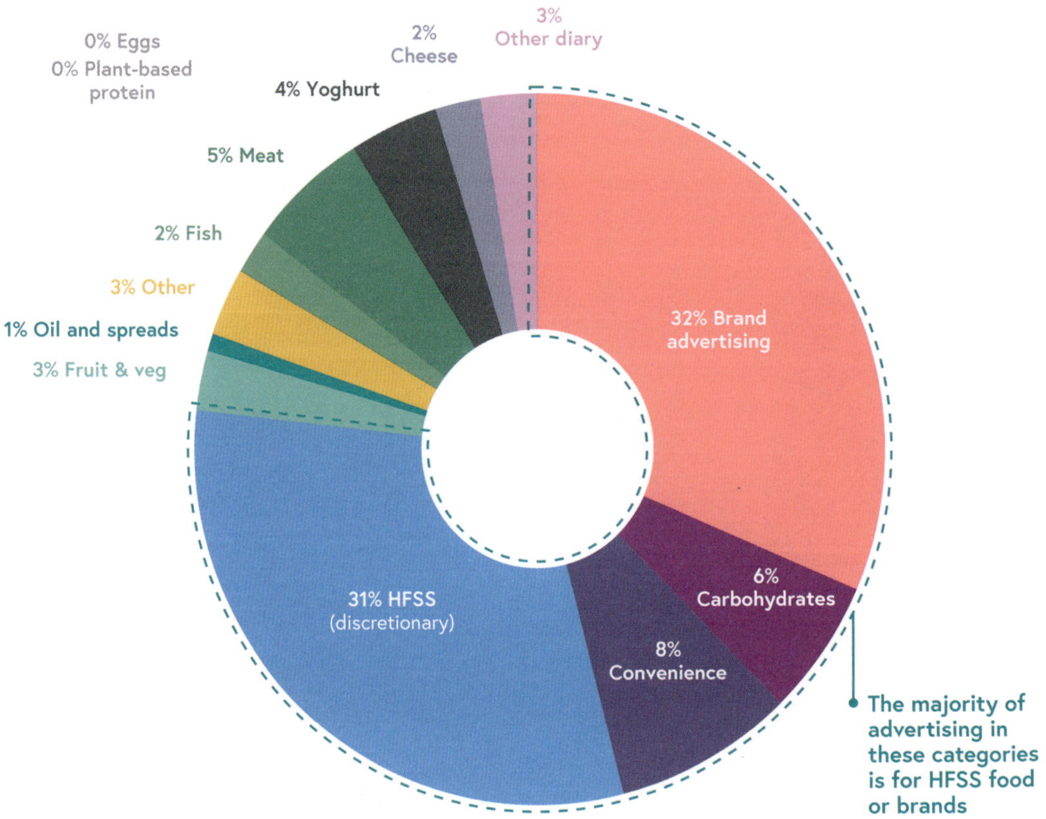

Chocolate, for example, has an "expandability" of 93%.[24] This means that if you run a buy-one-get-one-free on chocolate, customers will on average consume almost twice as much as they would have without the BOGOF.

Readers of a libertarian bent may be thinking: so what? If a person wants to spend their hard-earned cash on junk food – even if they keep eating such food until they make themselves ill – that is nobody's business but their own.

In fact, though, very few people who are overweight or suffering from diet-related disease are happy with their situation. And even if they were, the state cannot afford to keep picking up the tab.

In systems terms, we have become stuck in a reinforcing feedback loop – a vicious circle. Let's call it the Junk Food Cycle. We have a predilection for calorie dense foods, which means food companies invest more time and money creating these foods, which makes us eat more of them and expands the market, which leads to more investment, which makes us eat more.

It's not just the consumer who is trapped in this cycle: food companies are too. Of the manufactured food products sold in the UK, 85% are deemed to be so unhealthy they are unsuitable for marketing to children.[25] (In 2018, the home-grown fruit and vegetables market in the UK was worth £2.2bn, whereas confectionery alone – one small section of the processed food market – was worth £4.2bn.[26]) The booming market in online food deliveries is heading down the same route; Kantar reports that a third of all online delivery orders included pizza in 2019/20.[27]

But what are company bosses supposed to do? If they stop making and selling unhealthy foods, someone else will. They will lose their competitive edge, and their shareholders will have a conniption.

This is why several company bosses have told us they would actually welcome legislation designed to improve the food they sell. They want to do the right thing, but they need a level playing field. Tim Rycroft, a spokesman for the Food and Drink Federation, hinted at this dilemma in the recent BBC documentary "What are we Feeding our Kids?" Asked whether the priority of food companies should be profit or public health, he answered without hesitation: "Profit". But, he added, "The industry has to be guided by the Government. If the Government says there is a reason why these [foods] are no longer acceptable, of course we will change."[28]

We will not succeed in transforming the food system until we break the most destructive feedback loops between appetite and commerce, and make it harder to make money from foods that make us ill.

You can't outrun a bad diet

We have seen how the Junk Food Cycle overrides both education and willpower. But what about exercise? Is it possible to outrun a bad diet?

It seems logical to assume that one of the major causes of the rise in obesity has been a steep decline in physical activity. At the start of the 20th century, 28% of Britons worked in manufacturing, most of them doing manual labour, and 11% in agriculture.[29] They would have used up a huge number of calories just getting through the working day. (The Institute for Fiscal Studies has calculated that to burn the same number of calories as a coal miner, you would have to jog for over ten hours a week.)[31]

By the end of the 20th century, working patterns had changed dramatically: just 14% of the population remained in manufacturing, and 2% in agriculture.[30]

Technology has taken the sweat out of household chores, and even getting from A to B has become more sedentary. The average person in the UK walked 255 miles per year in the mid-seventies, but only 179 miles in 2010.[32] All this amounts to a fundamental change in the way humans interact with the world. We used to do it with muscle power; now we do it with machines.

It may seem obvious, therefore, that we are burning fewer calories than previous generations. But it turns out this isn't the case. In the eighties, scientists developed a new technique for measuring people's exact energy expenditure as they went about their daily lives, rather than making an estimate based on observation. This new technique, the doubly labelled water method,[†] allowed scientists to calculate exactly how much carbon dioxide a subject breathed out over the course of a day by measuring changing levels of oxygen and hydrogen isotopes in their urine. The CO_2 we breathe out is directly correlated to the energy we burn.

As soon as they started using this method, researchers found a weirdly counterintuitive pattern emerging. The daily energy expenditure of very physically active populations turned out to be almost the same as that of more sedentary industrialised populations.

A study of Hadza hunter-gatherers in Tanzania found that they burned the same number of calories per day as urban-dwelling Americans.[33] Another study showed that children of the indigenous Shuar people of Amazonian Ecuador burned the same number of calories regardless of whether they moved into towns and adopted a more sedentary life, or lived like their parents as foraging horticulturalists.[34] Women in rural farming populations in Nigeria have been shown to have similar calorie expenditures to women in metropolitan Chicago.[35] And a global meta-study found that across the board, people in less developed, more physically active populations have the same daily calorie expenditures as their more sedentary counterparts in rich countries.[36]

There is clearly a balancing feedback loop in play here, whereby the body seeks to regulate its daily energy expenditure just as it regulates body temperature, blood glucose levels and so forth. It works to keep daily calorific output within a narrow range, regardless of lifestyle.

There are (at least) two possible mechanisms for this. The first – proposed by the evolutionary anthropologist Herman Pontzer, who conducted many of the doubly labelled water experiments – is that if you burn less energy through exercise, your body will use much of the leftover energy elsewhere, particularly on boosting your immune system and reproductive system.

In evolutionary terms, our bodies are still lagging at the hunter-gatherer stage: a condition in which lives could be cut short by violence or illness at any moment. The evolutionary imperative, therefore, is to invest as much energy as possible into your health and reproduction. Live fast, pass on your genes, die in a hunting accident. Pontzer suggests this might explain why diseases of the immune and reproductive systems have become so common in developed societies.

[†] They do this using the double water method which measures how much carbon dioxide they produce during the day by measuring hydrogen and oxygen concentrations in their urine.

We eat so much and move so little that our bodies are investing too much surplus energy into these systems, leading to chronic inflammation, stress and reproductive cancers in industrialised populations.[37]

The second widely accepted theory is that our bodies simply compensate for increased exercise.[38] So when we consciously increase our deliberate exercise – by going for a run, say – we then unconsciously limit our physical activity for the rest of the day. We may fidget less, for example, or drive to the shops instead of walking.

It is possible, of course, that both these mechanisms are at work simultaneously. What is clear is that exercise is not a good way to lose weight. If you increase your exercise level, your body will soon adapt to moderate your calorie output. Studies examining the relative effects of exercise and diet on weight loss have consistently shown that diet is by far the most important factor (see Figure 4.6).

Even the small weight loss benefits that might come from exercise – the body doesn't appear to offset all changes in energy expenditure – are compromised by changes in our appetite. When we exercise we tend to get hungry and eat more.[39] Our body's feedback mechanisms work hard to stop us losing weight, because historically starvation has been a much bigger threat to humanity than obesity.

The idea that exercise is a good way to lose weight is not just incorrect: it is actively harmful. Every January, people take out gym memberships in droves, hoping to lose weight.[40] When the scales don't budge, they become disheartened and give up.

But there are so many other benefits to exercising. It lowers blood pressure, reduces the risks of cancer, diabetes and osteoporosis, boosts the immune system and has a huge impact on mental health.[41] Exercise benefits just about everyone, regardless of weight. It is also the case that – for reasons scientists have not yet fully understood – exercising does seem to help people maintain a healthy BMI once they have lost weight (see Figure 4.6).

If exercise could be prescribed it would be one of our most powerful and multi-functional drugs. But in the public imagination it is associated almost exclusively with weight loss. And because it doesn't work for that purpose, people think it doesn't work. The amazing things that exercise can do are eclipsed by the one thing it can't.

Figure 4.6

Exercise had a minimal impact helping Boston's policemen lose weight, but it was effective in preventing weight gain (after the weight-loss phase)[42]

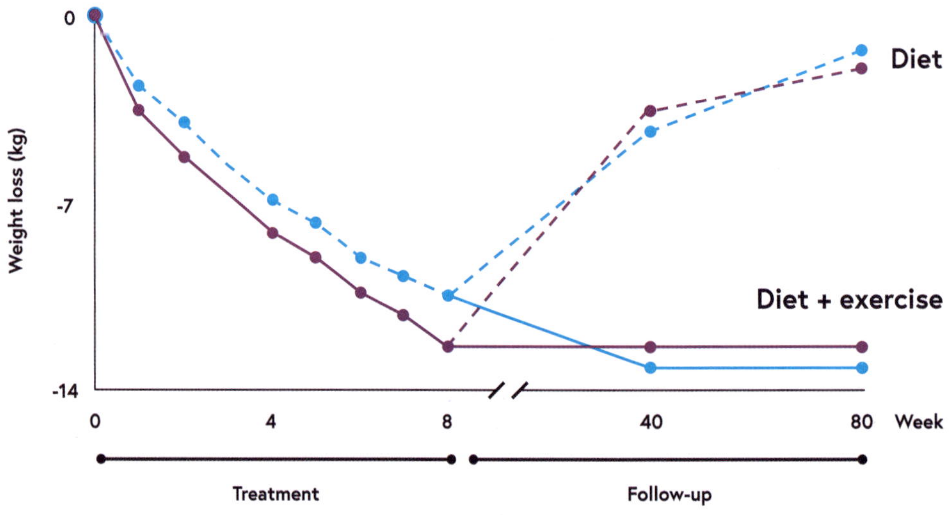

A 1989 study of Boston policemen showed that adding exercise to a reduced calorie diet only marginally improved weight loss during the two-month active weight-loss phase. However, men who exercised afterwards kept the weight off. Those who didn't exercise in the months following the weight-loss phase gained all the weight back.[43]

Ultra-processed food

What if it's not just the ingredients in processed food that interfere with our appetite? What if the processing itself is part of the problem?

This idea was first developed by the Brazilian physician Carlos Monteiro and his team at the Centre for Epidemiological Research on Nutrition and Health (NUPENS) at the University of São Paulo. It is now being investigated by scientists in many other countries.

Monteiro devised a categorisation system, known as NOVA,[44] to divide commercially available foods into four groups:

Group 1: Unprocessed or minimally processed foods. This group includes anything from a tomato to a bunch of mint, a pork chop to a walnut. They are obtained directly from plants or animals and go through minimal processing (such as cleaning or freezing) before reaching our kitchens.

Group 2: Processed culinary ingredients. This includes things like butter, sugar and honey. They are extracted from nature by processes such as pressing, grinding, crushing, pulverizing, and refining. They are often used sparingly to make other foods delicious.

Group 3: Processed foods. These contain elements from groups one or two, processed by manufacturers – often salted, fermented, or pickled. They include bacon, cheeses, canned fruit and vegetables, smoked salmon, and traditionally made bread.

Group 4: Ultra-processed foods. These are quite different from the other groups. They tend to contain the sugars, oils and starches from group 2, but instead of being used sparingly, these ingredients make up the bulk of the dish. Ultra-processed foods also contain ingredients unfamiliar to domestic kitchens, such as soy protein isolates or dextrose. Colourings, emulsifiers, flavourings and other additives are added to make the products better-looking, tastier, more stable and longer-lasting. This makes them extremely moreish – or "hyperpalatable", in Monteiro's jargon. Foods in this group include most shop-bought biscuits and cakes, mass-produced bread, reconstituted meat products, mass produced desserts, and many ready meals.

Based on these definitions, 50% of UK household food purchases are ultra-processed. This compares to 46% for Germany, 14% for France and 13% for Italy.[45]

Monteiro argues that ultra-processed food has a particularly acute effect on weight and health, compared to equivalent food cooked from scratch. In 2015 – to the fury of large food manufacturers – his food group definitions were adopted into the Brazilian government's "Dietary Guidelines for the Brazilian Population".[46] Since then other countries have encouraged their citizens to reduce the amount of ultra-processed food they eat: Canada, Ecuador, Peru and Uruguay have introduced dietary guidance recommending citizens eat less ultra-processed food, and the Pan American Health Organization, has introduced a new approach to "profiling" food which includes looking at whether products are high in fat, salt and sugar, (or sweeteners), to determine whether a product is healthy.[47]

The science of all this is still uncertain. Studies show a high correlation between consumption of ultra-processed food and a range of non-communicable diseases. An incremental 10% increase in the proportion of ultra-processed foods in a person's diet is correlated with a 12% increase in cancers, a 21% increase in depressive symptoms and a 12% increase in cardiovascular disease risk.[48]

Sceptics, however, argue that "ultra-processed" is just another way to describe foods that are sugary or fatty, or both at once. Why not blame the contents of the food, rather than the degree of processing in its manufacture?

One former sceptic, Dr Kevin Hall of the US National Institute of Diabetes and Digestive and Kidney Diseases ran a study that attempted to adjust for these factors. Hall gathered ten men and ten women at the National Institute of Health Clinical Center just outside Washington DC.[49] Over a four-week residential stay, they were fed different diets under controlled conditions. For two weeks, the participants ate mostly ultra-processed meals, such as turkey sandwiches with crisps, and for another two weeks they ate mostly unprocessed food such as spinach omelettes with sweet potato hash.

The diets were broadly matched for fat, sugar, calories and fibre. The researchers also worked hard to design both sets of meals to be tasty and familiar to all participants. When participants were asked to rate the food for pleasure, there was little difference.

Blood tests showed that levels of the appetite suppressing hormone PYY were significantly lower when participants were on the processed food diet. By contrast, levels of the hunger hormone, ghrelin, were lower on the unprocessed diets decreased. On the unprocessed diet, participants lost weight: an average of 0.9kg. On the ultra-processed diet, they ate an average of 500 calories more per day than on the unprocessed diet, and they gained an average of 0.9kg.

The exact mechanism responsible for these differences is not yet fully understood. Hall has received a deluge of suggestions since publishing his report. Could it be linked to the gut microbiome, or the satiating effect of specific types of protein? Hall himself thinks that it might be because the ultra-processed food was more calorie-dense, contained less water and, although matched for fibre, contained less insoluble fibre than the unprocessed food. In other words, it's about the ingredients rather than the process. He is about to embark on a new trial to test this theory.

The Boston-based physicist Albert-László Barabási, who specialises in the topography of networks, has his own theory about ultra-processed foods. Having already mapped the complex reactions between different proteins inside human cells, Barabási and fellow physicist Giulia Menichetti have turned their attention to nutrition.

Scientists, they note, have recorded 70,296 distinct biochemicals across the entire range of foods eaten by humans.[50] Yet most nutritional research is centred on the 150 key nutritional components tracked and catalogued by the United States Department of Agriculture. Some of this research has been vital, transforming our understanding of the role of calories, sugar, fat vitamins and other nutrients. But without studying how the thousands of other chemicals within any given food interact, how can we properly understand its impact on health?

Consider garlic, a key ingredient of the Mediterranean diet. The USDA quantifies 67 nutritional components in raw garlic, but each clove actually contains more than 2,306 distinct chemical components – from allicin, an organosulfur compound responsible for the distinct aroma of the freshly crushed clove, to luteolin, a colourless crystalline compound with reported protective effects against cardiovascular disease.

Barabási and Menichetti are using machine learning to search and draw from all the academic papers and nutritional databases available online. In this way, they hope to build a digital catalogue of every nutritional biochemical, along with all the research done on each so far, to better understand how they react with each other and with our bodies to make us healthy or sick. They call this a study of "the dark matter of nutrition".

They have compared the chemical composition of a range of ultra-processed foods with similar home-cooked dishes and raw ingredients. They found that, even where the macronutrient profiles looked similar – sugars, vitamins, fatty acids, minerals, and flavonoids – the other chemical components of ultra-processed foods were different in quantity and type. The reason for this is still unknown. Is it the processing that causes the difference or the specific selection of ingredients and recipes?

What all this shows us is how little we still understand about the way food works. Nutrition has long been the Cinderella of scientific research, perhaps because diet-related disease is a slower, more stealthy killer than, say, cancer. There is a huge amount of work to be done to unravel the full complexity of our diets. As Barabási says: "We are as close to knowing everything there is to know about the pieces. But we are as far as we have ever been from understanding nature as a whole."

Changing Diets

The dietary choices we make as individuals are influenced by multiple factors, often highly personal. At a population level, however, it is possible to identify five major factors that have combined to change the way we eat since the Second World War:

- **Price/Affordability** Rising incomes and more efficient (and intensive) farming techniques have made some products much cheaper relative to household income. Foods made from refined flour, sugar and vegetable oil have become especially cheap.
- **Availability** The range of products on offer affects what people choose.[51] The proliferation of supermarkets in the 1960s meant it became possible to stock a larger variety of produce from across the world at more affordable prices. Consumers could compare products and select their preferred choice.[52] We now buy four times as much pasta and rice, half as much bread and two-thirds less potatoes than we did in the 1970s.[53]
- **Convenience** The enormous social changes that followed the Sexual Revolution – in particular, the rise in women working and in people living alone – have made convenience a much bigger priority. Modern technology – freezers, microwaves and, most recently, delivery apps – has accelerated this trend. Once you factor in the time it takes to cook a meal from scratch, the cost of home-cooked food has risen since the 1980s, whereas the cost of processed convenience food has declined.[54] This has helped create a four-fold rise in ready meals and takeaway food.[55] The pandemic has reinforced this shift: during lockdown the delivery market increased by 41%, and many people say they will stick with it.[56]
- **Marketing** Both commercial marketing (promoting new products or maintaining brand loyalty) and public health marketing can play an important part in shaping our food choices. Since 2007, studies have shown that food and drink advertising contributes to increased calorie intake in children.[58]
- **Taste** Learned behaviours, family culture and individual preferences all contribute to our food choices. But modern processed foods are designed to appeal to the broadest possible base. They tend to be simultaneously bland (no strange or unfamiliar flavours) and highly moreish, packed full of the salt, sugar and fat that our evolutionary appetites crave. Large food companies spend a huge amount of money perfecting the flavour and "mouth feel" of every product. The more of this kind of food we eat, the more we prefer it.

Some countries have done better than others at stopping themselves getting caught in the Junk Food Cycle. South Korea and Japan, for example, have much lower rates of obesity than most developed countries and diets which are still high in fish and plants and low in meat and sugary drinks.[58] Both countries have achieved this by bringing in policies to protect their traditional cuisines, such as compulsory school lunches, Government-funded lessons on how to prepare traditional food, and strong marketing campaigns.[60] However, even with these protective measures, obesity is rising in these countries as citizens shift to more Western style diets.[61]

Unfortunately, it is too late for the UK to take similar preventative measures. Junk food has already become embedded in our food culture and childhood memories. For example, our packed lunches and picnics invariably include a packet of crisps and a chocolate bar, and our religious festivals – most notably Easter – are dominated by junk food marketing. Even activities such as gaming are closely linked with consumption of unhealthy foods, with KFC recently launching a games console with an inbuilt chicken warmer.[62]

So far, Government attempts to shift diets have relied heavily on interventions – such as labelling, leaflets and marketing campaigns – which require individuals to make a conscious effort to change their behaviour. But as we have seen, it is unrealistic to expect the junk food cycle to be broken solely through individual willpower.[63]

Voluntary schemes developed with the food industry have also had limited sustained impact because companies have been allowed to opt out and thus secure a competitive advantage.

Mandatory interventions have had much more impact, over a shorter period. The UK's Soft Drinks Industry Levy led to a 29% reduction in the average sugar content of soft drinks within three years.[64] Similar results can be seen in Hungary and Mexico, where taxes on unhealthy foods have encouraged food companies to reformulate their products and have reduced purchases of unhealthy foods.[65] These taxes have been in place since 2011 and 2014 respectively, and there are now signs of detectable health impacts.[66]

But no country has successfully reversed the drift towards obesity. While some interventions are more effective than others, there is no silver bullet. Given the power of the Junk Food Cycle, multiple interventions are needed, much like those that have led to the decline in smoking since the 1950s.[67]

Even then we are unlikely to see immediate improvements. Changes in dietary behaviour across populations take time to reach a scale where the benefits (or otherwise) can clearly be seen. Today's dietary patterns have formed over a period of at least 70 years. We will need long-term political commitments to reverse them.

5

Inequality

AT Glasgow's book festival earlier this year, the BBC presenter Andrew Marr was asked about his student flirtation with Marxism, which earned him the nickname "Red Andy". He explained that in later life he had come to appreciate the power of the free market – albeit with reservations.

"The market is something we live in all the time," he said. "It's almost the water we swim in, and it gives us all the things we take for granted about ourselves. It's a great machine for inventiveness and ingenuity, but it presents two really serious problems. One is dirt: it produces filth and pollution. The second is that it produces huge and unacceptable levels of inequality. For me, the job of politics is to remove the dirt, and reduce inequality."

Much of this report will be about the "dirt" – or externalities, in economics jargon – created by the food system. But in this chapter, we want to focus on inequality

It isn't just capitalism that creates inequality. In fact, ever since humans began to farm, keep livestock, and pass on their assets to future generations, inequality has been a defining feature of human societies – regardless of their political structure. In his book The Great Leveler, the Stanford-based historian Walter Scheidel[1] showed that only the "Four Horsemen" of social levelling – mass-mobilisation warfare, transformative revolutions, state collapse, and catastrophic plagues – have ever significantly reduced inequality. It never goes peacefully.

COVID-19 has, so far, served mainly to exacerbate inequalities in the UK. But it has also generated a new sense of urgency about addressing them.

The inequalities within, and created by, our food system are stark. Analysis of the annual National Diet and Nutrition Survey shows that adults on low incomes are more likely to have diets which are high in sugar but low in fibre, fruits, vegetables and fish. Children from the least well-off 20% of families consume around 29% less fruits and vegetables, 75% less oily fish, and 17% less fibre per day than children from the most well off 20%.[2] The effects of this dietary disparity are all too predictable.

Figure 5.1 shows how the rates of different diet-related conditions vary according to the affluence of an area. People living in the most deprived decile are almost twice as likely to die from all preventable causes, compared to those in the richest decile. They are 2.1 times more likely to die from preventable heart disease; 1.7 times more likely to die from preventable cancer; and 3 times more likely to have tooth decay at age 5. Their children are nearly twice as likely to be overweight or obese at age 11.[3]

This pre-existing divide in diet-related health is one reason why people in the most deprived areas have been twice as likely to die from COVID-19, compared to those in the least deprived areas.[4]

Even before Covid, however, the upward trajectory of life expectancy in the UK had begun to slow – and in some areas, go into reverse.[5] Women in the most deprived 10% of neighbourhoods in England now die 3.6 months younger than they did in 2010.[6] Their life expectancy is 7.7 years shorter than that of women in the richest areas.

Figure 5.1

People on low incomes are more likely to suffer, and die from, diet-related conditions[7]

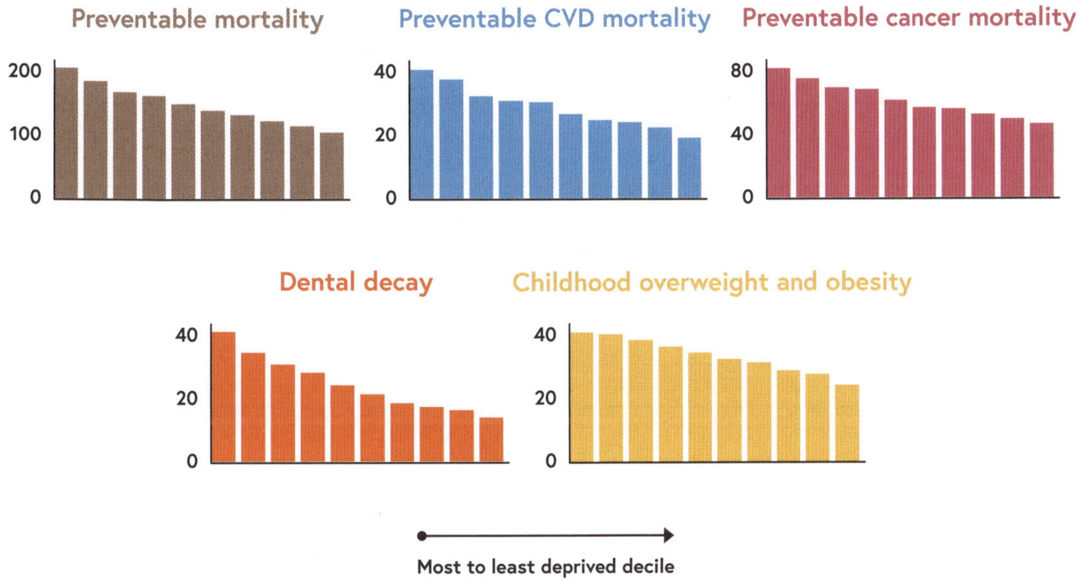

Y axis in all charts shows relative risk, expressed as percentages, rate per 100,000 people, or mortality per 100,000 people.

Figure 5.2

Poorer children tend to be shorter than their wealthier counterparts[8]

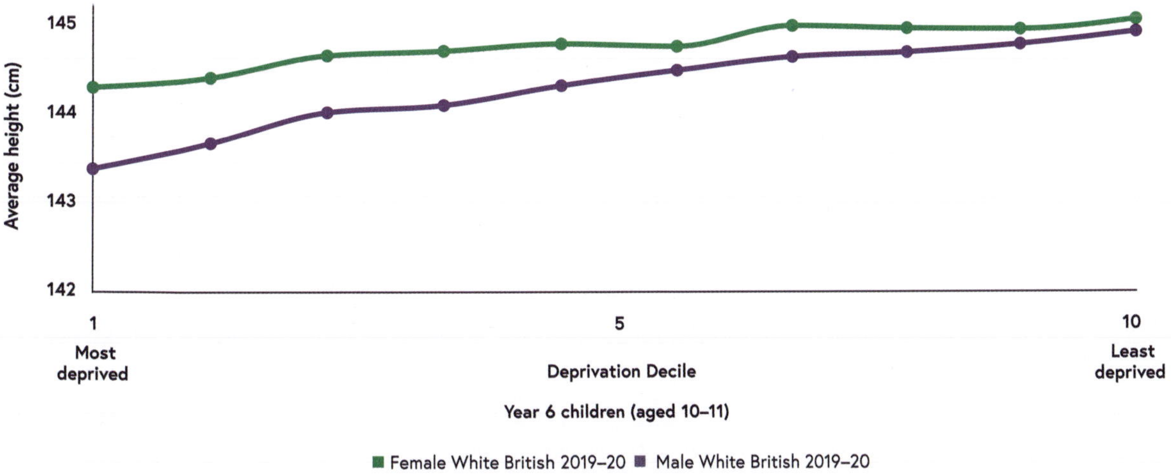

Figure 5.3

Average height in high income Western countries: female, aged 5, 2019[9]

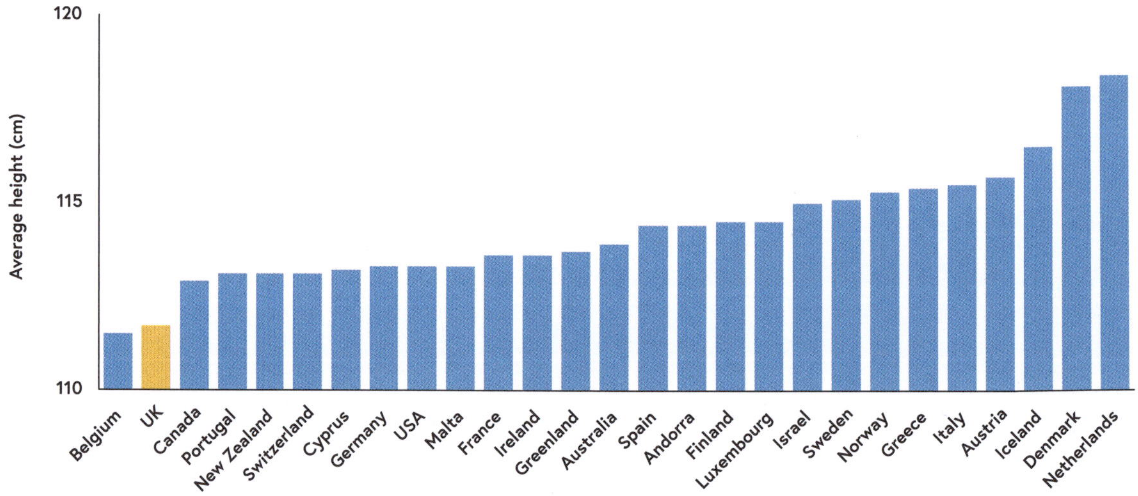

Figure 5.4

Average height in high income Western countries: male, aged 5, 2019[10]

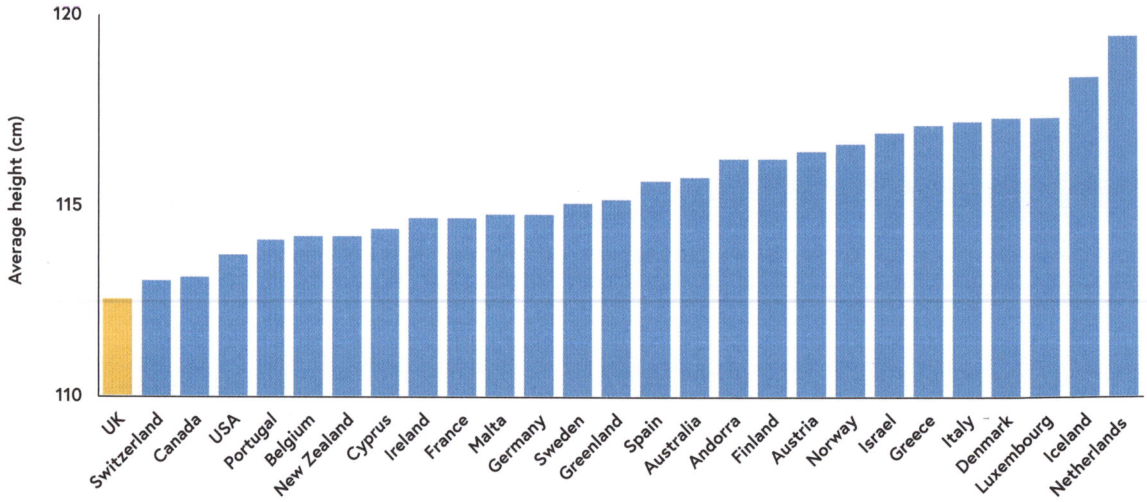

The differential for men is 9.5 years.[11] For healthy life expectancy there is an even greater disparity between rich and poor with a gap of 19 years.[12]

It shouldn't have taken a global pandemic to make us pay proper attention to dietary inequality. It has long been visible to the naked eye. A modern diet of cheap junk food has the peculiar quality that it can make you simultaneously overweight and poorly nourished. Children in the poorest areas of England are both fatter and significantly shorter than those in the richest areas at age 10–11 (see Figures 5.1 and 5.2). (This also has an impact at a national level. The average five-year-old in the UK is shorter than his or her peers in nearly all other high-income western countries.[13])

Figure 5.5

There is a strong correlation between income, educational attainment, and fruit and vegetable consumption[14]

Based on years 1–3 of the National Diet and Nutrition Survey (2008/09–2010/11). Note: Foods appear in this graphic only if they are consumed in quantities that exceed the 95% upper confidence interval of the population mean. The foods represented here are those which stand out on a statistical basis, and do not represent the totality of the diet within each demographic group. The size of the circle is proportional to the relative difference between the level of consumption within a specific income-education category and that of the population overall.

CEDAR Centre for Diet and Activity Research

Obesity can also co-exist with outright hunger. The same households that struggle to eat well may sometimes find themselves unable to eat at all. Data collected in 2019 by the Department of Work and Pensions found that, even before the pandemic, 4% of UK families experienced disrupted eating patterns or were forced to cut back on food due to a lack of resources.[15] (The Government calls this "very low food security".) Among those on Universal Credit, this proportion rose to 26%.[16] The economic disruption caused by the pandemic has increased the number of households struggling to put food on the table.[17]

By now some readers may be writhing irritably in their seats, wondering whatever happened to personal responsibility. The wartime generation managed to survive on scraps, through careful budgeting and menu planning. Lentils are cheap. Isn't eating badly a symptom of laziness, rather than just poverty?

It is true that a little can be made to go a long way – provided you know where to buy cheap ingredients, you have the means to get there and back, and you are skilled enough to turn raw ingredients into something appetising. But those are significant provisos. Culinary skills and knowledge have diminished across every social class since convenience food became widely available, and they are still diminishing as one generation after another grows up without seeing or trying cookery at home.[18] (This is another example of a reinforcing feedback loop.)

The fact is, we live in a completely different food landscape from that of our thrifty grandparents. As we saw in the previous chapter, unhealthy food is cheaper per calorie than healthy food. This is especially true when you factor in the opportunity cost of cooking from scratch. If you're tired and short of time – and especially if you're not a confident cook – it makes economic sense to buy a box of chicken and chips instead of toiling at the stove. Especially as you can be sure the kids will eat it, so there's no danger of it going to waste.

There are capital costs to eating well, too. Cooking requires technology, even at the most basic level. There are currently an estimated 1.9 million people in the UK living without a cooker, 2.8 million people without a freezer, and 900,000 people without a fridge.[19] Some households have the relevant white goods in place, but not enough money to run them.

There's also a strong psychological component to what people buy and eat.

Poverty causes high levels of stress, sleeplessness and cognitive overload.[20] Numerous studies have shown how scarcity of money, food or time affects cognitive processes, in effect narrowing mental "bandwidth".[21] This can result in people making decisions that go against their long-term interests.[22] People from the poorest households are much less likely to adopt healthy behaviours – such as planning and cooking meals from scratch – because all their energy is taken up with coping in the short term.[23]

The stress of poverty also interferes with the hormones that regulate appetite. The more exhausted and strung out you are, the harder it is to resist temptation.[24] Not coincidentally, people in deprived areas tend to be surrounded by the temptations of junk food. There is a clear correlation between poverty and the density of fast-food outlets, with almost twice as many in the most deprived areas compared to the least (see Figure 5.6). In one deprived area in North-West England, there are 230 fast food outlets for every 100,000 people, compared to an England-wide average of 96.[25]

In these so-called "food swamps, junk food is everywhere but fresh ingredients are harder to find. Roughly 3.3 million people cannot reach any food stores selling raw ingredients within 15 minutes by public transport, and 40% of the lowest income households lack access to a car – almost twice as many as the national average.[26] Without a local shop selling fresh ingredients, or a car to get you to the supermarket, or a fridge to keep perishables in, cooking from scratch becomes dauntingly difficult.

The economic inequalities in this country are not about to vanish overnight. Whatever the government's other "levelling up" priorities may be, there is a particular urgency to the problem of helping low-income families eat well. Improving the diets of the poorest households would have both immediate and long-term benefits, not just for those people who would live longer and in better health, but for the economic outlook of the whole country.

Figure 5.6

The most deprived areas tend to have more fast food outlets[27]

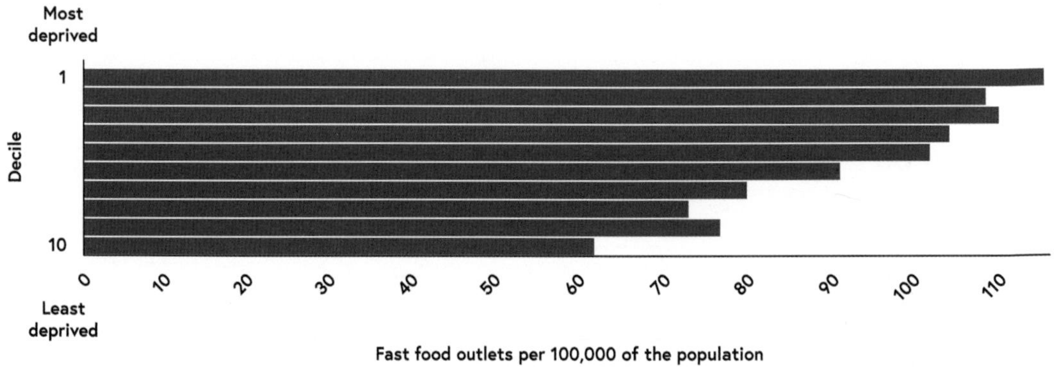

Welfare

Our Terms of Reference tasked us with creating a Food Strategy that, among other things, enables people to access "safe, healthy, affordable food; regardless of where they live or how much they earn". We have outlined in this chapter how social inequalities in the UK are reflected in, and exacerbated by, inequalities of diet. Our recommendations also set out how these can be alleviated, in part, by using taxation to encourage corporations to reformulate unhealthy food, and using some of that money to help the least affluent access healthy food.

Our scope does not cover the economic measures required to structure a fairer society, nor have we been asked to suggest changes to the benefits system more broadly. Ideally, of course, the true cost of eating healthily should be calculated into benefits payments.

There is a widespread notion that giving low-income households extra money to spend on food is a waste of time. We heard this again and again during our consultations with citizens – even from those who were themselves on benefits. "They'd just spend it on booze and fags" was a common refrain, only partially in jest.

But all the evidence suggests this is a myth. Studies in this country have shown that, as poorer families' income goes up, they spend more on fruit, vegetables, fibre, oily fish and other foods rich in vitamins and minerals. And families actually cut their spending on alcohol and tobacco as their income rises.

6

Exposing the invisibility of nature

"Statistics are the lens through which we see the world, but they have made nature invisible to policymakers. Twenty-first century progress cannot be measured using twentieth century statistics."

Diane Coyle, Bennett Professor of Public Policy at the University of Cambridge[1]

WE have seen how the Junk Food Cycle – a reinforcing feedback loop between commercial incentives and the human appetite – is damaging our health. Now we must turn our attention to the system failures that are causing so much harm to our environment.

The manufacture, production and distribution of food has become an ecological disaster. Globally (and domestically), it is the single largest contributor to the destruction of habitats, biodiversity and major abiotic systems (water, nitrogen and carbon).[2]

In systems terms, the reason for this is simple. There is no balancing feedback loop to stop us destroying nature. By almost all of the measurements that we use to value human activity, nature is invisible.

"Nature" is everywhere, yet almost impossible to measure. It doesn't sit in bank accounts or wallets, waiting to be counted. Much of it is silent, invisible or mobile. The biome of microscopic bacteria in the soil quietly breaks down nutrients to make them accessible to plants. Populations of deep water fish rise and fall unseen on the ocean floor. Winds blow, rivers flow, oceans circulate, and insects and birds flitter across national borders, belonging to no one but the Earth. (See Figure 6.1 drawn from Dasgupta's review.)

What we don't notice, we don't tend to value. It is no surprise that the most eye-catching parts of nature get the most attention. Campaigns to save charismatic megafauna, such as giant pandas, long preceded widespread concern for the biodiversity of life in our soil. If carbon dioxide smelled bad, you can be certain we would have done more about cutting down on greenhouse gas emissions.

> "I feel like [climate change is] the defining issue of our time and we'll look back on it like we look back on the slave trade and things like that. Almost in a way of, 'How could we not have seen sooner what was happening?'"
>
> "Deliberative dialogue" participant, South West England

Figure 6.1

Redrawn from Partha Dasgupta's "The Economics of Biodiversity"; Nature is silent, invisible and mobile

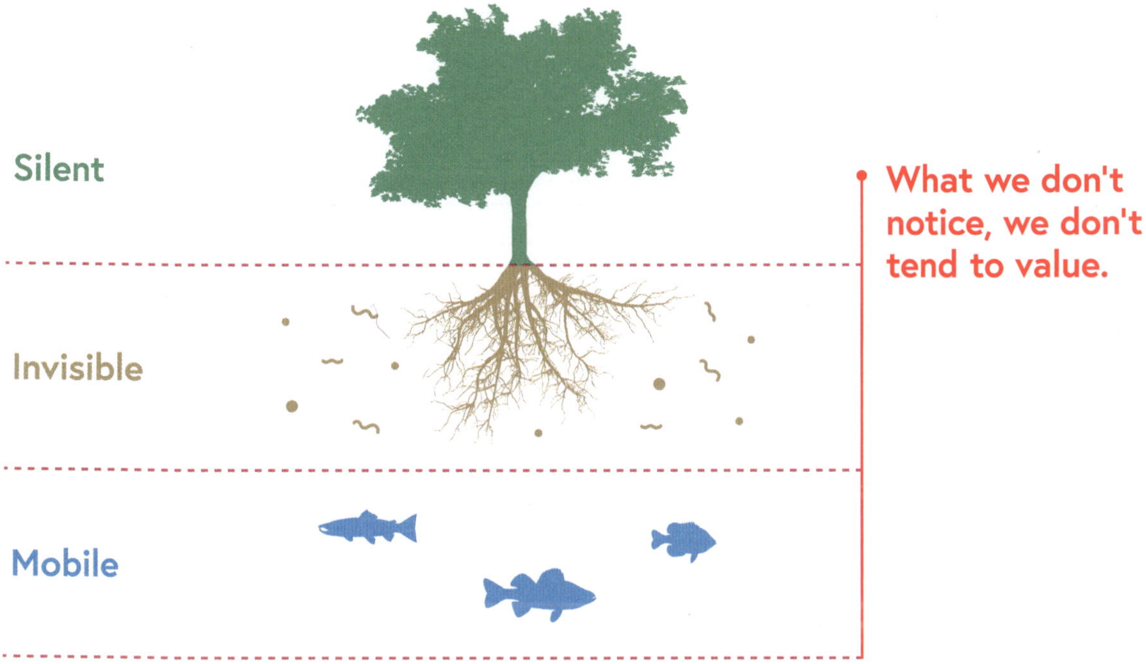

Crucially, we do not place a financial value on nature. A farmer who ploughs up an area of rich peatland, for example, does not have to pay for carbon that is emitted from the peat in the process, accelerating climate change. Nor is the cost passed on to the consumer. Intensive farming has made food unprecedentedly cheap, in terms of household outlay, even as the cost to the planet spirals out of control. No one pays for the damage, so everyone does.

Environmental destruction and climate change impose a huge financial burden on the taxpayer. Yet none of this is recorded on our financial spreadsheets. It is not factored into the GDP with which we measure a nation's economic health, or the financial statements of our companies.

Nature has an intrinsic and universal value which exceeds any economic measurement. But the fact that it simply doesn't exist within the financial calculations that shape so much of human, and governmental, decision making, makes it extremely vulnerable to bad decisions.

Our economic systems treat natural resources as if they were both costless and infinite. In fact, it is worse than that. As the economist Partha Dasgupta pointed out in The Economics of Diversity, his recent review for the UK Treasury, Governments around the world actively encourage the destruction of nature.[3] Every year, $500 billion-worth of Government subsidies are spent globally on supporting practices – such as intensive agriculture, fisheries, fossil fuel mining and fertiliser manufacture – that destroy nature. These economic incentives are estimated to cause $4 to $6 trillion of environmental damage every year. In economic terms, we have actually given nature a negative value.

As Dasgupta's review makes plain, we are currently living way beyond the planet's means. Technological advances alone will not save us. Unless we make dramatic changes to our agricultural, industrial and consumer patterns, we will destroy the lives of future generations. Once ecosystems are lost it is hugely expensive – and often impossible – to rebuild them.

The world is slowly waking up to this reality. Farmers, for example, are increasingly paid by governments to deliver environmental benefits as well as food. But these interventions have been small compared to the scale of change required. Around 4% of the subsidy money provided by the Common Agricultural Policy goes on supporting low carbon, environmentally friendly farming.[4]

In 2011, the Government commissioned a team of economists and environmental academics to work out how we could become "the first generation to leave the environment in a better state than it inherited".[5] The final report of the Natural Capital Committee, published last year, set out three "guiding principles":[6]

1. **Net environmental gain** It is not enough to stop destroying nature, we need to start rebuilding it.
2. **Public money for public goods** The Government should spend taxpayers' money on things that benefit everyone in society. From a farming perspective, this might include habitats with better biodiversity, which capture water and prevent floods, or which are simply beautiful. By definition, public goods are non-excludable (their benefits cannot be confined just to those who have paid for them), and non-rivalrous (consumption by one person does not restrict consumption by others).
3. **The polluter pays** Any individual who destroys the natural habitat must be made to pay to restore the harm they have done.

As we pursue these principles, we need to be able to measure our progress. And to do that, we must decide which elements of the environment to measure, and how; what value to attach to each of these measurements; and finally, how to build that value into our food system (whether in the form of a public good, or by using the polluter pays principle). None of this is easy.

The Global Farm Metric (GFM) coalition has recently been wrestling with the first part of this problem: what to measure on farms, and how. A collaboration between farmers, food producers, supermarkets, environmental NGOs, banks and investors, the GFM is attempting to create an internationally agreed set of indicators for assessing the sustainability of any farm: the Global Farm Metric. That is the limit of their scope: just agreeing on the indicators, not assigning any value to them. They simply want to establish an international language for quantifying various elements of nature – much as the International Bureau of Weights and Measures in Paris defines the metrics used in science and engineering. (The precise length of a metre, for example.)

Figure 6.2, a work in progress, illustrates the many factors the GFM currently believe should be measured in order to understand the impact of a farm – not only on nature, but also on society. These range from water quality to soil structure, to animal welfare and the skills of the human workforce.

For each of these elements, and more, the GFM is devising a metric of measurement. This is easier in some cases than others. The methods for quantifying greenhouse gas emissions are already well debated (although, as we shall see in the next chapter, not fully agreed). But the science of measuring, say, carbon sequestration has a long way to go. No one has yet worked out how to measure the carbon stored in soils systematically and reproducibly over large areas. And we are only just beginning to think about how to quantify many other elements of nature, such as biodiversity.

Assuming the world can eventually agree on the metrics by which to measure nature, we still have to find a way to place values on these metrics. This, again, is fraught with difficulty.

In devising the £2.4 billion of subsidies that will be paid to farmers in place of the Common Agricultural Policy, our Government has pledged to only subsidise public goods.[7] (Not, say, the production of food, which is both excludable and rivalrous. I can stop you eating my apple; and once I have eaten it, you can't.) But how should it weigh up the various public goods against one another? What is a beautiful view of pasture and dry-stone walls worth, compared to a biodiverse riparian woodland along a stream, or a flood-preventing wetland?

There is also, still, intense debate over exactly how one makes the polluter pay. The British economist Arthur Cecil Pigou, in his 1920 work The Economics of Welfare, argued that this should be done through taxation.[8] But in 1960, the America economist Ronald Coase argued that such "Pigouvian" taxes could "lead to results which are not necessarily, or even usually, desirable".[9] Today, economists are still divided between these two camps. We will examine their arguments further in Chapter 12.

Politically, too, there are dangers in making the polluter pay. The cost is often born by the consumer, and tends to be felt most keenly by the poorest. Just look at the recent Gilets Jaunes protests in France, sparked by rises in fuel duty, or our own fuel protests in 2000.

Figure 6.2

A selection of the metrics for understanding the impact of a farm[10]

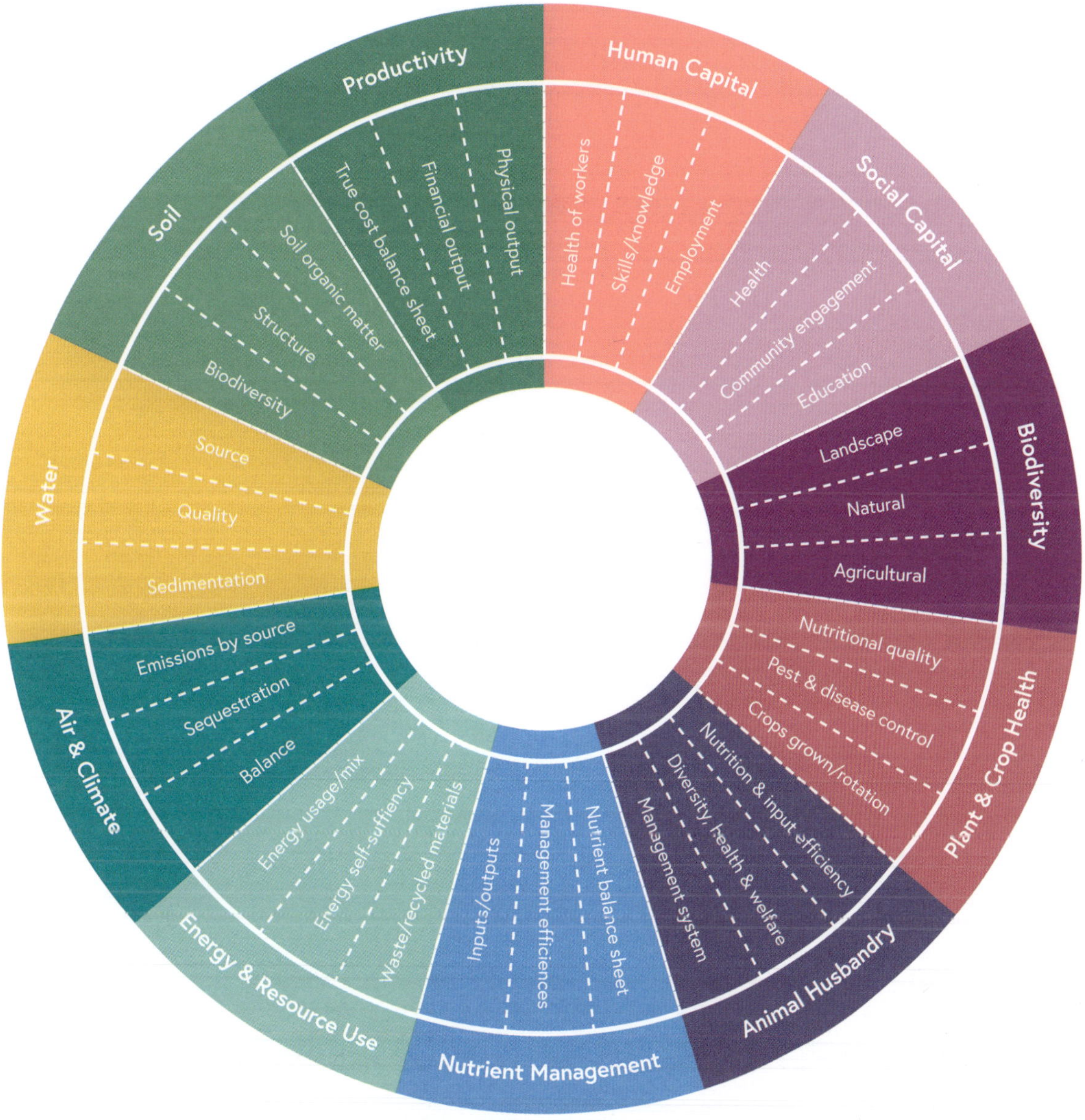

Finally, there are some environmentalists who dislike the very idea of putting a price tag on nature. The journalist George Monbiot, writing in The Guardian, derided the concept of "natural capital" as "morally wrong, intellectually vacuous, emotionally alienating and self-defeating".[11] It "reinforces the notion that nature has no value unless you can extract cash from it," he argued. It turns the natural world into just another tradeable commodity, subject to the corrosive values of the marketplace.

Dasgupta's report was criticised along similar lines, by people who don't appear to have read it. In fact, Dasgupta is keenly aware of the dangers of abandoning the environment to an unregulated free market. "Markets alone are inadequate for protecting ecosystems from overuse," he writes. He recognises that the value of some ecosystems may essentially be infinite, either because they have sacred value or because they are close to a tipping point past which they will be lost forever.

Dasgupta also accepts that often it will be impossible to measure and value the true harm done to a system. We know, for example, that the extraordinary complexity of mycelia, bacteria, protists, archaea, and the vast array of microorganisms and invertebrates in our soils, are essential to both agriculture and the natural world. But we are a long way from truly understanding this miniature ecosystem, let alone being able to put a price on it. If we just hazard a guess, and slap on a price tag that undervalues a vital part of the natural world by mistake, we might accelerate its destruction. In many cases, says Dasgupta, it would be simpler and safer to impose legal restrictions to stop people exploiting certain habitats, rather than relying on taxation.

The "invisibility" of nature is what makes it acutely vulnerable to human activity. But there is no straightforward way to make it visible. Clumsy reform could easily lead to unintended consequences.

Doing nothing, however, is more dangerous still. To properly disincentivise environmental destruction, we must find a way to build its true cost into the system – even if we can't value it to the last penny.

In the following chapters we will examine what a food system in which nature was visible and valued might look like. Is there a way of getting all the food we need from the land while simultaneously restoring nature and sequestering carbon? And if so, how do we reach this promised land?

"I think that as human beings we are short - sighted in a crisis. We need to take a longer view of our time here and what it means to be a citizen in modern society if we are to make any lasting changes."

"Deliberative dialogue" participant,
London & the South East

7

Food and climate

THE food system – agriculture, food production, distribution and retail combined – releases more greenhouse gases than any other sector apart from energy. It is responsible for 25–30% of global emissions: a tally that dwarfs, say, the 3.5% contributed by air travel.[1] In the UK, the food system accounts for a fifth of domestic emissions – but that figure rises to around 30% if we factor in the emissions produced by all the food we import.[2]

There are four major ways in which the food system contributes to climate change:

1. The damage done when wild areas are converted to farmland, or when farmland is prevented from reverting to forest.
2. The release of carbon from farmland soil – particularly peat soils.
3. The use of fossil fuels in every part of the food system.
4. The release of two potent greenhouse gases, methane and nitrous oxide, from agriculture – by far the largest factor in the UK.

Wherever land is converted for farming, it exacts a terrible toll on the environment. The most famous example is the deforestation of the Amazon rainforest, which – as well as destroying vast areas of ancient beauty and biodiversity – has released a vast amount of carbon into the atmosphere. During the 2010s, tree-burning in the Amazon released more carbon than seven years' worth of UK fossil fuel emissions.[3]

In this country, we destroyed our forests long ago. In 5,000 BC, 75% of the UK was covered in wildwoods.[4] But as human settlements spread and became more sophisticated, trees were chopped down to clear land, to build houses and boats, and to burn for fuel. By 1086, when the Doomsday Book was completed, the proportion of land in England covered by forest had shrunk to 15%. That figure currently sits at just 10% (up from a low point of 6% at the end of the Second World War).[5]

A more recent calamity in this country is the destruction of our peat bogs. Peat is created when plants growing on top of a bog – typically mosses, sedges and reeds – sink into wet, acidic and anaerobic conditions below. Under these conditions they do not fully decay. Instead of rotting and releasing carbon back into the atmosphere, like most dying things, these plants retain their carbon as they sink in layers down into the bog. By this process, a peat bog might sequester 0.4 to 1.1 tonnes of carbon per hectare per year.[6] (This compares to 5 to 40 tonnes for growing woodland, with temperate forests typically sequestering 10–20 tonnes per year.)[7]

It takes thousands of years for a peat bog to form, but a matter of days to plough it up. Because peat is so rich in nutrients, it makes wonderfully fertile farmland. Over the past couple of centuries, 56% of the UK's peat land has been drained and converted to agricultural use – either for grazing animals or for growing crops.[8] When peat dries out, the organic matter that has built up for thousands of years begins to be eaten by bacteria in the soil. This process converts the carbon in the peat into carbon dioxide, which is then released into the atmosphere.

Emissions from converted peat bogs can be huge – each hectare of lowland peat used for crop farming emits an average of around 4 tonnes of carbon dioxide equivalent per year.[9] And of course, this land doesn't just emit carbon; like deforested land, it also loses the ability to sequester carbon.[10]

Once a farm is up and running, it typically uses a lot of energy to produce crops. Most farming in this country relies heavily on man-made herbicides, pesticides and, above all, fertiliser. These days most fertiliser is not created from manure or nitrogen-fixing crops but from ammonia, which itself is produced in vast factories. Nitrogen from the atmosphere is synthesized with hydrogen atoms ripped from fossil fuels at high temperature and under high pressure. This process on its own accounts for 1% of global carbon emissions.[11†]

Once spread onto the land, any fertiliser that isn't taken up by plants sinks into the soil. From there, it is either washed into our rivers and underground aquifers, contaminating both, or converted by bacteria into nitrous oxide – a greenhouse gas roughly 265 times more potent than carbon dioxide. This adds a further 2% to global emissions.

Farm machinery and buildings require a lot of energy to run. And once the raw ingredients have left the farm, another long chain of energy consumption begins: processing, packaging, transport, retail, cold storage, cooking in homes and restaurants, waste disposal. The good news is that these parts of the food system increasingly benefit from innovations in clean and efficient energy. Now that we have made clean electricity cheaper than fossil fuels, many food manufacturers and retailers have been able to cut their carbon footprints dramatically. Nestlé UK and Ireland has, for example, reduced its operational emissions by more than 60% since 2007.[12]

Figure 7.1 shows how greenhouse gas emissions are distributed across the various parts of the food system. It is worth noting that the transport of food – the famous "food mile" – actually accounts for only 13% of the food system's total carbon footprint. Airfreight is a small percentage of that (estimated at around 1% and 1.5% of total emissions from food),[††] though flying does turn low carbon food into high carbon food: the carbon footprint of South American asparagus, for example, increases by more than 25 times when it is flown to the UK.[13]

Figure 7.1

Agriculture is the biggest contributor to GHG emissions in the food system[14]

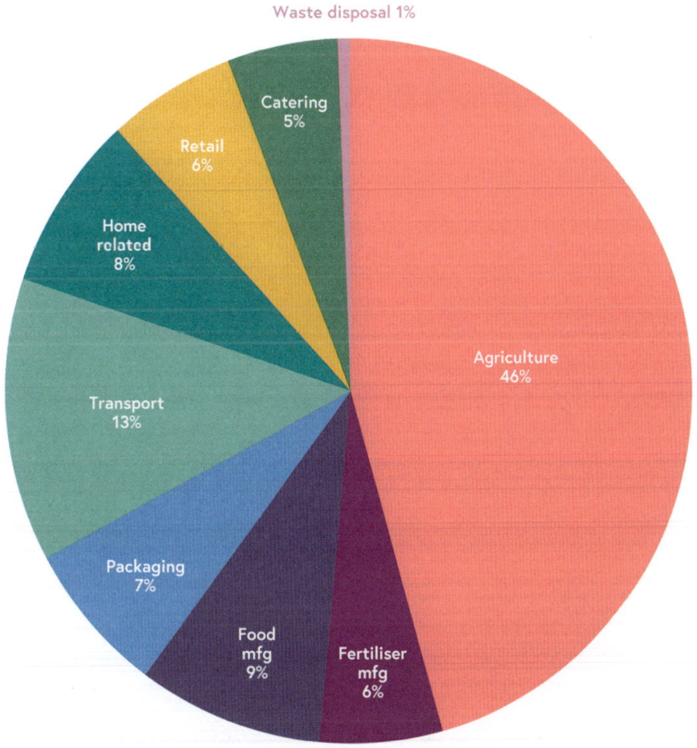

[†] 1% of global emissions come from ammonia production and 12% of total agricultural emissions (2.9% of total emissions) from synthetic ammonia use. In total, then, synthetic fertiliser is about 4% of global GHGs.

[††] Air freight only represents a very small percentage of food miles (estimated at 0.16%) as it is so expensive. Only 1.5% of UK fruit and vegetables are air freighted. Overall, air freighting accounts for 1–1.5% of food emissions.

The relative potency of CO_2, CH_4 and N_2O

Three man-made greenhouse gases account for the bulk of the warming associated with climate change: Carbon Dioxide (CO_2), Methane (CH_4), and Nitrous Oxide (N_2O). The food system is the only field of human activity that emits all three.

For a long time, it was thought water vapour and clouds were solely responsible for regulating the temperature of our planet. To a large degree this is true. The sun washes the Earth with every imaginable wavelength of light. A third of that light is reflected back by clouds and a sixth is absorbed by airborne water vapour. The remaining half – most of it visible – makes it to the Earth's surface and is almost all absorbed by the land, oceans and vegetation. The Earth heats up and emits this heat back into the atmosphere in the form of infra-red light, some of which gets trapped in the atmospheric water vapour, and some of which makes it back out into space. In total, the water vapour traps just enough heat to make the world warm enough for us to live in and releases enough to ensure we don't get too hot.

Man-made greenhouse gases, exist in our atmosphere in such tiny quantities (by comparison with water vapour) that for a long time no one imagined they could have any significant effect on our climate. If you were to fill a million balloons with air from the Earth's atmosphere, the total quantity of water vapour would be enough to fill 25,000 balloons. The carbon dioxide would fill only 300 balloons. The methane would fill less than one and a half balloons, and the nitrous oxide just under a quarter of one balloon.

Until the late 19th century, scientists believed that changes in water vapour alone must account for the world's hot and cold phases. It took an impulsive and energetic Swedish scientist, Svante Arrhenius, to prove them wrong.

Arrhenius realised that the wavelengths of light absorbed by carbon dioxide were different from those absorbed by water vapour. So carbon dioxide could theoretically "sweep up" the heat that got through those gaps in the absorption spectrum of the vapour. Without a computer to aid him, Arrhenius sat down on Christmas eve of 1894 to begin the "tedious calculations" required to work out whether this effect could be significant. They proved so tedious that by the time he finished, in December 1895, his new and pregnant wife (formerly his laboratory assistant) had left him to go to live alone on a remote island.

But Arrhenius had made a remarkable discovery. Small changes in airborne carbon dioxide, he concluded, could have a huge effect on the climate. The burning of fossil fuels would lead to the gradual warming of the planet over time. "In the future," he wrote from the perspective of Sweden's frigid climate, "our descendants [will] live under a warmer sky and a less harsh environment than we were granted."

We now know that it is not just carbon dioxide that has this effect but other gases too. They all have different qualities: each is better or worse at absorbing heat and each remains in the atmosphere for different periods of time.

In terms of volume, methane (CH_4) is only a middling player: there is 210 times less methane in the atmosphere than carbon dioxide, but five times more methane than nitrous oxide.[15†] The problem is that methane is a very potent greenhouse gas. A tonne of methane released into the atmosphere will trap 85 times more heat than carbon dioxide over a 20 year period.[16]

To enable us to compare their relative potency, and therefore to prioritise our actions to mitigate climate change, scientists have created the Global Warming Potential (GWP) scale. The GWP of a gas is calculated over a specific time horizon, commonly 20 or 100 years. The benchmark gas, carbon dioxide, is defined as having GWP of 1. Over twenty years, methane has a GWP of 85. But over 100 years its GWP is 34, because – unlike carbon, which lingers for centuries – methane disappears from the atmosphere relatively quickly. Nitrous Oxide has a GWP of 265 over both periods.[17]

So although methane and nitrous oxide fill many fewer balloons than carbon dioxide, each balloon created packs a much bigger punch.

† Approximately 1,900 and 330 parts per billion respectively vs 400,000 parts per billion for carbon dioxide.

But the food system's two biggest climate sins are methane and manure. Agriculture is responsible for 50% of global methane emissions.[18] Most of this is generated by just two foodstuffs: rice (fermenting bacteria in the wet soil of rice paddies give off large quantities of methane) and ruminant livestock, chiefly cows and sheep.[†]

Ruminant stomachs have to work hard to ferment plant cellulose into digestible starches. This process creates methane, which the animals burp out. Ruminant manure – the run-off from which pollutes watercourses and leads to freshwater eutrophication – also releases methane and nitrous oxide. Taken together, the burping and manure of ruminant animals account for two thirds of the UK's farming emissions.[19]

The methane produced by ruminants is estimated to have caused a third of total global warming since the industrial revolution.[20] And, as we have seen, there are currently more animals being reared for food than ever before. The combined mass of agricultural livestock is now 1.8 times bigger than all the humans on Earth.[21] Every year, around the world, around 1.3 billion ruminants are slaughtered for food.[22]

Methane is a much more potent greenhouse gas than carbon dioxide. (To understand the different qualities of the main greenhouse gases, please read the box above.) But it also has the singular quality of impermanence. While carbon dioxide and nitrous oxide both linger in the atmosphere,[††] methane transforms itself. It reacts with hydroxyl radicals (OH) – oxidising chemicals that are abundant in the upper atmosphere – to turn into water vapour or (much less potent) carbon dioxide.[†††] The average methane molecule is thought to remain in the atmosphere for only 12 years. (This is why the GWP – see box – of methane is 85 over twenty years, but only 34 over 100 years.)

This has two important implications.

The first is that, if we stopped increasing the number of ruminant animals on the planet, it would take around 12 years for the amount of methane in the atmosphere to stabilise.

Imagine a landscape with a herd of cows grazing on the left, and a power station on the right. As the cows keep burping, their total contribution to the amount of methane in the atmosphere keeps growing – but only for 12 years. After that, the methane they burped out in the early days will start to fall out of the atmosphere. As long as the herd stays the same size,[††††] its total methane contribution will stabilise, as new methane goes up and old methane vanishes from the atmosphere. The carbon dioxide emitted by the power station, by contrast, will keep building up because it lingers in the atmosphere for centuries.

As Figure 7.2 shows, the global demand for meat is in fact already slowing. In developed countries, consumption of beef and lamb seems to be in (modest) decline, perhaps because of perceived health or environmental concerns. Some commentators have suggested the world may be reaching "peak meat". If that is the case (which remains to be seen), it may be possible to cap methane emissions at their current level simply by eating the same number of ruminants as we do today.

It follows from this that if we actually reduced the number of ruminants on the planet (or the methane produced by each ruminant), over time the quantity of methane in the atmosphere would reduce. This would have a cooling effect. If all the ruminants on Earth mysteriously vanished tomorrow, it would take roughly twelve years for the methane they have already produced to leave the atmosphere almost completely. After a couple more decades, the temperature of the planet would have cooled to the same temperature as if those animals had never existed.[†††††]

There is no comparable vanishing trick that can be performed with carbon or nitrous oxide. Only methane can disappear like this. Cutting back on methane is therefore one of the very few methods by which we could put a relatively sharp brake on climate change. This is why, in recent years, meat-eating has risen up the environmental agenda.

Rapidly reducing methane emissions[††††††] from both agriculture and the fossil fuel industry, could reduce temperature rises this century by 0.25 degrees.[23]

....

† Pigs and chickens also produce methane and emissions from manure, though at much lower levels.

†† Nitrous oxide for around 120 years, CO_2 for at least several hundred years.

††† Hydroxyl radicals are often known as the detergent of the troposphere because they react with many pollutants to remove them from the atmosphere. The increase in methane in the atmosphere is leading to a reduction in these radicals. This has leads to the removal of methane in the atmosphere slowing down. In 1990 it took, an average of ten years, vs the twelve today.

†††† Strictly speaking and for reasons too complicated to go into here, you would need to reduce the amount of livestock by 1% per annum to stabilise methane.

††††† This thought experiment ignores the effect of carbon feedback loops, but is accurate enough as to make no difference.

†††††† Though there are a range of scenarios in the recent UN Global Methane Assessment, 45% less is achievable by 2030.

Figure 7.2

There are tentative signs that the world may be reaching peak meat consumption[24]

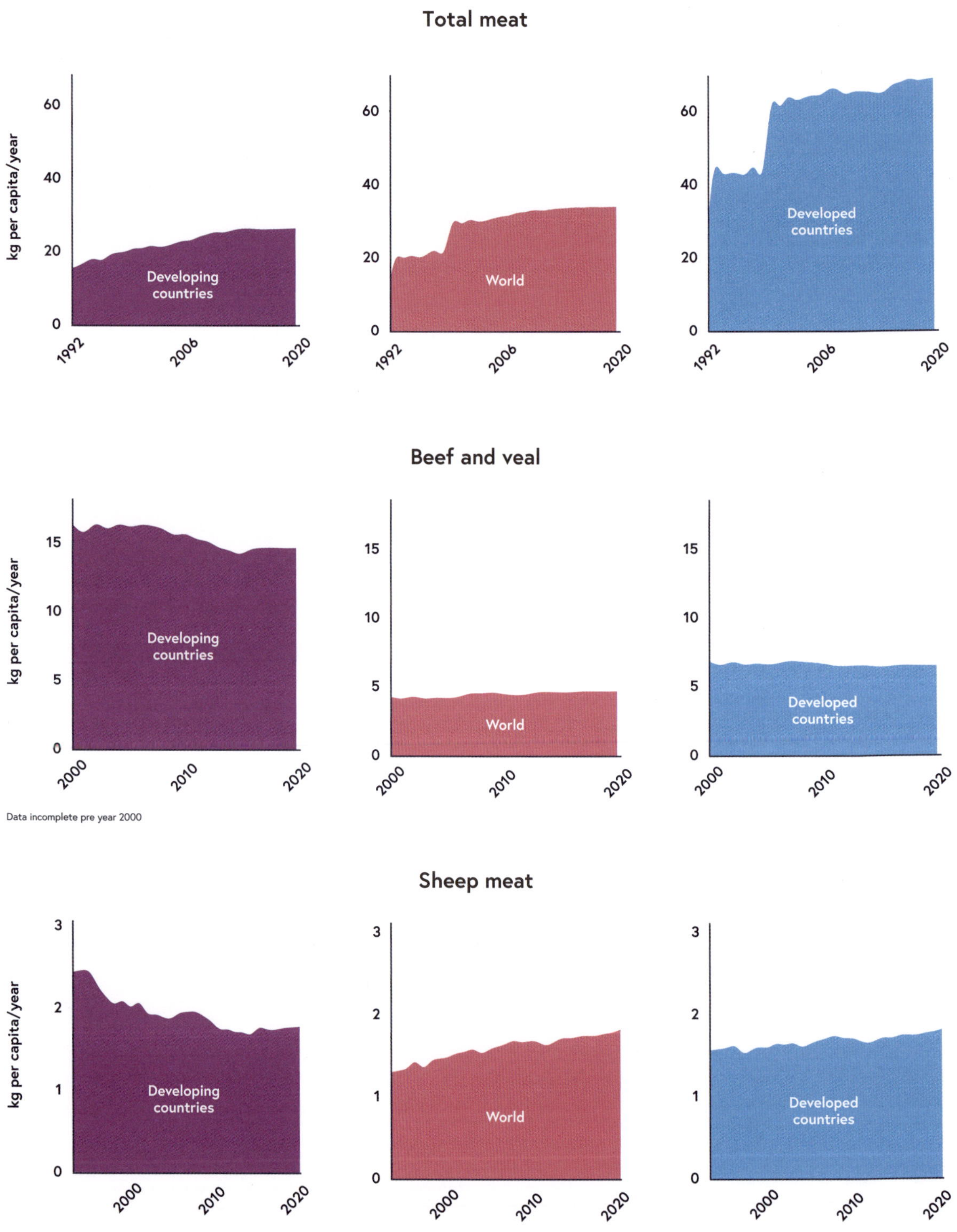

This is a huge deal when the world is striving to limit global warming to 1.5 degrees. Hence, the UK's Committee on Climate Change[†] has suggested a minimum reduction of 37% in methane levels from farming by 2050.[25††]

However, one could argue that – precisely because of its impermanence – methane is a less urgent problem than other greenhouse gases. Every tonne of carbon that gets released into the atmosphere stays there forever. Stopping carbon emissions now will have a much bigger cumulative effect in the future.

But going slow on methane reductions would be a missed opportunity. The magic disappearing qualities of methane mean early reductions can limit peak warming.[26]

Some farmers have already started experimenting with rearing ruminants in ways that reduce their emissions – by feeding them supplements that reduce their methane emissions, or by selectively breeding animals that do this naturally. Nestlé told us that by supporting their dairy farmers to change to regenerative practices, including mob grazing and the use of natural feed supplements, it believes it can halve the carbon footprint of its fresh milk supply in the UK, by 2025.[27]

The combined effect of reducing our overall meat consumption, while also buying meat and milk that has been reared in methane-reducing ways – could have a significant impact on overall emissions.

Structural change can be slow, however, and peak temperature is forecast to occur between 2050 and 2070. So while we may have a bit of time to work out what Net Zero farming looks like, we cannot afford to be complacent.

Figure 7.3 shows the implications of delaying short-lived climate pollutants (SLCP), which are mostly methane, and CO_2. It shows that reducing methane without also rapidly reducing CO_2 isn't very useful: this doesn't limit peak warming meaningfully (both purple lines go above 2°C by 2100). But it also shows that a climate strategy that cuts both methane and CO_2 over the course of the next decade can limit peak warming to 1.5°C (dashed pink line). Waiting to lower methane emissions for a decade or so (solid pink line) means that warming will peak above 1.5°C, with the attendant risks outlined above. The UK is cutting CO_2 emissions rapidly and early, and so it makes sense to also lower methane emissions quickly.

Figure 7.3

Reducing CO_2 early is essential to preventing harmful warming, but early methane reduction plays a crucial role in keeping emissions below 1.5°C[28]

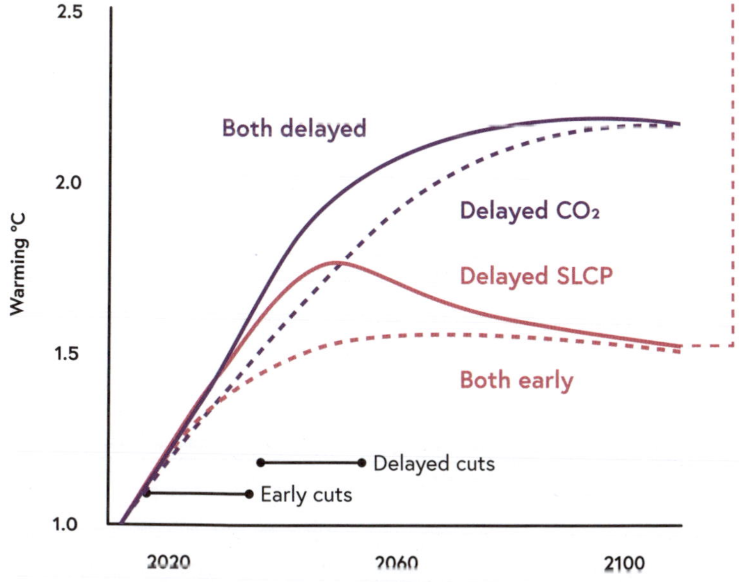

Climate strategy that cuts both methane and CO_2 over the course of the next decade can limit peak warming to 1.5°C.

"I don't know how many more statistics and David Attenborough documentaries there have to be ... we need to get on with this and produce our food in a different way and a much more sustainable way."

"Deliberative dialogue" participant, North West England

....

[†]See Glossary for Climate Change Committee.

[††]The CCC's "further ambition" scenario suggests a roughly 37% reduction in methane emissions, but this scenario does not quite reach net zero. Additional emissions reductions, possibly including further methane reductions, are needed to meet the UK's net zero target.

8

The complexities of meat

NOT all meat is created equal. Our taste for ruminants, as we have already seen, is a major contributor to climate change. But there are many other factors that make some meat more ecologically damaging than others – and not always in the ways you might expect.

Figure 8.1 shows the kilograms of carbon dioxide emitted in the production of 100 grams of protein from various foodstuffs. The undulations within each foodstuff occur where they are being farmed or processed in a particular way, with higher or lower resulting emissions. You can see, predictably, that vegetable proteins hug the left-hand side of the chart, meaning they are low in emissions, while meat and dairy extends much further towards the carbon-heavy right. But you can also see that the picture is complex.

Most fish farming, for example, ranks on the left-hand side of the chart. This is one of the lowest-carbon forms of animal protein. But if – as sometimes happens – ponds are left warm and unaerated, the feed and excreta that falls to the bottom can ferment and emit more methane per kg of protein than cattle. Hence, the long thin tail extending towards the right of the chart.

Chicken is also a relatively low-carbon protein, but the chart shows a bumpy tail to the right. This is because some methods of chicken farming are much higher in emissions than others. Instinctively, one would expect the villains to be intensive, indoor farms. Surely it must be more climate-friendly to raise chickens outside, rather than in huge temperature-controlled, strip-lit warehouses?

Alas, no: the more intensively you rear some animals, the more carbon-efficient they tend to be. Leaving aside other important concerns – including animal welfare, the pollution caused by manure run-off, and ammonia emissions into the atmosphere – intensively farmed chicken has a lower carbon footprint than free-range chicken. This is because the birds gain weight more quickly when housed indoors, they catch fewer viruses, get sick less often, and fewer die before they are ready to be slaughtered. This higher survival rate means you get more output (a portion of chicken) for less input (bags of chicken feed).

Figure 8.1 – Greenhouse gas emissions from protein-rich foods are shown per 100 grams of protein across a global sample of 38,700 commercially viable farms in 119 countries. The height of the curve represents the amount of production globally with that specific footprint. The white dot marks the median greenhouse gas emissions for each food product.

Figure 8.1

Vegetable proteins have low carbon footprints, while dairy and meat tends to be more carbon heavy[1†]

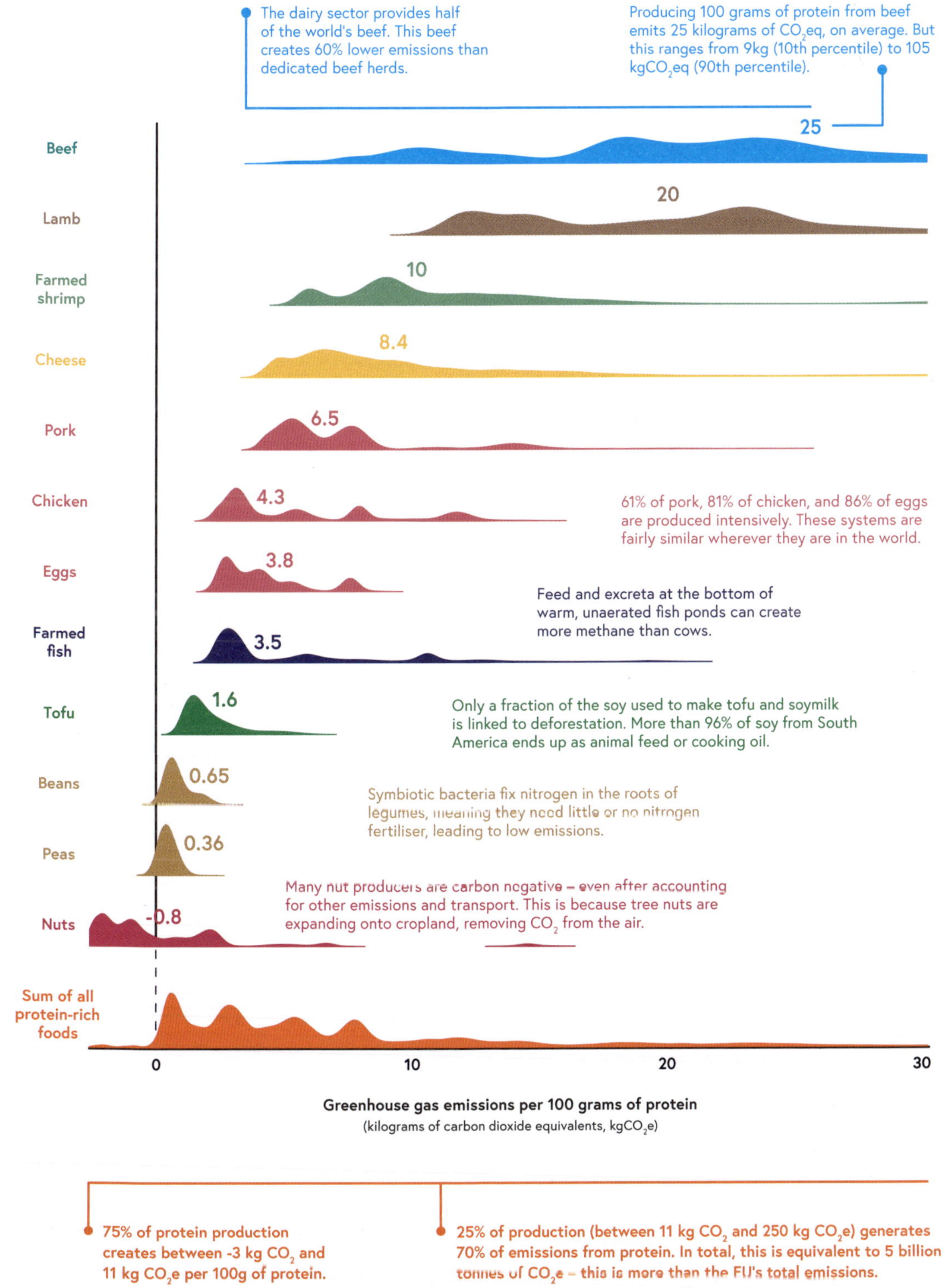

† Data refers to the greenhouse gas emissions of food products across a global sample of 38,700 commercially viable farms in 119 countries. Emissions are measured across the full supply chain, from land use change through to the retailer and includes on-farm processing, transport, packaging and retail emissions.

The livestock sector with the biggest variations in emissions is cattle. Figure 8.2 shows the average kg of carbon released per kg of beef† in various countries (overlaid with the amount of beef each country produces).

The range is huge, with Paraguay emitting over 200kg of carbon per kg of meat and Denmark emitting under 15kg. The reasons for this are various. Clearing forest to create pasture – which is still being done in many countries†† – massively increases emissions.[2] (This chart is somewhat unfair, as it doesn't reflect the historic deforestation done in the UK and elsewhere in the developed world. But that damage is a sunk cost.) Other factors include: how intensively the animals are reared; the suitability of the land for pasture (how much carbon-intensive fertiliser must be put on the land to create nutritious grass); and whether dairy cattle are subsequently used for beef.

While UK emissions from cattle farming are much lower than the worst producers, they are higher than some OECD countries - including the United States, with its vast and (to most British eyes) dystopian feedlot systems.[3] Once again, intensive livestock rearing has its carbon benefits. Feeding cows on grain (which is more calorific than grass), and giving them growth hormones, means they gain weight more quickly, go to the slaughterhouse younger and therefore have less opportunity to emit methane than cows reared on pasture. It may not be the life you would wish upon a sentient animal, but the methane cost is unquestionably lower.[4]

Figure 8.2

Carbon emissions from cattle vary significantly by country[5]

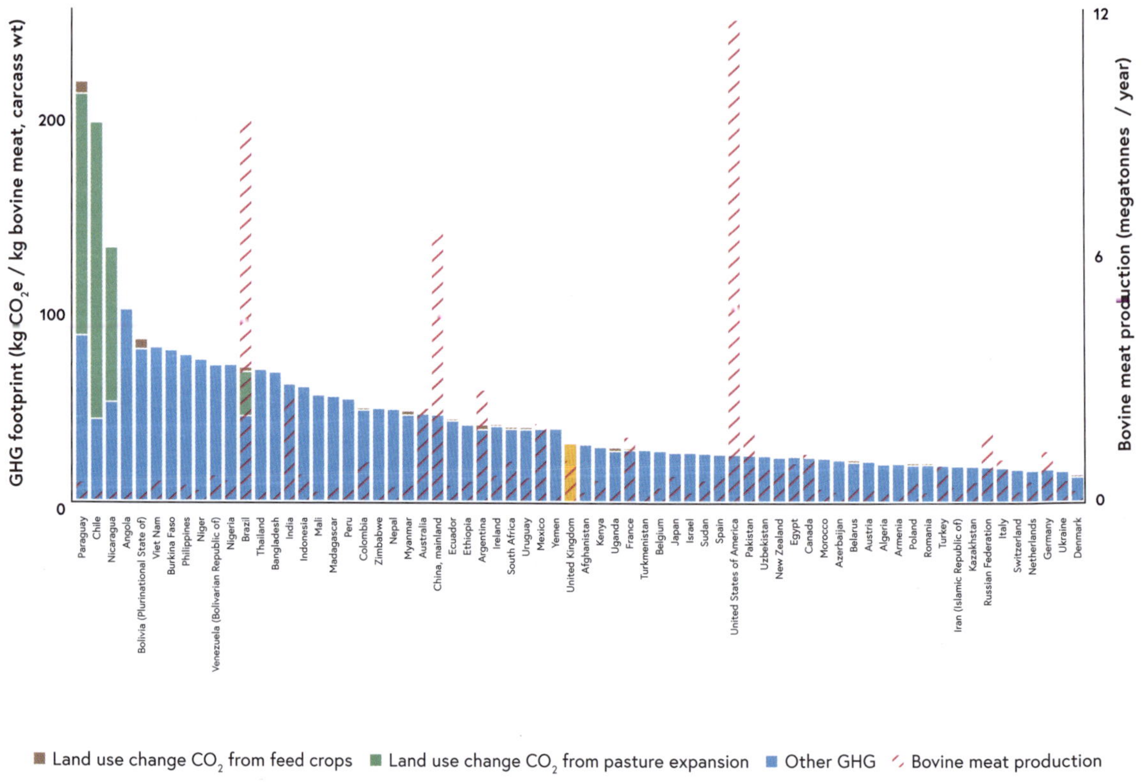

....

† Note that Figure 8.2 shows emissions per kg of beef. Figure 8.1 shows emissions per 100g of protein.
†† 73% of all deforestation in Queensland, Australia, for example, is due to beef production.

The countries with the lowest emissions from cattle, such as Denmark, combine intensive farming with an appetite for ex-dairy meat. Because dairy cattle produce protein throughout their lifetimes, in the form of milk, the overall ratio of emissions per kg of total protein is lower. Ex-dairy beef is a taste we haven't developed in this country, although on the continent the dense, highly marbled, strongly flavoured meat is often considered a delicacy.

The case for and against meat is further complicated by the fact that we get more than just sustenance from our livestock farmers. In this country, beef, dairy and lamb farming is largely responsible for the appearance of our "traditional" pastured countryside. These animals are, literally, part of the landscape.

They have their ecological uses, too. Some native breeds of cattle are being used in rewilding projects to create "pastured woodland". Where trees and scrub are being allowed to spread, the trampling and grazing of small herd of cows creates clearings in the budding forest: places where sunlight can get through, creating an abundance of biodiversity.[6]

Some conventional farmers, too, are reintroducing cows and sheep as part of a crop rotation system. This traditional practice, of allowing animals to graze on fallow land, fell out of favour after the Green Revolution. But growing numbers of farmers have realised that it can improve soil quality, reducing the need for expensive fertilisers and pesticides.

In the right circumstances, and used in the right way, cattle have even been shown to sequester carbon.

It is important to encourage this kind of imaginative, ecological livestock farming in the UK. Realistically, however, it could never produce enough meat to cater to our current appetite for beef and lamb. Neither, come to that, could large-scale intensive livestock farming – even if the British public were prepared to see their countryside transformed into giant American-style feedlots. We simply cannot reduce methane emissions to a safe level, nor free up the land we need for sequestering carbon, without reducing the amount of meat we eat.

I've made a decision based on some of what I've learned, and I am a great meat eater I love meat, but I'm only going to have red meat once a month"

East of England participant, deliberative dialogue

9

A nature-positive, carbon-negative food system

THE food system is about to be asked to perform a feat of acrobatics. In order to meet the UK's legal commitment to reach "net zero" emissions by 2050, the food system must first dramatically cut its own emissions: no small achievement in itself. On top of that, it must relinquish agricultural land to be used in ways that sequester carbon.

Every credible model for reaching net zero requires this. There are some industries that will remain heavily dependent on fossil fuels for years. (Steel production, for example, or air travel.) Using land – especially peat bogs and woodland – to sequester carbon is the only large-scale method we have for mopping up these emissions. And we must begin this work now. It takes around ten years for trees to grow big enough to sequester significant levels of carbon.[1]

The Government has also – rightly – committed to restoring the diminished biodiversity of our countryside. Since the 1970s, populations of wild animals and insects in the UK have been in continuous decline.[2] In September of last year, the Government made a pledge to protect 30% of UK land "for nature" by 2030. (The Government has since secured a similar "30x30" commitment from the leaders of all the G7 countries.)

Nature protection isn't incompatible with farming. In fact – as we will see in Chapter 10 – some species have evolved to thrive on the kind of old-fashioned farms that were, until the Green Revolution, the norm: plenty of hedgerows, mixed crops, low-density livestock and traditional rotations involving ruminant cattle to improve the soil.[3] Encouraging more of this kind of nature-friendly farming – sometimes called agroecological farming – must be part of the plan for restoring the UK's struggling wildlife.

But agroecological farming produces lower yields than modern intensive farming. We must somehow find a way to repurpose large areas of farmland, lowering yields in some places and returning others entirely to nature, while still producing enough to remain comfortably food-secure.

Various interpretations of this juggling act are visualised in the graph below (Figure 9.1). The bar on the left shows the situation today. Agriculture in the UK currently emits 54.6 million tonnes of carbon ($MtCO_2e$) per year. Land use – mainly carbon emissions from soil converted for agriculture – emits a further 12.8 $MtCO_2e$.[4] As the yellow stripe shows us, this tots up to total carbon emissions of just over 67 $MtCO_2e$ per year. (A figure, incidentally, that has remained virtually unchanged since 2008. Over the same period of time, emissions from the whole of our economy have decreased by 32%.)[5]

The next bar along shows what would happen if we followed all the recommendations made to Parliament by the Climate Change Committee (CCC), in its 2020 report *The Sixth Carbon Budget – The UK's Path to Net Zero*. In this future, the carbon emitted directly by agriculture would fall to 35 $MtCO_2e$. This would be achieved through a mixture of improved productivity, an overall reduction in meat-eating, and measures to reduce fertiliser use and prevent the release of nitrous oxide from slurry. (For example, the modern technique of injecting slurry into the soil, instead of spreading it over the top; or introducing perennial plants into arable crop rotations to increase microbial activity in the soil.)

The CCC model also has 21% of current farmland converted for carbon sequestration by 2050. This could be done by rewetting peat, planting trees and growing bioenergy crops. (These crops – which sequester carbon as they grow – would be burnt to generate electricity, using specialist power plants which capture all the carbon dioxide emitted in the process. This is known known as BECCS – bioenergy with carbon capture and storage.)

Figure 9.1

Different visions for the future of farming lead to different carbon emissions[6]

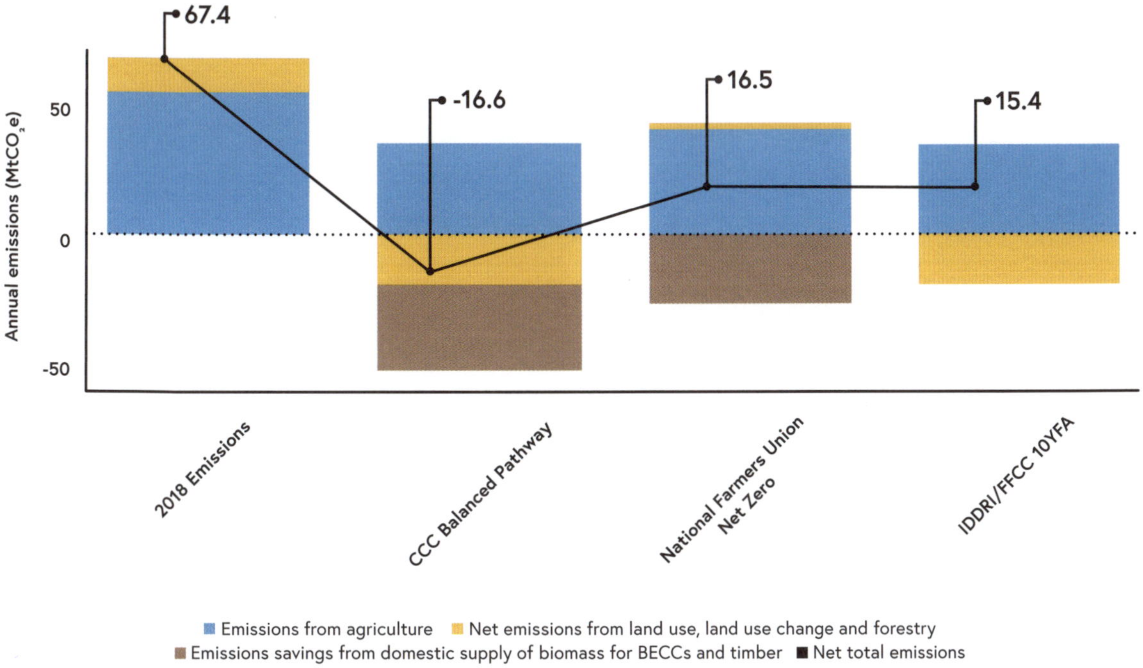

Under the CCC plan, net emissions from the land as a whole, including repurposed farmland, would go right down into negative figures: –16.6 $MtCO_2e$ per year.[7] This would be enough to soak up some of the projected emissions from other sectors.

This is more ambitious than the plan recently put forward by the National Farmers Union, represented by the third bar along.[8] Under the NFU's plan, farming itself would just about reach net zero – a huge turnaround, not to be sniffed at – but without providing enough carbon sequestration to offset remaining land emissions and mop up any of the pollution produced by other sectors. (The NFU's plan foresees farmers producing much more food from the land used for farming today, while sequestering more carbon in that soil, and growing more bioenergy.)

The fourth bar on Figure 9.1, based on the calculations of the Food, Farming and Countryside Commission (FFCC), shows what would happen if UK agriculture shifted en masse to lower-yield, nature-friendly agroecological farming.[9] In this future, there would be almost no need for fertilisers or pesticides. But emissions would remain relatively high, because this plan retains the most carbon-intensive livestock. By 2050, in the FFCC scenario, we would still have all of the beef and two-thirds of the lamb we produce today, whereas production of poultry, pigs, milk and eggs would be halved in order to eliminate imports of feed crops.

None of these three models quite succeeds in keeping all the necessary balls in the air. The CCC model is strong on carbon but says little about biodiversity. The NFU model is not ambitious enough on carbon and says little about nature. And the FFCC model is strong on farmland biodiversity but falls short on carbon.

Moreover, they all make radically different assumptions about our future diet. The CCC model lowers meat and dairy eating by at least a third and a fifth respectively. The NFU model assumes no change in our diet, and therefore no change in food production. The agroecological approach envisages significant – maybe unrealistic – changes to our eating habits: one and a half times more fruit and veg than we currently consume, five times more nuts, a third less beef (and no beef imports at all), half the chicken, two-thirds less pork and eggs, and 80% less sugar.[†]

....

[†] In this scenario, beef, milk, chicken, pork and egg consumption fall much more than UK production because imports of feed crops – broadly speaking, cereals, soya and rapeseed and palm oil – are eliminated. Sugar production falls by 95% and is offset by increased imports. The UK remains a net importer of fruit and vegetables, albeit with a higher domestic share of production.

All these models would reduce carbon emissions, albeit to varying degrees. But what about restoring nature? The good news is that – to use an unsuitable metaphor – it is possible to kill both these birds with one stone.

A 2013 research paper conducted a detailed analysis of which areas of UK farmland are best suited to each of these purposes – carbon storage or biodiversity restoration – using data collected by the Natural Environment Research Council and Natural England, among others.[10]

Although the two purposes don't overlap perfectly (the areas that are most important for biodiversity are more geographically diffuse than those with the greatest carbon sequestering potential), there is a significant area of land that is very well suited to both. Figure 9.2 shows the computer modelling for this, cropped to show England only. The red areas are where biodiversity and carbon sequestering projects could best be done simultaneously. Most are on the uplands, the downs and around the New Forest, as well as some in the Fens. This map shows that there doesn't have to be a conflict between nature and net zero.

What about food production, though? If we turn over some of this land to environmental projects, will we produce enough food to feed ourselves? To answer that, we need to look at how we currently farm our land.

Figure 9.3 shows, on the left, the different ways we use our land in the UK – not geographically, but as proportions of the whole. The hexagons on the right, which are drawn to the same scale, show the agricultural land abroad that is used to cater for the UK market. It includes not only the plants and animals that we import to eat directly, but also the land used to grow animal feed for UK livestock.

A few things immediately catch the eye. Agriculture currently takes up 70% of UK landmass. Yet golf courses occupy five times as much of our land as orchards. And all the UK's built-up areas combined are only two-thirds the size of our peat bogs. But what is most striking is how much land we use to rear lamb, beef and dairy cattle. The green coloured areas represent both pasture and the additional land used to grow feed for these animals. The total area of this land, here and abroad, is a bit larger than the entire landmass of Great Britain.

Figure 9.2

A significant area of land (red) is well suited simultaneously to sequester carbon and protect nature[11]

Figure 9.3

We use our land for a great diversity of purposes, but rearing lamb, beef and dairy cattle predominates[12]

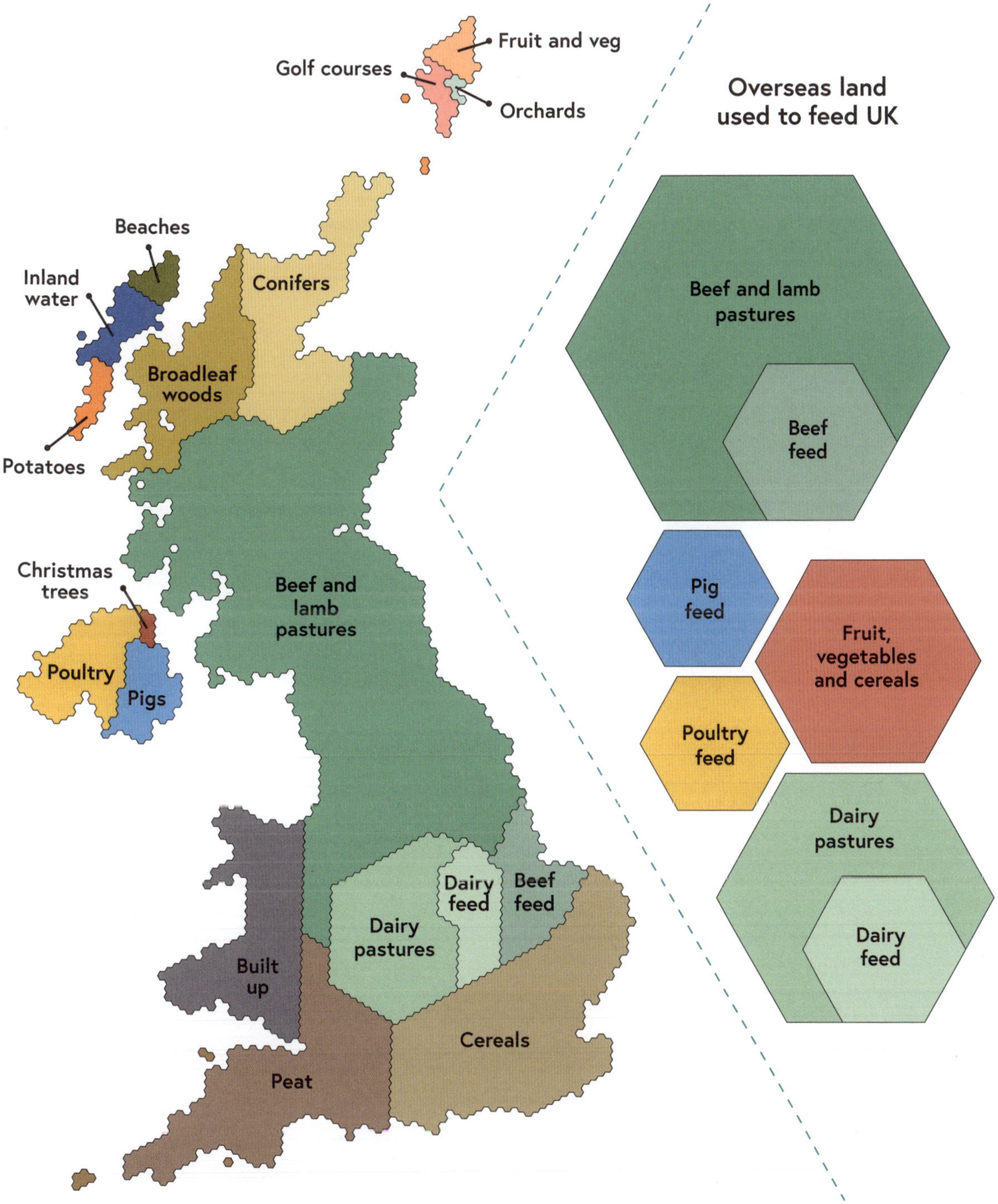

Note: this analysis draws on de Ruiter et al. (which uses a top-down methodology) and Poore and Nemecek (which uses a bottom-up methodology). These have a high degree of agreement other than for total land footprint and share of land footprint overseas. The overall size area of land associated with UK diets is estimated to be between 24 and 38 million hectares, and the relative share of this land that is in the UK versus overseas is around 50% (43–54%).

Figure 9.4

85% of the farmland that feeds the UK is used to rear animals[13]

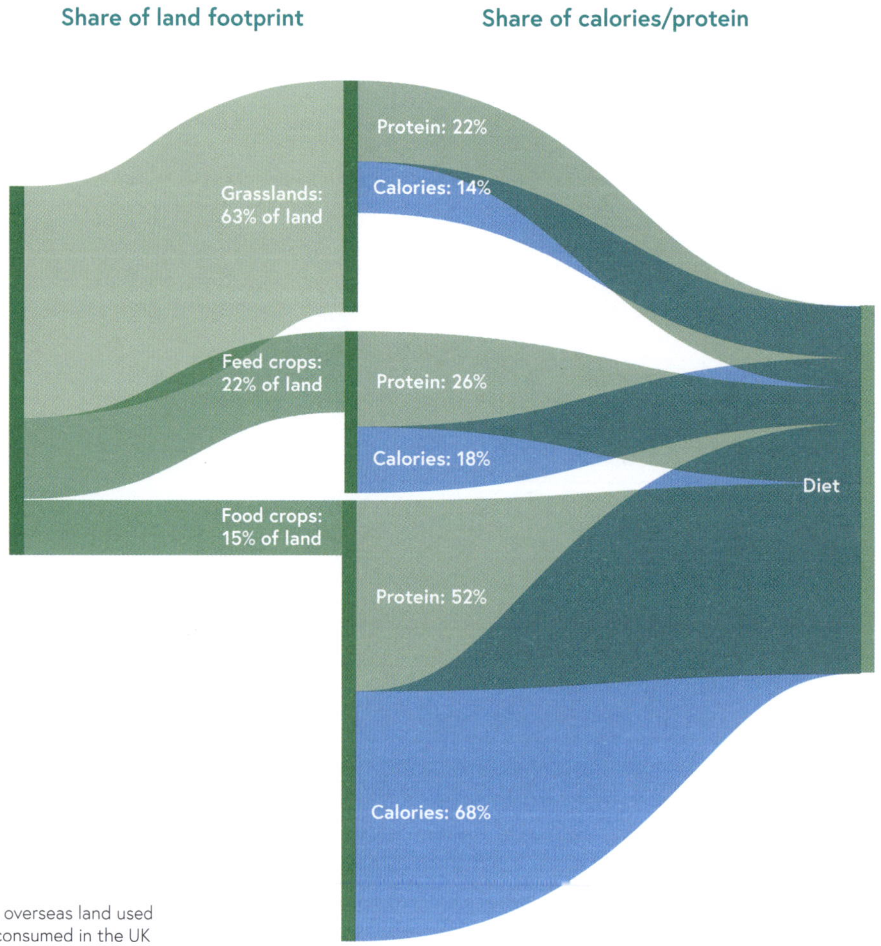

Note: includes overseas land used to grow food consumed in the UK

Looked at from a calorie perspective, this is a very inefficient way to use our land. Figure 9.4 shows that 85% of the farmland that feeds the UK, both here and abroad, is used to rear animals – even though meat, dairy and eggs only provide 32% of the calories we eat. By contrast, the 15% of farmland (roughly half in the UK, half overseas) that is used to grow plant crops for human consumption provides 68% of our calories.

It is true that much of the land in the UK is not viable for arable farming. "We have an excellent climate for growing grass" is a common refrain. But in fact much of the pasture in this country, even in the rolling uplands, is treated with fertiliser to make it grassy enough to sustain grazing animals profitably. And although ruminants are experts at turning grass into delicious meat, that is not the only useful purpose this land could serve.

Upland areas, as we have mentioned, provide bountiful opportunities for carbon sequestration. Most have peat bogs which could be rewetted, as well as areas that would be ideal for growing trees and shrubs. Many upland areas were once covered in temperate rainforests. Now they are covered in sheep, which nibble very close to the ground and make it difficult for tree saplings to grow.

Figure 9.5 shows how the carbon footprint of producing various foods increases when you add in the "opportunity cost" of not using that land to capture carbon. Globally, the biggest potential carbon benefit of eating less meat would not actually be the reduction in emissions, but the opportunity to repurpose land so that it sequesters carbon. Goats and sheep, both of which roam over large areas and have a taste for tree saplings, are reared at the greatest opportunity cost.

Unlike the environmentalist George Monbiot, who memorably denounced sheep as "woolly maggots", we believe there is a place for sheep farming in our countryside.[14] Culturally and aesthetically, it forms part of our national self-image – those rolling green hills covered in fluffy white dots. Sheep farming is a working tradition that in some communities goes back centuries.

But at present too much of our land is given over to livestock. The Climate Change Committee has said that we need to create new woodlands covering an area the size of East Anglia. This will mostly be land converted from agriculture. It makes sense to use the least productive farmland, so that we sacrifice as little food security as possible.

Figure 9.5

The biggest potential carbon benefit of eating less meat is the opportunity to repurpose land to sequester carbon[15]

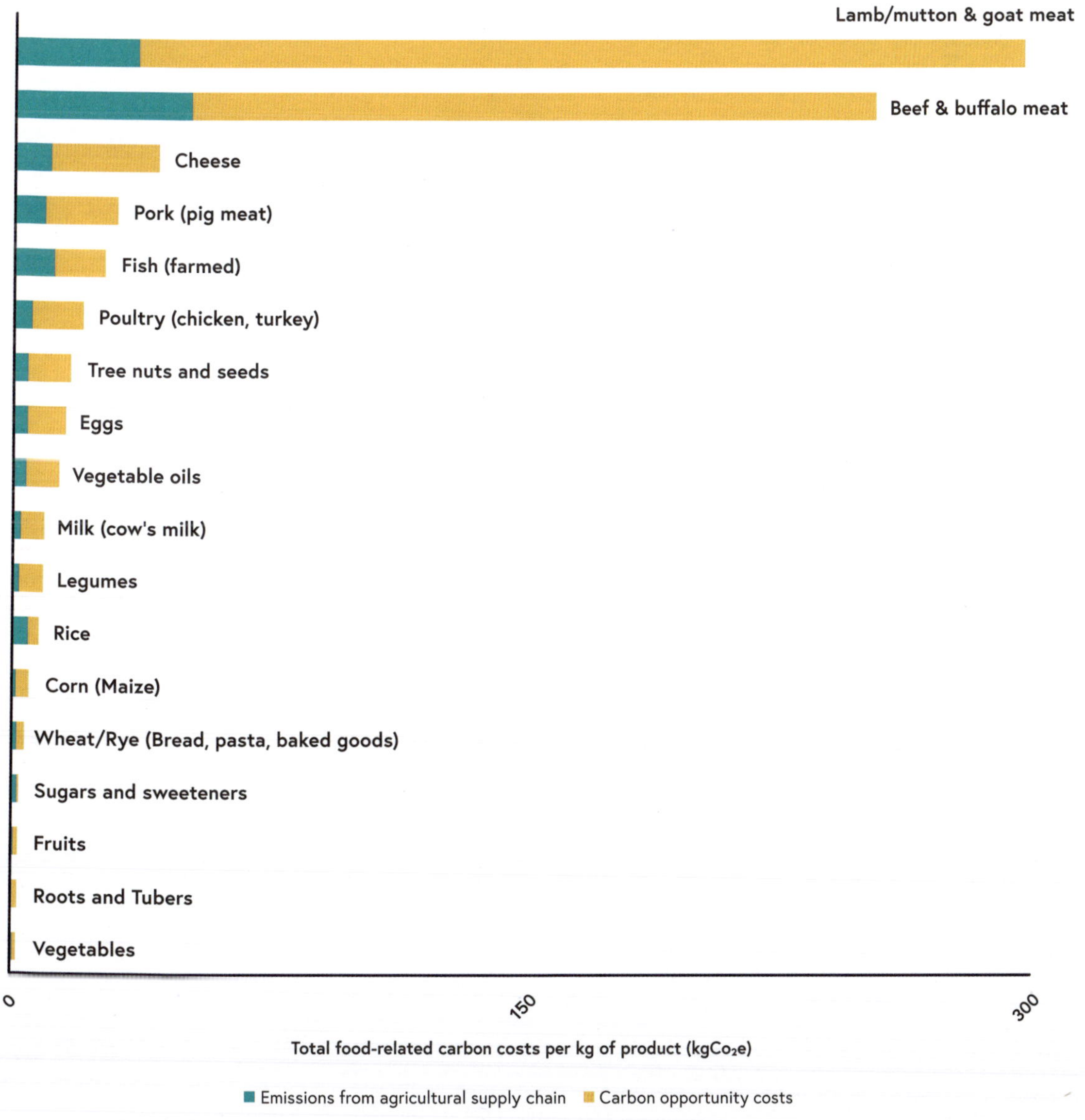

Figure 9.6 shows (in red) the areas of land most suited to carbon sequestration and biodiversity restoration, overlayed (in green) with our least productive farmland. There is a serendipitous overlap between some of the areas that produce the least food and those which are best suited to nature restoration and carbon removal.

This combination of low productivity and environmental potential is what makes our juggling act possible. The least productive 20% of our land produces only 3% of our calories.

If we properly incentivised farmers on this land, making environmental projects more attractive than conventional farming, we could meet the government's targets for both carbon sequestration and nature restoration. Most of this land could still be used for low intensity farming. We calculate that only 5%–8% of our total farmland would need to be freed from production almost entirely, largely to plant broadleaf woodland and restore peat bogs.

Figure 9.6

Much of the land that is best suited to nature restoration and carbon removal produces little food[16]

People and the land

We have talked a lot about land and food in this chapter. But what about people? Much of our agricultural land was created by sweeping people off the countryside to create sheep ranches – starting with the enclosures of the 13th century and ending with the brutal Scottish clearances of the 18th and 19th centuries. If you were to read the debate over restoring nature to farmland in some newspapers, you would imagine that turning land over to carbon sequestration and nature recovery might involve something similar.

This does not need to be the case. Many upland farmers are already reducing the number of sheep they graze, introducing hardy native cattle into their grazing, allowing areas of land to flood, building ponds and hedges, and planting trees.

This approach is described evocatively by the Cumbrian shepherd James Rebanks in his book *English Pastoral.*

"As we travel into the valley bottom, I see around me on all sides an ancient working landscape that still lives and breathes, but also with twenty years of changes written across its surface.

"I see ancient oak woodland above us trying to regenerate. Little mountain ash trees are sprouting up all over the wilding fell, trying to beat the deer. The vegetation is growing denser and deeper, with alder and thorny scrub creeping up the ghylls. The floodplain is half-abandoned and half-wild. The valley has become much shaggier and wilder than it ever was in my childhood, with far fewer sheep dotted around. Some of my neighbours are confused or angry about that, while others are adapting, keeping more cattle or finding other ways to earn a living from the land.

"I see farmers starting to work together to make this place even better, finding ways to farm around wilder rivers. Miles of hedges are being laid once more, drystone walls rebuilt, and old stone barns and field houses restored. I see river corridors fenced off and ponds dug; the blanket peat bog on our common land has been restored. Wild flower meadows liberated from artificial fertilisers and pesticides are now shimmering with clouds of insects, butterflies, moths and birds.

And I see other people in our community who aren't farmers also planting trees and hedges, or creating wetlands, or helping to coordinate our efforts. These things bring separate worlds together, and the old 'us' and 'them' divide is fading. There is a love of this place that unites us all".[17]

But all this depends on farmers getting sufficient Government support – cleverly targeted, and guaranteed for the long term. The way in which the Government's Future Farming programme is rolled out could make them or break them.

10

A Three Compartment Model

WHAT about the remaining farmland – the higher-yielding 80%? That's a huge chunk of our national surface area – 55%, in fact. How should it be managed for maximum food production and environmental benefit? There are currently two main schools of thought on this question, which – with dreadful inevitability – have become quite polarised.

One is the "land sparing" school. In this model, you make some farmland as productive as possible, thus freeing up other land for environmental projects. By producing more food from a smaller area, you create the necessary elbow room for all the other purposes required of our land.

This idea rings alarm bells among some environmentalists, who point out that pushing up productivity almost always comes at a heavy cost to nature. Since the Green Revolution, especially, farming has become what environmentalists call a "mining" operation: productivity has increased hugely, but we have achieved this in an entirely unsustainable way, by digging up fossil fuels to create manufactured fertilisers and pesticides while simultaneously wreaking havoc on water courses and wildlife habitats.

Proponents of the land-sparing school, however, say that emerging technologies are breaking the link between productivity and environmental damage. The future, they say, lies in "sustainable intensification". Thousands of new techniques are being trialled which promise to wean farming from its reliance on industrial fertiliser and "red diesel". (Diesel for agricultural machinery is not taxed in the UK; it is dyed red to prevent it being sold on the black market for other uses.)

In our researches, we have seen some amazing new technologies at work. We met engineers developing robots that zap weeds with powerful electric currents; botanists dipping maize seeds into a solution of nitrogen-fixing bacteria to reduce the need for fertiliser; and farmers using drones and AI to treat outbreaks of disease in their crops before the effects are even noticeable to the human eye.

We met one entrepreneur whose AI can already identify every one of millions of plants in a field, and alert the farmer to any change in their condition. Sam Watson-Jones, co-founder of the Small Robot Company, foresees a future of "per plant" farming where multiple different crops are mixed together. For example, arable crops could be planted with legumes (to fix nitrogen in the soil) and flowers (to attract pollinators). This kind of symbiotic farming dates right back to the Mesopotamians, and there are farmers in the UK experimenting with similar models today.[1] Agricultural robots could make it easier to harvest such fields, by separating the plants as they go.

There is no doubt that science and technology will be used to make high-yield farming much less destructive. But we can't know yet which of the techniques currently in development will turn out to be most transformational and cost effective, or when they will be ready for large-scale use.

In the meantime, there is a model of farming that we already know to have huge benefits for wildlife. Some people call this model "land sharing", because it performs two functions simultaneously: producing food and sustaining wildlife. Other people call it "high nature value farming" or "agroecological farming". It is an approach that overlaps with organic principles but covers a larger variety of farms. The terminology is unsettled and each of the categories is blurry at the edges.

But the basic principle of land-sharing is that farmers consciously and deliberately share their land with nature. Although some insects, birds and animals require a truly wild environment to thrive, others actually do better living on a certain kind of traditional, lower-yield farmland.[2]

For most of this country's history, we farmed in roughly the same way: on smaller plots of land, divided by trees and hedgerows, cultivating many different kinds of produce and using rotations of crops and livestock to ensure the health of the soil. We farmed like this for so long that some species have adapted to thrive alongside us. Skylarks, for example, flourish on farms that practise crop rotations, foraging in high cereal stubbles in the winter, but preferring lower and less dense crops for spring and summer breeding season.[3] Legume fallows – planted to restore the soil – offer habitats for butterflies and brown hares. The yellowhammer requires scrub for nesting (hedges are perfect), insect-rich open habitats in summer (such as flower-rich field margins) and seed-rich open habitats in winter (as provided by overwinter stubbles). These resources are generally most abundant on traditional, low-yield farmland.

The Green Revolution, in response to the post-War drive for food security, created a new kind of farming landscape which wiped out the habitats of many species. Even the most carefully-managed high-yield farms are currently, by necessity, inhospitable to much wildlife. They produce large monocultural crops or livestock herds, often in fields, without the weeds, trees, ponds and hedgerows that give rise to abundant biodiversity.

Land-sharing farmers – in all their many guises – farm in a gentler way. They use pesticides and fertilisers in much smaller quantities, if at all; maintain hedgerows, meadows and wild margins; and often deploy ruminant animals in rotations to help churn up and fertilise the soil. The end result is lower yields (typically 20–40% smaller), but a farmland that is much more hospitable to wildlife.[4]

However, this model does require more land to produce less food. It is kinder to those species that thrive on traditional farmland, but does not free up land to be restored to the kind of wilderness that some species prefer.

A detailed 2019 study considered the competing virtues of these two approaches.[5] Researchers studied the population levels of almost 200 species of birds in the Fenlands of Eastern England and on the Salisbury Plain, assessing how well the various species seemed to fare in different agricultural and wild terrains (see Figure 10.1). They then set a target of food production for each area of land, and ran mathematical models to work out how each bird species in these two areas would fare under three different scenarios: (1) land sparing (through conventional intensification); (2) land sharing, with all farms in the area switching to agroecological methods; and (3) a "Three Compartment Model" which had some agroecological farms, some conventional high-yield farms, and some land freed for nature (but not as much as in the land sparing model).

Unsurprisingly, the modelling predicted that species that rely on wilder ecosystems would fare best within the land sparing model, where some tracts of land could be returned to nature entirely. 59% of the bird species on the Fens and 37% of those on Salisbury Plain did best under this model.

However, the birds that prefer to live on sympathetically-managed farmland – 32% of species on the fens and 20% on the plain – would fare better under the land-sharing model. Some species – 9% in the fens and 43% on the plain – would do best with a mix of both approaches.

Figure 10.1

A combination of land sparing and land sharing produces the best outcomes for nature[6]

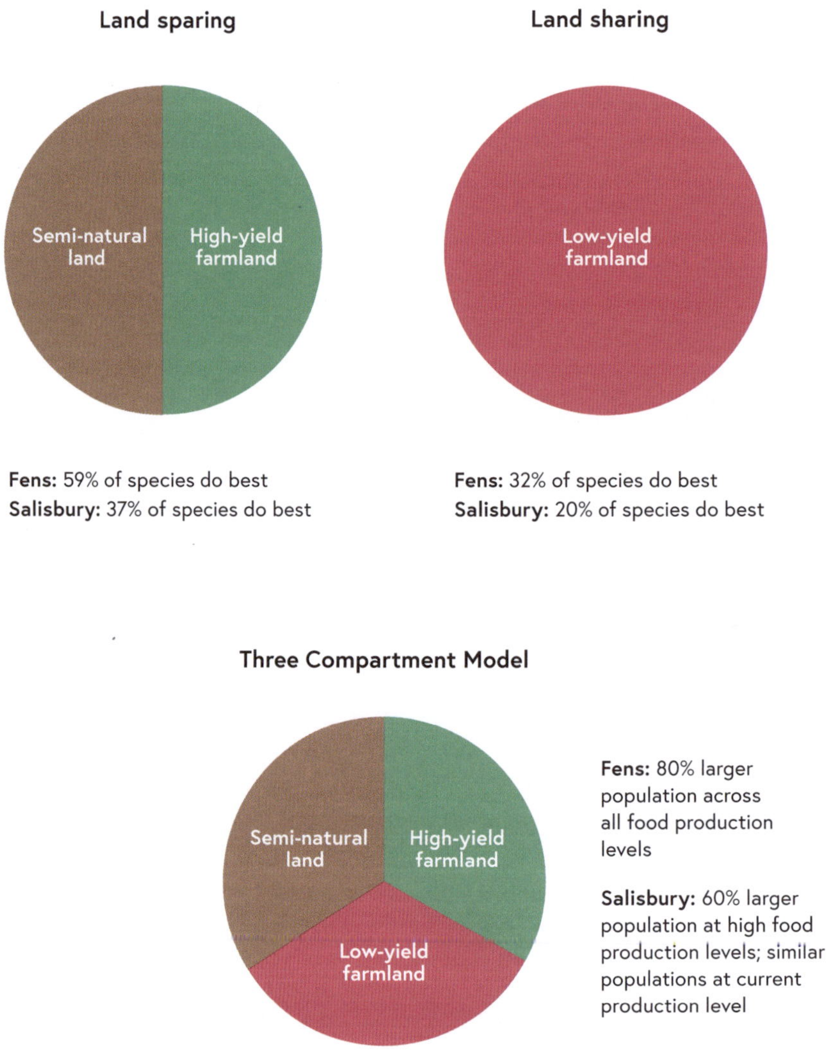

In terms of overall population numbers, however, the most successful model was often the Three Compartment Model. Creating a mosaic of different landscapes – wild land, low intensity farmland and higher intensity farming had the broadest beneficial effect for the most species.

In the past, land sharing and land sparing have been seen as conflicting schools of thought, when in fact the greatest benefits come from using both together. In much the same way, "agroecological" farming is often lined up against "sustainable intensification" as if the two were mutually incompatible. Yet both these newer models share a common goal: to end the agricultural system's reliance on fossil fuels and environmental destruction. Both schools are striving to create regenerative forms of farming, albeit by different routes.

We need an agricultural system that draws on traditional farming wisdom as well as cutting edge science. Diversity of method is a virtue in itself.

Farming in England[7]

Of the 106,000 farm holdings in England, 62% rear, or predominantly rear, livestock.

Figure 10.2

Farms in England by type

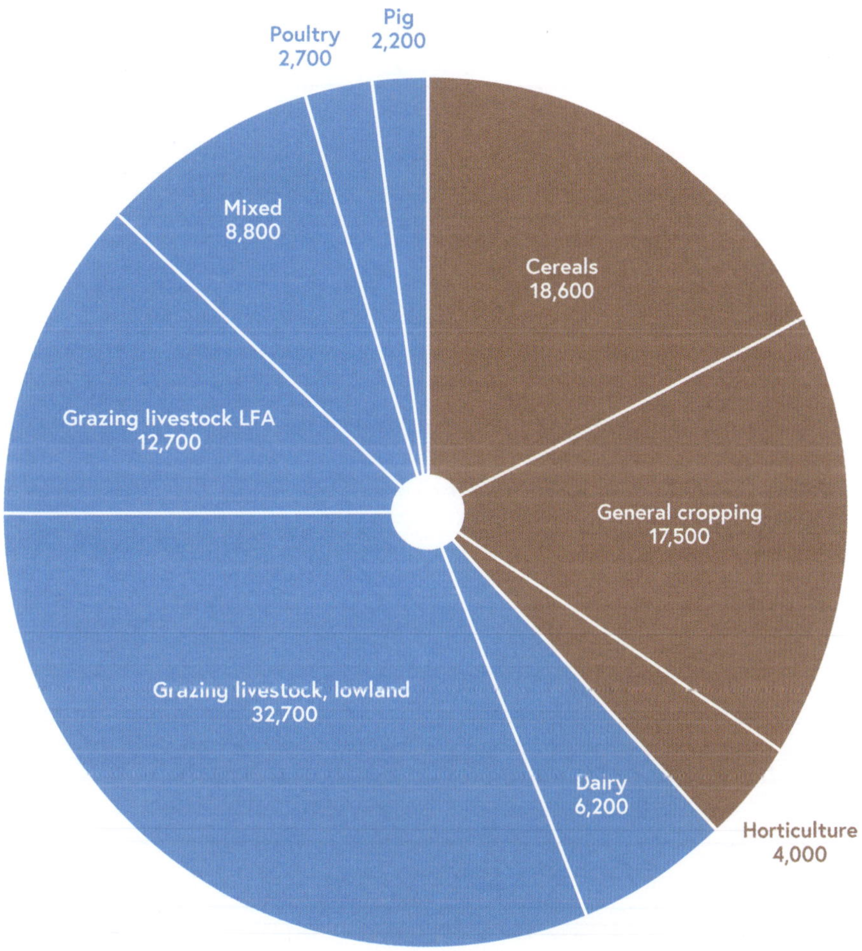

Figure 10.3

Large farms produce more output per area than other farm types

71% of English farms are small or very small, taking up 28% of the land in total and producing 13% of all agricultural output. The largest farms make up only 8% of farms but occupy 30% of farmland and produce 57% of farming output.†

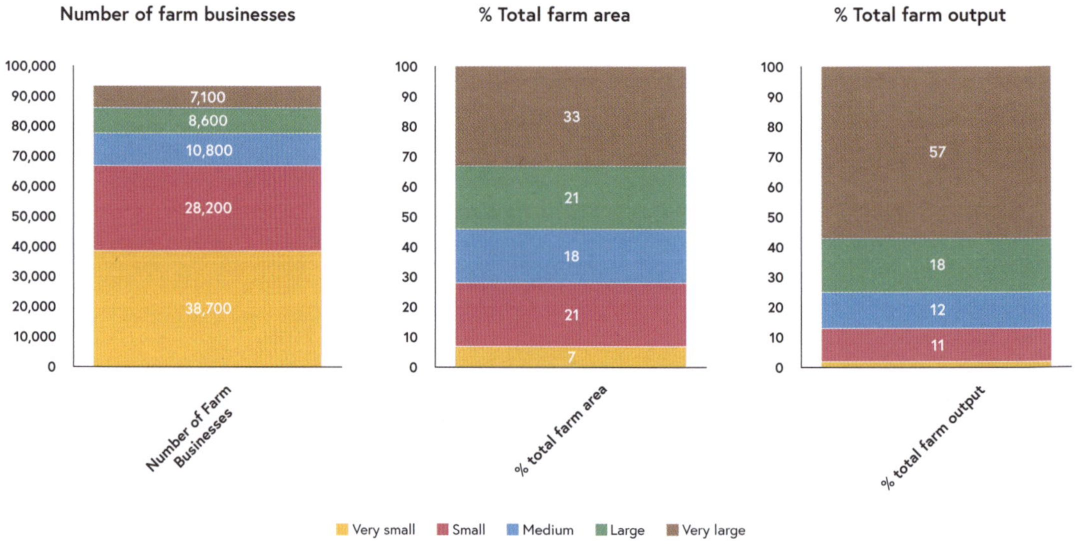

Figure 10.4

One in seven farms is exclusively tenanted, though nearly half of farms are partly tenanted

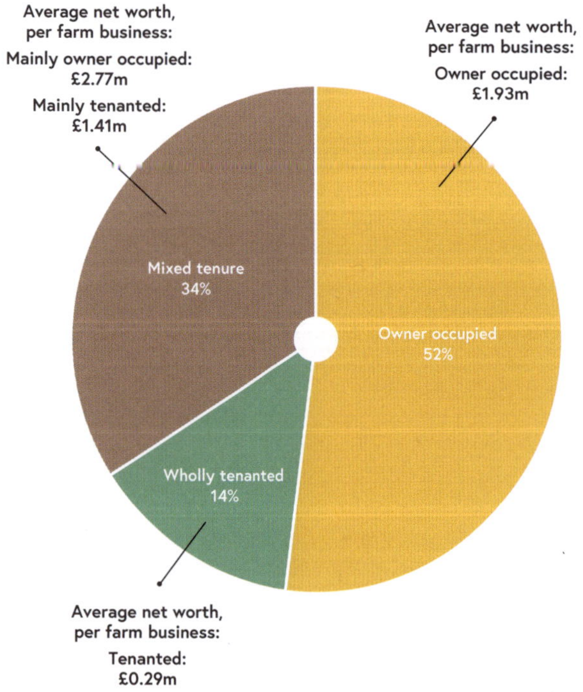

Nearly half of farms are fully or partly tenanted – although tenant farmland only occupies around a third of the total agricultural land area. Unsurprisingly, wholly tenanted farms have a comparatively small net worth: most of the value in most farms lies in the land.

....

† Farm size here is defined by Defra based on either farm business turnover or the theoretical number of workers required to run a holding, rather than physical size.

Figure 10.5

Farm profits

Income in farming is precarious. Across all farm types, more than half of income is from "direct payments" (subsidies that, using the old CAP format, pay for the land area farmed). Grazing and mixed farms on average made a loss from agricultural activities.[†]

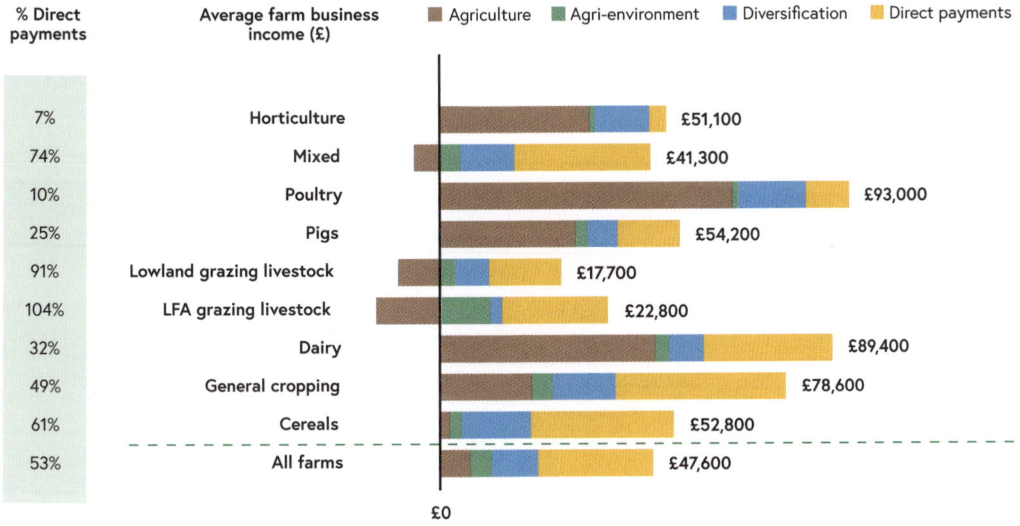

Figure 10.6

Average farm business income

On average small and part time farms make a loss on their agricultural activities. Large farms receive a greater share of direct payments.

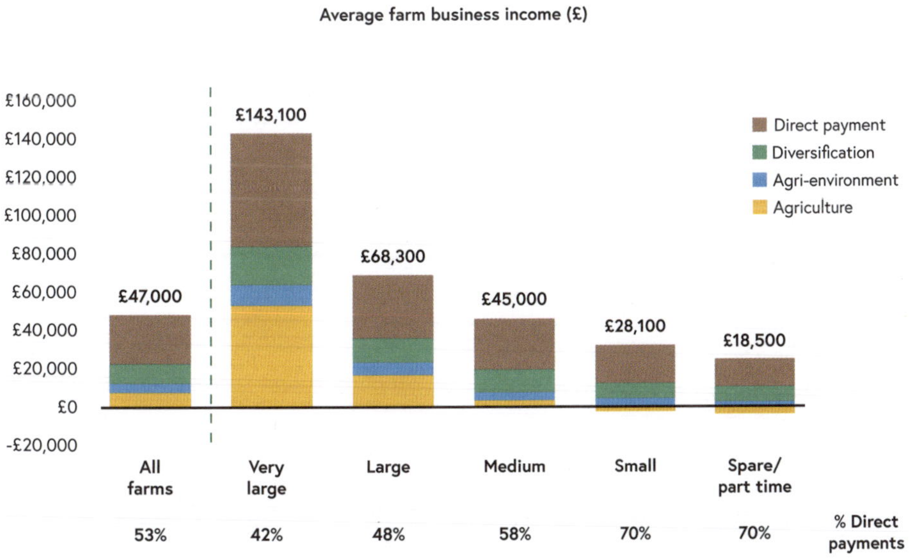

....

† LFA means "less favoured areas" – typically the uplands. "General cropping" refers to farms that produce both cereals and horticulture in broadly similar shares. Mixed farms produce cereals, horticulture, and livestock.

When split by income, half of farms make a significant loss on their agricultural activities – that is, the price they sell their produce for doesn't even cover the costs of growing or raising it. A further quarter make a tiny profit, with the bulk of their income coming from support payments. However, the top 25% of farms make a good income from agriculture.

Farms in England are unlike those on the continent in one major way: farmers in England tend not to work together. For example, co-operatives are widely used across Europe both to pool resources and to increase the share of the value chain they capture. In the UK, the combined turnover of co-operatives in in 2018 was £7.7 billion. That represents just 6% of business in relevant sectors where co-operatives are present (e.g. farming supply and farming), compared with 68% in the Netherlands, 55% in France, 45% in Spain and 17% in Germany.[8]

"I think the thing that's going to drive people to look more closely into collaboration will be the reduction in the BPS [Basic Payment Scheme] payments," says a leader of one of the UK's best-known farming co-operatives. "You can bumble along making profit some years and not making profit other years on your farming, but comfortable in the knowledge that come December or January you've got £20k coming to you… So I think without that money, suddenly farmers are going to think 'Oh Christ, I've got to make a profit out of this farming activity, what am I going to do?'"[9]

Figure 10.7

Relative contributions to farm business income (or profit)

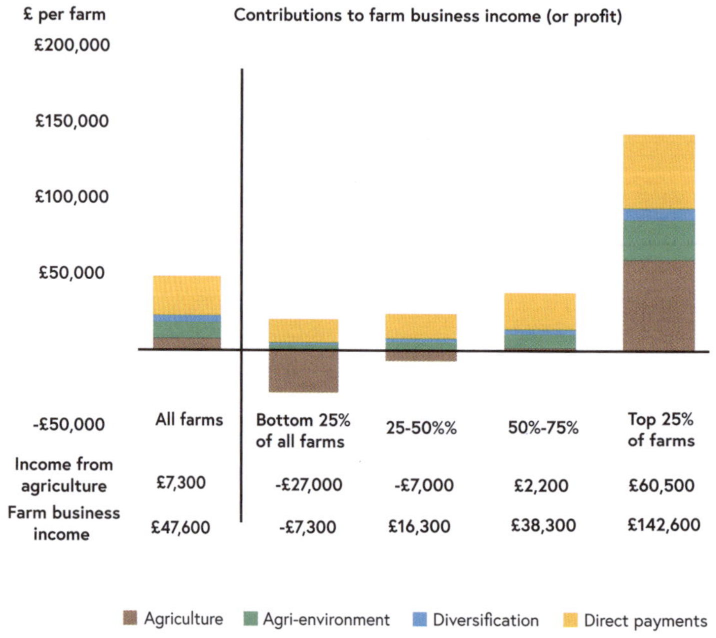

Regenerative farming

Craig Livingstone, who sits on our advisory board, farms what was previously a very conventional arable farm in Hampshire. Craig has set a target to reach net zero by January 2023 and not emit carbon at all.

Over the past five years, Craig has reduced pesticide use by 42% and industrial fertiliser by 32% without reducing yields. He has done this by focusing on soil health: diversifying the crops and varieties he grows; reintroducing a rotation system; growing cover crops and capturing solar energy; introducing grazing sheep back to the arable fields; and importing bulky organic fertilisers and soil conditioners, such as green waste compost and farm yard manure, to reduce his reliance on inorganic inputs.

After harvesting his commercial crops, Craig plants cover crops to protect his soil over winter. When the time comes to sow again, he brings in sheep to clear the field. (Many farmers would use the herbicide glyphosate.) Instead of ploughing up the whole field before sowing, he uses a shallow, "minimum-till" method which protects the integrity of his soil. In some fields he is doing "zero-till" sowing, which means drilling seed directly into the ground. He hopes eventually to use this method right across his farm, dispensing with manufactured fertiliser altogether. "Our soil isn't good enough to do that yet. It is like weaning yourself off drugs," he says.

Craig is a high-yield farmer, yet many of his priorities – and, increasingly, his methods – are similar to those of an agroecological farmer. In the future, and especially as more sustainable technologies feed into the mainstream, these two schools of thought will become more closely aligned.

Craig Livingstone, Farm and Estate Manager, Lockerley Estate

11

Can we have it all?

ONE way of freeing up enough land to meet our environmental targets is to tackle the vast amount of waste in the system. This isn't just the literal waste that first springs to mind: the excess lettuces ploughed back into the soil, the wonky carrots cast aside, the food we guiltily throw away at home because our eyes were bigger than our stomachs. It is systemic waste, which comes in three principal forms.

1. Food that's not eaten

The first form of waste is the one described above. Over a quarter of all the food grown in the UK is never eaten.[1] This wasted harvest accounts for between 6% and 7% of total UK greenhouse gas emissions.[2] Just under a third is wasted before it even leaves the farm gate because it doesn't meet specifications or because market fluctuations mean a crop suddenly becomes almost worthless. (Tomatoes, for example, are highly vulnerable to the vagaries of the British weather. A spell of hot weather will produce a glut of delicious ripe tomatoes. But if the skies suddenly cloud over, those tomatoes won't sell. People eat much less salad when it is cold.)

Beyond the farm gate, the biggest contributors to food waste are households (70%), followed by manufacturers (18%), the hospitality and food industry (10%) and then retailers (2%).[3]

The UK has committed to reducing food waste to 50% of 2007 levels by 2030.[4] The anti-waste charity WRAP estimates that we have already achieved half of this target, putting us on a promising trajectory.[5]

The Climate Change Committee also believes this target is feasible. It believes we could go further still – reaching 60% waste reduction by 2050 – by using policy levers such as increased household collection of food waste (which seems to make people more aware of what they are wasting), improving the clarity of best before labels and removing them from fruit and vegetables, and incentivising food manufacturers to reduce portions sizes.[6]

We can also draw confidence from the success of neighbouring countries (see Figure 11.1[7]).

"It ties in with what you were saying about best before dates. People throw away perfectly good food, because you panic. You panic it will make you ill. You never had those dates on before. You just ate what you ate."

"Deliberative dialogue" participant, North West England

Sources of post-farm-gate food waste

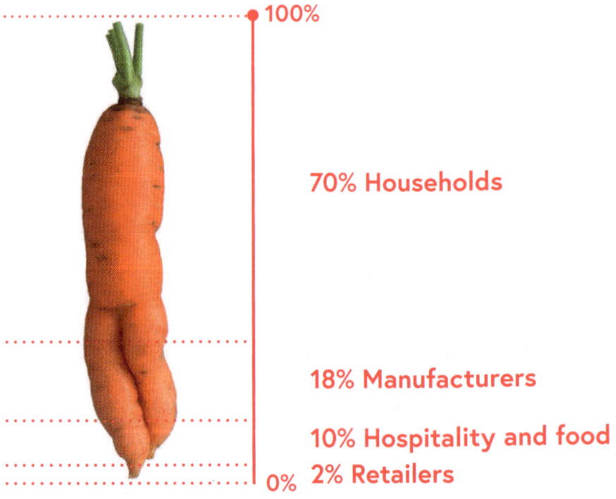

Figure 11.1

We produce more food waste than many of our European neighbours[8]

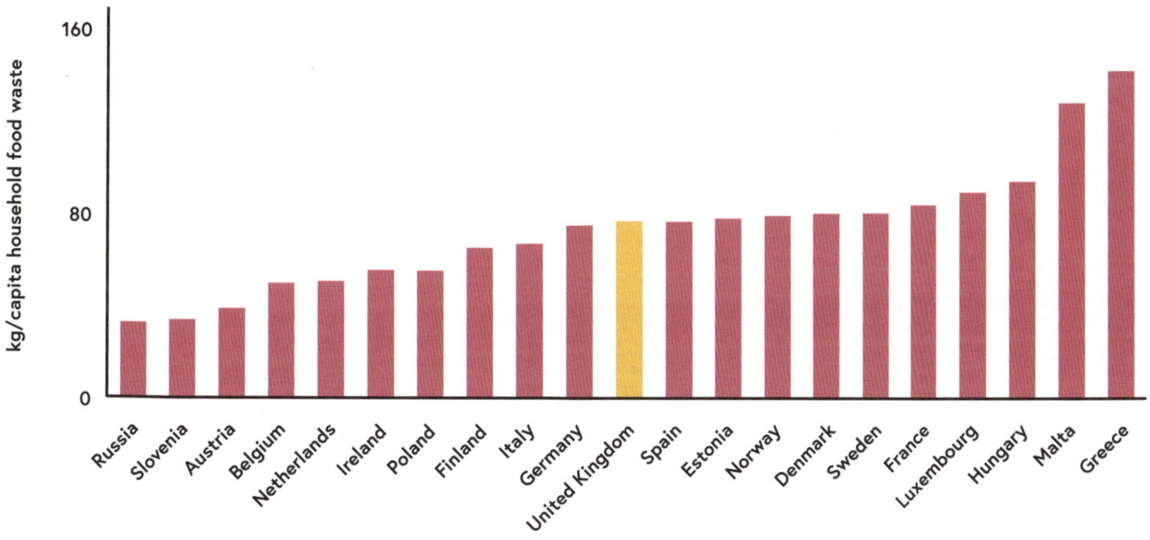

2. How we farm

The second form of reducible waste is caused by inefficient farming. In the UK we grow cereals on over 3 million hectares of land (13% of our total land).[9] Compared to most European countries we get a high yield out of this land. We have long summer days, good soil, and world-class rainfall. For wheat we average around 9 tonnes per hectare.[10] The UK record wheat yield, set in 2015 by Rod Smith, a farmer from Northumberland, is 16.5 tonnes per hectare. This was also the world record until 2017, when it was beaten by a New Zealander, Eric Watson, who managed to squeeze out an extra 0.9 tonnes per hectare.[11]

But there is a huge variation in how much food each farmer manages to produce from each hectare of land. A recent academic study concluded that the UK could realistically improve its yields by 13–15% if it were able to share best practice between farmers.[12]

And this estimate didn't consider the huge improvements that could be made through crop genetics. Another paper, in the science journal *Nature*, suggests that UK wheat production could rise by over 30% if you include possible advances through crop breeding.[13]

The Climate Change Committee, having studied detailed assessments of UK crop yields, concluded that they could be increased by 25% through crop breeding and improved farming practices.[14] It also believes that new precision technologies – such as AI which can monitor the health of every plant within a field – could increase yields further still.

"One of my concerns is food waste. There are always loads of promotions going on, multi-buy and so forth, and you do end up buying more than you need. When you get it home you don't necessarily finish them, so that does cause a lot of food waste."

South West England participant, deliberative dialogue

3. What we farm

The third kind of waste takes the form of land use. What we choose to grow and eat has a huge impact on how much land we need to feed ourselves.

As we saw in Chapter 9, meat and dairy make up only a third of the calories we eat. Yet 85% of UK farmland is used for feeding and rearing livestock.[15] Around one-sixth of this is used to grow crops for animal feed (although we buy a lot of feed in from abroad), and the remaining land is used for grazing.[16] This is a wildly inefficient use of land. Growing plants for human consumption generates around 12 times more calories per hectare than using the land for meat production.

Reducing meat consumption is the single most effective lever we can pull to improve the productivity of our land.

This is not a summons for everyone to go vegan. If we all just ate the amount of meat recommended by the government's Scientific Advisory Committee on Nutrition – most people do, but about a third of the population eats more – national meat consumption would fall by at least 15%, and our red and processed meat consumption by at least 27%.[17] The CCC says meat reduction will need to fall by 20–50% by 2050. Its central scenario calls for a 35% reduction in order for the UK to meet its net zero commitments.[18]

Eating less meat would be a lifestyle change for many, but it can hardly be described as a privation. If you usually eat meat and dairy at every meal, it could mean going without on Mondays and Tuesdays. Job done.

However, the idea of being forced to cut back on meat is unpopular with many consumers. There is something culturally sacred about a freeborn Englishman's right to a plate of bangers or a Sunday roast. It may prove easier to reduce the meat content in ready meals and convenience foods, where alternative proteins may soon match the taste and texture of, say, mince, but at a fraction of the price (see Chapter 13). Around half of the meat we currently consume is contained within processed foods.[19]

However we go about it, the rewards of eating less meat would be immense. Cutting our meat and dairy intake by one-third by 2050 could give us back a fifth of our farmland.

The route to having it all

The benefits of cutting all this systemic waste are hard to overstate. To take a perfectly plausible scenario, if we were to reduce our food waste by 50%, increase our farm yields by 15%, and reduce meat consumption by 30%, we could produce the same amount of calories from 30% less land (see Figure 11.2).

If we were to set our sights higher, increasing productivity by 30% and reducing meat eating by 35%, we could produce the same amount of food from 40% less land.

Both these scenarios free up enough land not just to achieve our climate goals but also to make space for nature, both in wilder areas and on our farms, without compromising our levels of food self-sufficiency.

But self-sufficiency is not the only issue. Price is just as important, if not more so. People will struggle to accept the transition to a sustainable food system if it makes it harder to feed their families. For that reason, it is politically risky too. Nothing brings down governments quicker than soaring food prices.

Figure 11.2

Halving food waste, increasing crop yields by 15% and eating 30% less meat would make it possible to feed the UK on a third less land[20]

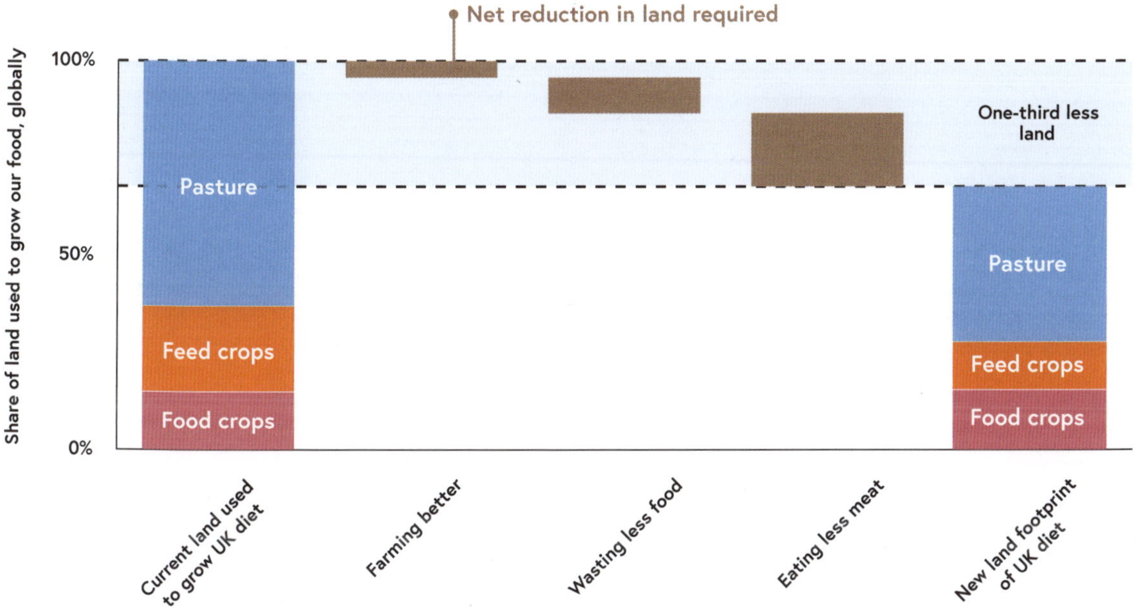

12

At what price?

"If you want to predict where political instability, revolution, coups d'état or interstate warfare will occur, the best factor to keep an eye on is not GDP, the human development index, or energy prices. If I were to pick a single indicator – economic, political, social – that I think will tell us more than any other, it would be the price of grain."

Lester Brown, President of the Earth Policy Institute, 2011

ON 2 October 1766, a riot broke out at the annual Nottingham Goose Fair. There were no geese involved. Instead, the row was about cheese, which was being sold by Lincolnshire traders for inflated prices. The locals, finding they could not afford the cheese, cut up rough. A mob began stealing cheese wheels and rolling them away.

According to *The Date Book of Remarkable and Memorable Events Connected with Nottingham and Its Neighbourhood (1880)*:

"The people were so exasperated that their violence broke loose like a torrent; cheeses were rolled down Wheeler-gate and Peck-lane in abundance, many others were carried away, and the Mayor, in endeavouring to restore peace, was knocked down with one in the open fair."

You can find a vivid account of The Great Cheese Riot on the website Amusingplanet.com. The name of the website is instructive in itself. In affluent nations, the idea of rioting over cheese prices now seems so unlikely as to be comic. But food riots were once a common part of our national life – especially in the 18th and early 19th centuries, when wars and harvest failures led to periods of excruciatingly high food prices. And elsewhere in the world, the price of food remains a pressing political problem. The Arab Spring of 2011 was preceded, and to some extent sparked, by food riots in Africa, the Middle East and Asia.[1]

The Covid pandemic caused global food commodity prices to rise sharply – by just under 40% between May 2020 and May 2021, according to UN figures – because of disruptions to production, labour and transport.[2] But bumper cereal harvests are expected to ease these price pressures, and the overall picture (at least in the developed world) looks relatively stable. For now.

In the UK, in the early part of the 21st century, the cost of food is about as low as it has ever been. Wheat, to take one example, costs a fifth of what it did in the fifties.[3] Chicken costs a third of what it did in 1970.[4] Food prices more broadly have fallen by 25% since the 1970s, while our average household incomes have doubled in real terms.[5] In 1957, the British spent 33% of our income on food. By 2017 that proportion had shrunk to 8%.[6]

America is the only major nation whose citizens spend a lower proportion of their income on food (see Figure 12.1). Both the US and the UK have very competitive wholesale and retail sectors which drive down farm margins. The same is true of countries such as Italy and France, but consumers in those countries spend more on higher quality produce, which pushes up the overall spend.[7]

This a luxurious position to be in. But it is also a dishonest one. As we saw in Chapter 1, our historically low food prices carry huge hidden costs, both to our planet and to our health.

Suppose, for example, a farmer has a contract to supply potatoes to a supermarket. In growing the potatoes, he pollutes a nearby watercourse with fertiliser. The cost of that pollution falls on us, the public, because our environment is polluted. If neither the farmer nor the supermarket (nor indeed the end consumer) is forced to cover the cost of cleaning

Figure 12.1

At 8%, UK households spend a relatively small proportion of their income on food[8]

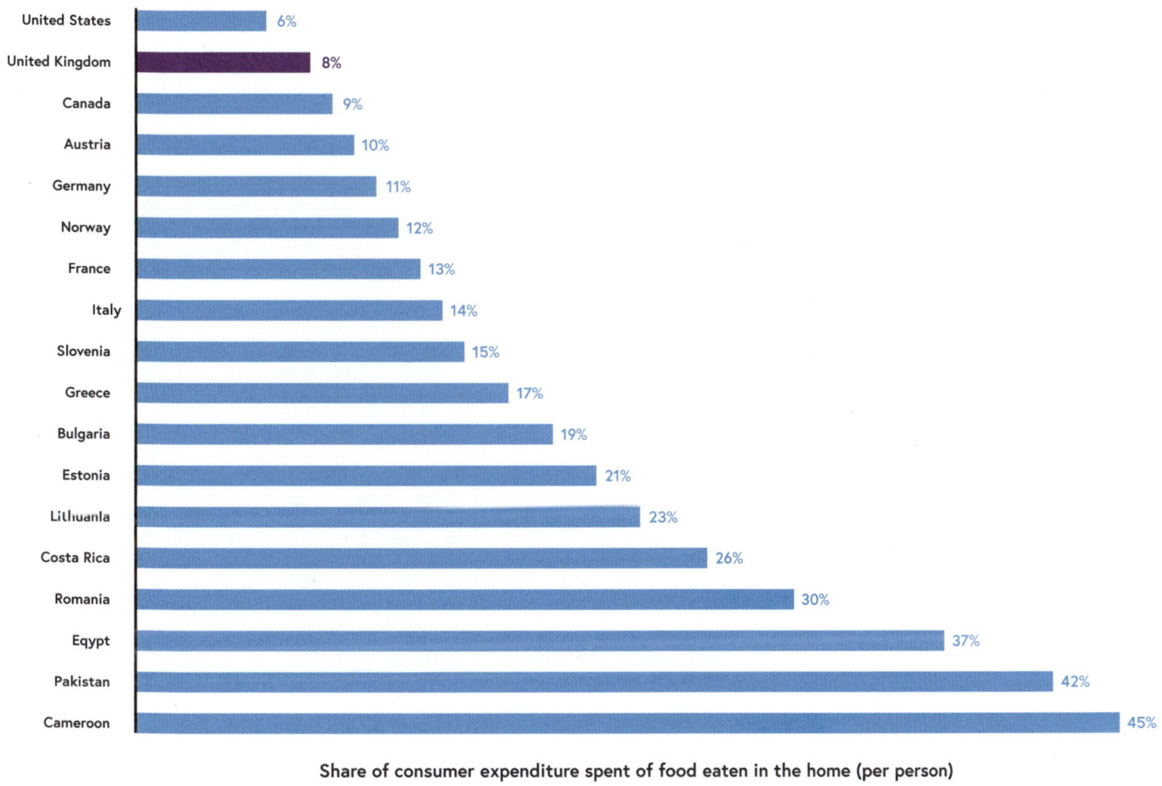

up the watercourse, there is no market incentive for the farmer to avoid such destructive practices. The cost to the environment is not factored in anywhere. The same is true of harm to animals, air pollution, biodiversity destruction and any number of deleterious side effects of food production.

These kinds of hidden costs – consequences of commercial activity that are not reflected in the price of that activity – are known by economists as externalities. Precisely because they are external, because their cost is not incorporated into the transactions of the free market, they are often allowed to run rampant. No one picks up the cost, but everyone pays the price.

In 1920, the British economist Arthur Pigou proposed that externalities should be dealt with by levelling taxes on the relevant goods. (The externalities that troubled Pigou were of their time. They included smoke from factory chimneys: "for this smoke in large towns inflicts a heavy uncharged loss on the community, in injury to buildings and vegetables, expenses for washing clothes and cleaning rooms, expenses for the provision of extra artificial light, and in many other ways".)[9]

Pigouvian taxes are designed to be equal to the cost of the externality so that the private and social costs of the transaction can be fully incorporated into the price tag. Once the true cost of a product is reflected in its price, argued Pigou, the free market can be left to work its magic. Producers have a built-in financial incentive to keep damaging externalities to a minimum.

Figure 12.2

Estimates put the hidden cost of food in the UK at £40bn–£96bn per year[10]

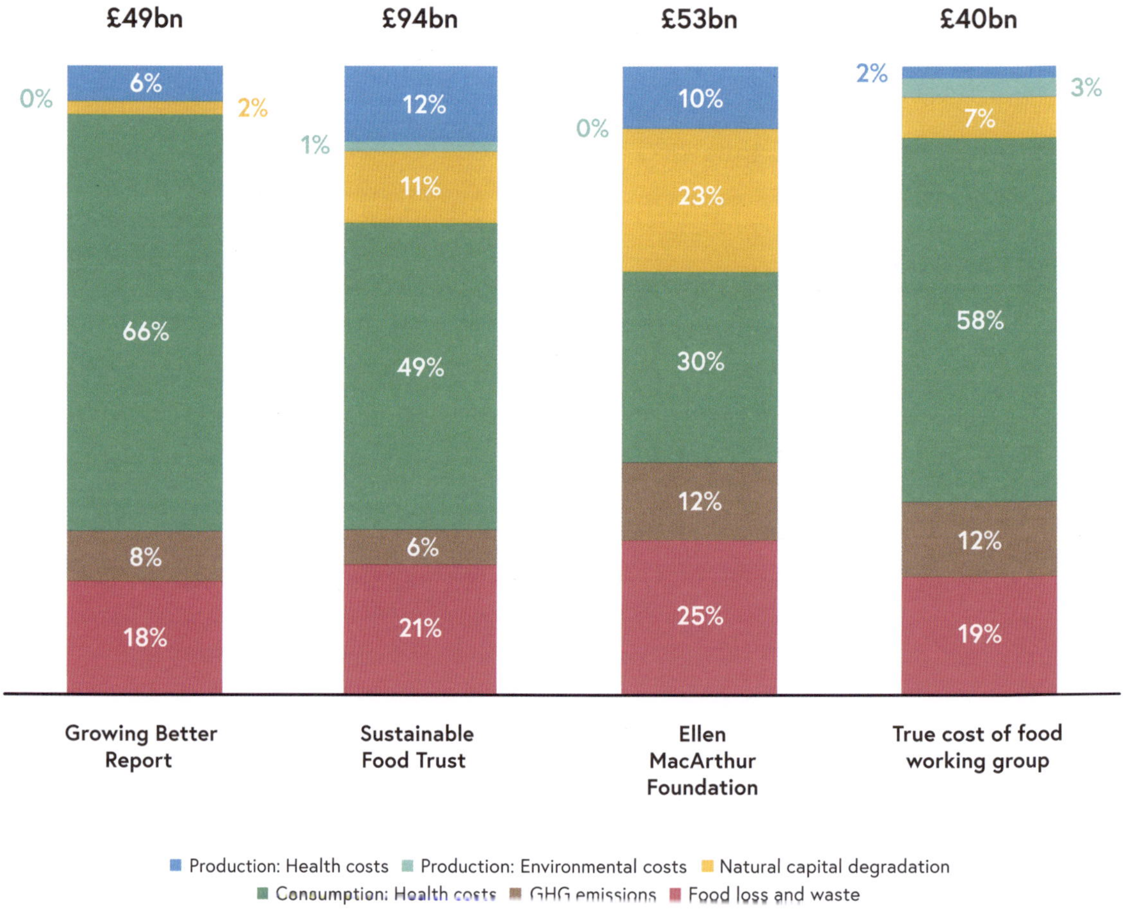

Imagine, however, the effect of adding Pigouvian taxes to food. A handful of recent studies (see Figure 12.2) have done just this for the UK. They found that if all the externalities of our food system – including the costs to the health service and to the environment – were factored into the price of our food, the price of the average weekly shop could double. If the Government were to inflict such a drastic price hike on its citizens, food riots would no longer be distant history. They would be front-page news.

This is one reason why many policy makers and commentators tend to be sceptical, verging on defeatist, about the possibility of radical change in the food system. They see it as a choice between two evils: we can either stick with our damaging but cheap food, or risk civil unrest.

But Pigouvian taxes are a blunt instrument, and not the only one available. In his response to Pigou, The Problem of Social Cost (1960), the American economist Ronald Coase pointed out that there are plenty of other methods for encouraging modes of production with fewer harmful externalities.[11] Grants and subsidies, legal rights, prohibitions and obligations are all existing tools in the legislator's box. The job of Government is to use the most effective tools for any given set of circumstances – the ones that it believes will do the job most effectively, that are the most politically acceptable and least likely to create unintended consequences.

A good example is the UK's transition from fossil fuels to more sustainable forms of energy. A strict Pigouvian approach would have been to slap a huge carbon tax on everyone's fossil fuel-powered energy bills. This would undoubtedly have encouraged companies to invest in renewable energy, which over time would have become cheaper and overtaken coal. But the political and social jeopardy of imposing such a big tax would have been prohibitive – or at least beyond the appetite of politicians.

Instead, the UK Government chose to introduce subsidies (for wind and solar energy providers), bans (no new coal-fired power stations) and legal obligations (an air pollution requirement that was almost impossible for coal-fired power stations to meet cost-effectively). As a result of these combined measures, the cost of wind power is now cheaper than the cheapest coal station (the cost of storing solar and wind energy for use on cloudy and still days is high, but in sunny places like California, solar-plus-storage† is already outcompeting new fossil power plants).[12] This has been achieved with only the most modest carbon tax.[13]

Would it be possible to pursue a similar approach to food? Rather than forcing the system to shift by suddenly adding the huge costs of externalities at the till – a burden that would fall hardest on the least affluent – could we use a similar portfolio of incentives and restraints to shift the food system to a more sustainable mode of production, without the need for drastic price increases?

Theoretically this is possible, but only if we can imagine a future model of farming that is sustainable without being significantly more expensive than our system today.

Figure 12.3

Organic food is sold at a premium[14]

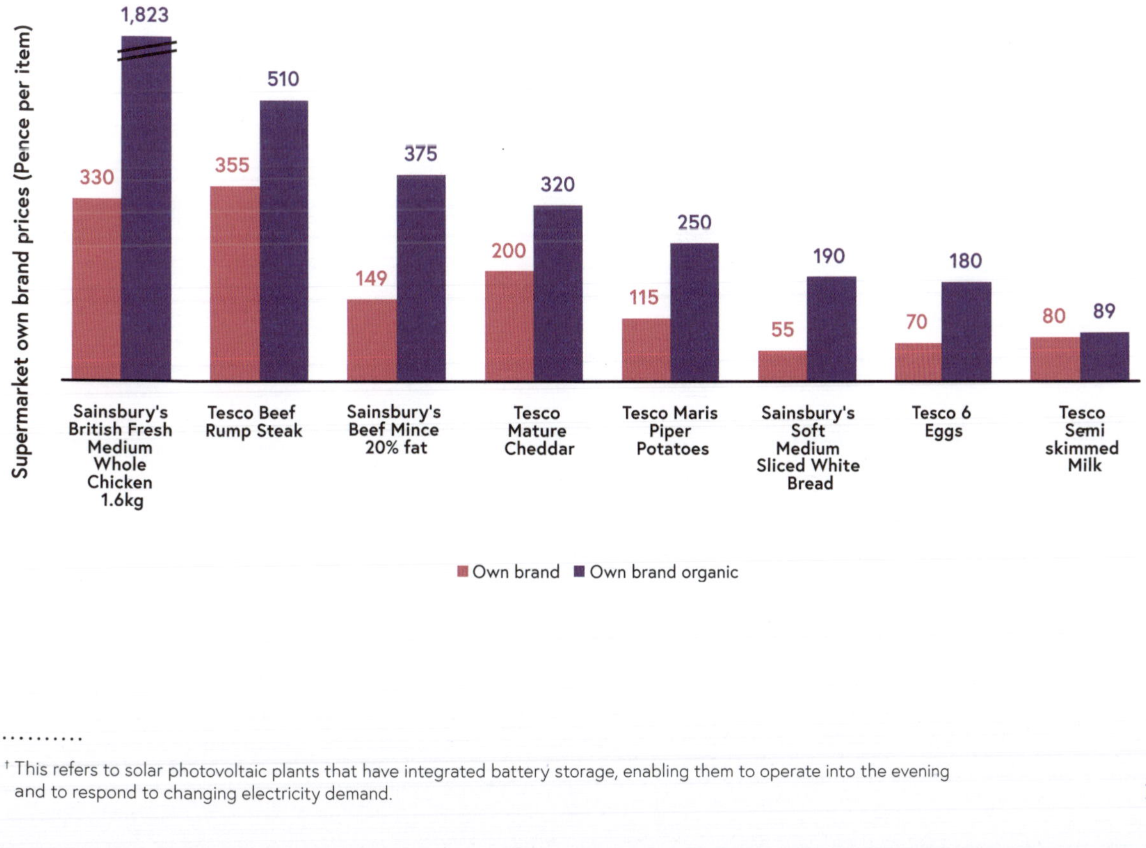

† This refers to solar photovoltaic plants that have integrated battery storage, enabling them to operate into the evening and to respond to changing electricity demand.

It is often assumed that this is hopelessly unrealistic. "Look at organic food," sceptics will say. "Most people can't afford it." And this is true. Figure 12.3 shows the cost of organic food relative to similar non-organic products in March 2021. The price premium for organic produce ranges from 11% (for organic milk) to over 400% (for organic chicken). Although the average UK household spend on food is, as we have said, historically low at 8%, that is only an average. For the least affluent 20% of the population the proportion goes up to 15%.[15] These households would not be able afford to feed themselves at organic prices.

But the current price of organic food is not an accurate benchmark for what the sustainable food of the future might cost. Organic food itself could certainly become cheaper through innovation and market growth. But it will not be the only source of sustainably farmed food in the future. There will also be more farms using modern science – robots, drones, improved genetics and AI – to produce carbon neutral and non-polluting crops. Other farms will combine new technology with traditional practices – for example, by using mixed crop rotations alongside modern no-till systems to keep carbon and moisture in the soil.

It is hard to predict exactly how the new wave of sustainable farming technology will affect food prices. Innovation moves in fits and starts, not smoothly or in a straight line. Nevertheless, our team has looked closely at current trends, and at the results of existing trials into new farming techniques, to extrapolate some numbers. It is reasonable to suppose that, for many crops, innovation will remove much of the expense of sustainable farming – and in some cases, actually make it cheaper than conventional farming.

We started by looking at the detailed economics of conventional farms today, using Defra's Farm Accounts: an annual report compiled by surveying farmers across England about their revenues, crop yields, livestock densities, costs of inputs for plants (such as fertiliser, seeds, pesticide and diesel) and for animals (such as feed and veterinary bills), and other costs such as rent, labour and machinery.

We then made assumptions about how these elements might change in future farming systems. What would happen to average yields and input costs if farms adopted more sustainable forms of higher yield farming or switched to an agroecological system? There is a wealth of available information to help with these estimates, including the accounts books of existing farms. For example, the regenerative advisory firm Soil Capital worked with a farmers' association in Belgium to help them improve the quality of their soil. They planted cover crops in their fields in winter, to stop the soil being washed away by heavy rain and improve its health, and used less invasive ploughing when readying the soil for planting. Over time this significantly improved soil quality, which meant they were able to reduce fertiliser and pesticide use by a third, at no cost to yields.[16] Research in the UK and US corn belt yielded similar results.[17]

Figure 12.4 shows the results of our analysis.[†] What you see is that in the future both kinds of sustainable farming methods – agroecological and higher yielding – should produce cheaper food than current organic prices. However, agroecological farming would remain more expensive than current conventional farming even if it went mass market. Sustainable forms of high-yield farming, by contrast, could produce even cheaper food than current conventional farming (a mirror of what has happened in the energy system), because it can maintain the same yields with lower input costs. (Of course unsustainable farming will probably become even cheaper too. That is always a danger until the costs of carbon and harms to the environment are properly built into the system.)

These findings, however, only apply to fruit, vegetables, and grains. Meat is a different story. As we showed in Chapter 11, there is currently no way to produce enough food, restore nature and sequester carbon while eating the same amount of meat. To get everything we need from the land, we will have to cut overall meat consumption by 30%. How on earth do we persuade a meat loving public to do that?

> **"Why do we have to be dictated to, that we need to stop eating meat and dairy products? Everybody likes a choice in life. We've seen what it's like when we don't have free democratic countries like, North Korea."**
>
> "Deliberative dialogue" participant, West of England

[†] This analysis is available as a supplementary document on https://www.nationalfoodstrategy.org/

Figure 12.4

Changing farming practices should not have a large impact on prices for plant-based products[18]

13

The protein transition

IN February of 2019, shortly before COVID-19 reached these shores, our team gathered in a small tearoom overlooking a graveyard in Bristol to discuss food policy with 36 strangers. This was the first of five "deliberative dialogues" that we staged around the country to get a better understanding of how the citizens of England feel about our food system, and how far they would be prepared to go to improve it.

Each panel was selected to be demographically-representative of their region. They came from all walks of life and every political affiliation (or none). They spent a total of 12.5 hours with us over four days – switching to Zoom once the pandemic took hold. They were able to question experts from different parts of the food system, as well as discussing their own experiences of its strengths and weaknesses. They also debated which political or commercial interventions they would be prepared to tolerate for the sake of improving the environment and public health.

Although there were differences of opinion within each panel and between the regions, some subjects elicited a remarkable degree of agreement. There was overwhelming support for much stronger restrictions on the advertising and promotion of junk food. Some participants wanted a ban on fast food joints opening near schools, and tougher regulations for retailers selling junk food.

Across the board, there was a higher tolerance for state intervention than we had anticipated – except in one respect. The idea of introducing a "meat tax" was a non-starter. Every time we raised it, the atmosphere would suddenly crackle with hostility. Although a minority of our panellists liked the idea, many more were vehemently opposed – and the arguments between these instantaneous tribes were fierce.

It is easy to understand why. A meat tax might be the quickest way to reduce consumption, but it would be expensive and regressive. If it were devised as a straightforward Pigouvian tax, and the cost of carbon emissions (as assessed by the Treasury) simply added to the price tag, the cost of beef and lamb would rocket overnight. This alone would cause public fury. To make matters worse, the biggest price increases would be on the cheapest cuts of meat. (Because carbon emissions are measured by the weight of the product, not the cut.) The cost of rump steak – which is already expensive – would rise by 31%. But the cost of mince – one of the most popular and economical ingredients for feeding a family – would rise by 145%. A kilo of lean beef mince would go from £4.80 per kilo to £11.76.[1]

After our deliberative dialogues, we ran a public poll on the idea of a meat tax, and got a similar response (Figure 13.1). Although 50% of people believe the Government should set a target for meat reduction, only 26% like the idea of a tax on fresh meat. 48% oppose the idea.

Figure 13.1

The public is suspicious of mandatory measures to reduce meat consumption[2]

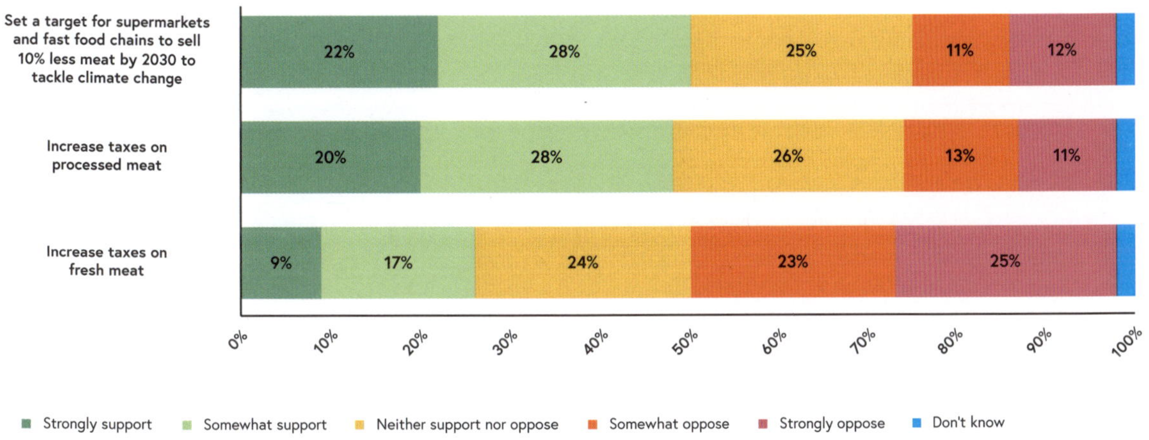

The Government is attuned to this public mood. When asked about the potential for a meat tax earlier this year, a Number 10 official was quoted as saying: "This is categorically not going to happen. We will not be imposing a meat tax on the great British banger or anything else."

Attitudes do change, and as the impact of climate change is increasingly felt, people's views about what interventions are acceptable might change. But we cannot afford to wait for the day the public ask for a meat tax. So what can we do in the meantime?

We propose a three-pronged approach: one that nudges people away from meat and makes alternatives cheaper. We should reduce the environmental impact of the meat we make, eat more alternatives to meat, and find ways for the government and supermarkets to help us cut down on our total meat consumption.

"I don't know about the rest of you, but the only time I ever have beef is in mince. I can't afford to buy a joint of meat unless it's been reduced, or is on special offer, because it's so expensive. I think that's the reason we buy cheap meat, the stuff that is mass produced, because it's cheap."

"Deliberative dialogue" participant, East of England

1. Cutting methane

We can assume that the vast majority of people will continue to eat some meat, milk and eggs for some time to come. Britain has always had an omnivorous food culture, and we produce some of the best meat, milk and cheese in the world. This feeds into our broader sense of identity. Once nicknamed "Les Rosbifs" by the French because of our appetite for red meat, we still invest considerable pride in "the great British banger".

The good news is that farmers and food companies are already developing ways to cut the carbon footprint of cows – the single largest source of emissions in our food system. For example, some breeds of cattle naturally emit less methane: a careful breeding programme could reduce emissions further still.[3] Augmenting cattle feed with certain ingredients, such as seaweed, can also reduce the amount of methane they produce – perhaps by up to 80%.[4]

Nestlé in the UK recently announced a plan to halve the carbon footprint of its milk supply by 2025 – in large part by working with their dairy suppliers to reduce methane emissions using feed supplements and regenerative farming practices.[5] This kind of commercial pressure is a powerful engine of change.

Providing government investment in research and innovation would speed things up further still, and have the added benefit of boosting the "green economy". But we must be realistic. There are drawbacks associated with methane reduction technologies, and limits to how they can be used.[6] Food additives need to be given regularly, which means they aren't suitable for cows that spend most of their days in fields. We estimate that the methane reduction techniques currently in development could cut farming emissions by around 10%.[7] A good start, but not enough on its own.

> "For us it is the whole smell, the taste, the look forward to the Sunday roast; it's all part of my heritage."
>
> "Deliberative dialogue" participant, West of England

2. Alternative proteins

One way to help consumers change their habits is to give them a cheaper alternative. In the 1960s, we ate four times more beef than chicken in the UK. (Although considerably less meat overall than we do today.)[8] By 1990, when intensive farmed chicken had massively reduced the price of chicken, sales matched those of beef. Now, 40% of all meat comes from chicken (see Figure 13.2).

Figure 13.2

We have changed our meat preferences significantly since 1961. We now eat much more chicken and less beef and lamb.[9]

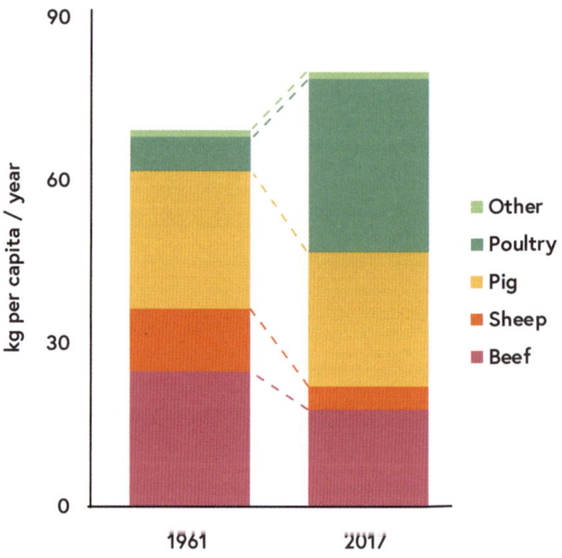

We may now be on the brink of an even more dramatic shift, this time from farmed meat to hi-tech alternatives.

The headline-grabber is lab-grown meat. This involves harvesting stem cells from a small stock of animals, which are then fed with a nutrient-rich solution typically including bovine fetal serum (blood drawn from the foetus of a cow), until they grow into a sort of meaty pulp.

No one has yet worked out how to manufacture lab-grown meat at scale. Last year's news stories about a Singapore restaurant serving lab-grown chicken nuggets neglected to mention that each £12 nugget only contained a tiny amount of lab grown meat, mixed with plant protein for bulk.[10]

Notwithstanding all this – and an inevitable degree of public squeamishness – lab-grown meat might yet turn out to be the tastiest alternative to farmed meat, so we shouldn't write it off.

For now, however, a more appealing (and commercial) option is using plants to create products that can take the place of meat. So far, most companies have been using wheat, soy or pea protein as their base, although other plants may follow. The British start-up SuSeWi has been developing a sustainable, protein-rich food source from algae held in huge pools in the desert, filled with water pumped from the Atlantic. (Their algal production plant, in Morocco, is pictured in Figure 13.3 below.)

> "Lab grown meat sounds unnatural. The compounds, the elements that make it up might be the same, but there's something that doesn't sit well with me."
>
> "Deliberative dialogue" participant, North West England

Figure 13.3

SuSeWi algae production plant in Morocco[11]

The American company Impossible Foods adds soy leghemoglobin to its products to give them a meaty flavour. This is a red protein, originally produced by nodules on the roots of soy plants but now fermented in tanks, which contains the same heme iron that gives meat its distinctive bloody taste. Leghemoglobin has not yet been approved for human consumption in the UK, but in America it has helped move plant-based products into the mainstream. The so-called Impossible Burger – a vegetarian patty that "bleeds" when cooked, like a real burger – already accounts for 10% of all the Whoppers sold by Burger King in the US.[12] Most of the people who buy Impossible Burgers will also eat the beef variety, according to US retail sales data.[13] A wholesale conversion to vegetarianism is not necessary if the plant-based option is appealing enough.

A third source of alternative protein comes from the science of "precision fermentation". This involves genetically engineering yeast cells so that they produce a particular kind of protein as a by-product of their fermentation. The yeast cells are then put in a vat and fed either a sugar solution or a mixture of carbon dioxide and hydrogen, so that they ferment and produce large amounts of protein.

This technique is already used to produce rennet for setting cheeses, and the insulin with which diabetics inject themselves. It is also similar to the process that makes Quorn. But in recent years, scientists have been engineering yeast to produce all sorts of new proteins in large fermentation tanks – including the leghemoglobin that goes into Impossible Burgers.

The Israeli start-up Imagindairy are starting to produce a "milk" protein from yeast which they say is indistinguishable from the real thing.[14] If this is true – and if the public is willing to accept the substitution – the commercial opportunities (and environmental benefits) could be massive. Almost 30% of Chinese milk imports, for example, are not drunk as a liquid or eaten as yoghurt or cheese, but converted into milk powder before being used in processed foods.[15] If milk powder produced by precision fermentation became cheaper than that from cows (a tipping point that some commentators believe is not far off) this would significantly disrupt the global dairy market.

We cannot know exactly how fast the alternative proteins industry will scale up, or what consumers will ultimately decide they want from these new foods. But a report in 2019 by the Royal Society predicted that 10% of the global meat industry could be replaced by alternative proteins within ten years.[16] The think tank RethinkX is even more bullish in its predictions, estimating that by 2030, 50% of dairy and beef products will have been replaced by alternative proteins.[17]

The environmental benefits of these new foods are clear; the health benefits, less so.[18] The Impossible Burger, for example, uses 96% less land than beef, 87% less water, and emits 89% less greenhouse gases.[19] But it also contains a quarter of your daily allowance of salt, and just as much saturated fat as a regular burger. This isn't really surprising: most alternative protein companies are targeting meat eaters and the fast food market, so one might expect them to be unhealthy.

Precision fermentation has its flaws too. Dr David Hanke, from the Department of Plant Sciences at the University of Cambridge, argues that ingredients made this way – in giant vats, often literally from thin air – will never match the nutritional richness of plants. "Unlike food from plants, no industrially generated food could provide the right mix of dietary constituents essential for health, such as balanced vitamins, minerals and bulk fibre," he wrote in a recent letter to The Guardian.[20]

Dr Hanke is surely right. For optimal health we should all be eating more plants, not fake meat. But we have to recognise how people actually behave, rather than just wishing they would behave differently. The UK is now a nation that eats vast quantities of burgers, processed meat and ready meals (see Figure 13.4). The trend towards convenience food has been at least five decades in the making, and will not be quickly reversed.

It so happens that this kind of food is particularly well-suited to alternative proteins. A processed ready meal may contain several ingredients – from mince to dairy powder – that could easily be replaced with more environmentally-friendly alternatives. There is, as yet, no novel protein that that can directly substitute or imitate a Sunday roast. But the meat in a ready-made lasagne, or even a takeaway sandwich, could plausibly be replaced.

The UK should be positioning itself at the forefront of this new industry. We have the right appetite for it, with our devotion to ready meals and our growing tendency towards "flexitarianism". Already, the UK buys a third of all the plant-based alternatives sold in Europe.[21] We estimate that developing and manufacturing alternative proteins in the UK, rather than importing them, would create an estimated 10,000 new factory jobs and secure 6,500 jobs in farming (to produce inputs for manufacturing processes).[22] It would also make it much easier to regulate this new industry, and to monitor its impact on health and the environment.

Figure 13.4

Over the last 50 years we have increased our consumption of ready meals and decreased our consumption of cuts of meat[23]

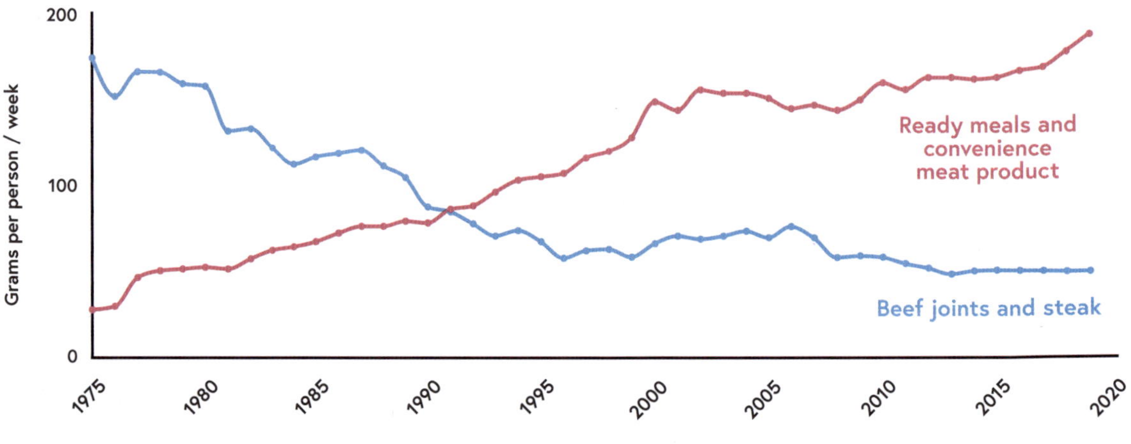

So far, the government has been slow to offer support and investment to companies developing novel proteins. As a result, most of this work is currently happening elsewhere (chiefly Singapore, Israel, The Netherlands and Canada), fostered by initiatives such as Canada's Protein Industries Supercluster.[24] We are in danger of missing a prime opportunity for green growth.

3. Government and industry leadership

Currently, 5.5% of all the food served outside the home is procured by state funded institutions.[25] This includes all the meals served in prisons, hospitals, government buildings, the armed forces, and of course schools.

When food is being produced in such bulk, small changes can have a big impact. Including minced mushrooms in beef burgers, for example, or putting more beans and less beef in a chilli, can significantly reduce the environmental impact of a dish.

In other words, the government has a big commercial lever at its fingertips. Making health and sustainability central to the government's food procurement guidelines would improve the food served in all state-funded institutions.

But most of the impetus to improve the food we eat will have to come from consumers, and from those who serve them. There is already a clear desire among the public to move towards a healthier, more sustainable diet (even if desire doesn't always translate into reality). In one recent poll 76% of UK adults said health is a major motivation for their choice of foods, and 53% cited the environment.[26] The retail industry, with its highly-developed powers of persuasion, can do a great deal to help consumers follow through on their good intentions. Consumer habits are affected by all sorts of subtle but deliberate factors, ranging from the layout of a supermarket aisle to the way in which dishes are ordered on a menu.

Supermarkets and chain restaurants sell us the majority of the meat we eat. They will therefore have a vital role to play in tempting us to eat more plants and a bit less meat.

In a complex system it is hard to predict the result of any single action. We have therefore placed three bets on meat: invest in technology to reduce the methane that ruminants emit; invest in alternative proteins which can replace some animal products, especially in processed foods; and nudge consumer behaviour through industry action and public sector procurement. The detail of all three recommendations is set out in Chapter 16.

What does this mean for our countryside?

The essence of rural England, wrote Stanley Baldwin, is "the sight of a plough team coming over the brow of a hill, the sight that has been in England since England was a land". But what will become of England's livestock farmers now? Where do they fit in this future of high-tech alternative proteins and vegetable-based diets? The answer is: right at the centre.

For one thing, the change we are recommending is not a wholesale transformation. Even if everything in this report happens exactly to plan, with a successful shift in land use and the commercial development of cheap alternative proteins, the overwhelming majority of England will still be farmed: 63–65% of total land area, compared to 70% today.[27]

Moreover, the recommendations in this strategy – particularly those concerning agricultural subsidies – are intended to broaden the range of good practise for which farmers can be paid. Rewarding better farming, rather than just carbon sequestration, will allow a continuation of the warp and weft of field and hedge that defines England.

Under the three-compartment model of farming described in Chapter 10, 2–4% of existing farmland might be given over to native woodland – and even this would contain large areas of semi-natural health and species-rich grassland maintained by extensive grazing. We would still use over 53% of England's total land area to farm beef, dairy, and lamb.

But these reassurances may not be enough to quell the deep – and understandable – anxieties of some farmers. Our team has spoken to many livestock farmers – especially those on tenant farms – who feel that red meat is being unfairly vilified, and that their jobs and way of life are at risk.

It's not just the call for reduced meat consumption that worries them. There is also the imminent loss of the "direct payments" which make up the majority of income for farmers in the uplands and in lowland livestock farming. And there appears to be a growing threat that new trade deals may allow in cheap, lower-standard imports of meat, which will undercut and potentially bankrupt our own livestock farmers.

There must be joined-up thinking across government to address all these issues, and create a new deal for livestock farming.

14

Food security

SECURING the nation's food supply has been a central role of all states since history began. It was a standing item at every meeting of the assembly in ancient Athens. In Genesis, we learn how Joseph – he of the multicoloured dreamcoat – saved the people of Egypt from famine (and in the process enslaved them).†

These days, in wealthy countries like the UK, food security has become one of those largely invisible political issues that the public tends not to think about much – until something goes wrong. The disruption to food supplies caused by the first wave of the COVID-19 pandemic was actually remarkably well-contained, thanks to the nimbleness of food businesses and their close collaboration with government. Yet even temporary shortages of a handful of products (tinned tomatoes, pasta, flour) caused consumers to panic, and in some cases to stockpile.

Behind the scenes, therefore, food security remains a major political issue. But the question of how best to achieve it is unresolved. Even the precise meaning of "food security" is disputed. One study on the topic identified over 200 definitions of the term in academic literature.[1]

In Part One of this Strategy, we distinguished between food security and self-sufficiency. Self-sufficiency is the ability to feed a nation from its own produce, rather than from imports. Food security, as we defined it, is being able to feed the population at a reasonable cost, even in the face of future shocks such as a global pandemic, massive harvest failure, or a general crisis of agricultural productivity caused by climate change.

As Tim Lang points out in his book Feeding Britain, food security is a many-tentacled beast.[2] It depends on an array of different factors, including the defence of supply lines (being confident they are not vulnerable to attack), the resilience of all parts of the food system, separately and combined (how quickly they can adapt in the face of sudden shocks), capacity (the skills and capabilities in the system) and control (how concentrated is ownership of the system and what risks might arise from high levels of concentration).

Being self-sufficient does not guarantee food security. In the event of a harvest failure or other local crisis, it is good to have alternative supply routes to fall back on. We have not been self-sufficient in Britain since 1846, when the hated Corn Laws – which protected farming landowners from cheap European grain imports, but led to high food prices and even famine – were repealed.[3]

Our self-sufficiency fell steadily after that as food imports grew (see Figure 14.1), accelerating with the development of new technologies such as refrigerated shipping.†† As we saw in Chapter 3, it reached a low point of 30% by the eve of the Second World War.[4] (The percentage figure for self-sufficiency is always a net total, allowing for the flow of exports as well as imports.) The huge wartime effort to grow more food

....

† It's a much less jolly story than the musical. Joseph, working on behalf of the Pharaoh, makes the starving Egyptians hand over all their money in exchange for the grain he has hoarded for seven years. When they run out of money he takes their livestock, and finally their land and freedom. "The land became Pharaoh's, and Joseph reduced the people to servitude, from one end of Egypt to another."

†† Contrary to received wisdom, the pre-war British food system was not based on the colonies. They played a relatively small role in imports until the first tariffs were imposed on food in 1931. Up until then, the majority of UK imports came from the US, South America and continental Europe (especially Denmark for pork and butter).

Figure 14.1

UK self sufficiency over time[5]

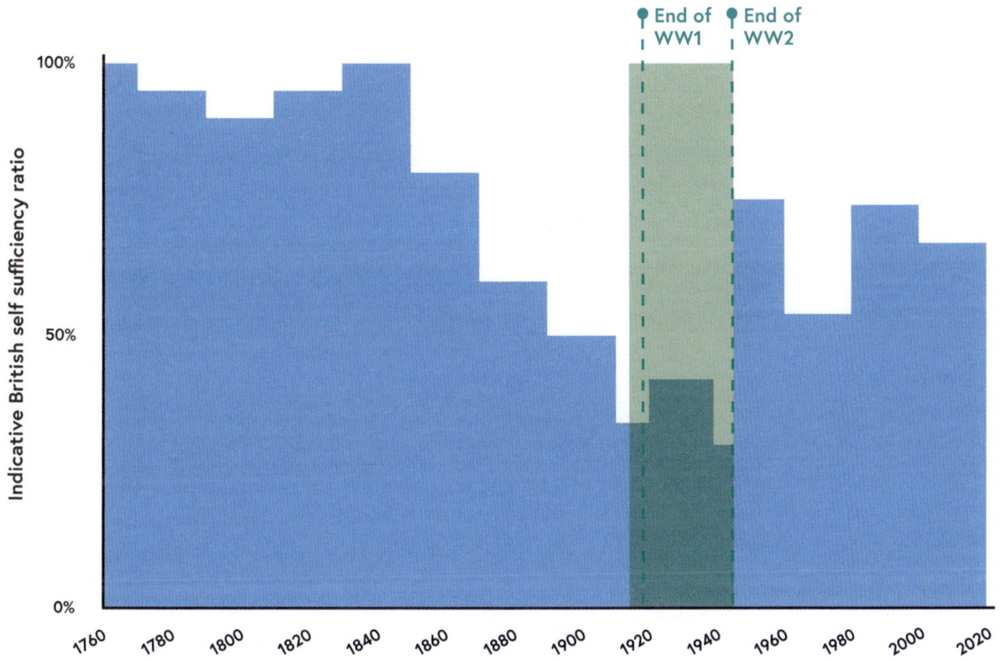

meant that Britain's self-sufficiency soared to 75% by 1945.[6] It dipped briefly after the War, but Government subsidies, combined with protective tariffs, pushed it back up.

And when Britain joined the Common Agricultural Policy (CAP), our farmers became entitled to European subsidies designed to encourage bigger yields, along with protectionist tariffs designed to keep out produce from beyond the Common Market. Once it was no longer cheaper to import, say, Canadian wheat, British farmers had a financial incentive to produce more of it themselves.

By the mid-eighties, when CAP subsidies and tariffs were at their height, Britain's self-sufficiency reached a peak of almost 80%. But this feat was achieved through distorted economics. Farmers within the Common Market were receiving twice as much for their produce as they would have done without such protectionist measures – with most of that bonus paid by the state and the rest by shoppers. Unsurprisingly, these incentives resulted in huge surpluses of food. The EU was sometimes forced to buy up produce just to maintain prices.[7] No one who was alive at the time can forget the headlines about warehouses full of "butter mountains" and "milk lakes".

Since then, subsidies and protective tariffs have been reduced, and our domestic food production has declined accordingly. We now produce about 65% of the total value of the food we eat.[8]

Our Government no longer sets a target for the amount of food that we should grow to feed ourselves, as it used to in the Seventies.[9] Instead, it relies on two methods to assess the nation's food security.

First, it conducts occasional reviews to understand whether we have what you might call "U-Boat food security". That's to say, if we were cut off completely from all other countries, but could rely on rationing and other forms of drastic Government intervention, would we be able to restore ourselves to full self-sufficiency before we starved?

Defra's 2010 UK Food Security Assessment concluded that we already grow much more of our own food than we did before the War, so we would have a better starting point. And a shift from livestock production to grains and vegetables could make up the remaining gap, "particularly if this extreme scenario included a reduction in the level of food waste … Maximising calorie production would require a dramatic reduction in livestock production, with all crop production used for human food where possible instead of animal feed."[10] In such a scenario, they estimated, we could produce more than enough calories per person per day.

Defra also conducts internal monitoring of food security. These are shorter but more wide-ranging than the 2010 report. They assess the risk of various dangers across the system: how global harvests might change because of climate change and other pressures; the geographical diversity of our food imports, and how exposed we would be in the event of a harvest failure in one region; the diversity and security of ports, roads and warehouses along our import routes; and so forth.

At the start of the pandemic, the market had to work closely with the Government to maintain food supplies. The particular circumstances of this crisis made that easier. Disruption to the food chain was mainly caused by the national lockdowns implemented across the world. Because governments had imposed these lockdowns, they were also well placed to mitigate them – for example, by exempting farm workers and lorry drivers from lockdown restrictions. In this country, the Government suspended elements of competition law to allow food companies to co-operate, share information and pool resources. (One example: the abrupt closure of all restaurants meant that meat suppliers suddenly had a huge surplus of steak on their hands. This surplus was sold into the retail system, with supermarkets agreeing to promote the "back half of the cow" so that it didn't go to waste.)

The next big shock to our food system, however, will probably be very different – and less easily mitigated. The most likely threat is widespread harvest failure caused by climate change. Figure 14.3 shows the UN's assessment of how climate change is likely to affect crop yields globally. Red means harvests are likely to shrink, green means they are likely to grow. It paints a picture of the kind of extreme inequality that is certain to have extreme consequences: famine, mass migration, even war.

Moreover, the "green" status of our own country is not assured. The additional warmth and wetness of climate change may lead to better harvests, but if melting glaciers cause the gulf stream to slow to a standstill, UK temperatures would fall abruptly – as would rainfall. This could dramatically reduce our yields.[11] This is one of many potential existential threats created by climate change (see box).

The known unknowns of climate change are the most dangerous uncertainties we face. But this country is itself in a state of transition. Our trading relationships and our agricultural system are both in flux. This creates potential for good, but we must also be alert to possible pitfalls.

Figure 14.2

The UK is 77% self-sufficient in foods that can grow in our climate and 64% self-sufficient overall[12]

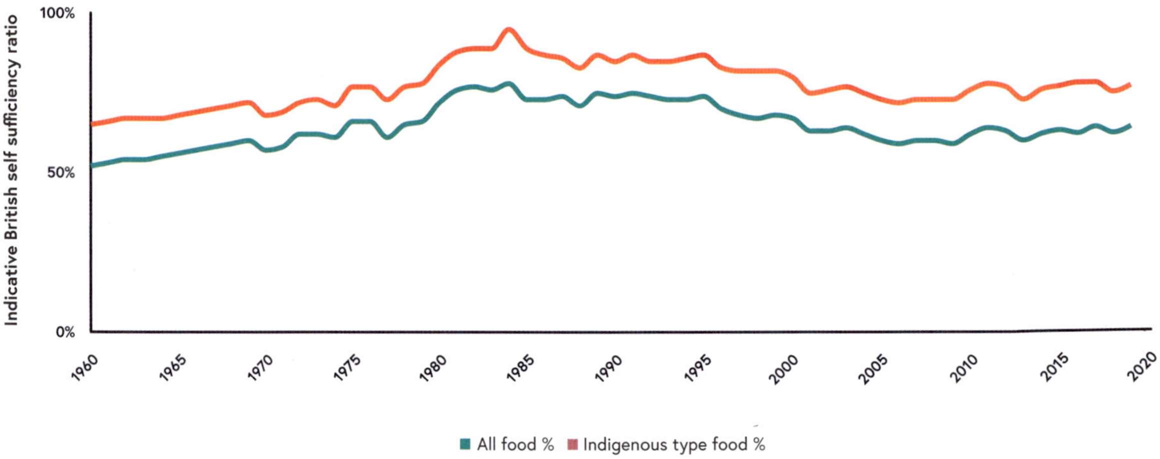

The 2020 Agriculture Act formalised Defra's food security review, creating a statutory duty to publish a report at least every three years. We will propose in Chapter 16 that that this review should in fact be annual, given the significant changes ahead, and that it should involve broader consultation, bringing in organisations responsible for nutrition, cybersecurity infrastructure, climate change and the environment. We need the widest possible foresight to help prepare us for the future.

Changing the way we farm is bound to create new uncertainties. But it is also, in itself, a food security measure. Modern agriculture is stuck in a vicious cycle of its own: the way we produce food is causing climate change, which in turn threatens our food supply. As we have seen in previous chapters, the UK is quite capable of building a better agricultural future, with high-yield, low-impact farming sitting alongside nature restoration and carbon sequestration.

But there is one critical problem: trade. There is no point trying to build a low-carbon, nature-friendly, world class food system in this country if it can be undercut by imported food produced to lower standards from abroad. We need to get trade right.

Figure 14.3

By 2050 large parts of the southern hemisphere will see crop yields fall while the northern hemisphere will see increases in yield[8]

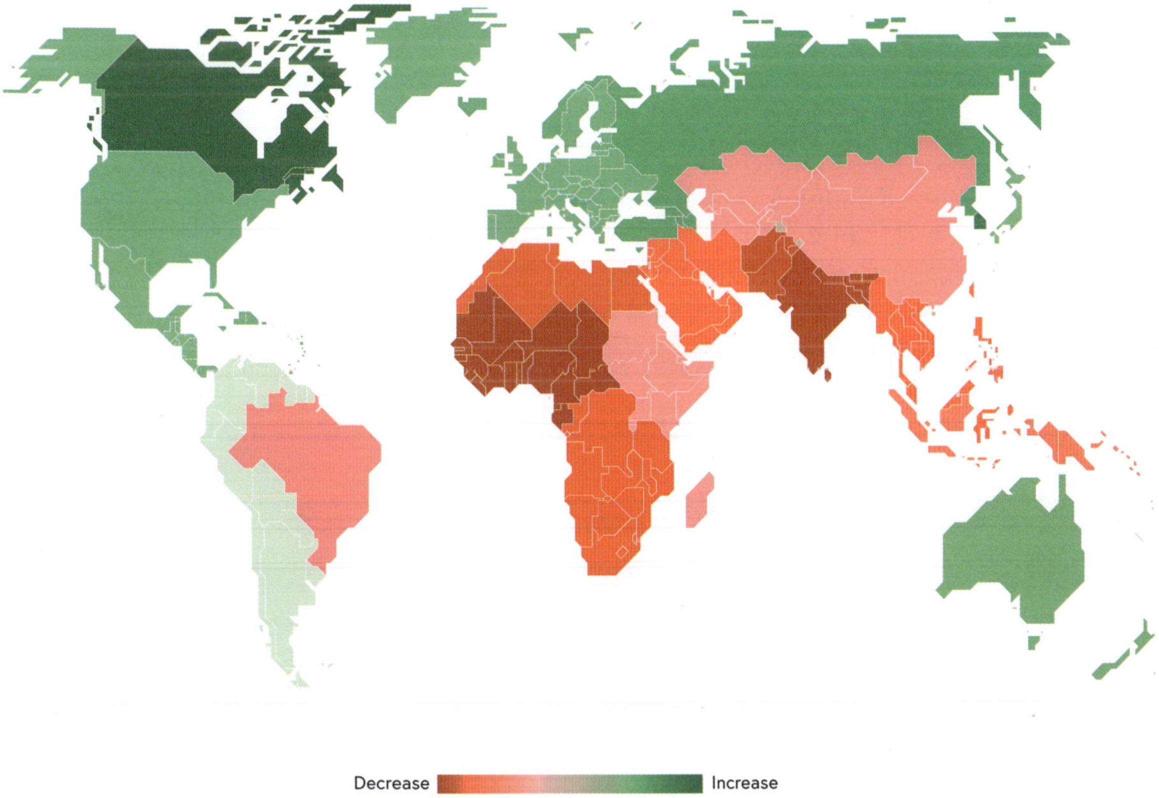

Existential threats to the food system

One paradox of modern food production is that the pursuit of food security has led to such high levels of environmental harm, it puts the entire food system at risk. Asaf Tzachor, a researcher at Cambridge University's Centre for the Study of Existential Risk, describes the problem thus.[13]

1. Demand for agricultural commodities worsens climate change

As the global population continues to grow, there is a greater demand for food, specifically wheat, maize, rice and soybean, which account for half of the global cropland under cultivation.[14] Increase in demand requires intensification of production, which has led to higher levels of deforestation and agrochemical use, both of which have significant contribution to greenhouse gas emissions.[15]

2. Demand for animal-source foods (meat, dairy, and eggs) drives the collapse of marine ecosystems and harms those who depend on them for their livelihoods

Fish consumption is also being driven by the demand for food, yet this has led to severe overexploitation which jeopardizes future fish stocks and livelihoods. 31% of marine fish stocks are rated as over exploited[16] by the FAO, 58% are fully exploited. Hundreds of millions of people depend on fisheries for their livelihoods around the globe.[17]

3. Climate change drives crop failures, migration and civil unrest

Some evidence suggests change in global climates will decrease crop yields, which could lead to higher prices and make societies more vulnerable to famine, food riots and conflict.[18]

4. Climate change will increase the volatility of global food supply chains

Crop pests and livestock diseases are likely to increase with warmer temperatures.[19] Extreme weather events will damage infrastructure for production, transportation and processing of food.

15

Trade

TRADE is a vital part of our food system. At the most basic level, foreign imports underpin our food security: the UK has not been self-sufficient in food since the early 19th century, in part because having a diverse supply of food creates resilience.

The quality as well as the quantity of our food is improved by trade. Over the past 30 years, Britain's restaurant scene has undergone a remarkable renaissance – due, in large part, to an expansion of tastes and skills created by generations of immigrants, and the diverse range of products we now import to serve those tastes. A similar flourishing of choice and quality has spread through our supermarket shelves.

Perhaps more surprisingly, trade can reduce the environmental impact of our diet. Importing tomatoes from Spain generates less carbon than growing them in greenhouses in the UK, because Spain has such a natural abundance of sun.

In other cases, though, food imports can have a sharply negative effect on our environmental balance sheet. The carbon footprint of Brazilian beef is almost twice as big as UK beef.[1] Australian beef, too, has a higher carbon footprint than our own, in part because Australian forests are still being cleared to create pasture.[2] This is already negating our attempts at reforestation at home: between 2010 and 2013, the UK consumed imported products that had been produced at a cost of 31,000 hectares a year of forest overseas, but we only managed to increase our own coverage by 17,000 hectares.[3]

It's not just about carbon. The UK is a global leader in animal welfare and livestock husbandry – unlike some of the countries that would like to sell us meat. Allowing cheap imports from such countries would undermine our own standards, as well as undercutting our farmers. This is something the British public feels very strongly about: 94% of the public want existing food standards to be maintained in any trade deals the UK does.[4]

Knowing the strength of public feeling, the Conservative Party pledged in its 2019 election manifesto that: "In all of our trade negotiations, we will not compromise on our high environmental protection, animal welfare and food standards".

In Part One of this strategy, published in July of last year, we proposed a mechanism that would allow the government to keep this promise without falling foul of the WTO's anti-protectionism rules. We suggested that the independent Trade and Agriculture Commission should be asked to define a set of core UK standards. In any future trade deals, the UK would then agree to remove import tariffs only on those products that meet these standards.

Our report was followed by a report from the Trade and Agriculture Commission (TAC), which made the same recommendation. It suggested that "if trading partners could not demonstrate equivalence with core standards, then they would not be considered for zero tariff, zero quota access for those products to which the core standards applied." The TAC was clear that these standards should cover not just food safety but "climate change, environmental, ethical and animal welfare measures".

> "My big thing really is getting back to some kind of British pride and standard in our food where we produce it from, you know, from rearing it to eating it, from farmyard to table, and supporting the local farmers."
>
> Tony, 56, Burnley

This conclusion was all the more notable because the TAC panel contained some devout free-traders, as well as farming representatives. There had been scepticism that such an ideologically disparate group would be able find a consensus on trade policy. But both sides agreed that it was vital to protect good farming practices from being undercut by cheap imports.

The Government is now facing the first significant test of its manifesto promise, in the form of the recently concluded trade deal with Australia. Australian farmers – although heavily regulated – are permitted to use practices that most reasonable observers would not deem to be in line with UK standards. For example, battery cages for laying hens are still legal in Australia, and cattle are held in greater densities than in the UK.

Perhaps most distressingly, the practise of "mulesing" is commonplace in Australia. This is when the skin is cut off a lamb's rump, in two crescent-shaped flaps, to encourage large scabs to form. The idea is to prevent flies infesting the area. It is done to female breeding lambs: those that will grow up to become ewes. Lambs destined for the supermarket shelves are slaughtered too young to require the practice. Around 30% of the time, no anaesthetic is used.[5]

When it announced the Australian deal, the Government said it would include measures to protect our standards. The deal does contain a chapter on animal welfare, which is in itself a world first, and we look forward to seeing the detail. Until we do, however, it is unclear how the government plans to maintain its commitments.

The way we do one trade deal inevitably feeds into how we do the next. Brazil – which has significantly worse environmental and welfare standards than our own, or indeed Australia's (see Figure 15.1) – is also being lined up for a trade deal. If we are seen to lower our standards for the Australia deal, it will make it much harder to hold the line with Brazil – or the next potential trading partner, or the next.

At a time when the government is asking our own farmers to raise their environmental standards higher than ever, this would be an extraordinary failure of joined-up thinking. It would make it much harder to achieve the other goals we have set for our food system and undermine many of the recommendations we have made elsewhere in this Strategy. Our true carbon footprint – including that from imports – would be larger than ever, as would the impact our food has on biodiversity. It would also imperil our own farming sector, by undercutting it with cheap imports made to lower standards than our own. And it would infuriate the British public, who could hardly have made their feelings clearer.

To protect farmers and ensure that the British people can have confidence in our imported food, the government must draw up a set of "core standards" that it can use for all future trade deals. It should then explain how it intends to enforce them and thereby help to raise standards both here and abroad.

Figure 15.1

Comparison of food standards with potential trade partners

■ Equal or better than UK
■ Lower standard that is less likely to distort competition
■ Likely trade distorting

	UK	US	Australia	Brazil
Laying hens	All cages must have a perch, nest box and litter and provide at least 750 cm² of space per bird.[4]	No federal standard; voluntary guidelines suggest cages should be at least 432 cm². California will require entirely cage-free housing from 2022, with other states expected to follow.	Legally binding federal standards for poultry welfare are in the final stages of development. Current voluntary guidelines suggest cages should have at least 550 cm² of space per bird.[6]	No legislation. Some laying hens are housed with as little as 357 cm² of space per bird.[7]
Broiler chickens	Stocking density may not be higher than 39 kg/m². Chemical washes banned.	No federal legal maximum stocking density. Chemical washes widely used.	Voluntary guidelines suggest stocking density should not be higher than 46 kg/m².[8]	No legislation.[9]
Beef cattle	Growth hormones banned since 1981.	Growth hormones widely used.	Growth hormones used on about 40% of cattle.[10]	Use of hormones in beef cattle prohibited by Normative Instruction No 55 of 2011.[11]
Dairy cattle	Bovine somatotropin (BST) hormone banned since 1990. Maximum somatic cell count (SCC) 400,000/ml. .	BST widely used. SCC maximum 750,000/ml.	BST banned. Industry standard maximum SCC 400,000/ml (but not in federal statute and may vary).[12, 13]	BST widely used.[14] Maximum SCC 1,000,000/ml.[15]
Sheep	Tail docking using rubber ring permitted in lambs under 7 days without anaesthesia, to prevent blowfly; after 7 days, anaesthetic required. Castration without anaesthetic permitted in lambs under 3 months. Mulesing and other mutilations prohibited.[16]	No federal legislation; the American Sheep Industry Association's Sheep Care Guide suggests that castration and tail docking may be performed without anaesthesia up to 8 weeks.[17]	Castration and tail docking may be performed without anaesthetic up to 6 months. Mulesing practised in sheep for wool production; anaesthesia should be used "where practical and cost-effective".[18]	No legislation or guidance.[19]
Animals in organic systems	Antibiotic use permitted for therapeutic use on a veterinarian's prescription.	Total ban on antibiotic use.	Antibiotic use permitted for therapeutic use on a veterinarian's prescription, but the meat cannot then be sold as organic and products (such as milk) may be sold as organic only after a waiting period.[20]	Antibiotics may be used therapeutically, but the animal products may not be sold as organic before a waiting period.[21]
Pigs	Sow stalls banned since 1999. Ractopamine (beta-agonist used as growth promoter) banned.	Sow stalls legal in 41 states (but banned in California and several others). Ractopamine used in 60-80% of pigs	Sow stalls banned in 2 states; elsewhere sows may be confined in stalls for no more than 6 weeks. Voluntary initiative to phase out use.[22] Ractopamine use legal.[23]	No legislation on sow stalls.[24] Ractopamine in use.[25]
Welfare in transport	Maximum legal journey time 12 hours; livestock density set by law.	Maximum journey time 28 hours; no maximum legal stock density.	Maximum journey times vary by species: eg 48 hours for adult sheep and cattle; 24 hours for pigs. Loading densities set in national guidelines, implemented in state legislation.[26]	Regulated by National Traffic Council Regulation No 675 of 2017. Basic standards for the construction of vehicles but no maximum journey time and no maximum stocking density.[27]
Antibiotic use	Average antibiotic use in food animals limited to 29.5 mg/kg.	Average antibiotic use in food animals limited to 160.7 mg/kg. (Except organic)	Administration of antibiotics as growth promoters legal.[28] Some high-priority human antibiotics banned for use in animals.[29] Use is concentrated in largely domestically-focused pig and poultry industries.[30]	Some antibiotics widely used as growth promoters, but many categories are prohibited. Average use is reported to be lower than some EU countries, but there is a lack of data.[31]
Carbon emissions from beef[32]	30 $kgCO_2e$/kg beef	25 $kgCO_2e$/kg beef	45 $kgCO_2e$/kg beef	70 $kgCO_2e$/kg beef
Tree cover loss due to shifting agriculture (2018)[33]	42 ha	2,970 ha	7,620 ha	835,000 ha

16

The Plan

IN this report we have examined at length the things that have gone wrong with the food system. Now we must address an even more urgent question: how do we put them right?

The food system of the future must meet these goals:

- **Make us well instead of sick**
- **Be resilient enough to withstand global shocks**
- **Help to restore nature and halt climate change so that we hand on a healthier planet to our children**
- **Meet the standards the public expect, on health, environment, and animal welfare**

This will require significant – although not necessarily painful – changes to our national diet, and to the way we grow our food. Figure 16.1 shows how our diets will need to change across the next ten years if we are to meet the Government's existing commitments on health, climate and nature.

We will need to use more of our countryside to sequester carbon and restore nature, which means encouraging diverse methods of land management. A small amount of our farming land will be given over to native woodland, peatland, heath and species-rich grassland maintained by conservation grazing. On the remaining farmland, lower intensity, agroecological farms will sit alongside higher-yielding farms that use the latest technology to maintain yields without polluting. And there will be any number of farms in between, drawing from both traditions.

Figure 16.1

Changes are needed to the national diet by 2032 (compared to 2019) to meet health, climate and nature commitments†

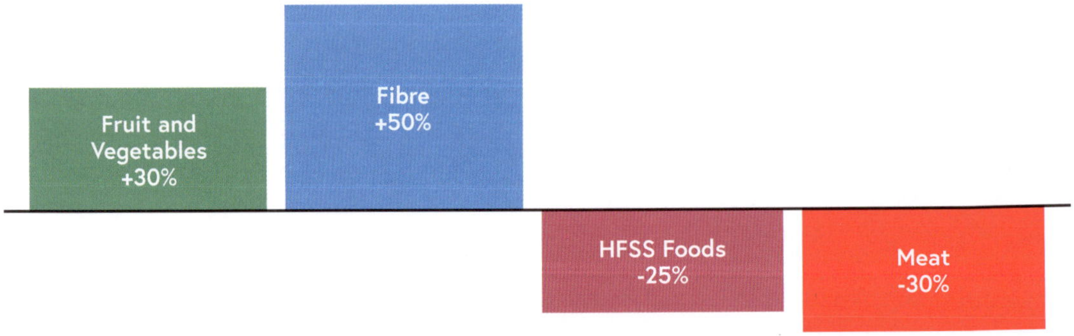

† Three of the diet-related targets are based on advice from the Scientific Advisory Committee on Nutrition. A 30% increase in fruit and vegetables would bring us in line with the Eatwell recommendation to eat five pieces of fruit and vegetables per day; a 50% increase in fibre would bring us in line with the SACN recommended 30g/day; a 25% reduction in consumption of HFSS foods will take us towards the required 60% reduction in salt, 20% reduction in saturated fat; and 50% reduction in free sugars. A 30% reduction in meat is required to achieve the fifth carbon budget and the 30x30 nature commitment – this represents the creation and maintenance of at least 410,000 hectares of woodland, maintaining and restoring 325,000 hectares of peatlands, and managing 200,000 hectares mainly for nature (for example, heathland and species-rich grassland, some of which would be managed through conservation grazing).

The recommendations in this strategy are designed to intervene in the system at multiple levels. We arrived at them after reviewing and assessing policy ideas from around the world, as well as the hundreds of proposals that were submitted to our public Call for Evidence. We narrowed these down to a few dozen, which we then analysed in detail, modelling their potential impact and cost, consulting our Advisory Panel along with other experts and stakeholders, and testing the most challenging ideas in focus groups and with citizens at the "deliberative dialogues" we held around the country.

This is not a wish list of ideas that we hope might help. These are concrete proposals for immediate action, which we have explored in depth and are confident will work. More detail and evidence on each recommendation can be found in Appendices 1 to 14.

Designed to be implemented over the next three years, they are essential first steps in a longer-term transition.

Recommendations

1. Escape the junk food cycle and protect the NHS

Recommendation 1
Introduce a Sugar and Salt Reformulation Tax. Use some of the revenue to help get fresh fruit and vegetables to low-income families.

Recommendation 2
Introduce mandatory reporting for large food companies.

Recommendation 3
Launch a new "Eat and Learn" initiative for schools.

2. Reduce diet-related inequality

Recommendation 4
Extend eligibility for free school meals.

Recommendation 5
Fund the Holiday Activities and Food programme for the next three years.

Recommendation 6
Expand the Healthy Start scheme.

Recommendation 7
Trial a "Community Eatwell" programme, supporting those on low incomes to improve their diets.

3. Make the best use of our land

Recommendation 8
Guarantee the budget for agricultural payments until at least 2029 to help farmers transition to more sustainable land use.

Recommendation 9
Create a Rural Land Use Framework based on the three compartment model.

Recommendation 10
Define minimum standards for trade and a mechanism for protecting them.

4. Create a long-term shift in our food culture

Recommendation 11
Invest £1 billion in innovation to create a better food system.

Recommendation 12
Create a National Food System Data programme.

Recommendation 13
Strengthen Government procurement rules to ensure that taxpayer money is spent on healthy and sustainable food.

Recommendation 14
Set clear targets and bring in legislation for long-term change.

1. Escape the Junk Food Cycle and protect the NHS

The way appetite malfunctions in the modern world has created a huge market for unhealthy foods.

We have a predilection for calorie dense foods, which means food companies invest more time and money creating these foods, which makes us eat more of them and expands the market, which leads to more investment, which makes us eat more. Company bosses do not dare to stop investing in these foods, in case they lose their competitive edge. Both consumers and food companies are stuck in a reinforcing feedback loop – a Junk Food Cycle.

The results are dire. Poor diet contributes to an estimated 64,000 deaths every year in England.[1] More than half of over-45s are living with diet-related health conditions.[2] This is putting an enormous strain on NHS resources.

One study has estimated that every unit of body mass index put on by every individual raises the UK's annual healthcare costs by £16.[3] As things stand, obesity is expected to continue increasing.[4] By 2035/36, Type 2 diabetes is projected to cost the NHS £15 billion a year, or one and a half times as much as cancer does today.[5] Halting this trajectory is the single biggest thing we can do to protect the future of our health service.

Education and willpower are not enough. We cannot escape this vicious circle without rebalancing the financial incentives within the food system.

Recommendation 1

Introduce a Sugar and Salt Reformulation Tax. Use some of the revenue to help get fresh fruit and vegetables to low-income families.

The Government should introduce a £3/kg tax on sugar and a £6/kg tax on salt sold for use in processed foods or in restaurants and catering businesses. This would create an incentive for manufacturers to reduce the levels of sugar and salt in their products, by reformulating their recipes or reducing their portion sizes.

The CEOs of major food companies have told us privately that they cannot make these changes without Government intervention. They need a level playing field if they are to start making their products healthier, otherwise the competition will simply move in and undercut them.

The public, too, supports this kind of intervention. One poll found that 63% of people in the UK would like the Sugary Drinks Levy to be expanded to include other sugary foods such as sweets and biscuits.[6]

Our modelling suggests this tax would lower the average sugar intake by 4–10g per person per day, and the salt intake by 0.2–0.6g per person per day. This would reduce the average calories eaten per person per day by 15-38 kcal.[7] According to the UK's expert group on calorie reduction, this could completely halt weight gain at a population level (which would require an average reduction of 24kcal per person per day).[8]

High salt intake raises blood pressure and increases the risk of stroke, heart disease, osteoporosis, stomach cancer and kidney disease.

An estimated 300,000 years of healthy life are lost to diet-related illness or disease in the UK every year, with all the worry, work and logistical strain that such a situation entails. Once the years lost to premature death are factored in, that rises to almost 1.5 million.[9] According to our modelling, the Sugar and Salt Tax would save 37,000–97,000 of those years.

On top of the enormous personal benefits of improving people's health, there are financial gains to be made. The Sugar and Salt Tax could raise £2.9–£3.9 billion per year for the Treasury (£2.3–£2.8 billion from sugar and £570–£630 million from salt).

We considered a wide range of fiscal and other mechanisms to break the Junk Food Cycle. The Sugar and Salt Reformulation Tax has the merit that it is technically feasible, it is simple for consumers and businesses to understand, and it enables industry to minimise the commercial impact and the impact on consumers wallets through reformulation.

It also has a clear and effective precedent in the form of the Soft Drinks Industry Levy (SDIL), which is estimated to have already resulted in 36,000 fewer cases of obesity in children and teenagers in England, and 6,200 fewer decayed and missing teeth.[10] (But because the SDIL only covers sugary drinks, it has not been enough to really change people's diets and the health consequences that follow from them. For example, it has reduced average sugar consumption by 1.8g per person per day, but adults still consume 20g too much sugar every day.[11])

This tax should be introduced in a 2024 Finance Bill, to enable Government and business to get implementation right. It should replace the current SDIL.

While this tax is intended to encourage reformulation,

it is possible that the price of some products – particularly those, such as value jam, that are almost entirely made from sugar – will rise. We do not want to place added financial pressures on those households that are already struggling to put food on the table. We especially want to avoid the possible unintended consequence that hard-pressed shoppers end up cutting back on healthy foods. As we discussed in Chapter 4, unhealthy food is significantly cheaper per calorie than healthy food – especially once you factor in the opportunity cost of having to cook from scratch.

We therefore propose a series of measures to get fresh food and ingredients to low-income households with children. Details of these measures are set out under Objective 2. They include expanding free school meals and extending the Holiday Activities and Food programme for the next three years (to support children during both term time and holidays); an expansion of the Healthy Start scheme (to support the diets of young children before they start school); and the trial of a "Community Eatwell" programme that enables GPs to prescribe fruit and vegetables to people suffering, or at risk of suffering, from diet-related illness or food insecurity.

Over three years, the average annual cost to Government of these four measures is £1.1 billion.

Recommendation 2

Introduce mandatory reporting for large food companies.

Substantial shifts in the nation's diet are required if we are to reduce the environmental and health impacts of our consumption.

Voluntary action alone will not be enough which is why we are calling for the world's first Sugar and Salt Reformulation Tax. However, we do detect a genuine desire for change within the food industry. The CEOs of several major food companies have told us that the pandemic shocked them into wanting to do things better.

Supermarkets and the hospitality sector are extremely adept at nudging consumers towards certain products and behaviours. They can do this by changing their layouts and menus, using discounts and promotions, reformulating their own products, changing their packaging and labelling, and using their enormous purchasing power selectively.

We do believe that food retailers and hospitality businesses want to be part of the solution. However, voluntary measures work best if they are monitored and subject to public scrutiny.

We therefore recommend that there should be a statutory duty for all food companies with more than 250 employees – including retailers, restaurant and quick service companies, contract caterers, wholesalers, manufacturers and online ordering platforms – to publish an annual report on the following set of metrics:

- Sales of food and drink high in fat, sugar or salt (HFSS) excluding alcohol
- Sales of protein by type (of meat, dairy, fish, plant, or alternative protein) and origin[†]
- Sales of vegetables[††]
- Sales of fruit
- Sales of major nutrients: fibre, saturated fat, sugar and salt
- Food waste
- Total food and drink sales.

Companies of this size already have a legal obligation to calculate calories on their foods, meaning the majority already produce the raw data required to calculate these figures.

Publishing these numbers will allow investors, Government, and others to track whether businesses are heading in the right direction. It will enable better scrutiny and maintain public pressure on companies to do the right thing.

Data reporting should be done via an online portal, and a summary of data by company made available to the public. The Food Standards Agency should develop the portal and ensure standardised reporting so that there is a common set of definitions and data standards in place. The data should form part of the Food Standards Agency's annual report to Parliament on the state of the food system (see Recommendation 14).

....

† For all protein this should include country of origin. For pork, poultry, dairy, eggs and fish, it should additionally include welfare or method of production accreditations (e.g. Red Tractor, RSPCA, Freedom Food, organic, pasture-fed, Better Chicken Commitment, MSC).

†† "Fruit and vegetables" includes frozen, tinned and composite meals as well as fresh.

Recommendation 3

Launch a new "Eat and Learn" initiative for schools.

Eating well is much easier if you know how to cook from scratch. But culinary skills and knowledge have declined across every social class since convenience food became widely available, and they are still declining, as one generation after another grows up without seeing or trying cookery at home.

Since the publication of the School Food Plan in 2014, schools have had a legal requirement to teach cookery and nutrition to all children up to the age of 14. The curriculum states that schools should attempt to "instil a love of cooking in pupils", while teaching them the kitchen skills necessary "to feed themselves and others affordably and well, now and in later life".[12] By 14, all pupils should be able to "understand the source, seasonality and characteristics of a broad range of ingredients" and "cook a repertoire of predominantly savoury dishes".

In too many schools, this is still not happening. "Food tech" remains a second-class subject – a fun but frivolous distraction from the real business of learning.

It is time to take food education seriously. The Eat and Learn initiative is a package of measures designed to achieve that. It includes five elements:

1. Curriculum changes.

a. **Sensory education for early years.** Children should start their food education as young as possible, while their minds and palates are still open to new experiences. Sensory food education should be added to the curriculum for nursery and reception classes. This teaching method – in which children are introduced to new foods and encouraged to explore them with all five senses – has been shown to increase children's willingness to try fruit and vegetables.

b. **Reinstate the food A level.** In 2016 the food A Level was axed alongside a number of other subjects. This means that pupils who are interested in food and nutrition – whether for vocational reasons or just for love of the subject – are cut off at the educational pass. It has also led to an inevitable slump in the number of cookery and nutrition teachers available to teach the subject in earlier years. This decision should be reversed, and the food A Level reinstated, with every school, primary and secondary, required to have a cookery subject lead.

c. **Review other qualifications.** The DfE should conduct a qualification review to ensure that existing and new qualifications such as T Levels in science and catering provide an adequate focus on food and nutrition, and a progression route for students after GCSEs. This is particularly important in light of the post-Brexit skills shortage in hospitality.

2. Accreditation.

The Government should require schools to work with accreditation schemes such as Food for Life to improve food and food education in schools. These schemes would also provide training and support for leaders and staff.

3. Inspection.

Cookery and nutrition lessons should be inspected with the same rigour as maths or English lessons. Whenever Ofsted inspectors visit a school, they conduct deep dives on four to six different subjects. (The only subject that is always inspected is reading in primary schools.) Ofsted should conduct deep dives on cookery and nutrition lessons as often as they do other subjects. Ofsted should also set up a team to create and publish a food and nutrition "research review", as they have started doing with other subjects. These reviews are a powerful influence on what is taught in schools and how it is taught.

4. Funding.

a. We recommend that the Government pays for the ingredients that children use in cooking lessons (as they do for schoolbooks). The current system leads to waste – it is hard for parents to buy ingredients in one-portion quantities – and to stigmatise children whose parents struggle to afford them.

b. We recommend that the Government doubles the current level of funding for the School Fruit and Vegetable Scheme (from £40.4 million to £80.8 million per year), but gives the money directly to schools rather than administering the scheme centrally. This will allow schools to procure higher quality produce from local suppliers.

5. Recruitment.

The Government should ensure there are sufficient training places, bursaries and recruitment strategies in place to address the current shortage of food teachers in secondary schools.[13]

The implementation of all of these things should be placed under a dedicated Eat and Learn team in DfE which works closely with the Office of Health Promotion.

One thing that schools who do food well have in common is that they adopt what is often called a "whole-school approach". This sounds like jargon, but is actually a very simple concept. It means integrating food into the life of the school: treating the dining hall as the hub of the school, where children and teachers eat together; lunch as part of the school day; the cooks as important staff members; and food as part of a rounded education.[14] The Eat and Learn initiative should actively champion this approach.

Over three years, the average annual cost to Government to deliver this recommendation is £206 million[†], of which £124 million is for food education ingredients.

[†] We have not included the cost of the first year (2022/23) in calculating this average because we assume that the implementation of this scheme will not be until autumn 2023.

2. Reduce diet-related inequality

Health inequality in England is stark – and getting worse. A man in one of the 10% most affluent postcodes will live, on average, 9.5 years longer than his peer living in one of the least affluent postcodes.[15] Women in the poorest areas of the UK are actually dying younger than they did in 2010.

Children living in the poorest areas are four times more likely than children from the richest areas to be severely obese when they arrive at primary school.[16] They are five times more likely to be severely obese when they leave it. Sixteen per cent of people in the lowest income group suffer from diabetes: this is more than twice the percentage of those in the highest income group.[17]

It is a peculiarity of the modern food system that obesity sometimes co-exists with hunger. Bad diets are, per calorie, much cheaper than healthy diets. The same households that cannot afford to eat healthily may sometimes find themselves struggling to put food on the table.

Data collected in 2019 by the Department of Work and Pensions found that, even before the pandemic, 4% of families experienced disrupted eating patterns or were forced to reduce their food consumption due to a lack of resources.[18] (This is known as "very low food security".) Among those on Universal Credit, this proportion rose to 26%.

The economic disruption caused by the pandemic has increased the number of households struggling to put food on the table. These people cannot wait around for the food system to be fixed: they need help now. The Government must give direct support to the poorest households to help them eat well. The first priority should be children.

Recommendation 4

Extend eligibility for free school meals.

In Key Stage 1 (Reception to Year 2), all children receive free school meals (FSM). After that, the eligibility threshold is set at an annual household income of less than £7,400 before benefits. In other words, you have to be extremely poor to qualify. This means there are some children from low-income households going hungry. Children with empty stomachs struggle at school: they find it hard to concentrate, their behaviour deteriorates, and they are more likely to be disruptive in class.[19]

In Part One of this strategy, published last July, we recommended that the Government extend free school meals to everyone on Universal Credit, up to the age of 16. We estimated this would cost £670 million. However, since the pandemic began, a further 230,000 households with children in the UK have registered for Universal Credit: an increase of 7%. This means that extending eligibility to everyone on Universal Credit would now cost £790 million, at a time when the public finances are already under extreme pressure.

We have therefore revisited the figures on food insecurity, to see if there is a way to target those in most urgent need of free school meals. We found that increasing the earnings threshold to £20,000 before benefits would ensure that 82% of children in households with "very low food security" (as defined by the Government) would be eligible for free school meals, as well as 70% of those facing "low food security".[20]

Even this modified ambition would be expensive. Over three years, the average annual cost to Government to deliver this recommendation is £544 million. This would extend free school meals to all the children in households currently earning less than £20,000, as well as those from households with No Recourse to Public Funds (NRPF), to whom the Government has extended free school meals during the pandemic. It would mean a total of 1.1 million additional children getting a freshly cooked, free lunch every day. As the economy recovers, and as earnings increase and fewer families become eligible, we expect this additional cost to fall.

Free school meals are extremely popular with the public. One recent poll found that 75% of UK adults agree with the statement "Parents are responsible for feeding their children, but Government must step in for children whose parents are unable to do so."[21] Over half (51%) of respondents went further still, saying that "school meals should be free for all students so that poor students are not stigmatised".

Recommendation 5

Fund the Holiday Activities and Food programme for the next three years.

In response to Part One of this strategy the Government made Holiday Activities and Food (HAF) clubs available to all children on free school meals for the duration of 2021. (They had previously been trialled in 17 local authorities.)

These programmes provide activities for children in the school holidays: four days a week for four weeks in summer, and a week over each of the Easter and Christmas holidays. Children on HAF programmes also receive at least one hot meal a day, which meets the School Food Standards. The majority of local authorities have also been offering the programmes to non-FSM children, for a small fee.

Holidays are a particularly hard time for households experiencing food insecurity. An estimated three million children are thought to be at risk of hunger during the school holidays, and data from food banks show a surge in demand for emergency supplies over the summer.[22]

As well as ensuring that children from the poorest households get at least one freshly cooked meal a day, HAF programmes provide social contact, exercise and enrichment activities. These are especially important in the wake of the pandemic, which has had such a detrimental effect on the emotional and social development of many children.

Currently, these programmes are funded to run until the end of 2021. We recommend that the Government extend them for at least the next three years, or until the next Spending Review. The programme should include children in households on qualifying benefits earning less than £20,000.

Over three years, the average annual cost to Government to deliver this recommendation is £449 million. This figure takes account of the uplift in the number of children that would be eligible for HAF if our recommendation were adopted on FSM eligibility. As the economy recovers, and as earnings increase and fewer families become eligible, we expect this additional cost to fall.

Recommendation 6

Expand the Healthy Start scheme.

Healthy Start is a means-tested scheme for low-income pregnant women and families with children under the age of four. It is also a universal entitlement for mothers under 18 years of age. The scheme provides coupons for vitamins and vouchers which can be used to buy fruit and vegetables, as well as milk.

As a response to our recommendations in Part One, the Government increased the value of the Healthy Start voucher from £3.10 per week to £4.25 per week (or double that for babies under 12 months). Several national supermarket chains also stepped forward to supplement the value of the vouchers. For example, Sainsbury's agreed to top up the vouchers by a further £2, Waitrose by £1.50, Lidl by £1.15 and Tesco, Iceland and Co-op by £1.

Studies on the effects of Healthy Start have shown that it plays an important role in helping pregnant women and their children access healthier foods. Women registered for the scheme report that it made them think more about their health and diet and led to better dietary choices.[23]

We propose that the Government use some of the proceeds from the Sugar and Salt Reformulation Tax to expand the financial eligibility for Healthy Start vouchers. The earnings threshold should be raised to £20,000 per year (before benefits).[†] This would bring it in line with our recommended eligibility for free school meals. The age limit should also be extended by a year, to cover children under the age of five. This would bridge the year-long gap in nutritional support that currently exists between the end of Healthy Start eligibility and the start of free school meal eligibility.

Over three years, the average annual cost to Government to deliver this recommendation is £82–£132 million.[††] This would bring the total cost of the scheme to £165–£285 million per year, depending on uptake.

Recommendation 7

Trial a "Community Eatwell" programme, supporting those on low incomes to improve their diets.

Before the pandemic, the Government spent £130 billion on the NHS every year. Of this, 95% was spent on treating illness, with just 5% going towards prevention.[24] Many medical professionals believe this is a topsy-turvy approach.[25] It would be more cost effective to increase spending on preventative measures so that fewer people get to the point where they need expensive medical treatments.

[†] Currently, due to the complexity of the benefits system, there are two thresholds. For example, if you receive the Child Tax Credit, your family's income must be less than £16,190 per year; if you are on Universal Credit, it has to be less than £5,000 per year.
[††] We have used the upper bound figure to calculate total aggregate costs elsewhere.

The Government has acknowledged this problem.[26] Its new "Green Social Prescribing" programme, currently being trialled in seven Primary Care Networks (PCNs) around England, is intended to improve patients' mental and physical health before they become acutely unwell. It enables GPs to prescribe therapeutic activities such as walking clubs, community gardening and food-growing projects.[27]

We recommend that the Government should trial a "Community Eatwell" programme, which would give GPs the option to prescribe fruit and vegetables – along with food-related education and social support – to patients suffering the effects of poor diet or food insecurity.

This recommendation is modelled on successful programmes from around the world. The Produce Prescription programme in Washington DC, for example, allows doctors to prescribe vouchers for fresh fruit and vegetables, along with cooking lessons, nutritional education and guided tours of shops and supermarkets to teach people how to shop cleverly. The scheme has been shown to increase consumption of fruit and vegetables and improve nutritional understanding. Of the 120 patients who received vouchers between 2012 and 2017, 50% lost weight over the course of a prescription.[28]

The Government should invite PCNs to bid for the chance to design their own pilot "Community Eatwell" programme, tailored to local needs and building on existing neighbourhood initiatives. Funds could also be used to invest in local infrastructure and facilities that make it easier to eat healthily and affordably, such as community kitchens, fruit and vegetable street markets, community farms and box schemes, and community cafes. If the evidence shows that these trials have significantly improved the diet and health of participants, while reducing the cost of medication, the "Community Eatwell" programme should be rolled out across all 1,250 PCNs in England.

Over three years, the average annual cost to Government to deliver this recommendation is £2 million.

3. Make the best use of our land

We already ask a lot from the land of this small and densely populated country. And in order to meet the UK's legal commitments on carbon emissions and nature restoration, we will have to ask a lot more.

Some farmland will have to be repurposed or adapted for environment projects. Some will have to be farmed at lower yields to enable nature to thrive. Some will have to become higher-yielding, low-carbon farms, using new technologies to increase productivity without polluting the Earth. This division of labour – sometimes known as the "three compartment model" of land use – is described in detail in Chapter 10.[29]

This is a major transition and will only be made possible by the knowledge, creativity and energy of farmers. Many farmers already opt to use methods for producing food that are better for the environment, while others are pioneering new approaches. But farms are not charitable enterprises. They are businesses, and some are already struggling with wafer-thin profit margins. Livestock farmers – some of whom manage land that is uniquely well-suited to both nature restoration and carbon sequestration – will need particular support.

Over the past 50 years, some farmers (particularly in the uplands) have seen their income and way of life eroded by forces beyond their control: declining lamb consumption, poorly designed subsidies, and underinvestment in communities and infrastructure. They have put in the hard graft – up at dawn and working into the night, 364 days a year – but have been left with some of the lowest incomes in the entire food system. Their farmland, too, has been degraded in the process. And now they fear a final blow. New trade deals could, unless very carefully finessed, put many of them out of business.

The Government is asking farmers to change the way they work for the public good. We must ensure they are properly recompensed. And we must protect them from unfair competition. The Government needs a trade policy that supports its environmental ambitions. Otherwise we will simply end up transferring damaging farming practices from one part of the planet to another and driving thousands of our own farmers to the wall in the process.

Recommendation 8

Guarantee the budget for agricultural payments until at least 2029 to help farmers transition to more sustainable land use.

Under the Common Agricultural Policy, most farmers in the UK received the bulk of their subsidies in the form of what are called basic payments. These were allocated according to the amount of land being farmed rather than the way it was farmed. Although the EU was (and still is) increasing the amount of money available for environmental projects, the balance of the payment system rewarded farms mainly according to their size.

Since our exit from the EU, the UK has been in an "Agricultural Transition Period". This means that the Government has been maintaining agricultural subsidies at the same levels as under the Common Agricultural Policy. However, it has begun the process of transforming the payment system to one of "public money for public goods". Under the new Environmental Land Management scheme (ELMs), farmers will no longer receive payments for commercial activities (producing crops) or simply for owning land, but for activities that contribute to the common good. These include nature restoration, managing woodland, flood prevention, soil improvement, animal welfare and carbon sequestration.

ELMs is being gradually introduced between now and 2027. But it is not yet clear exactly how the money will be distributed, which makes it hard for farmers to plan ahead. Moreover, the total budget is only guaranteed up to the end of this Parliament, in 2024.

We recommend that Defra should guarantee at least the current level of funding for agricultural payments until 2029 (the end of the next Parliament). At present, 40% of all farmers depend on basic payments to remain solvent. The transition to ELMs must be managed extremely carefully if the economy and culture of the countryside is to survive. The Government must ensure that ELMs payments are sufficiently generous to make it worthwhile for farmers to switch from conventional farming to more sustainable practices. Otherwise the temptation will be to farm even more intensively to make up for lost revenue – or to throw in the towel altogether.

We recommend that roughly a third of the ELMs budget – £500–£700 million per year – should go on paying farmers to manage the land in ways that actively sequester carbon and restore nature. Our calculations (see Appendix 8) suggest this would provide a fair return for the work involved in managing the land required for these projects: roughly 400,000 hectares of broadleaf woodland, 325,000 hectares of restored upland peat, and around 200,000 hectares of heath and species-rich grassland.

Accessing the schemes that support land use change will need to be as straightforward for farmers as it is to access the Government's Sustainable Farming Incentive. Otherwise uptake will be limited by bureaucracy, despite the interest of farmers. This is as true for owner-occupied farms as for tenants, but tenants face particular challenges: short tenancy agreements can prohibit them from making long-term changes such as planting trees.[30]

Defra should ensure that it is easy for tenant farmers to enter the schemes, as well as for farmers who own their land. Each scheme should be carefully proofed to ensure it does not inadvertently disadvantage tenants or commoners.

As well as rewarding such changes of land use, ELMs will pay farmers to improve the environmental conditions of working farms, by (among other things) enriching and protecting the soil,[†] increasing hedgerows and encouraging biodiversity.

Our models suggest the cost of adequately paying farmers for both on-farm nature improvements and changes to land use would be £2.2 billion per year. If we add to that Defra's 9–10% budget for measures to improve farm productivity, we get a total budget of £2.4–£2.5 billion. This means the Government will need, at the very least, to maintain its current budget commitment. This would not include money to improve people's enjoyment of the natural environment, which is a target in the 25 Year Environment Plan and a focus of public goods payments under the Agriculture Act 2020. That would have to be funded separately.

Recommendation 9

Create a Rural Land Use Framework based on the three compartment model.

The UK's net zero target is written into law, and its nature recovery commitments will soon follow. The only way to meet those targets is to change the way we use the land. This creates, de facto, a new land use strategy – but one that is unstructured, unstated and therefore unable to guide good local decision making. Crucially, it leaves farmers to second-guess the Government's priorities, further adding to the uncertainties they have to navigate.

We recommend that the Government should create a Rural Land Use Framework, setting out which areas of land would be best suited to the different functions of the "three compartment model" described in Chapter 10. This should inform the payments and regulations that are being designed to incentivise farmers across England to make the transition.

The Framework must be clear and explicit about what the Government is trying to achieve, which incentives, payments, and regulations it will use to achieve nature recovery, climate and food goals, and the metrics it will use to monitor progress.

At the heart of this strategy should be a National Rural Land Map (see Recommendation 12), which would supply detailed assessments of the uses to which any given area of land would be best suited.

The Rural Land Use Framework should be used to connect and inform the many existing incentive schemes and land-based strategies in Defra that inform the way land is used. There are currently at least eight different schemes – from the England Trees Action Plan to the ELM schemes – controlling funds ranging from £10 million to £2.4 billion per year.

Developing the Rural Land Use Framework should be one of the commitments in the upcoming green paper on how to protect 30% of UK land for nature by 2030.

Defra should seek input from the Ministry for Housing Communities and Local Government (MHCLG) and the Department for Business, Energy and Industrial Strategy (BEIS). Defra should publish its framework by March 2022 and then publish an annual progress report.

....

† The Government should conduct a review of small abattoirs to ensure that the capacity exists to serve the expected increase in numbers of farms using livestock in their rotations.

Recommendation 10

Define minimum standards for trade, and a mechanism for protecting them.

In its 2019 manifesto, the Conservative Party pledged that "in all of our trade negotiations, we will not compromise on our high environmental protection, animal welfare and food standards".[31]

In Part One of this strategy, published in July 2020, we proposed a mechanism that would enable the Government to achieve this without breaking the anti-protectionism rules of the WTO. When making new trade deals, the Government "should only agree to cut tariffs on products which meet our core standards".

A subsequent report from the Trade and Agriculture Commission made the same recommendation. It proposed that the UK should only lower import tariffs if the methods used to produce the imported food matched "a core set" of standards representing "the high standards of food production expected from UK producers".[32] These would include "climate change, environmental, ethical and animal welfare measures". If trading partners cannot "demonstrate equivalence with core standards, then they would not be considered for zero tariff, zero quota access".

So far, however, the Government has not specified which standards it wishes to protect, nor the mechanism with which it will protect them. (The trade deal with Australia has a chapter on animal welfare – a welcome first in international trade deals – but we do not yet know what it says.)

Without such a mechanism, there is serious peril in signing any trade deals with countries that have lower environmental and welfare standards than our own. A completely tariff-free trade deal on agriculture with, say, Brazil or the USA would seriously compromise our own attempts to protect animal welfare, restore nature and sequester carbon in this country. It would also allow cheap imported food to undercut – and potentially bankrupt – our own farming sector.

This is an issue on which public opinion is clear. Polls show that 93% want the UK's high food standards to be maintained in all post-EU Exit trade deals, and 81% are specifically worried about livestock farming standards being compromised in order to secure trade deals.[33]

The Government should, as a matter of urgency, draw up a list of core minimum standards which it will defend in any future trade deals. These should cover animal welfare, environment and health protection, carbon emissions, antimicrobial resistance and zoonotic disease risk.

It must then set out which mechanisms it intends to use to protect these standards.

4. Create a long-term shift in our food culture

We cannot make lasting changes to the food system without innovation in the widest sense. We need to change the way we use our land, reintroducing forgotten farming wisdom while simultaneously developing robots and AI to serve the farms of the future. We need businesses to innovate, creating new food products and reformulating old ones so that they do less damage. And we need to rethink how public policy works, finding more effective ways to improve our national eating habits.

Some of this is beyond the immediate remit of government. The state can never replace, or enforce, individual passion and entrepreneurialism. But it can invest to encourage creativity and help bring new products to the market. It can set targets and institutional goals, bring in legislation and collect and disseminate accurate data.

The importance of data cannot be overstated. Changing the outcomes of any complex system requires detailed, consistent and accurate data, arranged in such a way that it is easy to visualise and analyse. This is self-evident to those who spend their lives trying to influence complex systems, and yet it is rarely done.

In a 2018 article, the former UN Secretary General Kofi Annan described how detailed data maps developed by the University of Washington had transformed efforts to tackle malnutrition across Africa.[34] These interactive maps made it possible – easy – to find statistics on nutritional indicators such as childhood stunting, "almost down to the village level". Not only did "such fine-grained insight bring tremendous responsibility to act", but it also showed governments, NGOs and others precisely where to act, and which measures were likely to be most effective. "Without good data, we're flying blind," wrote Annan. "If you can't see it, you can't solve it."

During the COVID-19 pandemic our own Government discovered the true importance of accurate, well organised data. In order to get a better understanding of infection and hospitalisation rates across the country, and the various factors that may be creating regional disparities, the Government rapidly reorganised how it collects and visualises health data. One official told us this had massively improved the effectiveness of the pandemic response.

Changing the long-term culture of our food system will require a mixture of structural excellence and individual inspiration. We need the right ideas, the right evidence, the right laws and the right targets – all of which, together, will help change the food system on the ground.

Recommendation 11

Invest £1 billion in innovation to create a better food system.

It is fortuitous timing that the Government will soon launch its £22 billion innovation strategy, which aims to make the UK the world's most innovative nation by 2035. We recommend that one of the first official "missions" for the innovation strategy should be to create a better food system.

This mission should be backed by a new "challenge fund" worth £500 million over five years, with investment distributed by UK Research and Innovation (UKRI). Crucially, the money should be spent on projects that make the food system better in practice rather than simply on new ideas. At present, most of the Government money that goes into food-related innovation is directed towards scientists and academics. In many of the other areas where innovation happens – on farms, for example, or in start-up businesses or community projects – there has long been a funding drought.

The challenge fund money should be used to help shift the national diet to meet the targets set out at the beginning of this chapter. This might include accelerating work to reformulate processed foods, trying out new ways of helping customers change their habits, and boosting locally led initiatives to improve diet and health. But it should also be used to help develop new ways of growing food, such as vertical farming and precision fermentation.

Separately, Defra has already budgeted £280 million to support innovation as part of its Agricultural Transition Plan. The fund's welcome focus on "farmer-led" innovation recognises that the driving force behind regenerative agriculture has usually been the people on the ground, trying out new ideas. It is important that this funding should be used to support a wide range of methods, both high-tech and traditional, that can reduce carbon emissions and improve the natural environment. We specifically recommend targeting some investment towards methane reduction technologies, such as feed additives for sheep and cattle. But it is also important to get more support to the agroecological methods that have been starved of investment up to now.

Fruit and vegetable growing should be another priority for this innovation fund, and be applied across Defra's wider programme of investment to boost productivity. We need a less bureaucratic, more inclusive and better-funded successor to the previous EU Fruit and Vegetable Aid Scheme.

One of the most effective ways to reduce carbon emissions and free up land for nature is to cut back on animal proteins. Even though meat and dairy only account for one third of our calories, 85% of the land used to feed us is used for livestock farming. Plant-based proteins produce, on average, 70 times less greenhouse gas emissions than an equivalent amount of beef, and they use more than 150 times less land.[35]

The potential global market for alternative proteins is huge. The US is currently leading the world on the production front, with companies such as Impossible Foods, Memphis Meats and Perfect Day raising $700 million, $161 million and $300 million respectively in capital last year.[36] The Netherlands has developed one of the largest agribusiness regions in Europe – Food Valley – with universities, start-ups and multinationals working together to create new vegan foods.[37] Singapore and Israel have both proactively fostered alternative protein start-ups, and Singapore was the first country to give regulatory approval to a cultured meat product.[38]

The UK must do more to foster our own start-ups or they simply will migrate abroad.

The Government should put £50 million towards building shared facilities in a commercial "cluster" for entrepreneurs and scientists working on alternative proteins. Having a physical centre where many different players in the same field can set up base is known to encourage creativity and the cross-fertilisation of ideas. It should back this with annual grants for start-ups of £15 million for five years from the new Challenge Fund.

We estimate that developing and manufacturing alternative proteins in the UK, rather than importing them, would create around 10,000 new factory jobs and secure 6,500 jobs in farming (to produce protein crops and other inputs).[39]

Alongside innovation, we need evidence. Without good data, it is much harder to formulate good ideas, track their effectiveness or adjust them if they start to go off track. In writing this strategy, we found ourselves having to fight through thickets of jargon and dogma in order to get to the facts. We had to do a huge amount of data collection and analysis ourselves because so much of the evidence in circulation was not fit for purpose.

We recommend that, as well as the National Food System Data Programme (see Recommendation 12), the Government should establish two What Works Centres – modelled on the Education Endowment Foundation – to collect and analyse evidence on the effectiveness of food-related policies and business practices.

One of these centres should focus on diet, and the other on farming methods. The Evidence for Farming Initiative, already being piloted, could be expanded and formalised to take on the latter role. These centres should be endowed with £150 million and £50 million respectively, to guarantee funding over ten years.

Recommendation 12

Create a National Food System Data programme.

We recommend the Government creates a National Food System Data Programme, to collect and share data so that businesses and other organisations involved in the food system can track progress and plan ahead.

This programme should span and connect two main areas of evidence. The first is data about the land, as collected for the Rural Land Use Framework (Recommendation 9). The second is data from beyond the farm gate: on food production, distribution and retail, and the environmental and health impacts of that food. These two tasks should be connected through a single programme.

The Chief Scientific Advisers at Defra, DHSC, BEIS and the FSA should work together to establish a specialist team of civil servants – including IT experts and strategists – to develop and manage the National Food System Data Programme. Working with the Geospatial Commission and the Office for National Statistics, this team should start by setting baseline data definitions, standards and hierarchies, making it easier to collect consistent data across different areas and at different times, and to use it in multiple ways.

The team should then identify gaps in the existing data and broker agreements with third parties such as retailers or unions to fill in these gaps without breaching confidentiality.

The key data should be published using visualisation dashboards to make it easier for users to find and compare information, model future scenarios and assess the effectiveness of different policies or logistical models. These dashboards should include a National Rural Land Map (Recommendation 9).

The benefit to large businesses, which already collect extensive data, comes from making that data more reliable and comparable. The food sector's many small enterprises will benefit from having access to high-quality, free data, which they can use to shape their business models and project into the future.

Some data will be commercially sensitive, and businesses might be willing to share it with the Government, but not with industry competitors. There would therefore need to be a "layered" permissions model, to control access to different layers of information.

The food system is closely connected to many other systems, both national and international. Over time, data on transport, energy, environment, healthcare and so forth should be added to the programme. This would give the Government and the food industry an extremely powerful tool for devising, shaping and monitoring a better food system, to improve the nation's health, wellbeing and environment.

This will complement the Government's National Data Strategy, and contribute to the call from the Council for Science and Technology to improve analytical capability and flow of information across government.[40]

Over three years, the average annual cost to Government to deliver this recommendation is £3.5 million.

Recommendation 13

Strengthen Government procurement rules to ensure that taxpayer money is spent on healthy and sustainable food.

The Government spends £2.4 billion every year buying food for schools, hospitals, the Armed Forces, prisons and government offices.[41] This represents 5.5% of the total UK food service turnover.[42] Every year, a quarter of us will eat at least one meal provided by the state.[43] During term time children consume as much as 50% of their food at school, and for some, a free school lunch is their only substantial meal of the day.[44]

We recommend that the Government should redesign the Government Buying Standards for Food (GBSF) to ensure that taxpayer money is spent on food that is both healthy and sustainable. It should use the updated reference diet, discussed below in Recommendation 14, to set these standards. They should be made mandatory for all public sector organisations.

The Government should also introduce a mandatory accreditation scheme for all public institutions, working with existing certification bodies such as Food for Life, to help them reach baseline standards and encourage them to aim higher still.

At present, public food procurement is dominated by a small number of larger suppliers.[45] This quasi-monopoly means there is little incentive for innovation and improvement. To address this problem, the Government is already developing a trial scheme in South West England, in which local food suppliers can sell their produce via an online procurement page. Trials of this purchasing system suggest that it works extremely well, with users reporting more choice, better quality and no increase in costs.[46] The Government should accelerate the roll-out of this dynamic procurement scheme and use its new procurement standards to encourage caterers to try a broader range of suppliers.

In its annual report to Parliament (see Recommendation 14), the Food Standards Agency should include an assessment of how procurement budgets are being spent and the extent to which they are meeting the new standards.

Over three years, the average annual cost to Government to deliver this recommendation is £1 million.

Recommendation 14

Set clear targets and bring in legislation for long-term change.

The problems we have described in the food system have come about over decades, and solving them will be a long-term effort. To stay the course we need clear, long-term targets, ongoing political attention, and a joined-up approach not only within Government, but across the food industry and communities.

A strong framework of legal targets is essential to improve the food system. The Government has already set itself a statutory target for carbon emissions. The forthcoming Environment Act will do the same for the 30x30 pledge. We also recommend that it should include a legally binding target to halt biodiversity loss in England by 2030. And we recommend creating a statutory target to improve diet-related health through a Good Food Bill (see below).

To maintain political focus, we recommend that the role of the Food Standards Agency (FSA) should be expanded to cover healthy and sustainable food as well as food safety. Asking the FSA to take on these additional duties would be less confusing and expensive than establishing a whole new body to monitor progress. The FSA is governed independently and is well-placed to take a whole-system perspective. It is already established and has experience relevant to all the tasks that are required, although it would need additional resources to take on this responsibility.

Specific new duties would include:

- Reporting annually to Parliament on our national progress towards a healthier and more sustainable food system – using the goals defined in this plan and the metrics collected through the National Food System Data Programme (Recommendation 12) as a starting point. The report should also propose potential strategies the Government could adopt to accelerate progress, in the same way that the Climate Change Committee (CCC) gives advice on combating climate change. The FSA should explicitly seek input from the Climate Change Committee, and the newly established Offices for Environmental Protection and Health Promotion, in drawing up this report.
- Collecting and analysing the nutritional and environmental impacts of foods sold by food companies, as set out in Recommendation 2.
- Developing an updated "reference diet" for the nation, in line with our health and sustainability goals, working closely with the OHP and Defra. This would create a single reference point to underpin policies and advice.
- Working with Defra and the IGD to develop a harmonised and consistent food labelling system to describe the environmental impacts of food products.

All Local authorities should be required to put in place a food strategy, developed with reference to the goals and metrics set out above, and in partnership with the communities they serve. (Over 50 places are already doing this, with impressive results).[47]

The 2020 Agriculture Act requires Government to review the nation's food security at least once every three years. The Government should do this annually, with broad consultation, bringing in organisations responsible for nutrition, cybersecurity, infrastructure, climate change and the environment. Several of these measures – and others in this action plan – require primary legislation. We therefore recommend that Defra should put a Good Food Bill before Parliament in the fourth session of the 2019–2024 Parliament. A full list of the measures requiring primary legislation is shown in Table 16.2 below.

Over three years, the average annual cost to Government to deliver this recommendation is £5 million.

Figure 16.2

Legislative framework for creating a healthier, more sustainable food system

Bill	Provision	For	Duties (except where stated)
Good Food Bill	Health targets	Government	Define long-term health targets and put into secondary legislation
	Action plans and independent reports	Government	Prepare and publish a Good Food Action Plan every five years, which sets out interim food system targets and measures to meet them
		Government	Consult the FSA while developing its Good Food Action Plans
		FSA	Provide a regular independent progress report to Parliament on the Government's progress against the Good Food Action Plan
		FSA	Consult with the OEP, the CCC and the OHP in drawing up its advice and reports
		OEP, CCC and OHP	Advise the FSA on emerging issues within the remit of each body that are relevant to the scope of the FSA
	Other duties	FSA, working closely with the OHP and Defra	Establish and periodically update a healthy and sustainable Reference Diet, to be used by all public bodies in food-related policy making and procurement
		Government	Establish and periodically update a healthy and sustainable Reference Diet, to be used by all public bodies in food-related policy making and procurement
		Local authorities in England	Develop local food strategies, with reference to national targets and in partnership with the communities they serve
		Large food businesses	Expand obligation to promote consumer interest to include our collective interest in tackling climate change, nature recovery and health
Finance Bill	Levy	Government	Powers to apply a tax to sugar and salt

Over three years, the **average annual cost** to Government to deliver these recommendations is **£1.4 billion**.

In addition, there is a one-off cost, of **£250 million**, described under the innovation recommendation (Recommendation 11).

This is **new expenditure**. It does not include the costs of recommendations where funding has already been secured (ELMs funding, Recommendation 8, and Defra's £280 million fund to support innovation, part of Recommendation 11).

We estimate that the Sugar and Salt Reformulation Tax would raise **£2.9–£3.4 billion per year** for the Treasury. We propose using some of this money to fund a series of measures to support the diets of those in deprived communities.

These measures will have a long term economic benefit of up to **£126 billion**.

Chapter references

Introduction

[1] Department for Education. (2021). *Holiday activities and food programme 2021*. Available at: https://www.gov.uk/government/publications/holiday-activities-and-food-programme/holiday-activities-and-food-programme-2021

[2] NHS. (2021). *Applying for Healthy Start*. Available at: https://www.healthystart.nhs.uk/frequently-asked-questions/applying-for-healthy-start-faqs/

[3] Sainsbury's: Sainsbury's. (2021). *Sainsbury's tops up Healthy Start vouchers to help feed over half a million families*. 9 Feb 2021. Available at: https://www.about.sainsburys.co.uk/news/latest-news/2021/09-02-2021-sainsburys-tops-up-healthy-start-vouchers; Waitrose: John Lewis Partnership. (2021). *Waitrose to top up Healthy Start Vouchers for new families*. 3 February 2021. Available at: https://www.johnlewispartnership.co.uk/media/press/y2021/waitrose-to-top-up-healthy-start-vouchers.html; Tesco: Tesco PLC. (2020). *Tesco to offer free fruit and veg to 500,000 Healthy Start families*. 30 October 2020. Available at: https://www.tescoplc.com/news/2020/tesco-to-offer-free-fruit-and-veg-to-500-000-healthy-start-families/; Co-op: Co-operative Group Ltd. (2020). *Co-op's Christmas boost for families: retailer to top up Healthy Start vouchers by £1*. 21 December 2020. Available at: https://www.co-operative.coop/media/news-releases/co-ops-christmas-boost-for-families-retailer-to-top-up-healthy-start

[4] Tanzer, J. et al. (2015). *Living Blue Planet Report. Species, habitats and human well-being*. WWF. Available at: http://assets.wwf.org.uk/downloads/living_blue_planet_report_2015.pdf

[5] Thurstan, R. H. et al. (2010). *The effects of 118 years of industrial fishing on UK bottom trawl fisheries*. Nature Communications 1, 15. Available from: https://www.nature.com/articles/ncomms1013

[6] Harrabin, R. (2021). *Bottom trawling ban for key UK fishing sites*. BBC News. Available from: https://www.bbc.co.uk/news/science-environment-55894608

[7] See National Food Strategy. (2021). Evidence pack, page 66, available from: https://www.nationalfoodstrategy.org

[8] Foreign & Commonwealth Office. (2019). *Britannia Protects the Waves: £7 million extra funding to protect UK marine life*. HMG. Available at: https://www.gov.uk/government/news/britannia-protects-the-waves-7m-extra-funding-to-protect-uk-marine-life

[9] South Africa MPA: Kerwath, S. E. et al. (2013). *Marine protected area improves yield without disadvantaging fishers*. Nature Communications 4, 2347. Available from: https://doi.org/10.1038/ncomms3347; Scotland MPA: Stewart, B. D. et al. (2020). *Marine Conservation Begins at Home: How a Local Community and Protection of a Small Bay Sent Waves of Change Around the UK and Beyond*. Frontiers in Marine Science. Available from: https://www.frontiersin.org/articles/10.3389/fmars.2020.00076/full; Global effect of MPAs: Cabral, R. B. et al. (2020). *A global network of marine protected areas for food*. Proceedings of the National Academy of Sciences 117 (45) 28134–28139. Available from: https://www.pnas.org/content/117/45/28134

[10] The National Federation of Fishermen's Organisations' (2021). *Prepare for Displacement*. NFFO. Available at: https://www.nffo.org.uk/prepare-for-displacement/

[11] The National Federation of Fishermen's Organisations' (2021). *40 Marine Protected Areas in 3 Years*. NFFO. Available at: https://www.nffo.org.uk/40-marine-protected-areas-in-3-years/

[12] Turner, P. et al. (2020). *Food anaphylaxis in the United Kingdom: analysis of national data, 1998–2018*. British Medical Journal. Available at: https://doi.org/10.1136/bmj.n251

[13] Food Standards Agency. (2017). *Food Standards Agency Board meeting – 15 March 2017*. FSA. Available at: https://www.food.gov.uk/sites/default/files/media/document/fsa170306.pdf

[14] Department for Business, Energy & Industrial Strategy. (2021). *UK enshrines new target in law to slash emissions by 78% by 2035*. HMG. Available at: https://www.gov.uk/government/news/uk-enshrines-new-target-in-law-to-slash-emissions-by-78-by-2035

[15] Biodiversity loss: Benton, T. G. et al. (2021). *Food system impacts on biodiversity loss*. Chatham House. Available at: https://www.chathamhouse.org/sites/default/files/2021-02/2021-02-03-food-system-biodiversity-loss-benton-et-al_0.pdf; Rainforest destruction: Hosonuma, N. et al. (2012). *An assessment of deforestation and forest degradation drivers in developing countries*. Environmental Research Letters, Volume 7, Number 4. Available at: https://iopscience.iop.org/article/10.1088/1748-9326/7/4/044009/pdf; GHG Emissions: Our World in Data. (2020). *Sector by sector: where do global greenhouse gas emissions come from?* Available at: https://ourworldindata.org/ghg-emissions-by-sector

Executive summary

[1] Bahadue, K. C. et al. (2018). When too much isn't enough: Does current food production meet global nutritional needs? PLoS ONE 13(10). Available at: https://doi.org/10.1371/journal.pone.0205683

[2] Agriculture produces 10% of UK emissions: Climate Change Committee. (2020). Sixth carbon budget. Available at: https://www.theccc.org.uk/wp-content/uploads/2020/12/The-Sixth-Carbon-Budget-The-UKs-path-to-Net-Zero.pdf; Less than 1% of GDP: Farming income from: Defra. (2021). Total Income from Farming in the United Kingdom, first estimate for 2020. HMG. Available at: https://assets.publishing.service.gov.uk/government/uploads/system/uploads/attachment_data/file/989701/agricaccounts-tiffstatsnotice-27may21.pdf; GDP from: Office for National Statistics. (2021). Gross Domestic Product: chained volume measures: Seasonally adjusted £m. HMG. Available at: https://www.ons.gov.uk/economy/grossdomesticproductgdp/timeseries/abmi/ukea

[3] ~80 per cent of manufactured foods are unhealthy: Access to Nutrition Initiative. (2019). U.K. Product Profile 2019. Access to Nutrition Initiative. Available at: https://accesstonutrition.org/app/uploads/2020/02/UK-Product-Profile_Full_Report_2019.pdf and Euromonitor International. (2018). Consumers in 2019. Available at: https://www.euromonitor.com/consumers-in-2019/report

[4] Food Foundation. (2020). The Broken Plate 2020. Food Foundation. Available at: https://foodfoundation.org.uk/wp-content/uploads/2020/09/FF-Broken-Plate-2020-DIGITAL-FULL.pdf

[5] UK is the third fattest country in the G7: World Health Organization. (2016). Global Health Observatory data repository: Prevalence of obesity among adults, BMI ≥ 30, age-standardized – Estimates by county. Available at: https://apps.who.int/gho/data/node.main.A900A?lang=en; 28% of adults are obese: NHS Digital. (2020). Health Survey for England, 2019: Adult and Child Overweight and Obesity. NHS Digital. Available at: https://digital.nhs.uk/data-and-information/publications/statistical/health-survey-for-england/2019/health-survey-for-england-2019-data-tables

[6] 2019 data: Global Burden of Disease, accessed March 2021: Global Health Data Exchange. (2021). GBD Results Tool. Institute for Health Metrics and Evaluation. Available at: http://ghdx.healthdata.org/gbd-results-tool

[7] NFS analysis. See National Food Strategy Evidence Pack pages 42 and 56 for details. Available from https://www.nationalfoodstrategy.org

[8] Across the full range of scenarios considered under the 6th carbon budget. See Committee on Climate Change. (2020). Land use: Policies for a Net Zero UK. Committee on Climate Change. Sixth carbon budget. Available at: https://www.theccc.org.uk/publication/sixth-carbon-budget/

1. Why it matters

[1] https://twitter.com/waiterich/status/1382001123595276290

[2] Broughton, J. and Weitzel, E. (2018). *Population reconstructions for humans and megafauna suggest mixed causes for North American Pleistocene extinctions.* Nat Commun 9, 5441. Available at: https://doi.org/10.1038/s41467-018-07897-1

[3] Ruiter, H, et al. (2017). *Total global agricultural land footprint associated with UK food supply 1986–2011.* ScienceDirect. Available at: https://doi.org/10.1016/j.gloenvcha.2017.01.007

[4] National Food Strategy analysis based on: Bar-On, Y. M. et al. (2018). *The biomass distribution on Earth.* Proceedings of the National Academy of Sciences, 115(25), 6506–6511.

[5] National Food Strategy analysis based on: Bar-On, Y. M. et al. (2018). *The biomass distribution on Earth.* Proceedings of the National Academy of Sciences, 115(25), 6506–6511.

[6] Ritchie, H. and Roser, M. (2019). *Land Use.* Our World In Data. Available at: https://ourworldindata.org/land-use

[7] Ritchie, H. (2021). *Wild mammals have declined by 85% since the rise of humans, but there is a possible future where they flourish.* Our World in Data. Available at: https://ourworldindata.org/wild-mammal-decline

[8] IUCN. (2021). *The IUCN Red List of Threatened Species. Version 2021-1.* IUCN. Available at: https://www.iucnredlist.org

[9] Wilson, E. O. (1992). *The Diversity of Life.* London, UK. Penguin Press Science.

[10] FAO. (2020). *The State of World Fisheries and Aquaculture 2020.* Sustainability in action. Available at: www.fao.org/3/ca9229en/ca9229en.pdf

[11] Barnett, A. (2015). *The Nature of Crops: Why do we eat so few of the edible plants?* New Scientist. Available at: https://institutions.newscientist.com/article/mg22730301-400-the-nature-of-crops-why-do-we-eat-so-few-of-the-edible-plants/

[12] World Wildlife Fund. (2021). *Freshwater Systems.* World Wildlife Fund. Available at: https://www.worldwildlife.org/industries/freshwater-systems

[13] FAO. (2017). *Water for sustainable food and agriculture.* FAO. Available at: http://www.fao.org/3/i7959e/i7959e.pdf

[14] Global map: Mekonnen, M. & Hoekstra, A. (2016). *Four billion people facing severe water scarcity.* Science Advances, 2(2). Available at: https://advances.sciencemag.org/content/2/2/e1500323.full; UK inset map: World Resources Institute. (2021). *Aqueduct tools.* WRI. Available at: https://www.wri.org/aqueduct accessed June 2021.

[15] European Environment Agency. (2018). *European waters Assessment of status and pressures 2018.* Available at: https://www.eea.europa.eu/publications/state-of-water

[16] 1% of global emissions come from ammonia production: Gilbert, P. and Thornley, P. (2010). *Energy and carbon balance of ammonia production from biomass gasification.* In host publication. Available at: https://www.research.manchester.ac.uk/portal/files/33615474/FULL_TEXT.PDF; 12% of total ag emissions (2.9% of total emissions) from synthetic ammonia use: Smith P., M. et al. (2014). *Agriculture, Forestry and Other Land Use (AFOLU).* Climate Change 2014: Mitigation of Climate Change. Contribution of Working Group III to the Fifth Assessment Report of the Intergovernmental Panel on Climate Change. Available at: https://www.ipcc.ch/site/assets/uploads/2018/02/ipcc_wg3_ar5_chapter11.pdf; In total then synthetic fertiliser is about 4% of global GHGs and 12% of total ag emissions (2.9% of total emissions) from synthetic ammonia use.

[17] Food system: Crippa, M. et al. (2021). *Food systems are responsible for a third of global anthropogenic GHG emissions.* Nat Food 2, 198–209. Available at: https://doi.org/10.1038/s43016-021-00225-9; Aviation: Lee, D. and Forster, P. (2020). *Guest post: Calculating the true climate impact of aviation emissions.* Carbon Brief. Available at: https://www.carbonbrief.org/guest-post-calculating-the-true-climate-impact-of-aviation-emissions

[18] UK emissions: Garnett, T. et al. (2016). *Food systems and greenhouse gas emissions.* Food Climate Research Network. Available at: https://www.tabledebates.org/chapter/food-systems-and-greenhouse-gas-emissions

[19] National Food Strategy analysis based on: Garnett, T. (2008). *Cooking up a storm.* In: Food, greenhouse gas emissions and our changing climate. Food Climate Research Network, Centre for Environmental Strategy; BEIS. (2019). *Final UK greenhouse gas emissions national statistics.* Data Tables; WRAP. (2020). *Courtauld Commitment* 2025, 2020 Annual Report.

[20] Kellehear, A. (2007). *A Social History of Dying.* UK: Cambridge University Press.

[21] Change in the price of fresh chicken: Office for National Statistics. (2021). *Consumer price inflation time series.* Available from: https://www.ons.gov.uk/economy/inflationandpriceindices/datasets/consumerpriceindices. Change in chicken consumption: UN Food and Agriculture Organisation. (2020). *Meat food supply quantity – food available for human consumption.* Available from: http://www.fao.org/faostat/en/#data/FBS

[22] Global trends: Boeckel, T. et al. (2019). *Global trends in antimicrobial resistance in animals in low- and middle-income countries.* Science. Available at: DOI: 10.1126/science.aaw1944;

[23] Review on Antimicrobial Resistance. (2016). *Tackling Drug-Resistant Infections Globally Final Report and Recommendation.* Review on Antimicrobial Resistance. Available at: https://amr-review.org/sites/default/files/160518_Final%20paper_with%20cover.pdf

[24] For a broad assessment of zoonotic disease risk, see: Jones, B. A. et al. (2013). *Zoonosis emergence linked to agricultural intensification and environmental change.* Proceedings of the National Academy of Sciences of the United States of America. Available at: https://doi.org/10.1073/pnas.1208059110 For low genetic diversity enabling rapid viral spread in factory farms: United Nations Environment Programme. (2020). *Coronaviruses: are they here to stay?* United Nations Environment Programme. Available at: https://www.unep.org/news-and-stories/story/coronaviruses-are-they-here-stay; For cross-species pandemic-capable infection: A., Khatri, M. et al. (2012). *Identification of swine H1N2/pandemic H1N1 reassortant influenza virus in pigs, United States.* Veterinary Microbiology. Available at: https://doi.org/10.1016/j.vetmic.2012.02.014; For related poultry data: Rozins, C. and Day, T. (2016). *The industrialization of farming may be driving virulence evolution.* Evolutionary applications, 10(2), 189–198. Available at: https://doi.org/10.1111/eva.12442. For agricultural intensification's effect on pandemic risk: Willyard, C. (2019). *Flu on the farm.* Nature. Available at: https://www.nature.com/articles/d41586-019-02757-4.

[25] Johnson, C.. et al. (2020). *Global shifts in mammalian population trends reveal key predictors of virus spillover risk.* the Royal Society. Available at: https://doi.org/10.1098/rspb.2019.2736

[26] Boeckel, T. et al. (2015). *Global trends in antimicrobial use in food animals.* Proceedings of the National Academy of Sciences. Available at: https://doi.org/10.1073/pnas.1503141112.

[27] Loh, E. H. et al. (2015). *Targeting Transmission Pathways for Emerging Zoonotic Disease Surveillance and Control.* Vector Borne Zoonotic Dis. 2015 Jul;15(7):432–7. Available at: https://pubmed.ncbi.nlm.nih.gov/26186515/

[28] NHS Digital. (2020). *Health Survey for England, 2019: Adult and Child Overweight and Obesity.* NHS Digital. Available at: https://digital.nhs.uk/data-and-information/publications/statistical/health-survey-for-england/2019/health-survey-for-england-2019-data-tables

[29] Changulani et al. (2008). *The relationship between obesity and the age at which hip and knee replacement is undertaken.* The Journal of Bone and Joint Surgery. British volume, 90-B(3), pp.360–363. Available at: https://pubmed.ncbi.nlm.nih.gov/18310761/

[30] Global Burden of Disease: Global Health Data Exchange. (2021). *GBD Results Tool.* Institute for Health Metrics and Evaluation. Available at: http://ghdx.healthdata.org/gbd-results-tool

[31] Public Health England. (2020). *Excess weight and COVID-19: insights from new evidence.* HMG. Available at: https://www.gov.uk/government/publications/excess-weight-and-covid-19-insights-from-new-evidence

[32] Williamson, E. et al. (2020). *Factors associated with COVID-19-related death using OpenSAFELY.* Nature 584, 430–436 Available at: https://www.nature.com/articles/s41586-020-2521-4

[33] National Food Strategy analysis using data from: NHS Digital. (2020). Health Survey for England 2019: Adult's health. Available at: https://digital.nhs.uk/data-and-information/publications/statistical/health-survey-for-england/2019; NHS Digital. (2018). Health Survey for England 2017: Cardiovascular diseases. Available at: https://digital.nhs.uk/data-and-information/publications/statistical/health-survey-for-england/2017. Disease overlaps assumed to be the same across all age groups. Population data from: ONS. (2020). Population estimates for the UK, England and Wales, Scotland and Northern Ireland: mid-2019. ONS. Available at: https://www.ons.gov.uk/peoplepopulationandcommunity/populationandmigration/populationestimates/bulletins/annualmidyearpopulationestimates/latest

[34] Barron, E. et al. (2020). *Type 1 and Type 2 Diabetes and COVID-19 Related Mortality in England: A Whole Population Study.* SSRN Electronic Journal. Available at: https://www.england.nhs.uk/wp-content/uploads/2020/05/valabhji-COVID-19-and-Diabetes-Paper-1.pdf

[35] 2019 data: accessed March 2021: Global Burden of Disease: Global Health Data Exchange. (2021). GBD Results Tool. Institute for Health Metrics and Evaluation. Available at: http://ghdx.healthdata.org/gbd-results-tool

[36] NFS analysis of Family Food Surveys: Department for Environment, Food and Rural Affairs. (2020). *Family Food Surveys.* HMG. Available at: https://www.gov.uk/government/collections/family-food-statistics

[37] Griffith, R. et al. (2021). The decline of home cooked food. The IFS. Available at: https://ifs.org.uk/publications/15482

[38] Organisation for Economic Co-operation and Development. (2019). *The Heavy Burden of Obesity: The Economics of Prevention.* OECD Publishing. Available at: https://www.oecd.org/health/the-heavy-burden-of-obesity-67450d67-en.htm; The OECD model predicts that high BMI will cost the Government 8% of the total spend on healthcare on average per year between 2020–2050. They use an average annual figure over 30 years because results for a single year can be quite noisy due to a number of factors but have confirmed that the percentage can be used as the current figure.

[39] NHS Digital. (2021). *Statistics on Obesity, Physical Activity and Diet, England 2021.* NHS Digital. Available at: https://digital.nhs.uk/data-and-information/publications/statistical/statistics-on-obesity-physical-activity-and-diet/england-2021.

[40] Hofmarcher, T. et al. (2020). *The cost of cancer in Europe 2018.* European Journal of Cancer. Available at: https://doi.org/10.1016/j.ejca.2020.01.011. Hex, N. et al. (2012). *Estimating the current and future costs of Type 1 and Type 2 diabetes in the UK, including direct health costs and indirect societal and productivity costs.* Diabetic Medicine, 29(7), pp.855–862. Available at: https://pubmed.ncbi.nlm.nih.gov/22537247/

[41] 3.4% of GDP: Organisation for Economic Co-operation and Development. (2019). *The Heavy Burden of Obesity: The Economics of Prevention.* OECD Publishing. Available at: https://www.oecd.org/health/the-heavy-burden-of-obesity-67450d67-en.htm; The OECD model predicts that high BMI will reduce UK GDP by 3.4% each year between 2020 and 2030. UK GDP was £2.17 trillion in 2019. Source: *Gross Domestic Product in the United Kingdom from 1948 to 2020.* Statista. 3.4% of 2019 GDP is £73.78 billion: As above 3.4% of GDP is an average per year between 2020–2050.

[42] Organisation for Economic Co-operation and Development. (2019). *The Heavy Burden of Obesity The Economics of Prevention,* United Kingdom country note. OECD Publishing. Available at: https://www.oecd.org/unitedkingdom/Heavy-burden-of-obesity-Media-country-note-UK.pdf

[43] Department for Environment, Food and Rural Affairs. (2020). *Family Food Surveys.* HMG. Available at: https://www.gov.uk/government/collections/family-food-statistics

[44] 2019 data: accessed July 2021: Global Burden of Disease: Global Health Data Exchange. (2021). *GBD Results Tool.* Institute for Health Metrics and Evaluation. Available at: http://ghdx.healthdata.org/gbd-results-tool

[45] Organisation for Economic Co-operation and Development. (2019). *The Heavy Burden of Obesity: The Economics of Prevention,* OECD Health Policy Studies, OECD Publishing. Available at: https://doi.org/10.1787/67450d67-en

[46] NFS estimate: 58% of people in the lowest Index of Multiple Deprivation quintile have CVD, diabetes or obesity. National Food Strategy analysis using data from: NHS Digital. (2020). Health Survey for England 2019: Adult's health. Available at: https://digital.nhs.uk/data-and-information/publications/statistical/ health-survey-for-england/2019; NHS Digital. (2018). Health Survey for England 2017: Cardiovascular diseases. Available at: https://digital.nhs.uk/data-and-information/publications/statistical/health-survey-for-england/2017; NHS Digital. (2020). Healthy Survey for England 2019: overweight and obesity in adults and children. Available at: https://digital.nhs.uk/data-and-information/publications/statistical/health-survey-for-england/2019/health-survey-for-england-2019-data-tables. Population data from: ONS. (2017). Deaths and Populations by Index of Multiple Deprivation (IMD) decile, England and Wales, 2001 to 2015. ONS. Available at:https://www.ons.gov.uk/peoplepopulationandcommunity/birthsdeathsandmarriages/deaths/adhocs/006518deathsandpopulationsbyindexofmultipledeprivationimddecileenglandandwales2001to2015. Overlap between diabetes and obesity, diabetes and CVD and obesity and CVD from Health Survey for England. Assumptions: Very high waist circumference (>102cm for men, >88cm for women) assumed to be obese for purposes of CVD and obese overlap. The overlap between diseases is assumed to be the same across IMDs. Not including diet-related cancers as overlap data not available.

[47] O'Halloran et al. (2020). Obesity, BMI and Cause-Specific Hospital Admissions and Costs: The UK Biobank Cohort Study. Obesity. Available at: https://onlinelibrary.wiley.com/doi/full/10.1002/oby.22812

[48] O'Halloran et al. (2020). Obesity. BMI and Cause-Specific Hospital Admissions and Costs: The UK Biobank Cohort Study. Obesity. Available at: https://onlinelibrary.wiley.com/doi/full/10.1002/oby.22812

[49] Historic trend: NHS Digital. Health Survey for England. Available at: https://digital.nhs.uk/data-and-information/publications/statistical/health-survey-for-england; Projection: Janssen, F., Bardoutsos, A., & Vidra, N. (2020). Obesity Prevalence in the Long-Term Future in 18 European Countries and in the USA. Obesity Facts, 13(5), 514-527. Available at: https://doi.org/10.1159/000511023

[50] Stoye, G. and Zaranko, B. (2019). UK Health Spending, Institute for Fiscal Studies. Available at: https://ifs.org.uk/uploads/R165-UK-health-spending1.pdf

2. Systems thinking

[1] Government Office for Science. (2007). *Tackling Obesities: Future Choices – Obesity System Atlas*. Department of Innovation Universities and Skills. Available at: https://assets.publishing.service.gov.uk/government/uploads/system/uploads/attachment_data/file/295153/07–1177-obesity-system-atlas.pdf

[2] Parsons, K. (2020). *Who Makes Food Policy in England? A Map of Government Actors and Activities*. Rethinking Food Governance 1. Food Research Collaboration. Available at: https://foodresearch.org.uk/publications/who-makes-food-policy-in-england-map-government-actors/

[3] Parsons, K. (2020). *Who Makes Food Policy in England? A Map of Government Actors and Activities*. Rethinking Food Governance 1. Food Research Collaboration. Available at: https://foodresearch.org.uk/publications/who-makes-food-policy-in-england-map-government-actors/

[4] Forrester, J. (1989). *The Beginning of System Dynamics*. Cambridge, USA: Massachusetts Institute of Technology. Available at: http://web.mit.edu/sysdyn/sd-intro/D-4165-1.pdf

[5] Shahinnia, F. et al. (2016). *Genetic association of stomatal traits and yield in wheat grown in low rainfall environments*. BMC Plant Biology, 16(1). Available at: https://core.ac.uk/download/pdf/81835099.pdf

[6] Wheat: Shiferaw, B. et al. (2013). *Crops that feed the world 10. Past successes and future challenges to the role played by wheat in global food security*. Food Security, 5(3), pp.291–317. Available at: https://link.springer.com/article/10.1007/s12571-013-0263-y#:~:text=Wheat%20is%20fundamental%20to%20human,dietary%20calories%20and%20proteins%20worldwide

[7] Forrester, J. (1989). *The Beginning of System Dynamics*. Cambridge, USA: Massachusetts Institute of Technology. Available at: http://web.mit.edu/sysdyn/sd-intro/D-4165-1.pdf

[8] Meadows, D. H. (2015). *Thinking in Systems*. White River Junction, VT: Chelsea Green Publishing.

[9] Hardin, G. (1968). *The Tragedy of the Commons*. Science, 162(3859), pp.1243–1248. Available at: https://science.sciencemag.org/content/162/3859/1243

[10] Quoted in The New Yorker. (2010). *The Scales Fall*. Available at: https://www.newyorker.com/magazine/2010/08/02/the-scales-fall

[11] Rose, G. and Sherrylynn, R., (2015). *Northern cod comeback*. Canadian Journal of Fisheries and Aquatic Sciences. 72(12): 1789–1798. Available at: https://cdnsciencepub.com/doi/10.1139/cjfas-2015-0346

[12] School Food Plan: Dimbleby, H. and Vincent, J. (2013). *The School Food Plan*. HMG. Available at: http://www.schoolfoodplan.com/

3. How did we get here?

1 Population data for 1800 (based on extrapolations form Madison): University of Groningen. (2018). *Maddison Project Database 2018*. Available at: https://www.rug.nl/ggdc/historicaldevelopment/maddison/releases/maddison-project-database-2018 ; Population data for 1950: UN.org. (2015). *Population 2030 Demographic challenges and opportunities for sustainable development planning*. Available at: https://www.un.org/en/development/desa/population/publications/pdf/trends/Population2030.pdf

2 UN.org. (2017). *World population projected to reach 9.8 billion in 2050, and 11.2 billion in 2100*. Available at: https://www.un.org/development/desa/en/news/population/world-population-prospects-2017.html

3 Department for Food and Rural Affairs. (2008) *Ensuring the UK's Food Security in a changing World: a Defra Discussion Paper*. HMG. Available at: http://data.parliament.uk/DepositedPapers/Files/DEP2008–2037/DEP2008–2037.pdf

4 Dimbleby, J. (2016). The Battle of the Atlantic: How the Allies Won the War. London UK: Penguin Books Ltd

5 Winston, C. (1948). "Chapter 30, Ocean Peril" in *The Second World War, Volume 2*. Bloomsbury: London. Available at: https://www.churchillarchive.com/explore/page?id=CHUR%204%2F176#image=5

6 Food Chain Analysis Group, Department for Environment Food and Rural Affairs. (2006). *Food Security and the UK: An Evidence and Analysis Paper*. National Archives. Available at: https://www.ipcc.ch/apps/njlite/ar5wg2/njlite_download2.php?id=8916

7 BAIN Analysis for the National Food Strategy (2019). Based on Population data for 1800–1950: University of Groningen. (2018). *Maddison Project Database 2018*. Available at: https://www.rug.nl/ggdc/historicaldevelopment/maddison/releases/maddison-project-database-2018; Population data for 1950: UN.org. (2015). *Population 2030 Demographic challenges and opportunities for sustainable development planning*. Available at: https://www.un.org/en/development/desa/population/publications/pdf/trends/Population2030.pdf; Global agricultural production data for 1960–2010: FAO. (2020). *Net Agricultural Production Index*. Available at: http://www.fao.org/faostat/en/; Global agricultural data 2010 onward: FAO. (2018). *The Future of food and agriculture: Alternative Pathways to 2050*. Available at: http://www.fao.org/global-perspectives-studies/resources/detail/en/c/1157074/

9 Quoted in Mann, C. (2018). *Wizard and the Prophet: Two Remarkable Scientists and their Battle to Shape Tomorrow's World*. London: Pac Macmillan, p.130.

10 Rajaram, S. and Hettel, G. (1995). *Wheat breeding at CIMMYT*. Mexico, D. F.: CIMMYT, p.iv-v.

11 Roser, M. et al. (2013). *Life Expectancy*. Our World in Data. Available at: https://ourworldindata.org/life-expectancy

12 Population: UN.org. (2015). *Population 2030 Demographic challenges and opportunities for sustainable development planning*. Available at: https://www.un.org/en/development/desa/population/publications/pdf/trends/Population2030.pdf; Mass starvation: Hasell, J. and Roser, M. (2020). *Famines*. Our World in Data. Available at: https://ourworldindata.org/famines

13 Ritche, H. and Roser, M. (2013). *Land Use*. Our World in Data. Available at: https://ourworldindata.org/land-use

14 Richtie, H. and Roser, M. (2021). *Crop Yields*. Our World in Data. Available at: https://ourworldindata.org/crop-yields

15 Nestle. (2019). *KitKat Chocolatory brings premium breaks to the UK*. Nestle. Available at: https://www.nestle.co.uk/en-gb/media/pressreleases/allpressreleases/kitkat-chocolatory-brings-premium-breaks-uk

16 Action on Salt. (2019). *A Summary: Access to Nutrition Initiative: U.K. Product Profile 2019*. Available at: http://www.actiononsalt.org.uk/news/news/2019/news-stories/-a-summary-access-to-nutrition-initiative-uk-product-profile-2019.html

17 Department for Food and Rural Affairs et al. (2018). *Agriculture in the United Kingdom 2018*. HMG. Available at: https://assets.publishing.service.gov.uk/government/uploads/system/uploads/attachment_data/file/848641/AUK_2018_09jul19a.pdf

18 Wildflower Meadows: Hayhow, D. B. et al. (2019). *The State of Nature 2019*. The State of Nature partnership. Available at: https://nbn.org.uk/wp-content/uploads/2019/09/State-of-Nature-2019-UK-full-report.pdf; Ancient Woodland (decline since 1900): Woodland Trust. (2000). *Why the UK's Ancient Woodland Is Still Under Threat*. pp 3–5. Available at: http://www.wbrc.org.uk/atp/Ancient%20Woodland%20Threats%20-%20Woodland%20Trust.pdf; Heathland (extrapolated from data on Dorset): Fagúndez, J. and Bot, A. (2013). *Heathlands confronting global change: drivers of biodiversity loss from past to future scenarios*. Feb; 111(2): 151–172. Available at: https://www.ncbi.nlm.nih.gov/pmc/articles/PMC3555525/; Lowland Ponds: Hayhow, D. B. et al. (2019). *The State of Nature 2019*. The State of Nature partnership. Available at: https://nbn.org.uk/wp-content/uploads/2019/09/State-of-Nature-2019-UK-full-report.pdf

19 Hayhow, D. B. et al. (2019). *The State of Nature 2019*. The State of Nature partnership. Available at: https://nbn.org.uk/wp-content/uploads/2019/09/State-of-Nature-2019-UK-full-report.pdf

20 Eurostat. (2021). *Common farmland bird index*. European Union. Available at: http://appsso.eurostat.ec.europa.eu/nui/show.do?dataset=env_bio2&lang=en

21 BAIN analysis for National Food Strategy. Based on: Department for Food and Rural Affairs. (2018). Agriculture in the UK. HMG. Available at: https://www.gov.uk/government/statistics/agriculture-in-the-united-kingdom-2018; Ritchie, H. and Roser, M. (2019). *Crop Yields*. Our World in Data. Available at: https://ourworldindata.org/crop-yields

22 Garnett, T. et al. (2016). *Food systems and greenhouse gas emissions*. Food Climate Research Network. Available at: https://www.tabledebates.org/chapter/food-systems-and-greenhouse-gas-emissions

23 UK emissions: Garnett, T. et al. (2016). *Food systems and greenhouse gas emissions*. Food Climate Research Network. Available at: https://www.tabledebates.org/chapter/food-systems-and-greenhouse-gas-emissions; Imports: WWF. (2010). *Emissions from UK Food Industry far Higher than Believed*. WWF. Available at: https://assets.wwf.org.uk/downloads/how_low_report_1.pdf

24 Garnett, T. (2008). *Cooking up a storm*. In: Food, greenhouse gas emissions and our changing climate. Food Climate Research Network. Available at: http://www.unscn.org/layout/modules/resources/files/Cooking_up_a_Storm.pdf

4. Escaping the Junk Food Cycle

[1] Cole, H. (2021). *Online junk food ad ban to be axed as it would have almost no effect on obesity.* The Sun. 25/3/2021. Available at: https://www.thesun.co.uk/news/14470325/online-junk-food-ad-ban-axed-cutting-700-calories/

[2] Public Health England. (2015). *Attitudes to obesity: Findings from the 2015 British Social Attitudes survey.* Public Health England. Available at: https://www.bsa.natcen.ac.uk/media/39132/attitudes-to-obesity.pdf

[3] Woywodt, A. and Kiss, A. (2002). *Geophagia: the history of earth-eating.* Journal of the Royal Society of Medicine, 95(3), pp.143–146. Available at: https://www.ncbi.nlm.nih.gov/pmc/articles/PMC1279487/

[4] Brunner, E. J. et al. (2021). *Appetite disinhibition rather than hunger explains genetic effects on adult BMI trajectory.* Int J Obes 45, 758–765. Available at: https://doi.org/10.1038/s41366-020-00735-9

[5] Bain analysis for the NFS. 1955 mean BMI interpolated from US historic BMI trends and UK BMI from 1977 onwards. Distribution before 1980 is directional using normal distributions around mean value and, therefore, is not an exact representation. Source: NHS Digital. (2018). *Health Survey for England 2017* [NS]. NHS Digital. Available at: https://digital.nhs. uk/data-and-information/publications/statistical/health-surveyfor-england/2017; Euromonitor. (2019); NHS Digital. (2019). *National Child Measurement Programme;* Gov.UK. (2018); Population Pyramid. (2019); Davey, R. (2003) *The obesity epidemic: too much food for thought?;* The trend of BMI values of US adults by centiles, birth cohorts 1882–1986, National Bureau of Economic Research, 2010.

[6] National Food Strategy analysis of: NHS Digital. (2018). *Health Survey for England 2017* [NS]. NHS Digital. Available at: https://digital.nhs.uk/data-and-information/publications/statistical/health-survey-for-england/2017; Euromonitor. (2019); NHS Digital. (2018). *The National Child Measurement Programme.* Available at: https://digital.nhs.uk/services/national-child-measurement-programme/; and National Bureau of Economic Research. (2010).

[7] National Food Strategy analysis of: NHS Digital. (2018). *Health Survey for England 2017* [NS]. NHS Digital. Available at: https://digital.nhs.uk/data-and-information/publications/statistical/health-survey-for-england/2017; Euromonitor. (2019); NHS Digital. (2018). *The National Child Measurement Programme.* Available at: https://digital.nhs.uk/services/national-child-measurement-programme/; and National Bureau of Economic Research. (2010).

[8] National Food Strategy analysis of: NHS Digital. (2018). *Health Survey for England 2017* [NS]. NHS Digital. Available at: https://digital.nhs.uk/data-and-information/publications/statistical/health-survey-for-england/2017; Euromonitor. (2019); NHS Digital. (2018). *The National Child Measurement Programme.* Available at: https://digital.nhs.uk/services/national-child-measurement-programme/; and National Bureau of Economic Research. (2010).

[9] Timper, K. and Brüning, J. C. (2017). *Hypothalamic circuits regulating appetite and energy homeostasis: pathways to obesity.* Disease Models & Mechanisms, 10(6), pp.679–689. Available at: https://www.ncbi.nlm.nih.gov/pmc/articles/PMC5483000/

[10] Blood Sugar: NHS Inform. (2021). *Hypoglycaemia (low blood sugar) symptoms and treatment.* NHS inform. Available at: https://www.nhsinform.scot/illnesses-and-conditions/blood-and-lymph/hypoglycaemia-low-blood-sugar; Fat: Allison, M. B. and Myers, M. G. (2014). *20 YEARS OF LEPTIN: Connecting leptin signaling to biological function.* Journal of Endocrinology, 223(1), pp.T25–T35. Available at: https://joe.bioscientifica.com/view/journals/joe/223/1/T25.xml; Gut and Stomach: Suzuki, K. et al. (2011). *The Gut Hormones in Appetite Regulation.* Journal of Obesity, 2011, pp.1–10. Available at: https://www.ncbi.nlm.nih.gov/pmc/articles/PMC3178198/

[11] Volkow, N. D. et al. (2011). *Reward, dopamine and the control of food intake: implications for obesity.* Trends in Cognitive Sciences, 15(1), pp.37–46. Available at: https://www.ncbi.nlm.nih.gov/pmc/articles/PMC3124340/

[12] Prior, G. et al. (2011). *Exploring food attitudes and behaviours in the UK: Findings from the Food and You Survey 2010.* FSA. Available at: https://www.food.gov.uk/sites/default/files/media/document/food-and-you-2010-main-report.pdf

[13] Lisle, D. J. and Goldhamer, A. (2006). *The pleasure trap: mastering the hidden force that undermines health & happiness.* Summertown, Tennessee: Healthy Living Publications.

[14] Hall, K. D. et al. (2019). *Ultra-Processed Diets Cause Excess Calorie Intake and Weight Gain: An Inpatient Randomized Controlled Trial of Ad Libitum Food Intake.* Cell Metabolism. Available at: https://www.sciencedirect.com/science/article/pii/S1550413119302487

[15] de Graaf, C. and Kok, F. J. (2010). *Slow food, fast food and the control of food intake.* Nature Reviews Endocrinology, 6(5), pp.290–293. Available at: https://www.nature.com/articles/nrendo.2010.41; Fardet, A. (2016). *Minimally processed foods are more satiating and less hyperglycemic than ultra-processed foods: a preliminary study with 98 ready-to-eat foods.* Food & Function, 7(5), pp.2338–2346. Available at: https://pubs.rsc.org/en/content/articlelanding/2016/FO/C6FO00107F#!divAbstract

[16] Gupta, S. et al. (2019). *Characterizing Ultra-Processed Foods by Energy Density, Nutrient Density, and Cost.* Frontiers in Nutrition, 6. Available at: https://www.ncbi.nlm.nih.gov/pmc/articles/PMC6558394/

[17] Cassidy, R. M. and Tong, Q. (2017). *Hunger and Satiety Gauge Reward Sensitivity.* Frontiers in Endocrinology, 8. Available at: https://www.ncbi.nlm.nih.gov/pmc/articles/PMC5435754/; Reichelt, A. C. et al. (2015). *Integration of reward signalling and appetite regulating peptide systems in the control of food-cue responses.* British Journal of Pharmacology, 172(22), pp.5225–5230. Available at: https://www.ncbi.nlm.nih.gov/pmc/articles/PMC5341214/

[18] Wise, R. A. (2006). *Role of brain dopamine in food reward and reinforcement.* Philosophical Transactions of the Royal Society B: Biological Sciences, 361(1471), pp.1149–1158. Available at: https://www.ncbi.nlm.nih.gov/pmc/articles/PMC1642703/

[19] Yau, Y. H. C. and Potenza, M. N. (2013). *Stress and eating behaviors.* Minerva endocrinologica, 38(3), pp.255–67. Available at: https://www.ncbi.nlm.nih.gov/pmc/articles/PMC4214609/

[20] Griffith, R. (2021). *How does the price of different food products vary with the healthiness of that product?* University of Manchester and the Institute for Fiscal Studies. Available at: https://ebbb60b1-6870-4254-bdfd-a62c9c625e15.filesusr.com/ugd/9e5bac_baedcfe760e54ecf9ed564258518dfdd.pdf

[21] Gómez, M. I. et al. (2013). *Post-green revolution food systems and the triple burden of malnutrition.* Food Policy, 42, pp.129–138. Available at: http://www.fao.org/fileadmin/templates/esa/Papers_and_documents/WP_13–02_Gomez_et_al.pdf

[22] Smithson, M. et al. (2015). *An analysis of the role of price promotions on the household purchases of food and drinks high in sugar. Public Health England.* Available at: https://assets.publishing.service.gov.uk/government/uploads/system/uploads/attachment_data/file/470175/Annexe_4._Analysis_of_price_promotions.pdf

[23] National Food Strategy analysis of Nielsen Ad Intel data, 2019.

[24] Kantar Worldpanel Division. (2016). *Expandability Study based on FMCG panel*. Kantar Worldpanel.

[25] Access to Nutrition Initiative. (2019). *UK Product Profile 2019*. Access to Nutrition Initiative. Available at: https://accesstonutrition.org/app/uploads/2020/02/UK-Product-Profile_Full_Report_2019.pdf

[26] Fruit and Vegetables: Department for Environment Food and Rural Affairs. (2020). *Horticulture Statistics 2019*. HMG. Available at: https://assets.publishing.service.gov.uk/government/uploads/system/uploads/attachment_data/file/901689/hort-report-17jul20.pdf; Confectionary: Office for National Statistics. (2020). *UK manufacturers' sales by product*. ONS. Available at: https://www.ons.gov.uk/businessindustryandtrade/manufacturingandproductionindustry/datasets/ukmanufacturerssalesbyproductprodcom.

[27] Just Eat. (2021). *Most popular Just Eat dishes across the UK*. Just Eat. Available at: https://www.just-eat.co.uk/explore/top-popular-dishes; Kantar: Link Q Wave 4 – continue to buy delivery more or same % share of consumers/trips is vs total consumers 52 w/e Oct 20.

[28] BBC. (2021). *What Are We Feeding Our Kids?* BBC. Available at: https://www.bbc.co.uk/programmes/m000wgcd

[29] Lindsay, C. (2003). *A century of labour market change: 1900 to 2000*. Labour Market Trends. 111. Available at: https://www.researchgate.net/publication/228480967_A_century_of_labour_market_change_1900_to_2000

[30] Lindsay, C. (2003). *A century of labour market change: 1900 to 2000*. Labour Market Trends. 111. Available at: https://www.researchgate.net/publication/228480967_A_century_of_labour_market_change_1900_to_2000

[31] Griffith, R. et al. (2016). *Gluttony and sloth? Calories, labor market activity and the rise of obesity*. Journal of the European Economic Association, 14(6), pp.1253–1286. Available at: https://onlinelibrary.wiley.com/doi/pdf/10.1111/jeea.12183

[32] Townsend, N. et al. (2012). *Physical activity statistics 2012*. British Heart Foundation. Available at: https://www.bhf.org.uk/~/media/files/research/heart-statistics/m130-bhf_physical-activity-supplement_2012.pdf

[33] Pontzer, H. et al. (2012). *Hunter-gatherer energetics and human obesity*. PLoS One. Available at: 10.1371/journal.pone.0040503

[34] Urlacher, S. S. et al. (2021). *Childhood Daily Energy Expenditure Does Not Decrease with Market Integration and Is Not Related to Adiposity in Amazonia*. J Nutr. 2021 Mar 11;151(3):695–704. Available at: 10.1093/jn/nxaa361

[35] Ebersole, K. E. et al. (2008). *Energy expenditure and adiposity in Nigerian and African-American women*. Obesity (Silver Spring). 2008 Sep;16(9):2148–54. Available at: 10.1038/oby.2008.330

[36] Dugas, R. et al. (2011). *Energy expenditure in adults living in developing compared with industrialized countries: a meta-analysis of doubly labeled water studies*. Am J Clin Nutr. 2011 Feb;93(2):427–41. Available at: 10.3945/ajcn.110.007278

[37] Pontzer, H. (2018). *Energy Constraint as a Novel Mechanism Linking Exercise and Health*. Physiology (Bethesda). Available at: https://doi.org/10.1152/physiol.00027.2018

[38] Melanson, E. L. et al. (2013). *Resistance to Exercise-Induced Weight Loss*. Medicine & Science in Sports & Exercise, 45(8), pp.1600–1609. Available at: https://www.ncbi.nlm.nih.gov/pmc/articles/PMC3696411/

[39] Stensel, D. J. et al. (2016). *Role of physical activity in regulating appetite and body fat*. Nutrition Bulletin, 41(4), pp.314–322. Available at: https://onlinelibrary.wiley.com/doi/full/10.1111/nbu.12234

[40] Poon, L. (2019). *The Rise and Fall on New Year's Fitness Resolutions, in 5 charts*. Bloomberg. Available at: https://www.bloomberg.com/news/articles/2019-–01-–16/here-s-how-quickly-people-ditch-weight-loss-resolutions

[41] Obesity Prevention Source. (2016). *Physical Activity: Exercise Can Help Control Weight*. Harvard School for Public Health. Available at: https://www.hsph.harvard.edu/obesity-prevention-source/obesity-causes/physical-activity-and-obesity/

[42] Pavlou, K. N., et al. (1989). *Exercise as an adjunct to weight loss and maintenance in moderately obese subjects*. The American Journal of Clinical Nutrition, 49(5), pp.1115–1123. Available at: https://academic.oup.com/ajcn/article-abstract/49/5/1115/4651822?redirectedFrom=-fulltext

[43] Pontzer, H. (2021). *Burn: the misunderstood science of metabolism*. London: Allen Lane. p255; Pavlou, K. N. et al. (1989). *Exercise as an adjunct to weight loss and maintenance in moderately obese subjects*. The American Journal of Clinical Nutrition, 49(5), pp.1115–1123. Available at: https://academic.oup.com/ajcn/article-abstract/49/5/1115/4651822?redirectedFrom=fulltext

[44] Monteiro, C. et al. (2018). *The UN Decade of Nutrition, the NOVA food classification and the trouble with ultra-processing*. Public Health Nutrition, Available at: https://www.cambridge.org/core/journals/public-health-nutrition/article/un-decade-of-nutrition-the-nova-food-classification-and-the-trouble-with-ultraprocessing/2A9776922A28F8F757BDA32C3266AC2A

[45] Monteiro, C. et al. (2018). *Household availability of ultra-processed foods and obesity in nineteen European countries*. Public Health Nutrition. Available at: https://doi.org/10.1017/S1368980017001379

[46] Ministry of Health of Brazil. (2015). *Dietary Guidelines for the Brazilian Population*. Ministry of Health of Brazil. Available at: https://bvsms.saude.gov.br/bvs/publicacoes/dietary_guidelines_brazilian_population.pdf

[47] Government of Canada (2018). *Canada's Food Guide*. Canada.ca. Available at: https://food-guide.canada.ca/en/; Food and Agriculture Organization of the United Nations. (2021). *Food-based dietary guidelines – Ecuador*. Available at: http://www.fao.org/nutrition/education/food-dietary-guidelines/regions/countries/ecuador/en/, Food and Agriculture Organization of the United Nations. (2021). *Food-based dietary guidelines – Uruguay*. Available at: http://www.fao.org/nutrition/education/food-dietary-guidelines/regions/countries/uruguay/en/; Food and Agriculture Organization of the United Nations. (2021). *Food-based dietary guidelines – Peru*. Available at: http://www.fao.org/nutrition/education/food-dietary-guidelines/regions/countries/peru/en/; Pan American Health Organization. (2016). *Pan American Health Organization Nutrient Profile Model*. Available at: https://iris.paho.org/bitstream/handle/10665.2/18621/9789275118733_eng.pdf

[48] Cancer: Fiolet, T. et al. (2018). *Consumption of ultra-processed foods and cancer risk: results from NutriNet-Santé prospective cohort*. BMJ. Available at: https://doi.org/10.1136/bmj.k322; Depressive: Adjibade, M. et al. (2019). *Prospective association between ultra-processed food consumption and incident depressive symptoms in the French NutriNet-Santé cohort*. BMC Med. Available at: https://doi.org/10.1186/s12916-019-1312-y; Cardiovascular disease: Srour, B. et al. (2019). *Ultra-processed food intake and risk of cardiovascular disease: prospective cohort study (NutriNet-Santé)*. BMJ. Available at: https://doi.org/10.1136/bmj.l1451

[49] Hall, K. D. et al. (2019). *Ultra-Processed Diets Cause Excess Calorie Intake and Weight Gain: An Inpatient Randomized Controlled Trial of Ad Libitum Food Intake.* Cell metabolism. Available at: https://doi.org/10.1016/j.cmet.2019.05.008

[50] Barabási, A. L. et al. (2019). *The unmapped chemical complexity of our diet.* Nat Food 1, 33–37. Available at: https://doi.org/10.1038/s43016-019-0005-1

[51] Garnett, E. E. et al. (2019). *Impact of increasing vegetarian availability on meal selection and sales in cafeterias.* Proceedings of the National Academy of Sciences. Available at: https://www.pnas.org/content/pnas/early/2019/09/24/1907207116.full.pdf

[52] Foster, R. and Lunn, J. (2007). *Food Availability and Our Changing Diet.* British Nutrition Foundation. Available at: https://www.nutrition.org.uk/attachments/201_Food%20availability%20and%20our%20changing%20diet%20summary.pdf

[53] Department for Environment, Food and Rural Affairs. 2020. *Family Food Statistics.* HMG. Available at: https://www.gov.uk/government/collections/family-food-statistics

[54] Griffith, R. et al. (2021). *The decline of home cooked food. Institute for Fiscal Studies.* Available at: https://ifs.org.uk/uploads/WP202114-The-decline-of-home-cooked-food.pdf

[55] Department for Environment, Food and Rural Affairs. 2020. *Family Food Statistics.* HMG. Available at: https://www.gov.uk/government/collections/family-food-statistics

[56] NFS Analysis of Office for National Statistics. (2018). *Annual Business Survey.* ONS. Available at: https://www.ons.gov.uk/businessindustryandtrade/business/businessservices/methodologies/annualbusinesssurveyabs

[57] Lock, S. (2021). *Just Eat group revenue worldwide 2011–2018.* Statista. Available at: https://www.statista.com/statistics/579165/just-eat-group-revenue/#:~:text=This%20statistic%20presents%20the%20total,to%20779.5%20million%20in%202018

[58] Mytton, O. T. et al (2020). *The potential health impact of restricting less-healthy food and beverage advertising on UK television between 05.30 and 21.00 hours: A modelling study.* PLOS Medicine, 17(10), p.e1003212. Available at: https://journals.plos.org/plosmedicine/article?id=10.1371/journal.pmed.1003212#sec007

[59] World Health Organization. (2021). *Prevalence of obesity among adults, BMI >= 30 (age-standardized estimate) (%).* WHO. Available at: https://www.who.int/data/gho/data/indicators/indicator-details/GHO/prevalence-of-obesity-among-adults-bmi-=-30-(age-standardized-estimate)-(-); Kim, S. et al. (2016). *Korean diet: Characteristics and historical background.* Journal of Ethnic Foods, Volume 3, Issue 1. Pages 26–31, ISSN 2352-6181. Available at: https://doi.org/10.1016/j.jef.2016.03.002; Tsugane, S. (2021). *Why has Japan become the world's most long-lived country: insights from a food and nutrition perspective.* Eur J Clin Nutr 75, 921–928. Available at: https://doi.org/10.1038/s41430-020-0677-5

[60] Walton, S. and Hawkes, C. (2020). *What We Can Learn: A Review of Food Policy Innovations in Six Countries.* Available at: https://www.nationalfoodstrategy.org/wp-content/uploads/2020/07/What-we-can-learn.pdf

[61] International Food Policy Research Institute (IFPRI). (2015). *Global Nutrition Report 2015: Actions and accountability to advance nutrition and sustainable development.* IFPRI. Available at: https://www.ifpri.org/publication/global-nutrition-report-2015; Kagawa, Y. (1978). *Impact of westernization on the nutrition of Japanese: Changes in physique, cancer, longevity and centenarians.* Preventive Medicine, 7(2), pp.205–217. Available at: https://www.sciencedirect.com/science/article/abs/pii/0091743578902463; NHS. (2020). *Part 3: Adult overweight and obesity.* NHS Digital. Available at: https://digital.nhs.uk/data-and-information/publications/statistical/statistics-on-obesity-physical-activity-and-diet/england-2020/part-3-adult-obesity-copy

[62] Packed Lunches: Evans, C. E. L., et al. (2020). *A repeated cross-sectional survey assessing changes in diet and nutrient quality of English primary school children's packed lunches between 2006 and 2016.* BMJ Open, 10(1), p.e029688. Available at: https://bmjopen.bmj.com/content/10/1/e029688; KFC Games Console: Cooler Master. (2020). *Introducing the KFConsole.* Cooler Master. Available at: https://landing.coolermaster.com/kfconsole/

[63] Adams, J. et al. (2016). *Why Are Some Population Interventions for Diet and Obesity More Equitable and Effective Than Others?* The Role of Individual Agency. PLOS Medicine, 13(4) .Available at: https://journals.plos.org/plosmedicine/article?id=10.1371/journal.pmed.1001990

[64] Scarborough, P. et al. (2020). *Impact of the announcement and implementation of the UK Soft Drinks Industry Levy on sugar content, price, product size and number of available soft drinks in the UK, 2015–19: A controlled interrupted time series analysis.* PLOS Medicine, 17(2), p.e1003025. Available at: https://journals.plos.org/plosmedicine/article?id=10.1371/journal.pmed.1003025

[65] Soft Drinks: Scarborough, P. et al. (2020). *Impact of the announcement and implementation of the UK Soft Drinks Industry Levy on sugar content, price, product size and number of available soft drinks in the UK, 2015–19: A controlled interrupted time series analysis.* PLOS Medicine, 17(2). Available at: https://journals.plos.org/plosmedicine/article?id=10.1371/journal.pmed.1003025; Hungary: Martos, E., et al. (2015). *Assessment of the impact of a public health product tax: Final report.* World Health Organization. Available at: https://www.euro.who.int/__data/assets/pdf_file/0008/332882/assessment-impact-PH-tax-report.pdf?ua=1; Mexico: Taillie, L. S. et al. (2017). *Do high vs. low purchasers respond differently to a nonessential energy-dense food tax? Two-year evaluation of Mexico's 8% nonessential food tax.* Preventive medicine 105S, S37–S42. Available at: https://www.ncbi.nlm.nih.gov/pubmed/28729195

[66] Mexico: Hernández-F, M. et al. (2021). *Taxes to Unhealthy Food and Beverages and Oral Health in Mexico: An Observational Study.* Caries Research, 55(3), pp.183–192. Available at: https://www.karger.com/Article/Abstract/515223; Soft Drinks Industry Levy: Cobiac, L. et al. (2021). *Impact of the Soft Drink Industry Levy on health and health inequalities of children and adolescents in England.* [Pre Publication]

[67] Multiple policies needed to tackle obesity: Cecchini, M. and Sassi, F. (2012). *Tackling obesity requires efficient government policies.* Israel Journal of Health Policy Research, 1(1). Available at: https://www.ncbi.nlm.nih.gov/pmc/articles/PMC3424968/; Decline in smoking: Cancer Research UK. (2015). *Tobacco statistics.* Available at: https://www.cancerresearchuk.org/health-professional/cancer-statistics/risk/tobacco#heading-Three

5. Inequality

[1] Scheidel, W. (2018). *The Great Leveler.* Princeton, USA: Princeton University Press.

[2] National Food Strategy analysis of NDNS: Public Health England & Food Standards Agency. (2020). *National Diet and Nutrition Survey: Rolling programme Years 9 to 11 (2016/2017 to 2018/2019).* HMG. Available at: https://assets.publishing.service.gov.uk/government/uploads/system/uploads/attachment_data/file/943114/NDNS_UK_Y9-11_report.pdf

[3] National Food Strategy Analysis of PHE Public Health Outcomes Framework: Public Health England. (2013). *Public Health Outcomes Framework.* HMG. Available at: Public Health Outcomes Framework – GOV.UK (www.gov.uk)

[4] Public Health England. (2020). *Disparities in the risk and outcomes of COVID-19.* HMG. Available at: https://assets.publishing.service.gov.uk/government/uploads/system/uploads/attachment_data/file/908434/Disparities_in_the_risk_and_outcomes_of_COVID_August_2020_update.pdf

[5] Marmot, M. et al. (2020). *Health equity in England: the Marmot review 10 years on.* Institute of Health Equity. Available at: https://www.health.org.uk/publications/reports/the-marmot-review-10-years-on

[6] Marmot, M. et al. (2020). *Health equity in England: the Marmot review 10 years on.* Institute of Health Equity. Available at: https://www.health.org.uk/publications/reports/the-marmot-review-10-years-on

[7] NFS Analysis of PHE Public Health Outcomes Framework: Public Health England. (2013). *Public Health Outcomes Framework.* HMG. Available at: https://fingertips.phe.org.uk/profile/public-health-outcomes-framework

[8] NCD Risk Factor Collaboration (NCD-RisC). (2020). *Height and body-mass index trajectories of school-aged children and adolescents from 1985 to 2019 in 200 countries and territories: a pooled analysis of 2181 population-based studies with 65 million participants.* The Lancet. Available at: https://doi.org/10.1016/S0140-6736(20)31859-6

[9] NCD Risk Factor Collaboration (NCD-RisC). (2020). *Height and body-mass index trajectories of school-aged children and adolescents from 1985 to 2019 in 200 countries and territories: a pooled analysis of 2181 population-based studies with 65 million participants.* The Lancet. Available at: https://doi.org/10.1016/S0140-6736(20)31859-6

[10] NCD Risk Factor Collaboration (NCD-RisC). (2020). *Height and body-mass index trajectories of school-aged children and adolescents from 1985 to 2019 in 200 countries and territories: a pooled analysis of 2181 population-based studies with 65 million participants.* The Lancet. Available at: https://doi.org/10.1016/S0140-6736(20)31859-6

[11] Office for National Statistics. (2021). *Health state life expectancies by national deprivation deciles, England and Wales: 2015 to 2017.* ONS. Available at: https://www.ons.gov.uk/peoplepopulationandcommunity/healthandsocialcare/healthinequalities/bulletins/healthstatelifeexpectanciesbyindexofmultipledeprivationimd/latest

[12] Office for National Statistics. (2021). *Health state life expectancies by national deprivation deciles, England and Wales: 2017 to 2019.* ONS. Available at: https://www.ons.gov.uk/peoplepopulationandcommunity/healthandsocialcare/healthinequalities/bulletins/healthstatelifeexpectanciesbyindexofmultipledeprivationimd/latest

[13] 13 NCD Risk Factor Collaboration (NCD-RisC). (2020). Height and body-mass index trajectories of school-aged children and adolescents from 1985 to 2019 in 200 countries and territories: a pooled analysis of 2181 population-based studies with 65 million participants. The Lancet. Available at: https://doi.org/10.1016/ S0140-6736(20)31859-6;

Public Health England. (2020.) Height by deprivation decile in children aged 10 to 11. (2020.) HMG. Available at: https://www.gov.uk/government/publications/height-by-deprivation-decile-in-children-aged-10-to-11

[14] UKCRC Centre for Diet and Activity Research. (2014). Food, income and education: who eats more of what? CEDAR. Available at: www.cedar.iph.cam.ac.uk/resources/evidence/food-income-education-graphic/

[15] Department for Work and Pensions. (2021). Family Resources Survey: financial year 2019 to 2020. HMG. Available at: https://www.gov.uk/government/statistics/family-resources-survey-financial-year-2019-to-2020/family-resources-survey-financial-year-2019-to-2020#household-food-security-1

[16] Department for Work and Pensions. (2021.) *Family resources survey: financial year 2019 to 2020.* HMG. Available at: https://www.gov.uk/government/statistics/family-resources-survey-financial-year-2019-to-2020/family-resources-survey-financial-year-2019-to-2020#household-food-security-1

[17] Food Foundation. (2021). *A crisis within a crisis: the impact of COVID-19 on household food security.* Food Foundation. Available at: https://foodfoundation.org.uk/wp-content/uploads/2021/03/FF_Impact-of-Covid_FINAL.pdf

[18] Time spent cooking: Adams, J. and White, M. (2015.) *Prevalence and socio-demographic correlates of time spent cooking by adults in the 2005 UK Time Use Survey. Cross-sectional analysis.* Appetite. Available at: http://dx.doi.org/10.1016/j.appet.2015.05.022; Cooking skills: Adams, J. et al. (2015). *Prevalence and socio-demographic correlates of cooking skills in UK adults: cross-sectional analysis of data from the UK National Diet and Nutrition Survey.* Int J Behav Nutr Phys Act 12, 99. Available at: https://doi.org/10.1186/s12966-015-0261-x

[19] Turn2Us. (2020). *Living Without: The scale and impact of appliance poverty.* Turn2Us. Available at: https://www.turn2us.org.uk/T2UWebsite/media/Documents/Communications%20documents/Living-Without-Report-Final-Web.pdf

[20] Laraia, B. M. et al. (2017). *Biobehavioral Factors That Shape Nutrition in Low-Income Populations: A Narrative Review.* American Journal of Preventive Medicine. Available at: https://doi.org/10.1016/j.amepre.2016.08.003

[21] Mani, A. et al. (2013). *Poverty impedes cognitive function.* Science. Available at: https://science.sciencemag.org/content/341/6149/976; Bell R. (2017). *Psychosocial pathways and health outcomes: Informing action on health inequalities.* The Institute of Health Equity: Available at: https://www.instituteofhealthequity.org/resources-reports/psychosocial-pathways-and-health-outcomes-informing-action-on-health-inequalities

[22] Social Work Degree Center. (no date). *How poverty burdens the brain.* Social Work Degree Center. Available at: https://www.socialworkdegreecenter.com/poverty/; Laraia, B. M. et al. (2017). *Biobehavioral Factors That Shape Nutrition in Low-Income Populations: A Narrative Review.* American Journal of Preventive Medicine. Available at: https://doi.org/10.1016/j.amepre.2016.08.003; Hemmingsson, E. (2014). *A new model of the role of psychological and emotional distress in promoting obesity: conceptual review with implications for treatment and prevention.* Obesity Etiology. Available at: https://doi.org/10.1111/obr.12197

[23] Mani, A. et al. (2013). *Poverty impedes cognitive function*. Science. Available at: https://science.sciencemag.org/content/341/6149/976; Bell, R. (2017). *Psychosocial pathways and health outcomes: Informing action on health inequalities*. The Institute of Health Equity. Available at: https://www.instituteofhealthequity.org/resources-reports/psychosocial-pathways-and-health-outcomes-informing-action-on-health-inequalities; Benzeval, M. et al. (2014). *How does money influence health?* Joseph Rowntree Foundation. Available at: https://www.jrf.org.uk/report/how-does-money-influence-health

[24] Laraia, B. A. et al. (2017). *Biobehavioral Factors That Shape Nutrition in Low-Income Populations: A Narrative Review*. American Journal of Preventive Medicine. Available at: https://doi.org/10.1016/j.amepre.2016.08.003

[25] Public Health England. (2018). *Obesity and the Environment – Density of fast food outlets at 31/12/2017*. HMG. Available at: https://www.gov.uk/government/publications/fast-food-outlets-density-by-local-authority-in-england

[26] Lucas, K. et al. (2019). *Inequalities in Mobility and Access in the UK Transport System*. Government Office for Science. Available at: https://assets.publishing.service.gov.uk/government/uploads/system/uploads/attachment_data/file/784685/future_of_mobility_access.pdf

[27] Data from PHE. *Public Health Profiles 2020;* Presented in: Marmot, M. et al. (2020). *Health equity in England: the Marmot review 10 years on*. Institute of Health Equity. Available at: https://www.health.org.uk/publications/reports/the-marmot-review-10-years-on

6. Exposing the invisibility of nature

[1] In an address to the UN: United Nations. (2020). *Building Back Better: Natural Capital Accounting for a Green Recovery.* United Nations. Available at: https://seea.un.org/events/building-back-better-natural-capital-accounting-green-recovery; Quote available here: Bennett Institute for Public Policy. (2020). *Green recovery must end the reign of GDP, argue Cambridge and UN economists.* Bennett Institute for Public Policy. Available at: https://www.bennettinstitute.cam.ac.uk/news/green-recovery-must-end-reign-gdp-argue-cambridge-/

[2] For full details of the claims underlying this statement, see NFS Evidence Pack – in particular pages 6-29. Available from: https://www.nationalfoodstrategy.org

[3] HM Treasury. (2021). *The Economics of Biodiversity: The Dasgupta Review – Reactions.* HM Treasury. Available at: https://www.gov.uk/government/publications/final-report-the-economics-of-biodiversity-the-dasgupta-review/the-economics-of-biodiversity-the-dasgupta-review-reactions

[4] Scown, M. et al. (2020). *Billions in Misspent EU Agricultural Subsidies Could Support the Sustainable Development Goals.* One Earth. Available at: https://doi.org/10.1016/j.oneear.2020.07.011

[5] Comptroller and Auditor General. (2020). *Achieving government's long-term environmental goals.* National Audit Office. Available at: https://www.nao.org.uk/wp-content/uploads/2020/11/Achieving-governments-long%E2%80%91term-environmental-goals.pdf

[6] Natural Capital Committee. (2020). *Natural Capital Committee's seventh annual report.* Department for Environment, Food & Rural Affairs. Available at: https://www.gov.uk/government/publications/natural-capital-committees-seventh-annual-report

[7] Citation for £2.4bn: Department for Environment, Food & Rural Affairs. (2020). *The Path to Sustainable Farming: An Agricultural Transition Plan 2021 to 2024.* Defra. Available at: https://assets.publishing.service.gov.uk/government/uploads/system/uploads/attachment_data/file/954283/agricultural-transition-plan.pdf

[8] Pigou, A. C. (1921). *The Economics of Welfare.* London, UK: Macmillan & Co.

[9] Coase, R. H. (1960). *The Problem of Social Cost.* In: Gopalakrishnan C. (eds) Classic Papers in Natural Resource Economics. London, UK: Palgrave Macmillan. Available at: https://doi.org/10.1057/9780230523210_6

[10] Sustainable Food Trust. (no date). The Global Farm Metric. Available at: https://sustainablefoodtrust.org/key-issues/sustainability-metrics/the-global-farm-metric/

[11] Monbiot, G. (2018). *The UK government wants to put a price on nature – but that will destroy it.* Guardian News. Available at: https://www.theguardian.com/commentisfree/2018/may/15/price-natural-world-destruction-natural-capital

7. Food and climate

[1] Air travel: Lee, D. and Forster, P. (2020). *Guest post: Calculating the true climate impact of aviation emissions.* Carbon Brief. Available at: https://www.carbonbrief.org/guest-post-calculating-the-true-climate-impact-of-aviation-emissions; Food system: Allen, M. (2015). *Short-Lived Promise? The Science and Policy of Cumulative and Short-Lived Climate Pollutants.* Oxford Martin Policy Paper. Available at: https://www.oxfordmartin.ox.ac.uk/downloads/briefings/Short_Lived_Promise.pdf

[2] UK emissions: Garnett, T. et al. (2016). *Food systems and greenhouse gas emissions.* Food Climate Research Network. Available at: https://www.tabledebates.org/chapter/food-systems-and-greenhouse-gas-emissions; Imports: WWF. (2010). *Emissions from UK Food Industry far Higher than Believed.* WWF. Available at: https://assets.wwf.org.uk/downloads/how_low_report_1.pdf

[3] Qin, Y. et al. (2021). *Carbon loss from forest degradation exceeds that from deforestation in the Brazilian Amazon.* Nat. Clim. Chang. 11, 442–448. Available at: https://doi.org/10.1038/s41558-021-01026-5; European Space Agency. (2021). *Forest degradation primary driver of carbon loss in the Brazilian Amazon.* European Space Agency. Available at: https://www.esa.int/Applications/Observing_the_Earth/Space_for_our_climate/Forest_degradation_primary_driver_of_carbon_loss_in_the_Brazilian_Amazon

[4] Whitehouse, N. and Smith, D. (2010). *How fragmented was the British Holocene wildwood? Perspectives on the "Vera" grazing debate from the fossil beetle record.* Quaternary Science Reviews, Volume 29, Issues 3–4. Available at: https://doi.org/10.1016/j.quascirev.2009.10.010

[5] Forest Research. (2021). *Provisional Woodland Statistics 2021 edition.* Edinburgh: Forest Research. Available at: https://www.forestresearch.gov.uk/documents/8092/PWS_2021.pdf; Forest Research. (2021). *Area of Woodland: Changes Over Time.* Forest Research. Available at: https://www.forestresearch.gov.uk/tools-and-resources/statistics/forestry-statistics/forestry-statistics-2018/woodland-areas-and-planting/woodland-area/area-of-woodland-changes-over-time/

[6] Anderson, R. (2020). *Peatlands, forestry and climate change: What role can forest-to-bog restoration play?* Forest Research. Available at: https://www.forestresearch.gov.uk/documents/7912/20_0041_Leaflet_CC_factsheet_Peatlands_wip06_ACC.pdf

[7] Bernal, B. et al. (2018). *Global carbon dioxide removal rates from forest landscape restoration activities.* Carbon Balance Manage 13, 22. Available at: https://doi.org/10.1186/s13021-018-0110-8

[8] UK Centre for Ecology & Hydrology. (no date). *Peatlands factsheet.* UK Centre for Ecology & Hydrology. Available at: https://www.ceh.ac.uk/sites/default/files/Peatland factsheet.pdf

[9] Brown, P. et al. (2021). UK Greenhouse gas inventory, 1990 to 2019: annual report for submissions under the framework convention on climate change. Ricardo Energy & Environment. Annex 3. Available at: https://uk-air.defra.gov.uk/assets/documents/reports/cat09/2106091119_ukghgi-90-19_Annex_Issue_2.pdf

[10] IUCN. (2018). *UK Peatland Strategy.* IUCN National Committee United Kingdom. Available at: https://portals.iucn.org/library/sites/library/files/documents/2018-015-En.pdf, page 30.

[11] Gilbert, P., and Thornley, P. (2010). *Energy and carbon balance of ammonia production from biomass gasification.* In host publication. Available at: https://www.research.manchester.ac.uk/portal/files/33615474/FULL_TEXT.PDF; Synthetic ammonia use: Smith, P. et al. (2014). *Agriculture, Forestry and Other Land Use (AFOLU).* Climate Change 2014: Mitigation of Climate Change. Contribution of Working Group III to the Fifth Assessment Report of the Intergovernmental Panel on Climate Change. Available at: https://www.ipcc.ch/site/assets/uploads/2018/02/ipcc_wg3_ar5_chapter11.pdf

[12] Private correspondence with Nestlé UK.

[13] Validity of food miles: Department for Environment, Food & Rural Affairs. (2005). *The Validity of Food Miles as an Indicator of Sustainable Development.* Report prepared by AEA Technology PLC. Available at: https://webarchive.nationalarchives.gov.uk/20130125041710/http:/www.defra.gov.uk/statistics/files/defra-stats-foodfarm-food-transport-foodmiles-050715.pdf; Flying: Asparagus: Ritchie, H. (2020). *Very little of global food is transported by air; this greatly reduces the climate benefits of eating local.* Our World in Data. Available at: https://ourworldindata.org/food-transport-by-mode

[14] National Food Strategy analysis based on: Garnett, T. (2008). *Cooking up a storm.* In: *Food, greenhouse gas emissions and our changing climate.* Food Climate Research Network, Centre for Environmental Strategy. Available at: http://www.unscn.org/layout/modules/resources/files/Cooking_up_a_Storm.pdf; Department for Business, Energy and Industrial Strategy. (2019). Final UK greenhouse gas emissions national statistics. Data Tables. Available at: https://data.gov.uk/dataset/9568363e-57e5-4c33-9e00-31dc528fcc5a/final-uk-greenhouse-gas-emissions-national-statistics; WRAP. (2020). Courtauld Commitment 2025, 2020 Annual Report. Available at: https://wrap.org.uk/sites/default/files/2021-01/The-Courtauld-Commitment-2025-Annual_Report-2020.pdf

[15] World Meteorological Organization. (2019). *Greenhouse gas concentrations in atmosphere reach yet another high.* Available at: https://public.wmo.int/en/media/press-release/greenhouse-gas-concentrations-atmosphere-reach-yet-another-high

[16] GWP20 for methane is 84–87: IEA. (2020). *Methane Tracker 2020.* IEA. Available at: https://www.iea.org/reports/methane-tracker-2020

[17] There is some difference in assessments of methane's GWP, with recent studies suggesting 84–96 for GWP20 and 28–34 for GWP100. For a recent analysis see: M, Etminan. et al. (2016). *Radiative forcing of carbon dioxide, methane, and nitrous oxide: A significant revision of the methane radiative forcing.* Geophysical Research Letters. Available at: https://doi.org/10.1002/2016GL071930

[18] Getabalew, M. et al. (2019). *Methane Production in Ruminant Animals: Implication for Their Impact on Climate Change.* Con Dai & Vet Sci 2(4) 2019. Available at: https://lupinepublishers.com/dairy-veterinary-science-journal/pdf/CDVS.MS.ID.000142.pdf

[19] Enteric fermentation and wastes and manure management account for 68.4% of UK agricultural emissions. Available at: Committee on Climate Change. (2020). *Sixth Carbon Budget – Dataset.* Committee on Climate Change. Available at: https://www.theccc.org.uk/publication/sixth-carbon-budget/

[20] Reisinger, A. and Clark, H. (2017). *How much do direct livestock emissions actually contribute to global warming?* Global Change Biology. Available at: https://doi.org/10.1111/gcb.13975

[21] Bar-On, Y. et al. (2018). *The Biomass Distribution on Earth.* Proceedings of the National Academy of Sciences. 115 (25) 6506–6511. Available at: https://www.pnas.org/content/115/25/6506

[22] McCarthy, N. (2019). *How Many Animals Do We Eat Each Year?* Statista. Available at: https://www.statista.com/chart/16888/number-of-animals-slaughtered-for-meat-each-year/ (originally FAO stats).

[23] Methane's importance in 1.5°C: Collins, W. et al. (2018). *Increased importance of methane reduction for a 1.5 degree target.* Environ. Res. Lett. 13 0540. Available at: https://iopscience.iop.org/article/10.1088/1748-9326/aab89c; Rapid reduction potential: United Nations Environment Programme and Climate and Clean Air Coalition. (2021). *Global Methane Assessment: Benefits and Costs of Mitigating Methane Emissions.* Nairobi: United Nations Environment Programme. Available at: https://wedocs.unep.org/bitstream/handle/20.500.11822/35917/GMA_ES.pdf

[24] Organisation for Economic Co-operation and Development. OECD-FAO Agricultural Outlook. Meats – 1992 – 2028. Available at: https://stats.oecd.org/index.aspx?queryid=76854 accessed 2021.

[25] Committee on Climate Change. (2020). *Land Use: Policies for a Net Zero UK.* Committee on Climate Change. Available at: https://www.theccc.org.uk/wp-content/uploads/2020/01/Land-use-Policies-for-a-Net-Zero-UK.pdf, pages 41–46.

[26] Buis, A. (2019). *A Degree of Concern: Why Global Temperatures Matter.* NASA Global Climate Change. Available at: https://climate.nasa.gov/news/2865/a-degree-of-concern-why-global-temperatures-matter/

[27] Private correspondence with Nestlé UK.

[28] Allen, M. (2015). *Short-Lived Promise? The Science and Policy of Cumulative and Short-Lived Climate Pollutants.* Oxford Martin Policy Paper. Available at: https://www.oxfordmartin.ox.ac.uk/downloads/briefings/Short_Lived_Promise.pdf

8. The complexities of meat

[1] Ritchie, H. (2020). *Less meat is nearly always better than sustainable meat, to reduce your carbon footprint*. Our World in Data. Available at: https://ourworldindata.org/less-meat-or-sustainable-meat

[2] Wilderness Society. (2019). *Drivers of Deforestation and land clearing in Queensland*. Wilderness Society. Available at: https://www.wilderness.org.au//images/resources/The_Drivers_of_Deforestation_Land-clearing_Qld_Report.pdf

[3] 6 of the 38 OECD countries have higher beef emissions than the UK: Australia, Chile, Colombia, Ireland, Korea, and Mexico: Kim, B. et al. (2020). *Country-specific dietary shifts to mitigate climate and water crises*. Global Environmental Change, Volume 62. Available at: https://doi.org/10.1016/j.gloenvcha.2019.05.010

[4] Hayek, M. and Garrett, R. (2018). *Nationwide shift to grass-fed beef requires larger cattle population*. Environ. Res. Lett. 13 084005. Available at: https://iopscience.iop.org/article/10.1088/1748-9326/aad401

[5] Kim, B. et al. (2020). *Country-specific dietary shifts to mitigate climate and water crises*. Global Environmental Change, Volume 62. Available at: https://doi.org/10.1016/j.gloenvcha.2019.05.010

[6] For the overall productivity of these systems, see: Pent, G. (2020). *Over-yielding in temperate silvopastures: a meta-analysis*. Agroforest Syst 94, 1741–1758. Available at: https://doi.org/10.1007/s10457-020-00494-6; Biodiversity benefits are highly dependent on agroforestry management techniques, see: Torralba, M. et al. (2016). *Do European agroforestry systems enhance biodiversity and ecosystem services? A meta-analysis*. Agriculture, Ecosystems & Environment, Volume 230. Available at: https://doi.org/10.1016/j.agee.2016.06.002; Mupepele, A. et al. (2020). *European agroforestry is no universal remedy for biodiversity: a time-cumulative meta-analysis*. bioRxiv. Available at: https://doi.org/10.1101/2020.08.27.269589 (though note that the latter analysis has not yet undergone peer review). Water and air quality benefits are highly context dependent, though soil erosion benefits are commonly seen, see Jordon, M. et al. (2020). *Implications of Temperate Agroforestry on Sheep and Cattle Productivity, Environmental Impacts and Enterprise Economics. A Systematic Evidence Map*. Forests 2020, 11, 1321. Available at: http://dx.doi.org/10.3390/f11121321

9. A nature-positive, carbon-negative food system

[1] Gregg, R. et al. (2021). *Carbon storage and sequestration by habitat: a review of the evidence (second edition).* Natural England. Available at: http://publications.naturalengland.org.uk/publication/5419124441481216

[2] See NFS Evidence Pack, page 26, available from: https://www.nationalfoodstrategy.org

[3] Poux, X. and Schiavo, M. (2021). *Modelling an agroecological UK in 2050.* IDDRI for FFCC. Draft report available at: https://ffcc.co.uk/assets/downloads/Modelling-An-Agroecological-UK-in-2050-Working-Draft-V5_January-20.pdf; Calculations based in part on private correspondence with the report authors and sponsors.

[4] Committee on Climate Change. (2020). *Sixth Carbon Budget – Dataset.* Committee on Climate Change. Available at: https://www.theccc.org.uk/publication/sixth-carbon-budget/; Emissions are net LULUCF emissions for the UK. We follow UNFCCC conventions on separating agricultural emissions from land use emissions – for more information on the relationship between agriculture, LULUCF and AFOLU: Iversen, P. et al. (2014). *Understanding Land Use in the UNFCCC.* Available at: https://ghginstitute.org/wp-content/uploads/2015/04/Understanding_Land_Use_in_the_UNFCCC.pdf

[5] Department of Business, Energy and International Strategy. (2021). *2019 UK Greenhouse Gas Emissions, Final Figures.* HMG. Available at: https://assets.publishing.service.gov.uk/government/uploads/system/uploads/attachment_data/file/957887/2019_Final_greenhouse_gas_emissions_statistical_release.pdf

[6] National Food Strategy analysis based on: Committee on Climate Change. (2020). *The Sixth Carbon Budget – The UK's path to Net Zero.* Committee on Climate Change. Available at: https://www.theccc.org.uk/wp-content/uploads/2020/12/The-Sixth-Carbon-Budget-The-UKs-path-to-Net-Zero.pdf; NFU. (2019). *Achieving Net Zero, Farming's 2040 goal.* NFU. Available at: https://www.nfuonline.com/nfu-online/business/regulation/achieving-net-zero-farmings-2040-goal/; IDDRI. (2018). *An agroecological Europe in 2050: multifunctional agriculture for healthy eating, Findings from the Ten Years For Agroecology (TYFA) modelling exercise.* IDDRI. Available at: https://www.iddri.org/sites/default/files/PDF/Publications/Catalogue%20Iddri/Etude/201809 ST0918EN tyfa.pdf

[7] NFS analysis of: CCC 6th Carbon Budget dataset; Committee on Climate Change. (2020). *Sixth Carbon Budget – Dataset.* Committee on Climate Change. Available at: https://www.theccc.org.uk/publication/sixth-carbon-budget/; Includes data provided via private correspondence.

[8] NFU. (2019). *Achieving Net Zero, Farming's 2040 goal.* NFU. Available at: https://www.nfuonline.com/nfu-online/business/regulation/achieving-net-zero-farmings-2040-goal/; Plus private correspondence.

[9] Poux, X. and Schiavo, M. (2021). *Modelling an agroecological UK in 2050.* IDDRI for FFCC. Draft report available at: https://ffcc.co.uk/assets/downloads/Modelling-An-Agroecological-UK-in-2050-Working-Draft-V5_January-20.pdf

[10] Thomas, C. D. et al. (2013). *Reconciling biodiversity and carbon conservation.* Ecology Letters. 16 (s1), 39–47. Available at: https://www.academia.edu/3746511/Reconciling_Biodiversity_and_Carbon_Conservation

[11] Thomas, C. D. et al. (2013). *Reconciling biodiversity and carbon conservation.* Ecology Letters. 16 (s1), 39–47. Available at: https://www.academia.edu/3746511/Reconciling_Biodiversity_and_Carbon_Conservation

[12] National Food Strategy based on: Poore, J. and Nemecek, T. (2018). *Reducing food's environmental impacts through producers and consumers.* Science 360:987–992. Available at: https://doi.org/10.1126/science.aaq0216; de Ruiter, H. et al. (2017). *Total global agricultural land footprint associated with UK food supply 1986–2011.* Global Environmental Change. 43. 72–81. Available at: http://dx.doi.org/10.1016/j.gloenvcha.2017.01.007; ONS. (2019). *UK natural capital: urban accounts.* ONS. Available at: https://www.ons.gov.uk/economy/environmentalaccounts/bulletins/uknaturalcapital/urbanaccounts; WWF. (2020). *Bending the Curve: The Restorative Power of Planet-Based Diets.* WWF. Available at: https://wwfint.awsassets.panda.org/downloads/bending_the_curve__the_restorative_power_of_planet_based_diets_full_report_final_pdf.pdf; Forestry Commission. (2020). *Forestry Statistics 2020: A compendium of statistics about woodland, forestry and primary wood processing in the United Kingdom.* National Statistics. Available at: https://www.forestresearch.gov.uk/documents/7806/CompleteFS2020.pdf; Centre For Ecology & Hydrology. (2000). *LAND COVER MAP 2000.* CEH. Available at: https://www.ceh.ac.uk/sites/default/files/LCM2000 Final Report.pdf; European Environment Agency. (2016). *Corine Land Cover 2012.* EEA. Available at: https://www.eea.europa.eu/data-and-maps/data/external/corine-land-cover-2012; BBC. (2017). *Five mind-blowing facts about what the UK looks like.* BBC. Available at: https://www.bbc.co.uk/news/uk-41901297

[13] de Ruiter, H. et al. (2017). *Total global agricultural land footprint associated with UK food supply 1986–2011.* Global Environmental Change. 43. 72–81. Available at: http://dx.doi.org/10.1016/j.gloenvcha.2017.01.007

[14] Monbiot, G. (2013). *Meet the greatest threat to our countryside: sheep.* The Spectator. Available at: https://www.spectator.co.uk/article/meet-the-greatest-threat-to-our-countryside-sheep

[15] Searchinger, T. D. et al. (2018). *Assessing the efficiency of changes in land use for mitigating climate change.* Nature 564, 249–253. Available at: https://doi.org/10.1038/s41586-018-0757-z

[16] NFS analysis based on: Department for Environment, Food & Rural Affairs. (2019). June Agricultural Survey Holding Data; USDA, Economic Research Service. (2021). *USDA ERS – Food Availability (Per Capita) Data System.* USDA, Economic Research Service. Available at: https://www.ers.usda.gov/data-products/food-availability-per-capita-data-system; Department for Environment, Food & Rural Affairs. (2020). *Agriculture in the United Kingdom data sets.* HMG. Available at: https://www.gov.uk/government/statistical-data-sets/agriculture-in-the-united-kingdom; Department for Environment, Food & Rural Affairs. (2021). *Monthly statistics on the activity of UK hatcheries and UK poultry slaughterhouses.* HMG. Available at: https://www.gov.uk/government/statistics/poultry-and-poultry-meat-statistics. (data for December 2019); Department for Environment, Food & Rural Affairs. (2020). *UK Slaughter Statistics, December 2019.* HMG. Available at: https://assets.publishing.service.gov.uk/government/uploads/system/uploads/attachment_data/file/865357/slaughter-statsnotice-16jan20.pdf; Agriculture and Horticulture Development Board. (2021). *UK milk yield.* AHDB. Available at: https://ahdb.org.uk/dairy/uk-milk-yield; FAO. (2021). Food Composition Tables. FAO. Available at: http://www.fao.org/3/X9892E/X9892e05.htm#P8217_125315 accessed December 2021; Meat Promotion Wales. (2014). *Feeding the ewe for lifetime production.* Available at: https://meatpromotion.wales/images/resources/Feeding_the_ewe_final.pdf; Hyde, R. M. et al. (2020). *Quantitative analysis of calf mortality in Great Britain.* J Dairy Sci. 2020 Mar;103(3):2615–2623. Available at: https://doi.org/10.3168/jds.2019-17383; Department for Environment, Food & Rural Affairs. (2020). *Horticulture Statistics 2019.* HMG. Available at: https://assets.publishing.service.gov.uk/government/uploads/system/uploads/attachment_data/file/901689/hort report 17jul20.pdf

[17] Rebanks, J. (2020). *English Pastoral.* London, UK: Penguin Books

10. A Three Compartment Model

[1] Innovative Farmers. (2019). *Intercropping and Companion Cropping in Arable Systems Field Lab 2018–19 report.* Available at: https://www.agricology.co.uk/sites/default/files/if-final-report-intercropping-2019.pdf

[2] See, for example: Balmford, B. et al. (2018). *How imperfect can land sparing be before land sharing is more favourable for wild species?* Journal of Applied Ecology, 56 (1), pp. 73–84. Available at: https://besjournals.onlinelibrary.wiley.com/doi/full/10.1111/1365-2664.13282; Feniuk, C. et al. (2019). *Land sparing to make space for species dependent on natural habitats and high nature value farmland.* Proceedings of the Royal Society B Biological Sciences, 286(1909). Available at: https://royalsocietypublishing.org/doi/10.1098/rspb.2019.1483

[3] Sausse, C. et al. (2015). *Do the effects of crops on skylark (Alauda arvensis) differ between the field and landscape scales?* PeerJ, 3 (1097). Available at: https://peerj.com/articles/1097/

[4] Lower yields: Smith, L. G. et al. (2019). *The greenhouse gas impacts of converting food production in England and Wales to organic methods.* Nat Commun 10(4641). Available at: https://www.nature.com/articles/s41467-019-12622-7

[5] Finch, T. et al. (2019). *Bird conservation and the land sharing-sparing continuum in farmland-dominated landscapes of lowland England.* Conservation Biology, 33(5), pp. 1045–1055. Available at: https://www.cb.iee.unibe.ch/e58878/e337393/e337410/e604441/e876095/Finch_ConBio2019_eng.pdf

[6] Finch, T. et al. (2019). *Bird conservation and the land sharing-sparing continuum in farmland-dominated landscapes of lowland England.* Conservation Biology, 33(5), pp. 1045–1055. Available at: https://www.cb.iee.unibe.ch/e58878/e337393/e337410/e604441/e876095/Finch_ConBio2019_eng.pdf

[7] All statistics and graphics in this box other than those specifically cited separately are derived from Department for Environment Food & Rural Affairs. (2019). *The Future Farming and Environment Evidence Compendium*, available from: https://assets.publishing.service.gov.uk/government/uploads/system/uploads/attachment_data/file/834432/evidence-compendium-26sep19.pdf; Department for Environment Food & Rural Affairs. (2020). *Agriculture in the UK Evidence Pack*, available from: https://assets.publishing.service.gov.uk/government/uploads/system/uploads/attachment_data/file/955918/AUK-2019-evidencepack-28jan21.pdf; Department for Environment Food & Rural Affairs. (2020). *Farm performance and productivity: analysis of farm business survey*, available from: https://assets.publishing.service.gov.uk/government/uploads/system/uploads/attachment_data/file/955919/fbs-evidencepack-28jan21.pdf

[8] Cogeca. (2014). *Development of agricultural cooperatives in the EU.* Report PUB(14)9112:2. www.copa-cogeca.eu/cogeca.

[9] Macmillan, T. and Cusworth, G. (2019). *Farmer co-operation in the UK. Opportunities for the industry.* Co-operatives UK. Available at: https://www.uk.coop/sites/default/files/2020-11/farmer_co-operation_in_the_uk_report.pdf

11. Can we have it all?

[1] 22% of post-farm gate food is wasted: WRAP. (2021). *Food surplus and waste arisings in the UK*. WRAP. Available at: https://wrap.org.uk/sites/default/files/2021-06/Food Surplus and Waste in the UK Key Facts June 2021.pdf; Estimates of food grown but never harvested are more uncertain, but likely adds around 7% to this figure: Bajzelj, B. et al. (2019). *Food waste in primary production in the UK*. WRAP. Available at: http://dx.doi.org/10.13140/RG.2.2.36134.14400

[2] Edible but wasted post farm-gate food adds 17.5 $MtCO_2e$ (5%) to UK emissions. Pre farm-gate waste is estimated to add between 3 MtCO2e (0.8%) and 7.7 $MtCO_2e$ (2.1%) to UK emissions. WRAP. (2019). *Food surplus and waste in the UK: Key facts*. Available from: http://www.wrap.org.uk/sites/files/wrap/Food%20Surplus%20and%20Waste%20in%20the%20UK%20Key%20Facts%20%2822%207%2019%29_0.pdf. For pre farm-gate GHGs, these are estimated based on the figures in Table 3 of WRAP. (2020). *Food surplus and waste in the UK – key facts*. WRAP. Available at: https://archive.wrap.org.uk/sites/files/wrap/Food-surplus-and-waste-in-the-UK-key-facts-Jan-2020.pdf, multiplied by average $kgCO_2e$/kg analysis from Poore, J. and Nemecek, T. (2018) *Reducing food's environmental impacts through producers and consumers*. Science 360, 6392. Available from: https://science.sciencemag.org/content/360/6392/987/tab-figures-data

[3] WRAP. (2020). *Food surplus and waste in the UK – key facts*. WRAP. Available at: https://archive.wrap.org.uk/sites/files/wrap/Food-surplus-and-waste-in-the-UK-key-facts-Jan-2020.pdf

[4] Dray, S. (2021). *Food waste in the UK*. Parliament. Available at: https://lordslibrary.parliament.uk/food-waste-in-the-uk/

[5] WRAP. (2020). *Food surplus and waste in the UK – key facts*. WRAP. Available at: https://archive.wrap.org.uk/sites/files/wrap/Food-surplus-and-waste-in-the-UK-key-facts-Jan-2020.pdf

[6] Carmichael, R. (2019). *Behaviour change, public engagement and Net Zero*. Imperial College London. Available at: https://www.chapterzero.org.uk/wp-content/uploads/2019/11/Behaviour-change-public-engagement-and-Net-Zero-Imperial-College-London.pdf

[7] Forbes, H. et al. (2021). *Food waste index report 2021*. United Nations Environment Programme. Available at: https://www.unep.org/resources/report/unep-food-waste-index-report-2021

[8] Forbes, H. et al. (2021). *Food waste index report 2021*. United Nations Environment Programme. Available at: https://www.unep.org/resources/report/unep-food-waste-index-report-2021

[9] Department for Environment, Food & Rural Affairs. (2020). *Farming Statistics – provisional arable crop areas, yields and livestock populations at 1 June 2020 United Kingdom*. HMG. https://assets.publishing.service.gov.uk/government/uploads/system/uploads/attachment_data/file/931104/structure-jun2020prov-UK-08oct20i.pdf

[10] Department for Environment, Food & Rural Affairs et al. (2020.) *Agriculture in the UK 2019*. HMG. Available at: https://assets.publishing.service.gov.uk/government/uploads/system/uploads/attachment_data/file/950618/AUK-2019-07jan21.pdf

[11] Crop Science Bayer. (2018.) *How do you grow a record-breaking wheat crop? We spoke to the current and former record-holders to find out*. Crop Science Bayer. Available at: https://cropscience.bayer.co.uk/blog/articles/2018/03/record-wheat-yield/

[12] Schils, R. et al. (2018). *Cereal yield gaps across Europe*. European Journal of Agronomy. Available at: https://doi.org/10.1016/j.eja.2018.09.003

[13] Senapati, N. and Semenov, M.A. (2019). *Assessing yield gap in high productive countries by designing wheat ideotypes*. Sci Rep 9, 5516. Available at: https://doi.org/10.1038/s41598-019-40981-0

[14] Committee on Climate Change. (2020). *Sixth Carbon Budget*. Committee on Climate Change. Available at: https://www.theccc.org.uk/publication/sixth-carbon-budget/

[15] NFS analysis based on Poore, J. and Nemecek, T. (2018) and de Ruiter, H. et al. (2017). See National Food Strategy Evidence Pack, pages 42 and 56, for details. Available from https://www.nationalfoodstrategy.org

[16] NFS analysis based on Poore, J. and Nemecek, T. (2018) and de Ruiter, H. et al. (2017). See National Food Strategy Evidence Pack page 42 and 56 for details. Available from https://www.nationalfoodstrategy.org

[17] NFS analysis based on NDNS data. See National Food Strategy Evidence Pack, pages 122 and 123, for details. Available from https://www.nationalfoodstrategy.org

[18] Across all 2050 net zero scenarios, as outlined in: Committee on Climate Change. (2020). *Sixth Carbon Budget*. Committee on Climate Change. Available at: https://www.theccc.org.uk/publication/sixth-carbon-budget/

[19] NFS analysis based on Defra Family Food Survey data. See National Food Strategy Evidence Pack, page 61, for details. Available from https://www.nationalfoodstrategy.org

[20] NFS analysis based on Poore, J. and Nemecek, T. (2018) and de Ruiter, H. et al. (2017). See National Food Strategy Evidence Pack, pages 42 and 56, for details. Available from https://www.nationalfoodstrategy.org; Scenario assumes land released is split equally across the overseas and domestic land footprint of UK diets.

12. At what price?

[1] Johnstone, S. and Mazo, J. (2011). *Global Warming and the Arab Spring.* Survival, 53:2, 11–17. Available at: https://doi.org/10.1080/00396338.2011.571006

[2] Food and Agriculture Organization of the United Nations. (2021). *Global food prices rise at rapid pace in May.* FAO. Available at: http://www.fao.org/news/story/en/item/1403339/icode/

[3] Roser, M. and Ritchie, H. (2013). *Food Prices.* Our World in Data. Available at: https://ourworldindata.org/food-prices#wheat-prices-since-the-13th-century

[4] ONS. (2021). RPI: *Ave price – Chicken: roasting, ovn ready, frsh/chilld, Kg.* ONS. Available at: https://www.ons.gov.uk/economy/inflationandpriceindices/timeseries/czom

[5] Cribb, J. et al. (2012). *Jubilees compared: incomes, spending and work in the late 1970s and early 2010s.* Institute for Fiscal Studies. Available at: https://ifs.org.uk/bns/bn128.pdf

[6] Avison, A. (2020). *Why UK consumers spend 8% of their money on food.* AHDB. Available at: https://ahdb.org.uk/news/consumer-insight-why-uk-consumers-spend-8-of-their-money-on-food

[7] Since per capita food consumption (in calories) is similar in all three countries, and in 2018 all three countries were subject to the same trade and agricultural subsidy regimes, differences in consumer preferences are the most plausible explanation for the significant divergence in food spending (amounting to an extra thousand pounds or so per year).

[8] Our World in Data. (2017). *Share of consumer expenditure on food (USDA (2017)).* Our World in Data. Available at: https://ourworldindata.org/grapher/share-of-consumer-expenditure-spent-on-food?tab=table

[9] Pigou, A. (2013). *The Economics of Welfare.* London, UK: Palgrave Classics in Economics.

[10] SYSTEMIQ analysis for the National Food Strategy, based on FOLU (2019), Sustainable Food (2017), Ellen MacArthur Foundation (2019), WBCSD (2021). Available at https://www.nationalfoodstrategy.org

[11] Coase, R. (1960). *The Problem of Social Cost.* In: Gopalakrishnan C. (eds) *Classic Papers in Natural Resource Economics.* London, UK: Palgrave Macmillan.

[12] Service, R. (2019). *Solar plus batteries is now cheaper than fossil power.* Science. Available at: https://science.sciencemag.org/content/365/6449/108/

[13] UCL. (2020). *Impact of Carbon Price Support on British energy bills.* UCL. Available at: https://www.ucl.ac.uk/bartlett/sustainable/sites/bartlett/files/annex_-_cps_-_final_-_20102019.pdf

[14] SYSTEMIQ analysis commissioned for the National Food Strategy, based on Tesco.com and Sainsburys.com, accessed 23 March. Available from https://www.nationalfoodstrategy.org

[15] Department for Environment Food & Rural Affairs. (2020). *Family Food 2018/19.* HMG. Available at: https://www.gov.uk/government/statistics/family-food-201819/family-food-201819

[16] SYSTEMIQ and Soil Capital. (2019). *Regenerating Europe's Soils.* SYSTEMIQ and Soil Capital. Available at: https://www.systemiq.earth/wp-content/uploads/2020/01/RegeneratingEuropessoils-FINAL.pdf

[17] See, for example, Earthwatch Europe: Head. J. (2019). *Soil Health, Biodiversity and the Business Case for Sustainable Agriculture.* Oxford, UK: Earthwatch Europe. Available at: https://earthwatch.org.uk/images/SustAgriculture/Soil_Report.pdf; Soil Health Partnership: Soil Health Partnership, Environmental Defense Fund, K·Coe Isom. (2021). *Conservation's Impact on the Farm Bottom Line.* Soil Health Partnership. Available at: https://www.soilhealthpartnership.org/wp-content/uploads/2021/02/Conservation-Impact-On-Farm-Bottom-Line-2021.pdf

[18] SYSTEMIQ analysis commissioned for the National Food Strategy, based on Tesco.com and Sainsburys.com, accessed 23 March. Available at https://www.nationalfoodstrategy.org

13. The protein transition

[1] SYSTEMIQ analysis for NFS, to be published on www.nationalfood-strategy.org

[2] NFS Commissioned polling – Fleetwood. (2021). *National Food Strategy polling.* Fleetwood.

[3] López-Paredes, J. et al. (2020). *Mitigation of greenhouse gases in dairy cattle via genetic selection: 2. Incorporating methane emissions into the breeding goal.* Journal of Dairy Science. 103(8). pp.7210–7221. Available at: https://www.sciencedirect.com/science/article/pii/S0022030220303994?casa_token=mFbenf4pgYEAAAAA:px-Z3oLqaLKqJqhR26HpVKtKDEZGhBA6qV6AEWKWOWKlgF2tmFiMSa-jL14B66PYRztBhXWyWLqwfm-Q

[4] Roque, B. et al. (2021). *Red seaweed* (Asparagopsis taxiformis) *supplementation reduces enteric methane by over 80 percent in beef steers.* PLOS ONE 16(3). Available at: https://journals.plos.org/plosone/article?id=10.1371/journal.pone.0247820

[5] Nestle. (2021). Nestlé's Net Zero Roadmap. Available at: https://www.nestle.com/sites/default/files/2020-12/nestle-net-zero-road-map-en.pdf

[6] Abbot, D. W. et al. (2020). *Seaweed and Seaweed Bioactives for Mitigation of Enteric Methane: Challenges and Opportunities.* Animals. 10(2432). Available at: https://www.mdpi.com/2076-2615/10/12/2432

[7] NFS analysis. See NFS evidence pack, pages 77–78.

[8] FAOSTAT. (2021). *Meat food supply quantity.* Available at: http://www.fao.org/faostat/en/#data/FBS See also page 145 of the evidence pack.

[9] FAOSTAT. (2021). *Meat food supply quantity.* Available at: http://www.fao.org/faostat/en/#data/FBS See also page 145 of the evidence pack.

[10] BBC News. (2020). Singapore approves lab-grown 'chicken' meat. Available at: https://www.bbc.co.uk/news/business-55155741

[11] Susewi. (2021). *Algae Based Products.* Available at: https://www.susewi.life/our-process/

[12] Based on data from Carrols Restaurant Group, the largest Burger King franchisor in the US, in 2019; Seeking Alpha. (2020). *Impossible Whopper momentum slows down.* Available at: https://seekingalpha.com/news/3531766-impossible-whopper-momentum-slows-down

[13] NPD Group. (2019). Checkout Data for year Ending May '19.

[14] Food Navigator. (2021). *Israeli start-up Imagindairy eyes lab-made milk launch after precision fermentation breakthrough.* Available at: https://www.foodnavigator.com/Article/2021/06/10/Israeli-start-up-Imagindairy-eyes-lab-made-milk-launch-after-precision-fermentation-breakthrough

[15] Daxue Consulting. (2020). *The dairy market in China will be the world's largest by 2022.* Available at: https://daxueconsulting.com/china-dairy-market/

[16] The Royal Society. (2019). *Future food: health and sustainability (Conference Report).* The Royal Society. Available at: https://royalsociety.org/-/media/events/2019/12/tof-future-foods/Future-of-Food-ToF-conference-report.pdf?la=en-GB&hash=23A54C1F233745C70A-FA42545A883422

[17] RethinkX. (2021). *Food and Agriculture.* Available at: https://www.rethinkx.com/food-and-agriculture

[18] Tso, R. et al. 2021. *A Critical Appraisal of the Evidence Supporting Consumer Motivations for Alternative Proteins.* Foods. 10(24). https://www.mdpi.com/2304-8158/10/1/24

[19] UNFCCC. (no date). *Impossible Foods: Creating Plant-Based Alternatives to Meat | Singapore, Hong Kong, USA, Macau.* Available at: https://unfccc.int/climate-action/momentum-for-change/planetary-health/impossible-foods

[20] Head Topics. (2020). *Can lab-grown food save the planet? | Letters.* Available at: https://headtopics.com/uk/can-lab-grown-food-save-the-planet-letters-10607553

[21] ING Research. (2020). *Growth of meat and dairy alternatives is stirring up the European food industry.* Available at: https://think.ing.com/uploads/reports/ING_report_-_Growth_of_meat_and_dairy_alternatives_is_stirring_up_the_European_food_industry.pdf

[22] NFS analysis based on feed conversion ratios in: Good Food Institute. (2021). *Anticipatory life cycle assessment and techno-economic assessment of commercial cultivated meat production.* Available at: https://gfi.org/wp-content/uploads/2021/03/cultured-meat-LCA-TEA-technical.pdf; tonnes per hectare of input in: Department for Environment, Food & Rural Affairs. (2019). *Farming Statistics Final crop areas, yields, livestock populations and agricultural workforce at June 2019 – United Kingdom.* HMG. Available at: https://assets.publishing.service.gov.uk/government/uploads/system/uploads/attachment_data/file/865769/structure-jun2019final-uk-22jan20-rev_v2.pdf; and agricultural workers per hectare in: Nation Master. (no date). Agricultural workers per hectare. Available at: https://www.nationmaster.com/country-info/stats/Agriculture/Workers-per-hectare

[23] National Food Strategy analysis based on: Department for Environment, Food & Rural Affairs. (2020). *Family Food 2018/19.* HMG. Available at: https://www.gov.uk/government/statistics/family-food-201819

[24] Government of Canada. (2021). *Canada's Protein Industries Supercluster.* Available at: https://www.ic.gc.ca/eic/site/093.nsf/eng/00012.html

[25] Department for Environment, Food & Rural Affairs. (2014). *A plan for public procurement: food and catering.* HMG. Available at: https://www.gov.uk/government/publications/a-plan-for-public-procurement-food-and-catering-the-balanced-scorecard

[26] Culliford, A. and Bradbury, J. (2020). *A cross-sectional survey of the readiness of consumers to adopt an environmentally sustainable diet.* Nutrition Journal. 19(138). Available at: https://nutritionj.biomedcentral.com/track/pdf/10.1186/s12937-020-00644-7.pdf

[27] NFS analysis. See NFS Evidence pack, pages 43, 47, 77–78.

14. Food security

[1] Gibson M. (2012). *Food Security-A Commentary: What Is It and Why Is It So Complicated?* Foods 1(1), 18–27. Available at: https://doi.org/10.3390/foods1010018

[2] Lang, T. (2020). *Feeding Britain: Our Food Problems and How to Fix Them.* London, UK: Penguin Books.

[3] Food Chain Analysis Group, Department for Environment Food & Rural Affairs. (2006). *Food Security and the UK: An Evidence and Analysis Paper.* National Archives. Available at: https://webarchive.nationalarchives.gov.uk/20130404001020/http://archive.defra.gov.uk/evidence/economics/foodfarm/reports/documents/foodsecurity.pdf; Barnett, M. (1985). *British Food Policy During the First World War.* Australia: Allen & Unwin; Department for Environment, Food & Rural Affairs. (2013). *Agriculture in the United Kingdom.* HMG. Available at: https://www.gov.uk/government/collections/agriculture-in-the-united-kingdom

[4] Food Chain Analysis Group, Department for Environment Food & Rural Affairs. (2006). *Food Security and the UK: An Evidence and Analysis Paper.* National Archives. Available at: https://webarchive.nationalarchives.gov.uk/20130404001020/http://archive.defra.gov.uk/evidence/economics/foodfarm/reports/documents/foodsecurity.pdf; Barnett, M. (1985). *British Food Policy During the First World War.* Australia: Allen & Unwin; Department for Environment, Food & Rural Affairs. (2013). *Agriculture in the United Kingdom.* HMG. Available at: https://www.gov.uk/government/collections/agriculture-in-the-united-kingdom

[5] Food Chain Analysis Group, Department for Environment Food & Rural Affairs. (2006). *Food Security and the UK: An Evidence and Analysis Paper.* National Archives. Available at: https://webarchive.nationalarchives.gov.uk/20130404001020/http://archive.defra.gov.uk/evidence/economics/foodfarm/reports/documents/foodsecurity.pdf; Barnett, M. (1985). *British Food Policy During the First World War.* Australia: Allen & Unwin; Department for Environment, Food & Rural Affairs. (2013). *Agriculture in the United Kingdom.* HMG. Available at: https://www.gov.uk/government/collections/agriculture-in-the-united-kingdom

[6] Food Chain Analysis Group, Department for Environment Food & Rural Affairs. (2006). *Food Security and the UK: An Evidence and Analysis Paper.* National Archives. Available at: https://webarchive.nationalarchives.gov.uk/20130404001020/http://archive.defra.gov.uk/evidence/economics/foodfarm/reports/documents/foodsecurity.pdf; Barnett, M. (1985). *British Food Policy During the First World War.* Australia: Allen & Unwin; Department for Environment, Food & Rural Affairs. (2013). *Agriculture in the United Kingdom.* HMG. Available at: https://www.gov.uk/government/collections/agriculture-in-the-united-kingdom

[7] politics.co.uk. (2020). *Common agricultural policy.* politics.co.uk. Available at: https://www.politics.co.uk/reference/common-agricultural-policy, accessed 4 March 2020.

[8] Department for Environment, Food & Rural Affairs., et al. (2019). *Agriculture in the UK.* HMG. Available at: https://assets.publishing.service.gov.uk/government/uploads/system/uploads/attachment_data/file/950618/AUK-2019-07jan21.pdf

[9] Ministry of Agriculture, Fisheries and Food. (1975). *Food From Our Own resources.* London, UK: HMG.

[10] Department for Environment, Food an&d Rural Affairs. (2009). *UK Food Security Assessment: Detailed Analysis.* HMG. Available at: https://www.groupedebruges.eu/sites/default/files/publications/downloads/defra_foodsecurityassessment_2.pdf, p. 82.

[11] Timmer, J. (2020). *Modeling what would happen to the UK if the Gulf Stream shuts down.* Ars Technica. Available at: https://arstechnica.com/science/2020/01/modeling-what-would-happen-to-the-uk-if-the-gulf-stream-shuts-down/

[12] Based on data provided by Wageningen Economic Research. (2018). *Climate Change and Global Market Integration: Implications for global economic activities, agricultural commodities and food security.* SOCO 2018 Background Paper, Rome, Italy: FAO.

[13] Tzachor, A. (2019). *Down the Hunger Spiral: Pathways to the Disintegration of the Global Food System.* Centre for the Study of Existential Risk at the University of Cambridge. Available at: https://www.cser.ac.uk/news/down-hunger-spiral-pathways-disintegration-global-/

[14] University of Toronto. (2019). *A very small number of crops are dominating globally: That's bad news for sustainable agriculture.* ScienceDaily. Retrieved July 11 2021. Available at: https://www.sciencedaily.com/releases/2019/02/190206161446.htm

[15] Tzachor, A. (2019). *Down the Hunger Spiral: Pathways to the Disintegration of the Global Food System.* Centre for the Study of Existential Risk at the University of Cambridge. Available at: https://www.cser.ac.uk/news/down-hunger-spiral-pathways-disintegration-global-/

[16] Tzachor, A. (2019). *Down the Hunger Spiral: Pathways to the Disintegration of the Global Food System.* Centre for the Study of Existential Risk at the University of Cambridge. Available at: https://www.cser.ac.uk/news/down-hunger-spiral-pathways-disintegration-global-/

[17] Tzachor, A. (2019). *Down the Hunger Spiral: Pathways to the Disintegration of the Global Food System.* Centre for the Study of Existential Risk at the University of Cambridge. Available at: https://www.cser.ac.uk/news/down-hunger-spiral-pathways-disintegration-global-/

[18] Tzachor, A. (2019). *Down the Hunger Spiral: Pathways to the Disintegration of the Global Food System.* Centre for the Study of Existential Risk at the University of Cambridge. Available at: https://www.cser.ac.uk/news/down-hunger-spiral-pathways-disintegration-global-/

[19] Tzachor, A. (2019). *Down the Hunger Spiral: Pathways to the Disintegration of the Global Food System.* Centre for the Study of Existential Risk at the University of Cambridge. Available at: https://www.cser.ac.uk/news/down-hunger-spiral-pathways-disintegration-global-/

15. Trade

[1] Kim, B. et al. (2020). *Country-specific dietary shifts to mitigate climate and water crises.* Global Environmental Change, Volume 62. Available at: https://doi.org/10.1016/j.gloenvcha.2019.05.010

[2] Kim, B. et al. (2020). *Country-specific dietary shifts to mitigate climate and water crises.* Global Environmental Change, Volume 62. Available at: https://doi.org/10.1016/j.gloenvcha.2019.05.010

[3] Pendrill, F. et al. (2019). *Deforestation displaced: trade in forest-risk commodities and the prospects for a global forest transition.* Environ. Res. Lett. 14(5). Available at: https://iopscience.iop.org/article/10.1088/1748-9326/ab0d41

[4] Which?. (2020). *Trade deals and our future.* Available at: https://campaigns.which.co.uk/trade-deals/

[5] Windsor, P. and Lomax, S,. (2013). *Addressing welfare concerns in control of ovine cutaneous myiosis in sheep in Australia.* Small Ruminant Research 110 (2–3) pp.165–169. Available at: https://www.sciencedirect.com/science/article/pii/S0921448812004877

[6] SCARM. (2002). *Primary Industries Standing Committee Model Code of Practice for the Welfare of Animals Domestic Poultry 4th Edition.* Australia: CSIRO Publishing. Available at: https://www.publish.csiro.au/ebook/download/pdf/3451

[7] Oliveira da Silva, I.J., 2019. *Sistemas de produção de galinhas poedeiras no Brasil* [Laying hen production systems in Brazil]. Diálogos União europeia–Brasil. Available at: http://www.sectordialogues.org/documentos/proyectos/adjuntos/b26c49_X-GUIA-GALINHAS-2019.pdf

[8] SCARM. (2002). *Primary Industries Standing Committee Model Code of Practice for the Welfare of Animals Domestic Poultry 4th Edition.* Australia: CSIRO Publishing. Available at: https://www.publish.csiro.au/ebook/download/pdf/3451

[9] World Animal Protection. (2020). *Animal Protection Index (API) 2020.* Available at: https://api.worldanimalprotection.org/country/brazil

[10] Food Standards Australia New Zealand. (2011). *Hormonal growth promotants in beef.* Available at: https://www.foodstandards.gov.au/consumer/generalissues/hormonalgrowth/Pages/default.aspx

[11] Ministry of Agriculture. (2011). *NORMATIVE INSTRUCTION No. 55, DE.* Government of Brazil. Available at: https://www.gov.br/agricultura/pt-br/assuntos/insumos-agropecuarios/insumos-pecuarios/alimentacao-animal/arquivos-alimentacao-animal/legislacao/instrucao-normativa-no-55-de-1o-de-dezembro-de-2011.pdf/view

[12] Dairy Australia. (2021). *Is there an official upper limit for somatic cells in cow's milk production in Australia?* Available at: https://www.dairy.com.au/dairy-matters/you-ask-we-answer/is-there-an-official-upper-limit-for-somatic-cells-in-cows-milk-in-australia

[13] Food Standards Australia New Zealand. (2018). Compendium of Microbiological Criteria for Food. Available at: https://www.foodstandards.gov.au/publications/Documents/Compedium%20of%20Microbiological%20Criteria/Compendium_revised-Sep%202018.pdf

[14] Rodrigues, L. et al. (2017). *A time series analysis of bulk tank somatic cell counts of dairy herds located in Brazil and the United States.* Cienc Rural 47. Available at: https://doi.org/10.1590/0103-8478cr20160618

[15] Rodrigues, C. O. et al. (2005). *Milk quality and new regulations in Brazil.* Journal of Dairy Science 88:272.

[16] legislation.gov.uk. (2007). *Mutilations (Permitted Procedures) (England) Regulations 2007.* The Stationery Office. Available at: https://www.legislation.gov.uk/ukdsi/2007/9780110757797

[17] American Industry Sheep Association. (2005). *Sheep Care Guide.* Available at: http://d1cqrq366w3ike.cloudfront.net/http/DOCUMENT/SheepUSA/Sheep_Care_Guide_2006.pdf

[18] Animal Health Australia. (2016). *Australian Animal Welfare Standards and Guidelines for Sheep.* Available at: http://www.animalwelfarestandards.net.au/files/2011/01/Sheep-Standards-and-Guidelines-for-Endorsed-Jan-2016-061017.pdf

[19] de Freitas, A. et al. (2017). *Bem-estar de ovinos: Revisão [Sheep welfare: review].* Pubvet: Publicações em Medicina Veterinária e Zootecnia, 11(1), pp. 18–29. Available at: https://www.pubvet.com.br/uploads/7a5c41f5a1b85cb7e375fef1fa935c26.pdf

[20] Department of Agriculture and Water Resources (Australia). (2016). *National Standard for Organic and Bio-Dynamic Produce.* Available at: https://www.agriculture.gov.au/sites/default/files/sitecollectiondocuments/aqis/exporting/food/organic/national-standard-edition-3-7.pdf

[21] Ministry of Agriculture, Livestock and Supply. (2017). *Normative Instruction No. 46 of October 6, 2011 (Plant and animal production) – Regulated by IN 17-2014).* Ministry of Agriculture, Livestock and Supply. Available at: https://www.gov.br/agricultura/pt-br/assuntos/sustentabilidade/organicos/legislacao/portugues/instrucao-normativa-no-46-de-06-de-outubro-de-2011-producao-vegetal-e-animal-regulada-pela-in-17-2014.pdf/view

[22] Australian Pork. (no date). *Pigs.* Available at: https://aussiepigfarmers.com.au/pigs/our-housing/sow-stalls/

[23] legislation.gov.au. (2017). *Australia New Zealand Food Standards Code, Schedule 20, Maximum Residue Limits.* Available at: https://www.legislation.gov.au/Details/F2017C00105

[24] World Animal Protection. (2020). *Animal Protection Index (API) 2020.* Available at: https://api.worldanimalprotection.org/country/brazil

[25] Brazilian Agricultural Research Corporation. (2017). *Deposição de resíduos de ractopamina em tecidos de suínos alimentados com farinha de carne e ossos contendo este aditivo.* Available at: https://www.embrapa.br/busca-de-projetos/-/projeto/209276/deposicao-de-residuos-de-ractopamina-em-tecidos-de-suinos-alimentados-com-farinha-de-carne-e-ossos-contendo-este-aditivo

[26] Department of Agriculture, Fisheries and Forestry (Australia). (2012). *Australian animal welfare standards and guidelines: Land transport of livestock.* Available at: http://www.animalwelfarestandards.net.au/files/2021/06/Land-transport-of-livestock-Standards-and-Guidelines-Version-1.-1-21-September-2012.pdf

[27] Ministry of Cities/NATIONAL TRAFFIC COUNCIL. (2017). *OFFICIAL GAZETTE OF THE UNION.* Government of Brazil. Available at: https://www.in.gov.br/materia/-/asset_publisher/Kujrw0TZC2Mb/content/id/19137370/do1-2017-06-26-resolucao-n-675-de-21-de-junho-de-2017-19137266

[28] Langham, F. and Cheng, A. C. (2019). Antibiotic use in animals and humans in Australia. Medical Journal of Australia. 211(4). pp.159–160. Available at: https://www.mja.com.au/system/files/issues/211_04/mja250258.pdf#:~:text=In%20summary%2C%20a%20large%20volume%20of%20antibiotics%20is,be%20addressed%20in%20both%20hospital%20and%20community%20settings

[29] Australian Government. (no date). *AMR and animal health in Australia.* Available at: https://www.amr.gov.au/about-amr/amr-australia/amr-and-animal-health-australia

[30] Prescott, J. (2019). *Veterinary Antimicrobial Stewardship in Australia.* Canadian veterinary journal. 60(3). pp. 246–248. Available at: https://europepmc.org/article/MED/30872846

[31] Bokma-Bakker, M. H. et al. (2014). *Antibiotic use in Brazilian broiler and pig production: An indication and forecast of trends.* Wageningen UR Livestock Research. Available at: https://edepot.wur.nl/297414

[32] Kim, B. et al. (2020). *Country-specific dietary shifts to mitigate climate and water crises.* Global Environmental Change, Volume 62. Available at: https://doi.org/10.1016/j.gloenvcha.2019.05.010

[33] Global Forest Watch. Available at: https://www.globalforestwatch.org/

16. The Plan

[1] Global health data exchange. (2020). *Global Burden of Disease, 2019 data*. Available at: http://ghdx.healthdata.org/gbd-2019

[2] National Food Strategy analysis using data from: : NHS Digital. (2020). Health Survey for England 2019: Adult's health. Available at: https://digital.nhs.uk/data-and-information/publications/statistical/health-survey-for-england/2019; NHS Digital. (2018). Health Survey for England 2017: Cardiovascular diseases. Available at: https://digital.nhs.uk/data-and-information/publications/statistical/health-survey-for-england/2017; NHS Digital. (2020). Healthy Survey for England 2019: overweight and obesity in adults and children. Available at: https://digital.nhs.uk/data-and-information/publications/statistical/health-survey-for-england/2019/health-survey-for-england-2019-data-tables. Population data from: Office for National Statistics. (2020). Population estimates for the UK, England and Wales, Scotland and Northern Ireland: mid-2019. ONS. Available at:https://www.ons.gov.uk/peoplepopulationandcommunity/populationandmigration/populationestimates/bulletins/annualmidyearpopulationestimates/mid2019estimates. Overlap between diabetes and obesity, diabetes and cardiovascular disease and obesity and cardiovascular disease from Health Survey for England. Assumptions: Very high waist circumference (>102cm for men, >88cm for women) assumed to be obese for purposes of cardiovascular disease and obese overlap. Overlaps assumed to be the same across all age groups. Not including diet related cancers as overlap data not available.

[3] Tigbe, W. W. et al. (2013). *A patient-centred approach to estimate total annual healthcare cost by body mass index in the UK Counterweight programme*. Int Journal of Obesity 37 (8), 135–139. Available at: https://pubmed.ncbi.nlm.nih.gov/23164699/

[4] Obesity increases and peaks by the mid-2030s, based on an assumption that tobacco-control like policies (high taxes, regulation of marketing, food environments, and advertising, and significant public health spending) are introduced for unhealthy foods. Janssen, F. et al. (2020). *Obesity Prevalence in the Long-Term Future in 18 European Countries and in the USA*. Obesity Facts, 13(5), 514–527. Available at: https://www.karger.com/Article/Fulltext/511023

[5] Hex, N. et al. (2012). *Estimating the current and future costs of Type 1 and Type 2 diabetes in the UK, including direct health costs and indirect societal and productivity costs*. Diabetic Medicine, 29(7), pp.855–862. Available at: https://pubmed.ncbi.nlm.nih.gov/22537247/; Hofmarcher, T. et al. (2020). *The cost of cancer in Europe 2018*. European Journal of Cancer, 129, pp.41–49. Available at: https://ihe.se/publicering/the-cost-of-cancer-in-europe-2018/

[6] The Health Foundation. (2020). *Public perceptions of health and social care in light of COVID-19 (May 2020)*. Ipsos MORI. Available at: https://www.health.org.uk/publications/reports/public-perceptions-of-health-and-social-care-in-light-of-covid-19-may-2020

[7] We considered a tax on saturated fat, which also contributes to poor diets and diet-related diseases. However, saturated fat is not an added ingredient in the same way that salt and sugar are. It is part of lots of different foods, some of which we eat too much of e.g. processed meat, and others which we need to eat more of, e.g. nuts. You therefore end up in a quagmire of which products you want to tax and which you do not. Furthermore, it would target meat consumption and this, as we have established, is not politically feasible. The complexity of implementation coupled with the difficult political nature means that we do not believe a tax on saturated fat is feasible.

[8] Department of Health and Social Care. (2011). *Statement of the Calorie Reduction Expert Group*. HMG. Available at: https://www.gov.uk/government/publications/statement-of-the-calorie-reduction-expert-group

[9] Global Burden of Disease, 2019 data. Accessed July 2021. Available at: http://ghdx.healthdata.org/gbd-results-tool

[10] Cobiac, L. et al. (2021). *Impact of the Soft Drink Industry Levy on health and health inequalities of children and adolescents in England*. [Pre Publication]

[11] Sugar reduction: Pell, D. et al. (2021). *Changes in soft drinks purchased by British households associated with the UK soft drinks industry levy: controlled interrupted time series analysis*. British Medical Journal, 372. Available at: https://www.bmj.com/content/372/bmj.n254. Overconsumption: Buttriss, J. (2015). *Why 5%?* Public Health England. Available at: https://assets.publishing.service.gov.uk/government/uploads/system/uploads/attachment_data/file/769482/Why_5__-_The_Science_Behind_SACN.pdf

[12] Department for Education. (2014). *The national curriculum in England: framework document*. DFE. Available at: https://assets.publishing.service.gov.uk/government/uploads/system/uploads/attachment_data/file/381344/Master_final_national_curriculum_28_Nov.pdf

[13] Data provided by School Teachers Centre.

[14] Dimbleby, H. and Vincent, J. (2013). *The School Food Plan. Evidence pack*. HMG. Available at: http://www.schoolfoodplan.com/wp-content/uploads/2013/10/School-Food-Plan-Evidence-Pack-July-2013-Final.pdf

[15] Office for National Statistics. (2019). *Health state life expectancies by national deprivation deciles, England and Wales: 2015 to 2017*. ONS. Available at: https://www.ons.gov.uk/releases/healthstatelifeexpectanciesuk2015to2017

[16] NHS Digital. (2020). *National child measurement programme, England 2019/20 school year*. Available at: https://digital.nhs.uk/data-and-information/publications/statistical/national-child-measurement-programme/2019-20-school-year/deprivation

[17] NHS Digital. (2020). *Health survey for England*. Available at: https://digital.nhs.uk/data-and-information/publications/statistical/health-survey-for-england/2019/health-survey-for-england-2019-data-tables

[18] Department for Work and Pensions. (2021). *Family Resources Survey 2019–20*. Available at: https://www.gov.uk/government/statistics/family-resources-survey-financial-year-2019-to-2020/family-resources-survey-financial-year-2019-to-2020#household-food-security-1

[19] Dimbleby, H. and Vincent, J. (2013). *The School Food Plan*. HMG. Available at: http://www.schoolfoodplan.com/wp-content/uploads/2013/10/School-Food-Plan-Evidence-Pack-July-2013-Final.pdf

[20] Food insecurity measurement has been standardised internationally and DWP uses this internationally standardised approach. The FRS asks a series of questions to the person in charge of food purchasing and preparation about their experiences in the previous 30 days. Questions include whether they have always had enough money to buy food before it runs out, whether they have been able to afford balanced meals and whether they have had to change eating habits because of a lack of money. A ten-point household score is generated and households are classified as either having high, marginal, low or very low food security based on their score. Low food security (score 3 to 5) indicates the household reduced the quality, variety and desirability of their diets but the quantity or normal eating patterns were not substantially disrupted. Very low food security (score 6 to 10) indicates the household experienced disrupted eating patterns or reduced their food consumption due to a lack of money or resources.

[21] Lasko-Skinner, R. and Sweetland, J. (2021). *Food in a Pandemic.* Demos. Available at: https://demos.co.uk/wp-content/uploads/2021/03/Food-in-a-Pandemic.pdf

[22] The Trussell Trust. (2018). *Families, hunger, and the holidays.* Available at: https://www.trusselltrust.org/wp-content/uploads/sites/2/2018/08/Families-hunger-and-the-holidays-policy-brief.pdf

[23] Crawley, H. and Dodds, R. (2018). *The UK Healthy Start scheme. What happened? What next?* First Steps Nutrition, p56. Available at: https://static1.squarespace.com/static/59f75004f09ca48694070f3b/t/5b8e2d0e575d1f6f1e5d2dcd/1536044307456/Healthy_Start_Report_for_web.pdf

[24] Office for National Statistics. (2020). *Healthcare expenditure, UK health accounts: 2018.* Available at: https://www.ons.gov.uk/peoplepopulationandcommunity/healthandsocialcare/healthcaresystem/bulletins/ukhealthaccounts/2018

[25] Faculty of Public Health. (2019). *What the NHS thinks about prevention: results of opinion polling of 310 NHS leaders.* FPH. Available at: https://www.fph.org.uk/media/2515/fph-what-the-nhs-thinks-about-prevention-final.pdf

[26] NHS. (2019). *NHS Long term plan.* NHS. Available at: https://www.longtermplan.nhs.uk/wp-content/uploads/2019/08/nhs-long-term-plan-version-1.2.pdf

[27] Expression of interest process: National Health Service. (2021). *Green social prescribing.* NHS. Available at: https://www.england.nhs.uk/personalisedcare/social-prescribing/green-social-prescribing/

[28] Slagel, N. et al. (2018). *The Effects of a Fruit and Vegetable Prescription Program (FVRx)® for Low-Income Individuals on Fruit and Vegetable Intake and Food Purchasing Practices.* Journal of Nutrition Education and Behavior 50 (7). Available at: https://www.sciencedirect.com/science/article/pii/S1499404618303373; Huang, J. et al. (2019). Impact of Fruits and Vegetables Prescription Program in Wellness Group Visits. Pediatrics 144 (706). Available at: https://pediatrics.aappublications.org/content/144/2_MeetingAbstract/706; DC Greens. (2021). *Produce Prescription Program (Produce Rx).* DC Greens. Available at: https://www.dcgreens.org/produce-rx

[29] Finch T. et al. (2019). *Bird conservation and the land sharing-sparing continuum in farmland-dominated landscapes of lowland England.* Conservation Biology. 33(5). 1045–1055. Available at: https://www.cb.iee.unibe.ch/e58878/e337393/e337410/e604441/e876095/Finch_ConBio2019_eng.pdf

[30] Department for Environment, Food & Rural Affairs. (2019). *Farm evidence compendium.* HMG. Available at: https://www.gov.uk/government/publications/the-future-farming-and-environment-evidence-compendium-latest-edition

[31] Conservative and Unionist Party. (2019). *The Conservative and Unionist Manifesto 2019.* Available at: https://assets-global.website-files.com/5da42e2cae7ebd3f8bde353c/5dda924905da587992a064ba_Conservative%202019%20Manifesto.pdf

[32] Trade and Agriculture Commission. (2021). *Final report.* TAC. Available at: https://assets.publishing.service.gov.uk/government/uploads/system/uploads/attachment_data/file/969045/Trade-and-Agriculture-Commission-final-report.pdf

[33] Maintain our standards: Which? (2020). *Ensuring trade deals work for consumers.* Available at: https://campaigns.which.co.uk/trade-deals/wp-content/uploads/sites/31/2020/01/5e2f163d92b97-Trade-deals-v4-2.pdf; Concern over livestock: Unison. (2020). *Public fears a lowering of meat standards in future US trade deals, says UNISON.* Available at: https://www.unison.org.uk/news/article/2020/02/public-fears-lowering-meat-standards-future-us-trade-deals-says-unison/

[34] Annan, K. (2018). *Data can help to end malnutrition across Africa.* Nature 555 (7). Available at: https://pubmed.ncbi.nlm.nih.gov/32094884/

[35] NFS analysis based on feed conversion ratios in Good Food Institute (2021). *Anticipatory life cycle assessment and techno-economic assessment of commercial cultivated meat production.* Available at: https://gfi.org/wp-content/uploads/2021/03/cultured-meat-LCA-TEA-technical.pdf; Type of product: https://www.meatless.nl/

[36] Labiotech. (2021). *Global funding for meat alternative companies tripled in 2020.* Available at: https://www.labiotech.eu/trends-news/solar-foods-meat-alternatives/

[37] Live Kindly. (2020). *How the Netherlands is leading the vegan food industry.* Available at: https://www.livekindly.co/netherlands-leading-vegan-food-industry/

38 Israel: Good Food Institute. (2021). *Israel state of alternative protein innovation report 2021.* Available at: https://gfi.org.il/resources/israel-state-of-alternative-protein-innovation-report-2021/?_ga=2.142138290.1497374895.1622640835-1621113986.1612276626; Singapore: Singapore Food Agency. (no date). *Safety of alternative protein.* Available at: https://www.sfa.gov.sg/food-information/risk-at-a-glance/safety-of-alternative-protein

[39] NFS analysis based on feed conversion ratios in: Good Food Institute. (2021). *Anticipatory life cycle assessment and techno-economic assessment of commercial cultivated meat production.* Available at: https://gfi.org/wp-content/uploads/2021/03/cultured-meat-LCA-TEA-technical.pdf; Tonnes per hectare of input in: Department for Environment Food & Rural Affairs. (2019). *Farming Statistics Final crop areas, yields, livestock populations and agricultural workforce At June 2019 – United Kingdom.* Available at: https://assets.publishing.service.gov.uk/government/uploads/system/uploads/attachment_data/file/865769/structure-jun2019final-uk-22jan20-rev_v2.pdf; Agricultural workers per hectare in: NationMaster. *Agricultural workers per hectare.* Available at: https://www.nationmaster.com/country-info/stats/Agriculture/Workers-per-hectare

[40] National Data Strategy: Department for Digital, Culture, Media & Sport. (2020). *National Data Strategy.* Available at: https://www.gov.uk/government/publications/uk-national-data-strategy/national-data-strategy; Council for Science and Technology: Vallance, P. (2020). *Achieving net zero through a whole systems approach:* Council for Science and Technology letter. Available at: https://www.gov.uk/government/publications/achieving-net-zero-carbon-emissions-through-a-whole-systems-approach

[41] Department for Environment, Food & Rural Affairs. (2014). *A plan for public procurement: food and catering.* Defra. Available at: https://assets.publishing.service.gov.uk/government/uploads/system/uploads/attachment_data/file/332756/food-plan-july-2014.pdf

[42] £2.4bn, 5.5% – estimate based on 2014 data: Department for Environment, Food & Rural Affairs. (2014). A plan for public procurement: food and catering. Defra. Available at: https://assets.publishing.service.gov.uk/government/uploads/system/uploads/attachment_data/file/332756/food-plan-july-2014.pdf

[43] 13.3m people eat in public sector settings each year, which is 24% of the population. NFS Analysis. Sources – NHS: NHS Digital. (2021). *Estates Returns Information Collection Summary page and dataset for ERIC 2018/19.* Available at: https://digital.nhs.uk/data-and-information/publications/statistical/estates-returns-information-collection/england-2018-19; Schools: Office for National Statistics. (2021). *Schools, pupils and their characteristics, Academic year 2021/21.* Available at: https://explore-education-statistics.service.gov.uk/find-statistics/school-pupils-and-their-characteristics; Higher education: Higher Education Statistics Agency. (2021). *Table 1 – HE student enrolments by HE provider 2014/15 to 2019/20.* HESA. Available at: https://www.hesa.ac.uk/data-and-analysis/students/table-1; Prisoners: Ministry of Justice. (2020). *Prison population figures: 2020.* HMG Available at: https://www.gov.uk/government/statistics/prison-population-figures-2020; Care homes: ONS. (2020). *Care home and non-care home populations used in the Deaths involving COVID-19 in the care sector article, England and Wales.* ONS. Available at: https://www.ons.gov.uk/peoplepopulationandcommunity/birthsdeathsandmarriages/deaths/adhocs/12215carehomeandnoncarehomepopulationsusedinthedeathsinvolvingcovid19inthecaresectorarticleenglandandwales; Ministry of Defence: Ministry of Defence. (2020). *Quarterly Service Personnel Statistics 1 July 2020.* HMG. Available at: https://assets.publishing.service.gov.uk/government/uploads/system/uploads/attachment_data/file/920074/1_July_2020_SPS.pdf. Analysis does not include NHS staff and visitors to hospitals as data not available so is likely to be an under estimation.

[44] Breakfast, lunch and snacks at school = 2/3 of weekday food, therefore 0.47 over 7 days; Royston, S., Rodrigues, L. and Hounsell, D. (2012). *Fair and Square: A Policy Report on the Future of Free School Meals.* The Children's Society, p12. Available at: https://d3hgrlq6yacptf.cloudfront.net/5f3ecf1e68cdc/content/pages/documents/1429471607.pdf

[45] The latest available data tells us that in 2013 the top four contract caterers (Compass Group, Sodexo, Westbury Street Holding and Elior) had 61% of the contract catering market share. Source: UK Parliament. (2021). *Written evidence submitted by Dynamic Food Procurement National Advisory Board.* UK Parliament. Available at: https://committees.parliament.uk/writtenevidence/9762/pdf/; European Commission. (2015). *Task 2: Market Analysis (draft) Working Document.* European Commission. Available at: https://susproc.jrc.ec.europa.eu/product-bureau/sites/default/files/contentype/product_group_documents/1581683081/Task%202%20Food%20and%20catering_JRC151015%20clean%20(ammended).docx.pdf

[46] Information and data provided directly to NFS by Bath and North East Somerset Council

[47] King, S. (2017). *Making the case for a place based systems approach: public health professionals' assessment of Sustainable Food Cities.* University of West England. Available at: https://www.sustainablefoodplaces.org/Portals/4/Documents/Making%20the%20case%20for%20a%20place%20based%20systems%20approach-pp.pdf; Hills, S. and Jones, M. (2019). *Sustainable Food Cities: phase 2 evaluation final report. University of West England.* Available at: https://www.sustainablefoodplaces.org/resources/files/documents/Hills_and_Jones_2019_SFC_Final_Report.pdf

Appendices

Recommendation 1. Introduce a sugar and salt reformulation tax. Use some of the revenue to help get fresh fruit and vegetables to low income families.

What is it?

The Government should introduce a £3/kg tax on sugar and a £6/kg tax on salt sold for use in processed foods or in restaurants and catering businesses.

This would encourage manufacturers to reformulate their products to use less sugar and salt, in order to keep costs down. In some cases – where products cannot be reformulated, and therefore remain extremely high in sugar and salt – the increased cost might be passed on to the consumer. This would make such products less appealing.

The tax would apply to all sugar and other ingredients used for sweetening (such as syrups and fruit extracts, but not raw fruit) at a rate of £3/kg. This is approximately the same rate as the current Soft Drinks Industry Levy (SDIL), which the sugar tax would replace.[1] It would apply at a rate of £6/kg to all salt sold for use in food manufacturing. As salt is used in much smaller quantities than sugar, the rate needs to be higher in order to achieve an impact.

Neither tax would apply to ingredients used in home cooking. This exemption could be managed either by taxing sales to manufacturers and food service businesses, or by taxing all sales of sugar and salt when they leave the factory gate and then allowing supermarkets to claim a rebate for sales to consumers. Although small businesses could theoretically abuse this exemption, the quantities of sugar and salt larger businesses require are so great that serious evasion is unlikely in practice. If it did become a problem, retailers could be encouraged to restrict the amount of sugar or salt sold in a single purchase.

In order to stop food manufacturers relocating overseas to avoid these taxes, imports of processed food should also be taxed according to sugar and salt content when they enter the UK. Importers should be required to register for the tax, report the amount of added sugar or salt contained in their product, and pay the tax on that sugar or salt at the same rate as charged domestically.

The taxes should be introduced through primary legislation in the 2024 Finance Bill. There should be a three year period before implementation to facilitate adaptation. Research by the Food Standards Agency suggests that, even under normal circumstances, most food products are reformulated or reviewed by their manufacturers over that time frame.[2]

Rationale

People in the UK eat too much sugar and salt. Adults should consume no more than 30g of sugar a day, but on average we each eat 50g per day. Children eat even more, with teenagers aged 11–18yrs eating an average of 55g per day.[3] This means that, on average, sugar provides over 12% of children and teenagers' total calorie consumption[4] – over twice as much as the Scientific Advisory Committee on Nutrition (SACN) recommends.[5] Similarly, UK adults on average eat 8.4g of salt a day, 40% more than the recommended 6g a day.[6]

This contributes to poor health and costs us millions of disability-adjusted life years (DALYs) per year.[7] Sugar consumption is one of the main contributing factors in people becoming overweight or obese, which is estimated to account for over 1.4 million DALYs annually.[8] It can lead to conditions including diabetes, heart disease and stroke – not to mention tooth decay, which is the leading cause of hospital admissions in children aged 6–10yrs.[9]

Eating too much salt is strongly linked to high blood pressure, which can cause strokes and cardiovascular disease. A meta-analysis found that a high intake of salt was associated with a 23% increase in the risk of stroke and a 14% increase in the risk of cardiovascular disease.[10] Conversely, falls in salt consumption have been associated with substantial improvements in people's health: when salt consumption in northern Japan went down by 4g a day, stroke deaths fell by 80% in spite of the fact that the population's weight, fat intake, alcohol consumption and tobacco use all went up.[11]

People on low incomes and some ethnic minorities are the hardest hit by these harms.[12] The poorest fifth of the population get 12% of their energy from sugar, while the richest get 10%.[13] While this sounds small, over time it can make a significant difference to people's weight and their wider health. Deprivation is strongly linked with weight and diet-related ill health. For example, year six children living in deprived areas are almost twice as likely to be classed as obese or overweight.[14]

As well as the harm it does to individuals, eating too much sugar and salt is bad for the nation's finances. The Organisation for Economic Co-operation and Development (OECD) estimates that obesity already accounts for 8% of annual health expenditure in the UK. That amounts to approximately £18bn, or as much as we spend on the police and fire services combined.[15] Type 2 diabetes (the type linked to poor diet) cost the NHS £8.8bn in 2011/12.[16] And these costs will rise, given that obesity is expected to continue increasing until it peaks at 37% of the population in the mid-2030s.[17] One study estimated that every unit of body mass index put on by every individual raises the UK's annual healthcare costs by £16.[18] By 2035/36, Type 2 diabetes could cost the NHS £15.1bn a year, or one and a half times as much as cancer does today.[19]

It therefore seems clear that we should try to reduce individuals' sugar and salt consumption. We considered a range of mechanisms for doing so. Past policies focused strongly on voluntary measures and individual behaviour change – for example, handing out leaflets or running marketing campaigns to promote healthier diets. Of the 689 diet-related Government policies launched between 1992 and 2020, just under half (43%) put the onus on individuals to change their behaviour, and 37% were policies that supported healthier eating but still required individuals to make better choices (e.g. providing healthy options in canteens).[20] These programmes, especially the ones which required individuals to change their behaviour, have not worked well because they assume that people take balanced, rational decisions about what they eat, and have the motivation, means and ability to act.[21] In many cases – and especially when people are short of money, time and kitchen skills – this is wishful thinking.

Those policies which placed fewer demands on individuals, and more on manufacturers or other food businesses, were usually voluntary.[22] This reduced their effectiveness. While the voluntary salt reduction programme was successful in its early phase, with salt intakes reducing from an average of 9.5g/day in 2000 to 8.1g/day in 2011, progress has since stalled.[23] Only half of the targets for 2017 were met, in part because reporting requirements were weakened and enforcement was minimal.[24] A similar voluntary sugar reduction programme challenged food manufacturers to cut sugar in their products by 20% before 2020, but only achieved a reduction of 3%.[25]

Mandatory interventions have been more successful. Following the introduction of the Soft Drinks Industry Levy (SDIL), the average sugar content of soft drinks fell by 29%. Preliminary results from a study looking at the health impacts of the SDIL estimates it will result in 6,200 fewer decayed and missing teeth and 36,000 fewer cases of obesity in children and teenagers in England.[26] But because of the narrow range of products it covers, it is still not enough to really change people's diets and the health consequences that follow from them. Adults currently consume 20g too much sugar per day, and even if free sugars were totally eliminated from soft drinks, they would still be consuming around 15g too much sugar every day, and teenagers around 16g a day.[27] In reality, the SDIL has only cut average sugar consumption by 1.8g per person, per day.[28]

The evidence suggests, therefore, that we need a measure that places the onus on businesses and not on individuals; that is mandatory and not voluntary; and that covers a wide range of products. This led us to a tax similar to the SDIL, but covering a wider range of products.

Our proposed tax is mandatory for all companies, and places fewer demands on consumers than previous policies. It targets a wide range of processed and prepared foods, which are the principal source of sugar and salt in British people's diets:[29] 85% of the sugar sold in the UK is for use in manufacturing and 75% of the salt we eat comes from processed foods.[30] A tax on the amount of sugar and salt used in these foods will create a significant incentive for companies to reformulate their products so as to avoid having to put the price up, which would be damaging to their business in the UK's highly competitive and price-sensitive food market.[31] We know that industry responds to taxes on unhealthy foods by reformulating. As discussed above, the SDIL produced a reduction in the sugar content of soft drinks of 29%, while the Public Health Product Tax in Hungary encouraged 40% of manufacturers of unhealthy foods to reformulate their products.[32]

Similar measures have been shown to be effective around the world. Sugary drink taxes in Mexico, Barbados, South Africa and the UK have led to reformulation and reduced sales of drinks high in sugar.[33] In Mexico, an 8% tax on non-essential food items with a high calorie content relative to their weight led to a 6% decrease in purchases.[34] In Hungary, a tax on unhealthy foods produced a sustained fall in consumption of those foods by most consumers.[35]

In addition, the evidence suggests that food taxes do not lead to economic damage or job losses. The SDIL had no lasting negative impacts on the UK soft drinks industry: firms' turnover remained constant and share prices continued to grow.[36] A recent study of the food and soft drink tax in Mexico found that it had no impact on employment either in the manufacturing industry or in retail.[37]

There is strong public support for cutting the amount of sugar we eat through taxes on unhealthy food. 70% of respondents in a 2017 survey supported the existing SDIL, and this level of support remained constant after the tax had been in place for almost two years.[38] Half of respondents to a 2018 survey by the Food Standards Agency said they were concerned about the amount of sugar in food.[39] Roughly the same numbers supported taxes on unhealthy food in surveys by Demos and YouGov.[40] Recent polling by the Health Foundation found that 63% of people would support an extension of the SDIL to other sugary foods such as sweets and biscuits, while a survey by the Food, Farming and Countryside Commission found majority support for taxes on foods high in fat, salt and sugar.[41]

Costs and benefits

This tax would have two main effects: incentivising businesses to reformulate their products and driving up the cost of those products which are not reformulated. Costs would therefore be incurred by two main groups: businesses and consumers.

Businesses would incur costs in administering the tax and reformulating their products. Given the scope of the taxes, however, calculating an average cost of reformulation is next to impossible. Some larger manufacturers may achieve economies of scale. Some products are easier to reformulate than others. Sugar reduction is easier in liquid and semi-liquid products such as yoghurt than in biscuits or confectionery, while salt reduction is likely to be more challenging in products such as cured meats and cheeses, where it is used as a preservative as well as for flavour.[42] Nonetheless, there is considerable room for improvement in this area. The tax will incentivise further innovation and reformulation, such as the use of potassium chloride – which is less harmful to health than conventional salt.[43]

Where businesses do not reformulate, consumers will face price rises. This was seen with the SDIL: where drinks were not reformulated, businesses passed on an average of 105–108% of the tax to the consumer (that is, the price went up by slightly more than the tax).[44] Usually, price increases make products less appealing to the consumer – which is, in the case of unhealthy foods, a good thing. If consumers do not change the foods they purchase, the Sugar and Salt Reformulation Tax could produce average price increases of around 16p–20p per adult per day.[45] These price rises would be driven mostly by the tax on sugar, which would lead to price increases of 15–25% in desserts, biscuits, confectionery and juice. Products with little or no added sugar, such as vegetables, fruit, grains, dairy and meat, would not become more expensive. Some examples of price rises are set out in Table 1 below, while full details of our analysis of price rises are set out in the accompanying economic analysis.[46]

Since part of the purpose of the taxes is to change the way people shop, however, the actual price rise experienced by people would be smaller. Consumer responses to price increases differ depending on several factors, including the strength of individual tastes and how easy it is to substitute one product for a cheaper alternative.[47] More details on our methods of assessing price increases can be found in our economic analysis.[48]

Table 1

Examples of predicted price rises for non-reformulated, reformulated and other products

Product	Sugar content per pack	Salt content per pack	Price rise from sugar (per pack)	Price rise from salt (per pack)	Current cost of a pack	Cost of a pack after tax	Current price per 100g	Price per 100g after tax	% increase
Cadbury Dairy Milk [49]	25g	0.11g	7.5p	£0	£0.60	£0.68	£1.34	£1.51	13%
Cadbury Dairy Milk 30% less sugar 35g[50]	13g	0.06g	4p	£0	£0.60	£0.64	£1.72	£1.83	6%
Salt and Vinegar Pringles 200g[51]	3.6g	4.6g	£0 (not free sugars)	3p	£2.50	£2.53	£1.25	£1.26	1%
Tesco Salt and Vinegar Crisps (6x25g)[52]	0.2g	0.4g	£0 (not free sugars)	1p	£0.77	£0.78	£0.51	£0.52	2%
Apples (min. 5 pack)[53]	78.5g	0g	£0 (not free sugars)[54]	0	£1.60	£1.60	£0.27	£0.27	0%

Since people on lower incomes are likely to have diets higher in sugar than richer people, the tax could be seen as regressive: it could have a larger impact on the poor than on the rich. However, the health benefits it could deliver would be progressive, since poorer people are more likely to be overweight and suffer from diet-related diseases. Precisely because people with lower incomes are more sensitive to price changes, they are likely to make bigger changes to their diets to avoid the taxes. Such an effect has been seen in evaluations of the Mexican tax, which has delivered greater health benefits to people with lower incomes.[55]

However, we are concerned about one possible unintended consequence. If hard-pressed families find the cost of their food shop going up, they may actually cut back on healthy food – which, as we have seen, is more expensive per calorie than unhealthy food (especially when you factor in the opportunity cost and difficulty of cooking from scratch).

We have therefore put in place a series of measures to ensure that low-income households get financial support, prioritising healthier foods. The details of these measures are set out under Objective 2. They include expanding free school meals and making the Holiday Activities and Food programme permanent (to support children during term time and during the holidays); an expansion of the Healthy Start scheme (to support diets at home); and trialling a "Community Eatwell" programme that enables GPs to prescribe fruit and vegetables to less affluent families suffering, or at risk of suffering, from diet-related illness. We estimate the total annual cost of these to be £1.1bn, which would be paid for by the tax.

The main financial impact on the Government will be positive. Excluding the enormous long-term gains from improving public health, we estimate the tax could generate between £2.9bn–£3.4bn per year for the Treasury. This includes £2.3bn–£2.8bn from the sugar tax and £570m–£630m from the salt tax.[56] There could be significant administrative costs to the Government in implementing and collecting the tax, especially if the exemption of retail sales is implemented through the provision of rebates to retailers. (This could require additional resourcing from HMRC due to the number of retailers selling sugar and salt in the UK, and also impose administrative requirements on these businesses.) There would be further monitoring costs from ensuring imports of products containing added sugar and salt were subject to the tax too. To ease these costs, the Government may want to consider a "de minimis" threshold, meaning that businesses which use small amounts of sugar, ingredients used for sweetening or salt are not affected by the taxes. This is similar to the Soft Drinks Industry Levy, which only applies to manufacturers which produce over 1 million litres of soft drinks per year.[57] We have not estimated these costs in our modelling.

Further monitoring of the impact of the tax will be required, but these mechanisms largely exist and we do not expect significant increases in costs from these elements. For example, biannual sodium surveys, National Diet and Nutrition Surveys (NDNS) and ongoing analysis of Kantar data will all be required to make sure the taxes are achieving their intended effect. These are already carried out by Public Health England.

It is likely that the benefits of the tax will arise from a combination of the reformulation of products and from changes in people's buying habits in response to price increase. We estimate that, combined, these could lead to a reduction in sugar consumption of n 4–10g per person per day and in salt consumption of 0.2–0.6g per person per day. Given we are not quite certain how much reformulation or change in consumer behaviour there will be, or how these two factors might interact, we have estimated the impacts as ranges. These span scenarios where customers and businesses are relatively unresponsive to the taxes, to those where they are very responsive. Full details of these estimates can be found in our economic analysis.[58]

The estimated reduction in sugar consumption would bring us between 16% and 83% closer to the target level of 30g per person per day, and amount to a cut of between 1kg and 3.6kg of sugar annually.[59] It would reduce the average calories eaten per person per day by 15-38kcal.[60] According to the UK's expert group on calorie reduction, this could completely halt weight gain at a population level (which would require an average reduction of 24kcal per person per day).[61] Modelling by the Department of Health and Social Care (DHSC) suggests that this calorie reduction could save 400,000–1,030,000 quality-adjusted life years (QALYs) over 25 years. Additional modelling for the National Food Strategy by the London School of Hygiene and Tropical Medicine (LSHTM) estimates that the number of QALYs saved over 25 years could be even greater, at 900,000–2,300,000 (worth approximately £1.5bn–3.7bn).[62] Based on the DHSC modelling, the UK's economic output could be between £2.2bn and £5.7bn greater, thanks to a larger and healthier workforce. The NHS could save £1.6bn–£4.1bn and the social care system £1.9bn–£4.8bn. Combining all of these benefits, the total gain to the UK could be as much as £63bn over 25 years.[63]

Similarly, the reduction in salt consumption would bring us between 8% and 25% closer to the target level (6g per person per day). According to modelling by LSHTM for the National Food Strategy, this could save 537,000–1,400,000 QALYs over 25 years and increase the UK's average life expectancy by 0.6–1.8 months per person. The economic value of this could be £22.7bn–£59.3bn across the UK.

The above modelling indicates that of the estimated 1.5 million years of healthy life which are lost to diet-related illness, disease and premature death the Sugar and Salt Tax could save 37,000-97,000 of those years.[64]

These are all conservative estimates: more detail on why this is the case can be found in our economic analysis.[65] By way of example, we have not assessed the positive impact of reductions in portion sizes. Since the UK groceries market is competitive and price-sensitive, manufacturers sometimes choose to shrink the size of portions when the cost of ingredients goes up.[66] If they chose to do so in response to the taxes, it could lead to lower consumption, because consumers are not generally attentive to changes in the size of portions.[67] One estimate has suggested that eliminating larger portions from the diet could reduce the calories consumed by the average British adult by 12–16%.[68] The extent to which this happens will be determined by a range of factors – for example, how producers of similar products respond. But it seems likely that the beneficial impacts of the tax could be even greater than our conservative estimates.

Endnotes

[1] The current upper SDIL rates is 24p per litre if the drink has over 8g of sugar per 100ml. This is around 0.3p per g of sugar.

[2] Food Standards Agency. (2009). Impact assessment of the revised salt reduction targets. HMG. Available at: https://www.legislation.gov.uk/ukia/2009/86/pdfs/ukia_20090086_en.pdf

[3] Public Health England. (2020). NDNS: results from years 9 to 11 (2016 to 2017 and 2018 to 2019). HMG. Available at: https://www.gov.uk/government/statistics/ndns-results-from-years-9-to-11-2016-to-2017-and-2018-to-2019

[4] Public Health England. (2020). NDNS: results from years 9 to 11 (2016 to 2017 and 2018 to 2019). Available at: https://www.gov.uk/government/statistics/ndns-results-from-years-9-to-11-2016-to-2017-and-2018-to-2019

[5] Tedstone, A. et al. (2015) Sugar reduction: the evidence for action. Public Health England. Available at: https://assets.publishing.service.gov.uk/government/uploads/system/uploads/attachment_data/file/470179/Sugar_reduction_The_evidence_for_action.pdf

[6] Average consumption: Niblett, P. et al. (2020) Salt targets 2017: second progress report. Public Health England. Available at: https://www.gov.uk/government/publications/salt-targets-2017-second-progress-report;

Recommended: Scientific Advisory Committee on Nutrition (2003). Salt and health. The Stationery Office. Available at: https://assets.publishing.service.gov.uk/government/uploads/system/uploads/attachment_data/file/338782/SACN_Salt_and_Health_report.pdf

[7] DALYs measure the total years lost to early death, ill-health and disability, thus combining mortality and morbidity. Calculation of DALYs: Tedstone, A. et al. (2015) Sugar reduction: the evidence for action. Public Health England. Available at: https://assets.publishing.service.gov.uk/government/uploads/system/uploads/attachment_data/file/470179/Sugar_reduction_The_evidence_for_action.pdf;

Poor health: Global Burden of Disease Collaborative Network. (2019). Global Burden of Disease Study 2019. GBD Compare Available at: https://vizhub.healthdata.org/gbd-compare/;

Salt and disease: Strazzullo, P. et al. (2009). Salt intake, stroke, and cardiovascular disease: meta-analysis of prospective studies. British Medical Journal, 339. Available at: https://www.bmj.com/content/339/bmj.b4567

[8] DALYs from being overweight or obese: Global Burden of Disease Collaborative Network. (2019). Global Burden of Disease Study 2019. GBD Compare Available at: https://vizhub.healthdata.org/gbd-compare/

[9] Health issues: Changulani, M. et al. (2008). The relationship between obesity and the age at which hip and knee replacement is undertaken. The Journal of Bone and Joint Surgery 90-B(3), 360–363. Available at: https://online.boneandjoint.org.uk/doi/full/10.1302/0301-620X.90B3.19782;

Whitty, C. (2021) Obesity. Gresham College lecture. Available at: https://s3-eu-west-1.amazonaws.com/content.gresham.ac.uk/data/binary/3513/2021-03-24-1800_WHITTY_Obesity-P.pdf;

Cardiovascular disease: Carbone, S. et al. (2019). Obesity paradox in cardiovascular disease: where do we stand? Vascular Health and Risk Management 15, 89–100. Available at: https://pubmed.ncbi.nlm.nih.gov/31118651/;

Stroke: Antillon, D. and Towfighi, A. (2011). No time to "weight": the link between obesity and stroke in women. Women's Health 7(4), 453–463. Available at: https://pubmed.ncbi.nlm.nih.gov/21790338/;

Tooth decay: Tedstone, A. et al. (2015). Sugar reduction: the evidence for action. Public Health England. Available at: https://assets.publishing.service.gov.uk/government/uploads/system/uploads/attachment_data/file/470179/Sugar_reduction_The_evidence_for_action.pdf;

Institute for Quality and Efficiency in Health Care. (2006). Tooth decay: Overview. InformedHealth.org. Available at: https://www.ncbi.nlm.nih.gov/books/NBK279514/;

Hospital admissions in 6–10 year olds: Public Health England. (2019). Child oral health: applying All Our Health. Public Health England. Available at: https://online.boneandjoint.org.uk/doi/full/10.1302/0301-620X.90B3.19782

[10] Strazzullo, P. et al. (2009). Salt intake, stroke, and cardiovascular disease: meta-analysis of prospective studies. British Medical Journal 339. Available at: https://www.bmj.com/content/339/bmj.b4567

[11] Hyseni, L. et al. (2017). Systematic review of dietary salt reduction policies: Evidence for an effectiveness hierarchy? PLOS ONE 12(5). Available at: https://journals.plos.org/plosone/article?id=10.1371/journal.pone.0177535

[12] Sport England. (2020). Overweight adults. HMG. Available at: https://www.ethnicity-facts-figures.service.gov.uk/health/diet-and-exercise/overweight-adults/latest;

Leung, G. and Stanner, S. (2011). Diets of minority ethnic groups in the UK: influence on chronic disease risk and implications for prevention. Nutrition Bulletin 36(2), 161–198. Available at: https://onlinelibrary.wiley.com/doi/full/10.1111/j.1467-3010.2011.01889.x

[13] NFS Analysis of Public Health England. (2020). NDNS years 7-8. Available at: https://www.gov.uk/government/collections/national-diet-and-nutrition-survey

[14] NFS Analysis of PHE Public Health Outcomes Framework: Public Health England. (2013). Public Health Outcomes Framework. HMG. Available at: https://fingertips.phe.org.uk/profile/public-health-outcomes-framework

[15] Organisation for Economic Co-operation and Development. (2019). The heavy burden of obesity: The economics of prevention. OECD Publishing. Available at: https://www.oecd.org/health/the-heavy-burden-of-obesity-67450d67-en.htm

[16] Department of Health and Social Care. (2015). 2010 to 2015 government policy: cancer research and treatment. HMG. Available at: https://www.gov.uk/government/publications/2010-to-2015-government-policy-cancer-research-and-treatment

[17] Janssen, F. et al. (2020). Obesity prevalence in the long-term future in 18 European countries and in the USA. Obesity Facts 13(5), 514–527. Available at: https://www.karger.com/Article/Fulltext/511023

[18] Tigbe, W. W. et al. (2013). A patient-centred approach to estimate total annual healthcare cost by body mass index in the UK Counterweight programme. International Journal of Obesity 37(8), 135–139. Available at: https://pubmed.ncbi.nlm.nih.gov/23164699/

[19] Hex, N. et al. (2012). Estimating the current and future costs of Type 1 and Type 2 diabetes in the UK, including direct health costs and indirect societal and productivity costs. Diabetes Medicine 29(7), 855-862. Available at: https://pubmed.ncbi.nlm.nih.gov/22537247/; Hofmarcher, T. et al. (2020). The cost of cancer in Europe 2018. European Journal of Cancer 129, 41-49. Available at: https://pubmed.ncbi.nlm.nih.gov/32120274/

[20] Theis, D. R. Z. and White, M. (2021). Is obesity policy in England fit for purpose? Analysis of Government strategies and policies, 1992–2020. The Milbank Quarterly 99, 126–170. Available at: https://onlinelibrary.wiley.com/doi/10.1111/1468-0009.12498

[21] Adams, J. et al. (2016). Why are some population interventions for diet and obesity more equitable and effective than others? The role of individual agency. PLOS Medicine 13(4). Available at: https://journals.plos.org/plosmedicine/article?id=10.1371/journal.pmed.1001990

[22] Theis, D. R. Z. and White, M. (2021). Is obesity policy in England fit for purpose? Analysis of Government strategies and policies, 1992–2020. The Milbank Quarterly 99, 126–170. Available at: https://onlinelibrary.wiley.com/doi/10.1111/1468-0009.12498

[23] He, F. J. (2013). Salt reduction in the United Kingdom: a successful experiment in public health. Journal of Human Hypertension 28(6), 345–352. Available at: https://pubmed.ncbi.nlm.nih.gov/24172290/

[24] Half targets met in 2017: Tedstone, A. et al. (2018). Salt targets 2017: Progress report. Public Health England. Available at: https://assets.publishing.service.gov.uk/government/uploads/system/uploads/attachment_data/file/765571/Salt_targets_2017_progress_report.pdf;

No further intervention: Laverty, A. A. et al. (2019). Quantifying the impact of the Public Health Responsibility Deal on salt intake, cardiovascular disease and gastric cancer burdens: interrupted time series and microsimulation study. Journal of Epidemiology and Community Health 73(9), 881–887. Available at: https://jech.bmj.com/content/73/9/881

[25] Coyle, N. et al. (2020) Sugar reduction: progress report, 2015 to 2019. Public Health England. Available at: https://www.gov.uk/government/publications/sugar-reduction-report-on-progress-between-2015-and-2019

[26] Impact of SDIL: Scarborough, P. et al. (2020). Impact of the announcement and implementation of the UK Soft Drinks Industry Levy on sugar content, price, product size and number of available soft drinks in the UK, 2015–19: A controlled interrupted time series analysis. PLOS Medicine 17(2). Available at: https://journals.plos.org/plosmedicine/article?id=10.1371/journal.pmed.1003025;

Impact on children and adolescents: Cobiac, L. et al. (upcoming). Impact of the Soft Drink Industry Levy on health and health inequalities of children and adolescents in England.

[27] Sugar reduction: Pell, D. et al. (2021). Changes in soft drinks purchased by British households associated with the UK Soft Drinks Industry Levy: controlled interrupted time series analysis. British Medical Journal 372. Available at: https://www.bmj.com/content/372/bmj.n254;

Overconsumption: Public Health England. (2020). NDNS: results from years 9 to 11 (2016 to 2017 and 2018 to 2019). HMG. Available at: https://www.gov.uk/government/statistics/ndns-results-from-years-9-to-11-2016-to-2017-and-2018-to-2019

[28] Pell, D. et al. (2021). Changes in soft drinks purchased by British households associated with the UK soft drinks industry levy: controlled interrupted time series analysis. British Medical Journal 372. Available at: https://www.bmj.com/content/372/bmj.n254

[29] Salt in processed foods: Ni Mhurchu, C. et al. (2010). Sodium content of processed foods in the United Kingdom: analysis of 44,000 foods purchased by 21,000 households. American Journal of Clinical Nutrition 93(3), 594–600. Available at: https://pubmed.ncbi.nlm.nih.gov/21191142/;

Need for salt reduction: Nicholas, J. et al. (2020). Salt reduction targets for 2024. Public Health England. Available at: https://www.gov.uk/government/publications/salt-reduction-targets-for-2024;

Need for sugar reduction. Tedstone, A. et al. (2017). Sugar Reduction: Achieving the 20%. Public Health England. Available at: https://assets.publishing.service.gov.uk/government/uploads/system/uploads/attachment_data/file/604336/Sugar_reduction_achieving_the_20_.pdf

[30] Sugar: AB Sugar. (2021). The UK sugar sector. AB Sugar. Available at: https://www.absugar.com/sugar-markets/uk-sugar-sector;

Salt: Murray, C. et al. (2002). Cardiovascular death and Disability can be reduced by more than 50 percent. World Health Organization. Available at: https://www.who.int/news/item/17-10-2002-cardiovascular-death-and-disability-can-be-reduced-more-than-50-percent

[31] D'Angelo, C. et al. (2000). Food consumption in the UK: Trends, attitudes and drivers. RAND Corporation. Available at: https://www.rand.org/pubs/research_reports/RR4379.html

[32] Hungary: World Health Organization. (2015). Good Practice Brief – Public Health Product Tax in Hungary. WHO. Available at: http://www.euro.who.int/__data/assets/pdf_file/0004/287095/Good-practice-brief-public-health-product-tax-in-hungary.pdf

[33] Mexico: Colchero, M. A. et al. (2016) Beverage purchases from stores in Mexico under the excise tax on sugar sweetened beverages: observational study. British Medical Journal 352. Available at: https://www.bmj.com/content/352/bmj.h6704;

Barbados: Alvarado, M. et al. (2019). Assessing the impact of the Barbados sugar-sweetened beverage tax on beverage sales: an observational study. International Journal of Behavioral Nutrition and Physical Activity 16(1). Available at: https://ijbnpa.biomedcentral.com/articles/10.1186/s12966-019-0776-7;

South Africa: Stacey, N. et al. (2021). Changes in beverage purchases following the announcement and implementation of South Africa's Health Promotion Levy: an observational study. The Lancet Planetary Health 5(4), 200–208. Available at: https://www.thelancet.com/journals/lanplh/article/PIIS2542-5196(20)30304-1/fulltext;

UK: Coyle, N. et al. (2020) Sugar reduction report on progress 2015–2019. Public Health England. Available at: https://assets.publishing.service.gov.uk/government/uploads/system/uploads/attachment_data/file/925027/SugarReportY3.pdf

[34] Taillie, L. S. et al. (2017). Do high vs. low purchasers respond differently to a nonessential energy-dense food tax? Two-year evaluation of Mexico's 8% nonessential food tax. Preventive medicine 105S, S37–S42. Available at: https://www.ncbi.nlm.nih.gov/pubmed/28729105

[35] Martos, E. et al. (2015). Assessment of a public health product tax final report. World Health Organisation. Available at: https://www.euro.who.int/__data/assets/pdf_file/0008/332882/assessment-impact-PH-tax-report.pdf?ua=1

[36] Share prices and turnover: Law, C. (2020). An analysis of the stock market reaction to the announcements of the UK Soft Drinks Industry Levy. Economics & Human Biology 38, 100834. Available at: https://www.sciencedirect.com/science/article/pii/S1570677X19302096;

Sales volume: Pell, D. et al. (2021). Changes in soft drinks purchased by British households associated with the UK soft drinks industry levy: controlled interrupted time series analysis. British Medical Journal 372. Available at: https://www.bmj.com/content/372/bmj.n254

[37] Guerrero-López, C. M. et al. (2017). Employment changes associated with the introduction of taxes on sugar-sweetened beverages and nonessential energy-dense food in Mexico. Preventive Medicine 105, S43–S49. Available at: https://pubmed.ncbi.nlm.nih.gov/28890354/

[38] Initial support: Pell, D. et al. (2019). Support for, and perceived effectiveness of, the UK soft drinks industry levy among UK adults: cross-sectional analysis of the International Food Policy Study. British Medical Journal 9(3). Available at: https://bmjopen.bmj.com/content/bmjopen/9/3/e026698.full.pdf;

Support after 2 years: Adams, J. et al. (upcoming). Change in public acceptability of the UK Soft Drinks Industry Levy in UK adults from before to after implementation: repeat cross-sectional analysis of the international food policy study (2017–2019).

[39] Prior, G. et al. (2011). Exploring food attitudes and behaviours in the UK: Findings from the Food and You Survey 2010. HMG. Available at: https://www.food.gov.uk/sites/default/files/media/document/food-and-you-2010-main-report.pdf

[40] Demos: Demos. (2020). Major food reformulation should be at the centre of Boris Johnson's obesity strategy, says new report from Demos. Demos. Available at: https://demos.co.uk/press-release/major-food-reformulation-should-be-at-the-centre-of-boris-johnsons-obesity-strategy-says-new-report-from-demos/;

YouGov: YouGov. (2019). Generally speaking, do you approve or disapprove of government putting higher taxes on food and drinks that are high in fat, sugar and salt, as a way of combatting obesity and health problems? YouGov. Available at: https://yougov.co.uk/topics/health/survey-results/daily/2019/07/03/2cbe9/1

[41] Health Foundation. (2020). Public perceptions of health and social care in light of COVID-19. Ipsos Mori. Available at: https://www.health.org.uk/publications/reports/public-perceptions-of-health-and-social-care-in-light-of-covid-19-may-2020;

Food Farming and Countryside Commission. (upcoming). Shifting the food system: Frames to speed policy change. FFCC.

[42] Reformulation: Buttriss, J. (2013). Food reformulation: The challenges to the food industry. Proceedings of the Nutrition Society 72(1), 61–69. Available at: https://pubmed.ncbi.nlm.nih.gov/23228239/;

Sugar: van der Sman, R.G. M. and Renzetti, S. (2019). Understanding functionality of sucrose in biscuits for reformulation purposes. Critical Reviews in Food Science and Nutrition 59(14), 2225–2239. Available at: https://doi.org/10.1080/10408398.2018.1442315;

Salt: Taormina, P. J. (2010). Implications of salt and sodium reduction on microbial food safety. Critical Reviews in Food Science and Nutrition 50(3), 209–227. Available at: https://pubmed.ncbi.nlm.nih.gov/20301012/

[43] Tedstone, A. et al. (2015) Sugar reduction: the evidence for action. Public Health England. Available at: https://assets.publishing.service.gov.uk/government/uploads/system/uploads/attachment_data/file/470179/Sugar_reduction_The_evidence_for_action.pdf;

Scientific Advisory Committee on Nutrition, and the Committee on Toxicity of Chemicals in Food, Consumer Products and the Environment. (2017). SACN-COT statement on potassium-based sodium replacers: assessment of the health benefits and risks of using potassium-based sodium replacers in foods in the UK. HMG. Available at: https://assets.publishing.service.gov.uk/government/uploads/system/uploads/attachment_data/file/660526/SACN_COT_-_Potassium-based_sodium_replacers.pdf;

Nicholas, J. et al. (2020). Salt reduction targets for 2024. Public Health England. Available at: https://www.gov.uk/government/publications/salt-reduction-targets-for-2024

[44] O'Connell, M. and Smith, K. (2020) Corrective tax design and market power. CEPR. Available at: https://martinoconnell85.github.io/Mywebsite/CorrectiveTaxDesignandMarketPower.pdf

[45] Calculated based on the average household being 2.4 people: Office for National Statistics. (2021). Families and households in the UK: 2020. HMG. Available at: https://www.ons.gov.uk/peoplepopulationandcommunity/birthsdeathsandmarriages/families/bulletins/familiesandhouseholds/2020;

Tedstone, A. et al. (2017). Sugar Reduction: Achieving the 20%. Public Health England. Available at: https://assets.publishing.service.gov.uk/government/uploads/system/uploads/attachment_data/file/604336/Sugar_reduction_achieving_the_20_.pdf;

Nicholas, J. et al. (2020). Salt reduction targets for 2024. Public Health England. Available at: https://assets.publishing.service.gov.uk/government/uploads/system/uploads/attachment_data/file/915406/2024_salt_reduction_targets_070920-FINAL-1.pdf

[46] Griffith, R. et al. (upcoming). The impact of a tax on added sugar and salt. Institute of Fiscal Studies and University of Manchester.

[47] Dubois, P. (2020). How well targeted are soda taxes? American Economic Review 110(11), 3661–3704. Available at: https://www.aeaweb.org/articles?id=10.1257/aer.20171898

[48] Griffith, R. et al. (upcoming). The impact of a tax on added sugar and salt. Institute of Fiscal Studies and University of Manchester.

[49] Tesco. (2021). Cadbury Dairy Milk 45G. Tesco. Available at: https://www.tesco.com/groceries/en-GB/products/275565630

[50] Tesco. (2021). Cadbury Dairy Milk 30% Less Sugar Chocolate Bar 35G. Tesco. Available at: https://www.tesco.com/groceries/en-GB/products/302301194

[51] Tesco. (2021). Pringles Salt and Vinegar 200G. Tesco. Available at: https://www.tesco.com/groceries/en-GB/products/296734905

[52] Tesco. (2021). Tesco Salt & Vinegar Crisps 6x25g. Tesco. Available at: https://www.tesco.com/groceries/en-GB/products/254926691

[53] Tesco. (2021). Tesco Braeburn Apple Minimum 5 Pack. Tesco. Available at: https://www.tesco.com/groceries/en-GB/products/284475671

[54] Swan, G.E. et al. (2018). A definition of free sugars for the UK. Public Health Nutrition 21(9), 1636–1638. Available at: https://www.cambridge.org/core/journals/public-health-nutrition/article/definition-of-free-sugars-for-the-uk/2A2B3A70999052A15FD157C105B3D745

[55] Batis, C. et al. (2016). First-year evaluation of Mexico's tax on non-essential energy-dense foods: an observational study. PLOS Medicine 13(7). Available at: https://pubmed.ncbi.nlm.nih.gov/27379797/

[56] NFS Analysis. Based on population of England in: Office for National Statistics. (2020) Population estimates for the UK, England and Wales, Scotland and Northern Ireland: mid-2019. Available at: https://www.ons.gov.uk/peoplepopulationandcommunity/populationandmigration/populationestimates/bulletins/annualmidyearpopulationestimates/mid2019estimates;

Kilocalorie requirements, and estimated reduction in sugar consumption following tax based on: Griffith, R. et al. (upcoming). The impact of a tax on added sugar and salt. Institute of Fiscal Studies and University of Manchester.

[57] HM Revenue & Customs. (2020). Register for Soft Drinks Industry Levy. HMG. Available at: https://www.gov.uk/guidance/register-for-the-soft-drinks-industry-levy

[58] Griffith, R. et al. (upcoming). The impact of a tax on added sugar and salt. Institute of Fiscal Studies and University of Manchester.

[59] The wide range is because free sugar consumption differs according to gender and age. For example, adults aged 19–64yrs consume an average of 50g/day; teenagers aged 11–18yrs an average of 55g/day and adults aged 65+yrs 42g/day. Public Health England. (2020). NDNS: results from years 9 to 11 (2016 to 2017 and 2018 to 2019). HMG. Available at: https://www.gov.uk/government/statistics/ndns-results-from-years-9-to-11-2016-to-2017-and-2018-to-2019

[60] Calories calculated by multiplying the sugar reduction by 3.75. This is on the basis that there are 3.75 calories in 1 gram of sugar. Source: Public Health England. (2021). McCance and Widdowson's The Composition of Food Integrated Dataset 2021. HMG. Available at: https://assets.publishing.service.gov.uk/government/uploads/system/uploads/attachment_data/file/971021/McCance_and_Widdowsons_Composition_of_Foods_integrated_dataset_2021.pdf

[61] Department of Health and Social Care. (2011). Statement of the Calorie Reduction Expert Group. HMG. Available at: https://www.gov.uk/government/publications/statement-of-the-calorie-reduction-expert-group

[62] The difference between the estimates are mainly because DHSC use a smaller population than the LSHTM model and the LSHTM model considers the impact of sugars through putting on weight, but also through other mechanisms, e.g. sugar reducing the level of High Density Lipoprotein "good" cholesterol which increases the risk of heart attack. The DHSC model only looks at the impact of sugar through reduction in BMI.

[63] This model carries significant uncertainty and does not include all obesity-related conditions, e.g. stroke, so benefits are anticipated to be an underestimate. Full model details: Department of Health and Social Care. (2018). Technical consultation document: Department of Health and Social Care (DHSC) calorie model. HMG. Available at: https://assets.publishing.service.gov.uk/government/uploads/system/uploads/attachment_data/file/736417/dhsc-calorie-model-technical-document.pdf

[64] Global Burden of Disease Collaborative Network. (2019). Global Burden of Disease Study 2019. GHDx. Available at: http://ghdx.healthdata.org/gbd-results-tool

[65] Griffith, R. et al. (upcoming). The impact of a tax on added sugar and salt. Institute of Fiscal Studies and University of Manchester.

[66] Chocolate bars: Office for National Statistics. (2017). Shrinkflation and the price of chocolate. HMG. Available at: https://www.ons.gov.uk/economy/inflationandpriceindices/articles/shrinkflation-andthechangingcostofchocolate/2017-07-24;

SDIL: Wood, Z. (2018). Coca-cola to sell smaller bottles at higher prices in response to sugar tax. The Guardian. Available at: https://www.theguardian.com/society/2018/jan/05/coca-cola-to-sell-smaller-bottles-at-higher-prices-in-response-to-sugar-tax;

Size of soft drinks: Scarborough, P. et al. (2020). Impact of the announcement and implementation of the UK Soft Drinks Industry Levy on sugar content, price, product size and number of available soft drinks in the UK, 2015–19: A controlled interrupted time series analysis. PLOS Medicine 17(2). Available at: https://journals.plos.org/plosmedicine/article?id=10.1371/journal.pmed.1003025

[67] Portion size: Rolls, B. J. (2002). Portion size of food affects energy intake in normal-weight and overweight men and women. The American Journal of Clinical Nutrition 76(6), 1207–1213. Available at: https://pubmed.ncbi.nlm.nih.gov/12450884/;

Price changes rather than quality: Gourville, J. T. and Koehler, J. J. (2004). Downsizing price increases: a greater sensitivity to price than quantity in consumer markets. SSRN. Available at: https://papers.ssrn.com/sol3/papers.cfm?abstract_id=559482

[68] Marteau, T. M. et al. (2015). Downsizing: policy options to reduce portion sizes to help tackle obesity. British Medical Journal 351. Available at: https://www.bmj.com/content/bmj/351/bmj.h5863.full.pdf

Recommendation 2. Introduce mandatory reporting for large food companies.

What is it?

All food businesses with over 250 employees should have a legal duty to publish annual data on their sales of various product types as well as food waste.

This duty would extend to retailers, restaurants and fast food outlets, contract caterers, wholesalers, manufacturers and online ordering platforms.[1] Food businesses with a franchising model would be treated as the sum of their franchisees operating under the same brand.

The report should include figures (both value in sterling and volume in tonnes) for:

- Sales of food and drink high in fat, sugar or salt (HFSS) excluding alcohol.
- Sales of protein by type (of meat, dairy, fish, plant, or alternative protein) and origin.[2]
- Sales of vegetables.
- Sales of fruit.
- Sales of major nutrients: fibre, saturated fat, sugar and salt.
- Food waste.
- Total food and drink sales.

The metrics should be reviewed every five years. The legislative basis for mandatory reporting should be a Good Food Bill, which we recommend should be introduced in the fourth session of this Parliament (2023/2024) (see Recommendation 14).

The metrics should be captured as a percentage of the volume of all of food and soft drink sales, to allow like-for-like comparison, year on year. This will also allow for shifts in market share over time, so that any company which grows significantly over the reporting period is not punished for its success.

The data should be reported through an online portal and made publicly available at the company level, rather than at an aggregate sector level. The Food Standards Agency (FSA) should develop the portal and provide guidance required by companies to standardise reporting, so there is a common set of definitions and data standards in place. The data would form part of the FSA's annual report to Parliament on the state of the food system (see Recommendation 14).

In making this recommendation, we are keen to avoid a proliferation in the metrics on which businesses are already required to report. Therefore, the FSA should maximise opportunities for harmonisation with other data reporting initiatives, such as the World Benchmarking Alliance.

Rationale

Substantial shifts in the nation's diet are required if we are to reduce the environmental and health impacts of our consumption, while supporting the high standards of food, farming and animal welfare that the public expects.

Disclosure of data – and the public scrutiny that comes with it – encourages businesses to take action to improve their practices. For example, the Carbon Disclosure Project (which runs a global disclosure system to help companies manage their environmental impact) has found that when companies disclose data on their carbon emissions for the first time, just 38% of them have an emission reduction target in place. By the third year they disclose, however, this increases to 69%.[3] Transparency by itself incentivises companies to improve.[4]

Reporting data makes it easier for investors to know what is going on in the companies they own, and to pressure management for change. The ShareAction Workforce Disclosure Initiative led to 140 of the world's largest companies agreeing to publish data on their workforces.[5] This enabled 70 investors in Amazon to make their views known in relation to an attempt to form a trade union in Alabama.[6]

Experience shows that reporting has more of an impact when governments make it a legal requirement with precise specifications. For example, the introduction of mandatory reporting on the gender pay gap, and a standard method to assess it, has helped to narrow that gap.[7] But the scheme needs to be well designed: even where reporting is mandatory, as in the case of modern slavery, it can have a limited impact if enforcement is weak and there is a lack of transparency and accountability.[8] The design of this recommendation is based on lessons learned from previous similar efforts, including these two examples.

The ultimate aim of the proposal is to change sales and consumption patterns for the foods for which reporting is required. This is important because these foods account for the main discrepancies between what the Government recommends people eat and what they actually do. Two-thirds of the population eat less than the minimum recommended level of fruit and vegetables and a third eat more than the maximum recommended level of red and processed meat. Across the population, we would need to increase our fibre intake by 50% and cut our consumption of sugar, salt and saturated fat by 12–40% to meet the recommended levels.[9] These discrepancies have a number of serious consequences for our health and the environment, which are outlined under other recommendations.

We recommend exempting smaller food businesses (those with fewer than 250 staff) for three reasons: larger businesses make up the vast majority of the overall sector, the administrative burden for smaller businesses would be too onerous, and enforcement would be too difficult.

Costs and benefits

Reporting requirements will make it possible to identify where businesses are making progress in helping their customers to shift to healthier and more sustainable diets, and where they are not. It will encourage action by businesses to improve the figures they report. This action is likely to take three forms:

1. Increasing the availability of healthier products, which are currently lacking across a number of product categories. For example, only 0–9% of pasta, ready meals and sandwiches on sale are high in fibre.[10] Businesses wanting to improve their figures may invest in new products that are healthier and more sustainable.

2. Reformulating existing products, to reduce sales of less healthy foods and drive up sales of healthier ones. Some retailers are already taking steps in this direction: for example, Tesco's Beef Mince With Vegetables contains around a third less beef than normal mince and more fibre and vegetables.[11] Reporting requirements will create incentives for further such progress.

3. Improving the marketing of healthy products. Currently less than 2% of food and drink advertising spend goes on vegetables.[12] We know that when they are advertised, consumption goes up, as shown by the vegetable advertising campaign "Eat Them to Defeat Them".[13] If businesses have stronger incentives to increase consumption of healthy products, they are likely to spend more on promoting them.

We have not assessed the cost to businesses for this recommendation. We do not expect significant costs, as most businesses already track their sales and report Electronic Point of Sales (EPOS) data to the Office for National Statistics.[14]

Endnotes

[1] "'Food business' means any undertaking, whether for profit or not and whether public or private, carrying out any of the activities related to any stage of production, processing and distribution of food" – see https://www.legislation.gov.uk/eur/2002/178/article/3

[2] For all protein this should include country of origin. For pork, poultry, dairy, eggs and fish, it should additionally include welfare or method of production accreditations (e.g. Red Tractor, Royal Society for the Prevention of Cruelty to Animals, Freedom Food, organic, pasture-fed, Better Chicken Commitment, Marine Stewardship Council).

[3] Gleed, J. (2018). COP24: Time to ramp up the Paris Agreement. CPD. Available at: https://www.cdp.net/en/articles/governments/cop24-time-to-ramp-up-the-paris-agreement

[4] Food Foundation. (2020). Plating up progress 2020. Food Foundation. Available at: https://foodfoundation.org.uk/wp-content/uploads/2020/11/Plating-up-Progress-2020.pdf

[5] Share Action. (2020). Workforce disclosure initiative. Share Action. Available at: https://shareaction.org/workforce-disclosure-initiative/why-disclose-to-the-wdi/workforce-disclosure-initiative-2020-findings/

[6] Canales, K. (2021). Amazon's own investors are reportedly telling the company to stop pressuring warehouse workers who have begun to vote on forming the firm's first union. Insider. Available at: https://www.businessinsider.com/amazon-investors-tell-company-stop-interfere-union-vote-2021-2?r=US&IR=T

[7] Blundell, J. (2021). Wage responses to gender pay gap reporting requirements. Centre for Economic Performance Discussion Papers 1750. Centre for Economic Performance, London School of Economics. Available at: https://cep.lse.ac.uk/pubs/download/dp1750.pdf

[8] Field, F. et al. (2019). Independent review of the Modern Slavery Act 2015: Final Report. Home Office. Available at: https://assets.publishing.service.gov.uk/government/uploads/system/uploads/attachment_data/file/803554/Independent_review_of_the_Modern_Slavery_Act_-_final_report__print_.pdf

[9] Failing to meet dietary recommendations, NFS analysis of: Public Health England. (2020). NDNS. results from years 9 to 11 (2016 to 2017). HMG. Available at: https://www.gov.uk/government/statistics/ndns-results-from-years-9-to-11-2016-to-2017-and-2018-to-2019

[10] Data kindly provided by FoodDB. FoodDB is a University of Oxford research project funded by the NIHR Biomedical Centre in Oxford.

[11] Tesco. (2021). Tesco 5% beef mince with vegetables, 750g. Tesco. Available at: https://www.tesco.com/groceries/en-GB/products/303174883

[12] Food Foundation. (2016). Veg facts: a briefing by the Food Foundation. Food Foundation. Available at: https://foodfoundation.org.uk/wp-content/uploads/2016/11/FF-Veg-Doc-V5.pdf

[13] Veg Power and ITV. (2021). "Eat them to defeat them" campaign evaluation. Veg Power. Available at: https://www.gsttcharity.org.uk/what-we-do/our-projects/%E2%80%98eat-them-defeat-them%E2%80%99-campaign-evaluation

[14] Office for National Statistics. (2017). Consumer price indices, a brief guide: 2017. ONS. Available at: https://www.ons.gov.uk/economy/inflationandpriceindices/articles/consumerpriceindicesabriefguide/2017

Recommendation 3. Launch a new "Eat and Learn" initiative for schools.

What is it?

The Department for Education (DfE) should launch a new "Eat and Learn" initiative for all children 3–18 yrs, in partnership with the new Office of Health Promotion. This would make learning to eat well part of every child's school experience. It would involve the following elements:

1. Curriculum changes
2. Accreditation
3. Inspection
4. Funding
5. Recruitment and training

Curriculum changes

Although schools have had a legal obligation to teach since 2014, food education remains a second-class subject. To ensure that food is taken seriously there needs to be change at all levels of the education system, from teaching staff to Government.

a. Sensory education for early years: the DfE should update the Early Years Foundation Stage framework (the curriculum standards that apply to children in nursery and reception classes) to include sensory food education. This teaching method – in which children are introduced to new foods and encouraged to explore them with all five senses – has been shown to increase children's willingness to try fruit and vegetables.[1]

b. Reinstate the food A-level: This would ensure that beyond 16 there is a proper qualification available for students wishing to continue studying food and nutrition after their GCSEs, whether that is purely because of interest in the subject or in preparation for careers in hospitality and other food related professions. The A-Level should first undergo a substantial redesign, conducted in consultation with food education experts and specialists. The new A-level should include learning about the food system and where our food comes from, and how the food we eat affects the environment and our health.

c. Review other qualifications: the DfE should conduct a qualification review to ensure that existing and new qualifications such as T Levels in Science and Catering provide an adequate focus on food and nutrition, and a progression route for students after GCSEs. This is particularly important in light of the post EU Exit skills shortage in hospitality.

Accreditation

Schools should be encouraged to adopt a "whole-school approach" to food. This means integrating food into the life of the school: the dining hall should be treated as the hub of the school, where children and teachers eat together; lunch treated as part of the school day; the cooks as important staff members; and food as part of a rounded education.[2] The Government should require all schools to work with accreditation schemes - such as Food for Life - to improve school food and education using this whole school approach.

These accreditation bodies would provide training and support for leaders and staff. There are various organisations that provide, or are in the process of developing, suitable online training. For example, schools could use the online professional standards and training that the Local Authority Caterers' Association have developed.

As an absolute minimum, to achieve bronze certification, schools should be required to: account for how school food funds had been adequately spent; fully comply with the School Food Standards (for nutrition) and Government Buying Standards for Food (for procurement); demonstrate that the food and nutrition curriculum was being met; and ensure their catering staff (whether employed directly or through contractors) are adequately trained to deliver quality meals.

Inspection

Ofsted should assess the quality of food and nutrition lessons with the same rigour as they do English or Maths lessons. When Ofsted inspects a school, it conducts deep dives of a sample of the subjects taught. This involves meeting curriculum and subject leaders to understand the way that the curriculum has been designed, its strengths and weaknesses, and check how core topics are being covered. The only subject that is always inspected in this way is reading (in primary schools). Ofsted should ensure that inspectors conduct deep dives in food and nutrition classes as often as they do for other subjects, to ensure that all schools are taking the subject as seriously as they should.

Ofsted should also publish a regular food and nutrition "research review". Starting in April 2021 Ofsted uses research to establish an evidence-based understanding of the quality of a school subject. These reviews are based on existing literature and present research relevant to the specific curriculum. Reviewing food and nutrition will improve both the status and the quality of the subject.

Ofsted should ensure that mandatory certification under the accreditation scheme has been successfully executed, and should consider the certification award level in their overall school rating.

Funding

We recommend that the government should pay for the ingredients that children use in cooking lessons (as they do for schoolbooks), in early years settings as well as in schools. The current system leads to waste – it is hard for parents to buy ingredients in one-portion quantities – and to stigma for children whose parents struggle to afford them. Teachers must be given the time, equipment and support to be able to order, prepare and store these ingredients, including funding support staff where necessary.

We recommend that the government doubles the funding for the School Fruit and Vegetable Scheme, from £40.4m to £80.8m. But it should give the money directly to schools rather than administering the scheme centrally.

There should be an entitlement to at least one portion of local fruit or vegetables a day for every infant school pupil. Schools and their caterers should be encouraged to use the dynamic procurement scheme (see Recommendation 13) to purchase fruit and vegetables from local suppliers once this system is rolled out nationally. The Government should provide comprehensive guidance and training on how they can do so.

Recruitment and training

Primary school teachers should be given the training and guidance they need to be able to deliver the curriculum. At secondary level, an essential step is tackling the shortage of food teachers. The DfE should monitor the number of food teachers and actively recruit and attract more specialists to tackle the shortage, by improving the information available on how to become a food teacher and by reinstating the food teacher training bursary.[3]

Implementation

The implementation of all of these changes should be placed under a dedicated Eat and Learn team in DfE. The DfE should update the School Food Standards. These standards need to align with the Reference Diet when this becomes available (see Recommendation 14), so that school menus are both healthy and sustainable. In line with the Reference Diet, the requirement to serve meat three times a week should be removed from the School Food Standards. In the meantime, the DfE should also ensure that the Standards reflect the most recent scientific advice from the Scientific Advisory Committee on Nutrition (SACN) on sugar and fibre consumption in children.[4]

To support school leaders an interactive website for the initiative should be created by the DfE and the Office for Health Promotion. It should signpost schools and early years providers to the best materials available, and to expert organisations who can support the goals of the initiative. It should also create a space for exchanging best practice between schools. The initiative should be widely marketed and create opportunities for engaging parents in its goals and securing endorsements and support from celebrities and public figures.

Rationale

Children's diets are not good enough. Childhood obesity rates more than double during primary school.[5] On average, children of primary and secondary school age eat less than half of the recommended five portions of fruit and vegetables a day, and no age group or income quintile meets the recommendation.[6] The shortfall is worst in teenagers.[7] This is not only a problem in childhood but also leads to long-term issues: a childhood diet low in fruits and vegetables is linked to increased cardiovascular risk in adults.[8] Good nutrition and maintaining a healthy weight in childhood help prevent obesity and diet-related ill health later in life.[9]

The school closures that have punctuated the pandemic have worsened the situation. Evidence suggests that children's diets have deteriorated during the pandemic: 35% of secondary school pupils report consuming more cakes and biscuits, 41% more crisps and 28% more sugary drinks.[10] The effect is likely to be similar to that seen during summer holidays, with children having more access to unhealthy foods and behaviours (such as excessive screen time). Children in food-insecure families may also have lost out on the hot, nutritious meal they would have expected at school.

Under normal circumstances, schools and early years settings offer a prime opportunity to improve children's diets. School-aged children eat a substantial proportion of their meals in school during term time, and for some a free school lunch is their main meal of the day.[11] They also have to study food: the curriculum states that schools should attempt to "instil a love of cooking in pupils", and teach them the skills they need "to feed themselves and others affordably and well, now and in later life".[12] By 14, all pupils should be able to "understand the source, seasonality and characteristics of a broad range of ingredients" and "cook a repertoire of predominantly savoury dishes".

The Government has not been using this opportunity as well as it might. It intervenes inconsistently to promote good nutrition. There is a particular lack of focus on increasing fruit and vegetable consumption among very young children and also among teenagers, when consumption is lowest.[13] Sensory food education, which has been shown to increase children's willingness to try new fruit and vegetables, is not yet widespread.[14]

Food education more broadly is inadequate. With the publication of the School Food Plan in 2014, food education was incorporated into the school curriculum.[15] But its implementation has been weak. There is no national champion for food education, no team responsible in DfE or Ofsted, no monitoring at a national level, and no subject reviews or research as there are in other subjects. As a result, many schools are simply not meeting the requirements of the curriculum. A 2018 survey of primary schools conducted by Ofsted found that while 89% had timetabled some curriculum time for lessons on food and healthy eating, only 26% offered cooking activities, 21% grew food and 24% had whole-school assemblies about healthy living.[16] Many secondary schools report that gaps in funding for materials, support staff and a lack of specialist teaching staff prevent them meeting the requirements of the curriculum.[17]

This problem has been exacerbated by the withdrawal of the food A-level. Food is currently the only national curriculum subject without an A Level. This means that children with an interest in food cannot pursue it at school beyond 16. Students who might have continued into higher education and careers in the food sector – including teaching food in schools – have lost a vital route to training.[18] The absence of an A-level in the subject has inevitably led to a reduction in status, funding and the availability of good food teachers.[19]

Without an A-level to go on to, the number of children taking the food GCSE has also declined. This is particularly concerning as recent statistics show that a third of the UK food and drink industry workforce is due to retire by 2024, leaving the industry facing a shortage of about 140,000 recruits.[20] These are not jobs that can be filled by unskilled school leavers: one-third of jobs within the food industry require a degree or postgraduate degree/PhD.

As well as the quality of food education, we also need to see further improvements in the quality of food provision in schools. As we discuss in Recommendation 13, this is vital in order to increase their uptake. Only 39% of primary school children who do not receive free school meals choose to eat them, often because they are unappealing.[21] This is regrettable, because school meals are almost always healthier and more nutritious than the alternatives.[22] And they can – if well-cooked and appetising – help to broaden palates and develop good eating habits by introducing children to new tastes and healthier foods.

One reason why some school lunches aren't as good as they should be is staffing. A skilled and well-trained chef will make high-quality, healthy, sustainable food that children will eat, and will know how to do this on a budget. In practice, however, school catering staff are often undervalued and untrained, both within schools and in the catering profession.[23] Formal training for school catering staff is not consistent and there is an emphasis on food hygiene and safety, and not on cooking skills.[24] Investing more in training is vital to improve the quality of meals.

Finally, expanding and improving the School Fruit and Vegetable Scheme (SFVS) will also play an important role in increasing consumption of fruit and vegetables by children. The existing scheme has already shown clear benefits. Government evaluations of the SFVS in 2004, 2006, 2008 and 2010 concluded that the SFVS increased consumption, encouraged children to try new fruit and vegetables that they might not have tried otherwise, and increased knowledge about healthy eating, particularly among children from deprived areas.[25] Giving schools the autonomy to choose local products and deliver the initiative in a way that is best suited to local requirements will improve the quality of delivery.

Costs and benefits

The annual cost to Government to deliver this recommendation is £206m, of which £124m is for food education ingredients. Over the next three years the total is £411m, assuming implementation from autumn 2023.

The DfE and the OHP should bid to secure funding in the next Spending Review.[26]

The initiative should be formally evaluated after the first three years, with a view to continued investment for at least ten more years. The £40.4m per year funding for the existing DHSC school fruit and vegetable scheme should be folded into this initiative.[27]

This estimate includes the cost of:

- At least one portion of fruit or vegetables per child each day (for 190 days) prioritising local, seasonal produce where possible (Recommendation 13).
- Food education support materials and ingredients.
- Monitoring and evaluation of the initiative.
- The Eat and Learn website to support school and early years providers

We estimate that mandatory training for catering staff in child nutrition and school food standards will take four hours, undertaken around usual duties or during inset days.

We expect the initiative to yield the following benefits:

- Increased uptake rates of school and nursery meals.
- A reduction in food waste.
- At least 90% of children leaving primary school having been taught all elements of the Design and Technology Curriculum on Cooking and Nutrition.
- At least 90% of children leaving secondary school able to prepare and cook at least five healthy savoury dishes using a range of cooking techniques.
- All staff working in school and nursery kitchens having received training to deliver high-quality, nutritious meals.
- More children leaving secondary school with passes in food GCSE and A-levels.
- More teachers who are qualified to teach food courses.

Endnotes

[1] Nekitsing, C. et al. (2018). Developing healthy food preferences in preschool children through taste exposure, sensory learning, and nutrition education. Current obesity reports 7, 60-67. Available at: https://link.springer.com/article/10.1007/s13679-018-0297-8

[2] Dimbleby, H. and Vincent, J. (2013). The School Food Plan. Evidence pack. HMG. Available at: http://www.schoolfoodplan.com/wp-content/uploads/2013/10/School-Food-Plan-Evidence-Pack-July-2013-Final.pdf

[3] Bursaries are available for subjects including Physics, Chemistry, Computing, Mathematics, Biology, Classics and Languages: DfE. (2021). Funding your training. DfE. Available at: https://getintoteaching.education.gov.uk/funding-your-training?gclid=CjwKCAjwuIWHBhBDEiwACXQYsckfALhWvhiN6TQi3ow7zqJaqWZScj7WDEYJ3EzE8wOCqf4kNwERMhoCjPoQAvD_BwE&gclsrc=aw.ds

[4] Scientific Advisory Committee on Nutrition. (2015). Carbohydrates and Health: Scientific Advisory Committee on Nutrition. TSO. Available at: https://assets.publishing.service.gov.uk/government/uploads/system/uploads/attachment_data/file/445503/SACN_Carbohydrates_and_Health.pdf

[5] We have not included exact percentages for reasons explained in the annex on child measurement: NHS Digital. (2020). National Child Measurement Programme, England 2019/20 School Year. NHS. Available at: https://digital.nhs.uk/data-and-information/publications/statistical/national-child-measurement-programme/2019-20-school-year

[6] NFS analysis of NDNS Year 9/11, 2016 to 2017 and 2018 to 2019. Available at: https://www.gov.uk/government/statistics/ndns-results-from-years-9-to-11-2016-to-2017-and-2018-to-2019

[7] NFS analysis of NDNS Year 9/11, 2016 to 2017 and 2018 to 2019. Available at: https://www.gov.uk/government/statistics/ndns-results-from-years-9-to-11-2016-to-2017-and-2018-to-2019

[8] Craigie, A. M. et al. (2011). Tracking of obesity-related behaviours from childhood to adulthood: A systematic review. Maturitas. Available at: https://www.sciencedirect.com/science/article/pii/S0378512211002969?via%3Dihub

[9] Chung, S. T. et al. (2018). Cardiometabolic risk in obese children. Annals of the New York Academy of Sciences 1411(1), 166–183. Available at: https://www.ncbi.nlm.nih.gov/pmc/articles/PMC5931397/;

Reilly, J. J. and Kelly, J. (2011). Long-term impact of overweight and obesity in childhood and adolescence on morbidity and premature mortality in adulthood: Systematic review. International Journal of Obesity 35(7), 891–898. Available at: https://pubmed.ncbi.nlm.nih.gov/20975725/;

Umer, A. et al. (2017). Childhood obesity and adult cardiovascular disease risk factors: A systematic review with meta-analysis. BMC Public Health 17(1), 683. Available at: https://pubmed.ncbi.nlm.nih.gov/28851330/

[10] British Nutrition Foundation (2020). Many children feel healthier and are more active since the return to school, research finds. Available at: https://www.nutrition.org.uk/press-office/pressreleases/hew20.html

[11] Estimated 17% of meals per year. Total meals is 3 x 365 = 1095. Children eat 1 meal 190 days a year in school = 190. 190/1095 = 17.3%; Royston, S., et al. (2012). Fair and Square: a policy report on the future of free school meals. The Children's Society. Available at: https://d3hgrlq6yacptf.cloudfront.net/5f3ecf1e68cdc/content/pages/documents/1429471607.pdf

[12] Department for Education. (2014). The national curriculum in England: framework document. HMG. Available at: https://assets.publishing.service.gov.uk/government/uploads/system/uploads/attachment_data/file/381344/Master_final_national_curriculum_28_Nov.pdf

[13] NFS analysis based on Public Health England (2018). National Diet and Nutrition Survey: results from years 7 and 8 (combined). HMG. Available at: https://assets.publishing.service.gov.uk/government/uploads/system/uploads/attachment_data/file/699241/NDNS_results_years_7_and_8.pdf

[14] Sapere Sensory food education. (2018). Sapere, A science based method. Sapere Sensory food education. Available at: https://www.sapere-association.com/sensory-education/research;H oppu, U. et al. (2015). Impact of sensory-based food education in kindergarten on willingness to eat vegetables and berries. Food and Nutrition Research. Available at: https://www.tandfonline.com/doi/full/10.3402/fnr.v59.28795;

Mustonen, S. and Tuorila, H. (2010). Sensory education decreases food neophobia score and encourages trying unfamiliar foods in 8–12-year-old children. Food Quality and Preference 21(4), 353-360. Available at: https://doi.org/10.1016/j.foodqual.2009.09.001;

C, Reverdy. et al. (2010). Effect of sensory education on food preferences in children. Food Quality and Preference 21(7), 794-804. Available at: https://doi.org/10.1016/j.foodqual.2010.03.008;

Nekitsing, C. et al. (2019). Taste exposure increases intake and nutrition education increases willingness to try an unfamiliar vegetable in preschool children: a cluster randomized trial. Journal of the Academy of Nutrition and Dietetics. Available at: https://doi.org/10.1016/j.jand.2019.05.012;

Coulthard, H. and Sealy, A. (2017). Play with your food! Sensory play is associated with tasting of fruits and vegetables in preschool children. Appetite 113(1), 84-90. Available at: https://doi.org/10.1016/j.appet.2017.02.003;

Mustonen, S. et al. (2009). Effect of sensory education on school children's food perception: a 2-year follow-up study. Food Quality and Preference 20(3), 230-240. Available at: https://www.sciencedirect.com/science/article/abs/pii/S0950329308001353

[15] Department for Education. (2014). The national curriculum in England: framework document. HMG. Available at: https://assets.publishing.service.gov.uk/government/uploads/system/uploads/attachment_data/file/381344/Master_final_national_curriculum_28_Nov.pdf

[16] Office for Standards in Education, Children's Services and Skills. (2018). Obesity, healthy eating and physical activity in primary schools: A thematic review into what actions schools are taking to reduce childhood obesity. Ofsted. Available at: https://assets.publishing.service.gov.uk/government/uploads/system/uploads/attachment_data/file/726114/Obesity__healthy_eating_and_physical_activity_in_primary_schools_170718.pdf

[17] Data provided by Food Teachers centre.

[18] Davies, L. (n.d.). A Level Food: the gap that remains. A report on the impact of removing post 16 A-level examinations for Home Economics and Food Technology in schools in England in 2016. Under review by the International Journal of D&T. Unpublished.

[19] Ballam, R. and Davies, L. (2020) What's happened in schools since the removal of 'food' A-level? British Nutrition Foundation. Available at: https://www.foodafactoflife.org.uk/media/9430/a-level-survey-2020-final-report.pdf;

Davies, L. (n.d.). A Level Food: the gap that remains. A report on the impact of removing post 16 A-level examinations for Home Economics and Food Technology in schools in England in 2016. Under review by the International Journal of D&T. Unpublished.

[20] Natwest. (2020). Food sector faces skills and labour shortage. Natwest. Available at: https://natwestbusinesshub.com/articles/food-and-drink-sector-faces-labour-shortage

[21] 39%: Dewberry Redpoint. (2019). School meal uptake research. Dewberry Redpoint Ltd. Available at: https://laca.co.uk/sites/default/files/attachment/news/SMU%20Research%20Report%202019.pdf;

Unappealing: Dimbleby, H. and Vincent, J. (2013). The School Food Plan. Evidence pack. HMG. Available at: http://www.schoolfoodplan.com/wp-content/uploads/2013/10/School-Food-Plan-Evidence-Pack-July-2013-Final.pdf

[22] School meals are healthier than packed lunches: Spence, S., et al. (2013) The impact of food and nutrient-based standards on primary school children's lunch and total dietary intake: a natural experimental evaluation of government policy in England. PLoS One. Available at: https://journals.plos.org/plosone/article?id=10.1371/journal.pone.0078298;

Kitchen, S., et al. (2013). Evaluation of the free school meals pilot. Department for Education. Available at: https://assets.publishing.service.gov.uk/government/uploads/system/uploads/attachment_data/file/184047/DFE-RR227.pdf;

School meals help children maintain a healthy body weight: Holford, A. and Rabe, B. (2020). Impact of the universal infant free school meal policy. Nuffield Foundation. Available at: https://www.nuffieldfoundation.org/project/impact-of-the-universal-infant-free-school-meal-policy

[23] Dimbleby, H. and Vincent, J. (2013). The School Food Plan. HMG. Available at: http://www.schoolfoodplan.com/plan/

[24] Dimbleby, H. and Vincent, J. (2013). The School Food Plan. HMG. Available at: http://www.schoolfoodplan.com/plan/

[25] 2004: Teeman, D. et al. (2005). Evaluation of the school fruit and vegetable pilot scheme: final report. National Foundation for Educational Research. Available at: https://www.nfer.ac.uk/evaluation-of-the-school-fruit-and-vegetable-pilot-scheme-final-report/;

2006: Ranslet, J. K. et al. (2007). Does the school fruit and vegetable scheme improve children's diet? A non-randomised controlled trial. Journal of Epidemiology and Community Health 61(8), 699 –703. Available at: https://www.ncbi.nlm.nih.gov/pmc/articles/PMC2652997/;

2008 and 2010: Teeman, D. et al. (2010). The third evaluation of the school fruit and vegetable scheme. National Foundation for Educational Research. Available at: https://webarchive.nationalarchives.gov.uk/20130124054158/http:/www.dh.gov.uk/prod_consum_dh/groups/dh_digitalassets/@dh/@en/@ps/documents/digitalasset/dh_114345.pdf;

Were successful: Hughes, R. J. et al. (2012). Childhood consumption of fruit and vegetables across England: a study of 2306 6–7-year-olds in 2007. British Journal of Nutrition 108, 733742. Available at: https://www.cambridge.org/core/services/aop-cambridge-core/content/view/74806CCE2954B1B08DB3DAF95393CAC8/S0007114511005939a.pdf/div-class-title-childhood-consumption-of-fruit-and-vegetables-across-england-a-study-of-2306-6-7-year-olds-in-2007-div.pdf

[26] This is a completely new scheme of substantial size. It will involve lots of pre-work from the DfE to get it right therefore we have not included a cost for the first year as implementation will not be until autumn 2023. The cost for the accreditation scheme is included in the procurement recommendation.

[27] The cost of the scheme in 2018/19 was £40,405,075 – figures provided by the Department of Health and Social Care.

Recommendation 4. Extend eligibility for free school meals.

What is it?

The Government should:

- Raise the household earnings threshold for free school meals (FSMs) from £7,400 to £20,000.
- Extend eligibility to children who are undocumented or have No Recourse to Public Funds (NPRF).
- Enrol eligible children for free school meals automatically.

This would increase the number of children benefiting from free school meals by 1.1 million, at a cost of £544 million per year. The Department for Education (DfE) should bid for these funds in the upcoming Spending Review.

Rationale

The current income threshold for FSMs is too low. Children aged 7-18yrs only qualify if they belong to a family with after-tax earnings of £7,400 or less and receive qualifying benefits.[1] This threshold is so low that it excludes many families that are food insecure. Nearly half of food insecure families with children do not qualify for FSMs because of the earning threshold (see Figure 1).

In addition, children who have No Recourse to Public Funds or are undocumented are ineligible for FSMs however little their family earns (though exceptions have been made during the COVID-19 pandemic). There are almost 400,000 such children in the UK.[2]

Finally, even eligible children are often missing out. Currently, FSMs are "opt-in": parents have to know about the scheme and apply for it. The effect of this is that, according to a 2013 estimate by the DfE, 11% of children entitled to FSMs do not receive them.[3]

This has serious consequences for those children. In the most extreme cases, they are going hungry. In one study by the Unity Project, over half of parents of children with NRPF reported that on at least one occasion they had been unable to give their child a hot meal all day because they could not afford it.[4]

The harmful effects of hunger on children's behaviour and educational performance are well known from scientific research.[5]

Only 20% of children in the poorest socio-economic class who would have to pay for school meals do so.[6] The main reason for this is cost (although appeal and sub-standard school food are also an important factors – which we address in Recommendation 14).[7] Most children who do not eat school meals have a packed lunch instead, but this is almost always less healthy than even the most uninspiring school meal. Only 1.6% of packed lunches meet the nutritional standards required for a school meal.[8]

This contributes to the diets of poorer children being less healthy than those of their richer schoolmates. The National Dietary Nutrition Survey (NDNS) reveals that children from the least well-off families eat substantially less fruit and vegetables, oily fish, fibre and other healthy foods than children from the most well-off families.[9] Free school meals are the simplest, least intrusive way to ensure that all children have at least one well-balanced, healthy and nutritious meal a day.

In Part One of this strategy, published last July, we recommended that the Government should extend free school meals to everyone on universal credit, up to the age of 16. We estimated this would cost £670 million. However, since the pandemic began, a further 230,000 households in the UK have registered for qualifying benefits: an increase of 7%.[10] This means that extending eligibility to everyone on Universal Credit (including NRPF children and children aged 16–19yrs) would now cost £790 million, at a time when the public finances are already under extreme pressure.

We have therefore tried to target those households in most urgent need of free school meals. We found that increasing the income threshold to £20,000, and making FSMs available to children who are undocumented or have NRPF, would ensure that 82% of households with "very low food security" and

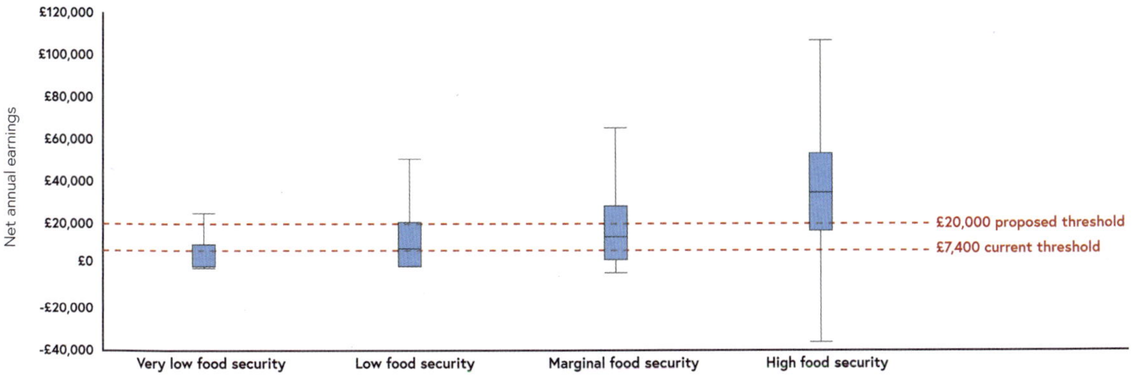

Figure 1

Food insecurity among families with an 8- to 19-year-old in England by annual earnings.[16]

70% of households with "low food security" would be eligible for FSMs. In total, almost three-quarters of food-insecure families with school children would receive FSMs.

We also recommend introducing automatic enrolment for FSMs. The Government has data on which families receive benefits that qualify them for FSMs, but this is not shared with schools. The Government has previously argued that this option is unviable for reasons of data protection. We urge the DfE to find a viable mechanism for automatic enrolment: it cannot be right to let paperwork stand between a child and a hot meal.

Free school meals are extremely popular with the public. In one recent poll 89% of the respondents agreed that: "Every child has the right to have a healthy meal at least once a day".[11] Three-quarters agree that: "Parents are responsible for feeding their children, but government must step in for children whose parents are unable to do so". Just over half (51%) of respondents went even further, saying that "school meals should be free for all students so that poor students are not stigmatised". Respondents to the National Food Strategy's Call for Evidence put forward similar recommendations.

Children in England are in danger of being disadvantaged in this respect compared to those elsewhere in the UK. In Northern Ireland, the eligibility threshold is already £14,000, almost double that in England. Scotland currently has a similar threshold to England, at £7,320 per year, but FSMs will start being rolled out to all primary school children from August 2021.[12] Wales has the same FSM threshold as England, but the Welsh Government is planning to review the criteria and extend eligibility.[13]

Costs and benefits

Based on current household incomes, expanding FSMs in the way we recommend would cost the Government an average of £544 million per year for three years.

Our recommendation would guarantee an additional 1.1 million children from low-income families a lunch in school. In total, 2.8 million disadvantaged children (including those aged under 7 who are eligible for means tested free meals) would benefit from a free school meal, covering 76% of families who are food insecure. For a full explanation of the methods used for estimating these figures, see online supplementary material.

This would have benefits for those children's health, but also for their educational achievement. Following one pilot of universal free school meals in 2009–11, primary school pupils made between four and eight weeks' more progress than expected.[14] Pupils from poorer families and those who had previously done less well at school showed the most improvement. Jamie Oliver's 2004 campaign to improve school food benefited children's achievement in English and maths, as well as reducing absences.[15]

In addition to the cost of free school meals themselves, eligibility for free school meals is linked to other funding streams. Schools are provided with a Pupil Premium for each child in receipt of FSMs. The purpose of the Pupil Premium is to help close the attainment gap of the most disadvantaged children. If the Government deems the cost attached to the larger number of Pupil Premiums once eligibility for FSMs is widened to be too high, the following two options would allow costs to be retained at current levels:

- The first option is to cap the Pupil Premium budget annually. The value of each Pupil Premium payment would then be determined by dividing the cap by the total number of eligible children.
- Alternatively, the Government could freeze the number of children eligible for Pupil Premium in each school at 2021/22 levels until the 2024 review following the completion of the Universal Credit transition. The review could address whether Pupil Premiums should continue to be linked to FSMs or if there is a better alternative for allocating them.

Endnotes

[1] Up to and including school year 2 (typically 6-7yrs), all children are eligible for FSMs under the national universal infant free school meals scheme.

[2] No Recourse to Public Funds: Fernández-Reino, M. (2020) Children of migrants in the UK. Migration Observatory briefing, COMPAS, University of Oxford. Available at: https://migrationobservatory.ox.ac.uk/wp-content/uploads/2020/08/Briefing-Children-of-Migrants-in-the-UK.pdf;

Undocumented: Institute for Community Research and Development at the University of Wolverhampton. (2020). London's children and young people who are not British citizens: A Profile. Greater London Authority. Available at: https://www.london.gov.uk/sites/default/files/final_summary_londons_children_and_young_people_who_are_not_british_citizens.pdf

[3] Lord, A. et al. (2013). Pupils not claiming free school meals – 2013. Department for Education. Available at: https://assets.publishing.service.gov.uk/government/uploads/system/uploads/attachment_data/file/266339/DFE-RR319.pdf

[4] Woolley, A. (2019). Access Denied: The cost of the "no recourse to public funds" policy. The Unity Project. Available at: https://static1.squarespace.com/static/590060b0893fc01f949b1c8a/t/5d0bb6100099f70001faad9c/1561048725178/Access+Denied+-+the+cost+of+the+No+Recourse+to+Public+Funds+policy.+The+Unity+Project.+June+2019.pdf

[5] Listed at Appendix C to Dimbleby, H. and Vincent, J. (2013). The School Food Plan. HMG. Available at: http://www.schoolfoodplan.com/plan/

[6] Dimbleby, H. and Vincent, J. (2013). The School Food Plan. HMG. Available at: http://www.schoolfoodplan.com/plan/

[7] Dimbleby, H. and Vincent, J. (2013). The School Food Plan. Evidence Pack. HMG. Available at: http://www.schoolfoodplan.com/wp-content/uploads/2013/10/School-Food-Plan-Evidence-Pack-July-2013-Final.pdf

[8] Packed lunches are common: Dimbleby, H. and Vincent, J. (2013). The School Food Plan. Evidence Pack. HMG. Available at: http://www.schoolfoodplan.com/wp-content/uploads/2013/10/School-Food-Plan-Evidence-Pack-July-2013-Final.pdf;

Packed lunches do not meet nutritional standards for school meals: Evans, C. et al. (2020). A repeated cross-sectional survey assessing changes in diet and nutrient quality of English primary school children's packed lunches between 2006 and 2016. BMJ Open. Available at: https://bmjopen.bmj.com/content/10/1/e029688

[9] Public Health England & Food Standards Agency. (2018). National diet and nutrition survey rolling programme years 7 to 8 (2014/2015 to 2015/2016). HMG. Available at: https://assets.publishing.service.gov.uk/government/uploads/system/uploads/attachment_data/file/699241/NDNS_results_years_7_and_8.pdf

[10] NFS analysis using Department for Work and Pensions. StatXplore. HMG. Available at: https://stat-xplore.dwp.gov.uk/webapi/jsf/login.xhtml;

Child and working Tax credit statistics November/December 2019: Her Majesty's Revenue and Customs. (2020). Child and working tax credits statistics: Provisional awards geographical analysis December 2019. Available at: https://assets.publishing.service.gov.uk/government/uploads/system/uploads/attachment_data/file/862232/Final_geo_tables.xlsx;

Child and working tax credit statistics November/December 2020: Her Majesty's Revenue and Customs. (2021). Child and working tax credits statistics: Provisional awards geographical analyses December 2020. Available at: https://assets.publishing.service.gov.uk/government/uploads/system/uploads/attachment_data/file/964651/Child_and_Working_Tax_Credits_December_2020__Geographical_Data_Tables_.ods

[11] Lasko-Skinner, R. and Sweetland, J. (2021). Food in a Pandemic. Demos. Available at: https://demos.co.uk/wp-content/uploads/2021/03/Food-in-a-Pandemic.pdf

[12] Seith, E. (2021). Free school meals rollout in primary to start in August. TES. Available at: https://www.tes.com/news/free-school-meals-rollout-primary-start-august

[13] Betteley, C. (2021). Free school meals for all children in Wales call. BBC News. Available at: https://www.bbc.co.uk/news/uk-wales-politics-56580568

[14] Kitchen, S. et al. (2013). Evaluation of the free school meals pilot. Department for Education. Available at: https://assets.publishing.service.gov.uk/government/uploads/system/uploads/attachment_data/file/184047/DFE-RR227.pdf

[15] Belot, M. and James, J. (2009). Healthy school meals and educational outcomes. Institute for Social and Economic Research. Available at: https://www.iser.essex.ac.uk/research/publications/working-papers/iser/2009-01.pdf

[16] NFS analysis of Department for Work and Pensions. (2021). Family Resources Survey: financial year 2019 to 2020. HMG. Available at: https://www.gov.uk/government/statistics/family-resources-survey-financial-year-2019-to-2020/family-resources-survey-financial-year-2019-to-2020#household-food-security-1

Recommendation 5. Fund the Holiday Activities and Food programme for the next three years.

What is it?

The Government should extend Holiday Activities and Food programme for the next three years.

The Holiday Activities and Food (HAF) programme offers a free holiday club to children who normally receive free school meals. This includes at least one hot meal a day, prepared in line with the School Food Standards. In most areas, children who do not receive free school meals have also been able to take part in HAF programmes, for a small fee. In response to a recommendation in Part One of this strategy, the Government rolled the programme out nationwide for 2021. (It had previously been trialled in 17 local authorities.) There is, however, currently no funding for the programme to continue beyond 2021.

The Government should commit to funding HAF programmes for the next three years. It should also evaluate the scheme to make sure that the current level of provision – four days a week for four weeks in the summer and a week at Christmas and Easter – is enough to make sure vulnerable children are not going hungry.

Rationale

Holidays are a particularly hard time for families experiencing food insecurity. Three million children are estimated to be at risk of hunger during the school holidays every year, and data from food banks shows a surge in demand for emergency supplies over the summer.[1] During the pandemic, the percentage of households experiencing food insecurity – as defined by the Government – increased from 7.6% to 9%.[2] Between April 2020 and March 2021, 17% of respondents to a nationally representative survey reported skipping meals or cutting down on portions because they could not afford enough food.[3] Households with at least one child were significantly more likely than the general population to have had to get help from a food bank or food charity.

As well as a cooked lunch every day, HAF programmes provide fun activities, exercise and social interaction. Even before the pandemic, children from poorer households were less likely to participate regularly in extra-curricular activities than children from higher income groups.[4] Eighty per cent of parents on low incomes report being unable to take their children out for activities during school holidays.[5] This makes them feel isolated and harms their health: children from the most deprived areas see their cardiovascular fitness go down over the summer holidays by more than their peers.[6]

HAF clubs also provide activities related to cooking and healthy eating. Children who are eligible for free school meals show more interest in these activities than children who are not eligible for free school meals.[7]

Evaluations of the pilot HAF programmes and similar schemes elsewhere have shown their positive impact on disadvantaged children. A 2019 assessment of HAF found that children's socialisation and wellbeing improved as a result of participating in the scheme.[8] Where local programmes have been evaluated in the UK, they have shown children have better diets and activity levels on the days they attend the programme.[9] Parents' wellbeing is also improved when children attend holiday clubs, and families say that they are better able to feed themselves healthily.[10] In the USA, summer food programmes for children have been running for more than 50 years. The programmes are associated with significantly lower rates of food insecurity and have benefits both for the diets and the academic performance of children from low-income and food-insecure families.[11]

There is a broad public consensus that the Government should provide children with healthy meals if their parents cannot afford to do so. In a nationally representative poll run in November 2020 89% of the respondents thought that "Every child has the right to have a healthy meal at least once a day" and 75% agreed that "Parents are responsible for feeding their children, but government must step in for children whose parents are unable to do so".[12] Respondents to the National Food Strategy's Call for Evidence proposed that disadvantaged children, including those from low-income households or with no recourse to public funds, should be provided with free, healthy and nutritious meals over school holidays as well as during term time.

Costs and benefits

If this proposal is combined with our recommendation to raise the income cap above which children become ineligible for free school meals, we estimate that an additional 1.375 million children of all ages will be eligible for HAF and that 985,000 children will take up the scheme in total.[13]

The average annual cost over three years to deliver this recommendation is £449m. This figure takes account of the uplift in the number of children that would be eligible for HAF to align with our recommendation on FSM eligibility. [14] The Department for Education should bid for these funds in the upcoming Spending Review.

Endnotes

[1] Three million children: Forsey, A. (2020). Hungry holidays: a report on hunger amongst children during school holidays. Available at: https://feedingbritain.files.wordpress.com/2015/02/hungry-holidays.pdf.

Food bank usage increases during holidays: The Trussell Trust (2018). Families, Hunger and the Holidays. Available at: https://www.trusselltrust.org/wp-content/uploads/sites/2/2018/08/Families-hunger-and-the-holidays-policy-brief.pdf.

[2] Food Foundation. (2021). The impact of Covid-19 on household food security. Available at: https://foodfoundation.org.uk/wp-content/uploads/2021/03/FF_Impact-of-Covid_FINAL.pdf

[3] Food Standards Agency (2021). Covid-19 consumer tracker survey. Available at: https://www.food.gov.uk/sites/default/files/media/document/covid-19-consumer-tracker-report-waves-9.-10-11-12.pdf

[4] The Sutton Trust. (2014). Extra-curricular Inequality Research Brief. Available at: https://dera.ioe.ac.uk/30273/;

Cullinane, C. and Montacute, R. (2017). Life Lessons: Improving essential life skills for young people. The Sutton Trust. Available at: https://www.suttontrust.com/wp-content/uploads/2017/10/Life-Lessons-Report_FINAL.pdf

[5] Kellogg's Foundation. (2015). Isolation and Hunger: the reality of the school holidays for struggling families. Kellogg's. Available at: https://www.kelloggs.co.uk/content/dam/europe/kelloggs_gb/pdf/HOLIDAY+HUNGER+REPORT.pdf

[6] Mann, S. et al. (2019). One-year surveillance of body mass index and cardiorespiratory fitness in UK primary school children in North West England and the impact of school deprivation level. Archives of Disease in Childhood 105. Available at: https://adc.bmj.com/content/early/2019/01/31/archdischild-2018-315567

[7] Lindley, L. et al. (2019). Omnibus survey of pupils and their parents or carers: Wave 5. Department for Education. Available at: https://assets.publishing.service.gov.uk/government/uploads/system/uploads/attachment_data/file/786040/survey_of_pupils_and_their_parents_or_carers-wave_5.pdf

[8] Campbell-Jack, D. et al. (2020). Evaluation of the 2019 holiday activities and food programme. Department for Education. Available at: https://assets.publishing.service.gov.uk/government/uploads/system/uploads/attachment_data/file/945255/Evaluation_of_the_2019_holiday_activities_and_food_programme_-_December_2020.pdf

[9] McConnon, L. et al. (2017). Food and fun school holiday enrichment programme 2016. Welsh Local Government Association. Available at: https://orca.cardiff.ac.uk/97619/

[10] Parental wellbeing: Long, M. A. et al. (2021). Examining the relationship between child holiday club attendance and parental mental wellbeing. Public health in practice 2. Available at: https://www.sciencedirect.com/science/article/pii/S2666535221000471;

Improved ability to feed family: O'Connor, J. et al. (2015). An evaluation of Holiday Kitchen 2014: Learning, food and play for families who need it most in the West Midlands. Accord Group. Available at: https://www.family-action.org.uk/content/uploads/2015/01/hk_bcu_report.pdf

[11] Ralston, K. et al. (2017). Children's food security and USDA child nutrition programs. United States Department of Agriculture. Economic Information Bulletin 174. Available at: https://www.ers.usda.gov/publications/pub-details/?pubid=84002

[12] Lasko-Skinner, R. and Sweetland, J. (2021). Food in a Pandemic. Demos. Available at: https://www.food.gov.uk/sites/default/files/media/document/fsa-food-in-a-pandemic-march-2021.pdf

[13] These numbers assume the uptake remains the same as the current scheme at 35%, and include existing and newly eligible children.

[14] The reduction in cost post-2024 assumes unemployment falls and household incomes rise after the pandemic.

Recommendation 6. Expand the Healthy Start scheme.

What is it?

The Government should expand the Healthy Start voucher scheme to all households earning under £20,000 with pregnant women or children under five. It should take steps to increase uptake among people who are eligible.

Healthy Start is a scheme which provides coupons for vitamins as well as vouchers that can be used to buy £4.25 worth of fruit, vegetables and milk per week.[1] The scheme is open to all pregnant women under 18yrs. It is also available to other pregnant women and families with children aged 3yrs or under, provided that they receive one of a number of qualifying benefits and have a low income.[2]

We recommend that all households with earnings under £20,000 should be made eligible. In addition, the age limit should be raised to include children aged under five. This would be accompanied by regular evaluations of the scheme, to understand its impact on fruit and vegetable consumption and to review the value of the voucher.

At the same time as expanding the scheme, the Government should attempt to increase uptake among eligible people by:

- Running a £5m communications campaign to publicise the expansion of the scheme.
- Making sure public information on the scheme (such as the website and leaflets) is up to date.
- Making the application process simpler.
- Making sure GPs, health visitors, midwives, social workers and early years workers are aware of the scheme and can help eligible families to apply. This could involve:
    - Updating the IT system GPs use so they are informed about Healthy Start.
    - Making it standard practice to give application forms to parents when they first record a pregnancy or when their children are born.
    - Making sure application forms are readily available in GP surgeries, children's centres and other settings where pregnant women and mothers are likely to be.
    - Encouraging local authorities, Clinical Commissioning Groups and hospital trusts to support people who work with pregnant women and young families (e.g. welfare rights workers, people working in food banks and community volunteers) to help them access the scheme.
- Continuing with plans to digitise the scheme (while ensuring alternative options are still available for those without digital devices).
- Considering how the scheme could be developed to allow purchases to be tracked, so as to allow more thorough evaluation of the scheme.

Rationale

Children do not eat enough fruit and vegetables. Children under five from families with low incomes eat on average only three portions of fruit and vegetables a day, instead of the five they need.[3] This can affect their health as adults. Eating too little fruit and vegetables as a child is linked to increased cardiovascular risk in adulthood.[4] Good nutrition and maintaining a healthy weight in childhood helps prevent obesity and diet-related ill health later in life.[5]

One of the main reasons for this is the affordability of fresh produce.[6] We set out the evidence for this in Recommendation 7. People consume more fruit and vegetables when they are cheaper or free.[7] A systematic review of 20 field studies found that discounts and vouchers for healthy foods increased purchases and consumption of them.[8] Another review of 14 studies concluded that food subsidy programs increase people's intake of targeted foods or nutrients by 10–20%.[9]

The current Healthy Start voucher scheme has been shown to increase spending on fruit and vegetables by 15%. This amounts to an additional 1.8kg of fruit and vegetables per month, or 22 portions.[10] Women receiving Healthy Start vouchers ate more fruit and vegetables and were more likely to get enough iron, folate, calcium and vitamin C than women who received vouchers for an earlier scheme that just provided milk.[11] Studies on the effects of Healthy Start have shown that it plays an important role in helping pregnant women and their children access healthier foods. It has increased the quantity and range of fruit and vegetables consumed, as well as establishing good habits.[12]

Healthy Start has also been shown to have an impact beyond financial support.[13] Women registered for the scheme report that Healthy Start made them think more about their health and diet, and this led to better dietary choices.[14]

However, the current scheme is too narrowly targeted. Just 530,000 pregnant women and children are eligible for it.[15] Over 250,000 children under five living in food insecurity cannot benefit from it.[16] Expanding the eligibility to any family earning less than £20,000 would reach 73% of food insecure families.[17] Extending the age eligibility to children under five would fill an existing nutritional gap where poorer children have stopped benefiting from Healthy Start but are not yet in school and receiving free school meals.

Furthermore, low uptake means that many eligible families are missing out. Current uptake is only around 50–60%.[18] This is thought to be due to a series of barriers which make it difficult for eligible people to find out about the scheme and to then apply successfully.[19] The application form is only available in English, can appear complicated, and there is little support for applicants to help them complete the form. The result is that almost a third of applications are rejected because the form is incorrectly filled in.[20]

Uptake has actually worsened during the pandemic, just when many families need this scheme most. At the start of the pandemic, the Government removed the requirement for the Healthy Start application form to be signed by a healthcare worker. The unintended consequence was that healthcare workers stopped alerting families to the scheme, leading to a drop in uptake.[21]

Other issues also contribute to low uptake. The scheme still relies on paper vouchers, which can be lost and damaged, although the switch to a digital card is underway. Only registered retailers accept the vouchers and there is currently a shortage of them in rural areas and in shops serving minority ethnic communities.[22] Some retailers are helping out by providing extra discounts and promotions for people using their vouchers, but they say that the scheme is currently too small to warrant significant investment.

A strong communication campaign can make a difference to uptake in just a short time. Since the End Child Food Poverty taskforce began its communication campaign in September 2020 Healthy Start uptake has risen by ten percentage points.[23] We would expect to see a further rise in uptake in response to the taskforce refreshing its communications campaign in April 2021 and the Government increasing the value of the voucher.

Costs and benefits

Under this recommendation, an additional 612,000 people would benefit from the scheme, taking the total number of beneficiaries to just under 1.15 million.[24] It is hard to estimate the benefits of increasing fruit and vegetable intake on very young children, since the impacts of poor diets often take years to materialise. However, introducing fruit and vegetables at an early age can help set habits which stay into adulthood. We anticipate that many of the benefits of the current Healthy Start scheme, including increasing the healthiness of household shopping baskets, would also apply to newly eligible households.[25]

The expansion of eligibility would cost an additional £82m–132m a year, depending on take up.[26] We also recommend a one-off £5m communications campaign. This would bring the total cost of the scheme to £165m-£285m per year, depending on uptake. Over three years the total additional cost is £245m – £395 m. The Department for Health and Social Care should bid for these funds in the upcoming Spending Review.

There would be additional costs to implementing and monitoring the scheme, but given the scheme already exists, we do not anticipate these to be significantly more than they are now.

To put this in context, it is estimated the sugar and salt tax (see Recommendation 1) could raise between £2.9bn–£3.4bn a year. The additional costs of expanding Healthy Start coverage would be more than covered by the revenues of the levy.

Endnotes

[1] The Government increased the value of the voucher in response to a recommendation in Part 1 of the National Food Strategy. The sum chosen (£4.25) was estimated to cover the cost of providing one child with five portions of fruit and vegetables and half a pint of milk each day for a week, as assessed in: Scottish Government. (2018). Welfare Foods – a consultation on meeting the needs of children and families in Scotland. Scottish Government, p6. Available at: https://consult.gov.scot/health-protection/welfare-foods/user_uploads/sct0218087754-1_welfarefoods_p4.pdf

[2] The exact income threshold varies depending on which qualifying benefit the family receives. For example, families on Universal Credit can earn no more than £408 per week from employment.

[3] One adult portion is 80g based on the recommended 400g a day of fruit and veg. For our calculations, we have used a portion size of 50g for children under 5. This is the midpoint value of the 40–60g recommended in the School Food Plan. NFS analysis of NDNS Year 9/11, 2016 to 2017 and 2018 to 2019. Available at: https://www.gov.uk/government/statistics/ndns-results-from-years-9-to-11-2016-to-2017-and-2018-to-2019

[4] Craigie, A. M. et al. (2011). Tracking of obesity-related behaviours from childhood to adulthood: A systematic review. Maturitas. Available at: https://www.sciencedirect.com/science/article/pii/S0378512211002969?via%3Dihub

[5] Chung, S. T. et al. (2018). Cardiometabolic risk in obese children. Annals of the New York Academy of Sciences 1411(1), 166–183. Available at: https://www.ncbi.nlm.nih.gov/pmc/articles/PMC5931397/;

Reilly, J. J. and Kelly, J. (2011). Long-term impact of overweight and obesity in childhood and adolescence on morbidity and premature mortality in adulthood: Systematic review. International Journal of Obesity 35(7), 891–898. Available at: https://pubmed.ncbi.nlm.nih.gov/20975725/;

Umer, A. et al. (2017). Childhood obesity and adult cardiovascular disease risk factors: A systematic review with meta-analysis. BMC Public Health 17(1), 683. Available at: https://pubmed.ncbi.nlm.nih.gov/28851330/

[6] Public Health England. (2015). Sugar Reduction: The evidence for action. HMG. Available at: https://assets.publishing.service.gov.uk/government/uploads/system/uploads/attachment_data/file/470175/Annexe_4._Analysis_of_price_promotions.pdf;

Scott, C. et al. (2018). Affordability of the UK's Eatwell Guide. The Food Foundation. Available at: https://foodfoundation.org.uk/wp-content/uploads/2018/10/Affordability-of-the-Eatwell-Guide_Final_Web-Version.pdf

[7] An, R. (2014). Effectiveness of subsidies in promoting healthy food purchases and consumption: a review of field experiments. Public Health Nutrition 16(7), 1215–1228. Available at: https://www.ncbi.nlm.nih.gov/pmc/articles/PMC3898771/;

Afshin, A. et al. (2017). The prospective impact of food pricing on improving dietary consumption: A systematic review and meta-analysis. PLoS One. Available at: https://pubmed.ncbi.nlm.nih.gov/28249003/;

Thow, A. M. et al. (2014). A systematic review of the effectiveness of food taxes and subsidies to improve diets: Understanding the recent evidence. Nutrition Reviews 72(9), 551–565. Available at: https://academic.oup.com/nutritionreviews/article/72/9/551/1859025;

Niebylski, M. L. et al. (2015). Healthy food subsidies and unhealthy food taxation: a systematic review of the evidence. Nutrition 31(6), 787–795. Available at: https://www.sciencedirect.com/science/article/pii/S0899900714005486?via%3Dihub

[8] An, R. (2014). Effectiveness of subsidies in promoting healthy food purchases and consumption: a review of field experiments. Public Health Nutrition 16(7), 1215–1228. Available at: https://www.ncbi.nlm.nih.gov/pmc/articles/PMC3898771/

[9] Black, A. P. et al. (2012). Food subsidy programs and the health and nutritional status of disadvantaged families in high income countries: a systematic review. BMC Public Health 12. Available at: https://bmcpublichealth.biomedcentral.com/articles/10.1186/1471-2458-12-1099

[10] Griffith, R. et al. (2018). Getting a healthy start: The effectiveness of targeted benefits for improving dietary choices. Journal of Health Economics 58, 176–187. Available at: https://www.sciencedirect.com/science/article/pii/S0167629616302533

[11] Ford, F. et al. (2009). Effect of the introduction of "Healthy Start" on dietary behaviour during and after pregnancy: early results from the "before and after" Sheffield study. British Journal of Nutrition 101(12), 1828–1836. Available at: https://pubmed.ncbi.nlm.nih.gov/19017424/

[12] McFadden, A. et al. (2014). Can food vouchers improve nutrition and reduce health inequalities in low-income mothers and young children: a multi-method evaluation of the experiences of beneficiaries and practitioners of the Healthy Start programme in England. BMC Public Health 14. Available at: https://bmcpublichealth.biomedcentral.com/articles/10.1186/1471-2458-14-148

[13] Griffith, R. et al. (2018). Getting a healthy start: The effectiveness of targeted benefits for improving dietary choices. Journal of Health Economics 58, 176–187. Available at: https://www.sciencedirect.com/science/article/pii/S0167629616302533

[14] Crawley, H. and Dodds, R. (2018). The UK Healthy Start scheme. What happened? What next?. First Steps Nutrition Trust, p56. Available at: https://static1.squarespace.com/static/59f75004f09ca48694070f3b/t/5b8e2d0e575d1f6f1e5d2dcd/1536044307456/Healthy_Start_Report_for_web.pdf

[15] National Health Service. (2021). Healthy start uptake data: England uptake data. HMG. Available at: https://www.healthystart.nhs.uk/healthcare-professionals/

[16] NFS analysis based on: National Health Service. (2021). Healthy Start uptake data. NHS. Available at: https://www.healthystart.nhs.uk/healthcare-professionals/;

Department for Work and Pensions. (2021). Family resources survey: financial year 2019 to 2020. HMG. Available at: https://www.gov.uk/government/statistics/family-resources-survey-financial-year-2019-to-2020/family-resources-survey-financial-year-2019-to-2020

[17] NFS analysis based on: Department for Work and Pensions. (2021). Households below average income, 1994/95–2019/20. HMG. Available at: https://www.gov.uk/government/statistics/households-below-average-income-199495-to-201819

[18] National Health Service. (2021). Healthy start uptake data: England uptake data. HMG. Available at: https://www.healthystart.nhs.uk/healthcare-professionals/

[19] McFadden, A. et al. (2014). Can food vouchers improve nutrition and reduce health inequalities in low-income mothers and young children: a multi-method evaluation of the experiences of beneficiaries and practitioners of the Healthy Start programme in England. BMC Public Health 14. Available at: https://bmcpublichealth.biomedcentral.com/articles/10.1186/1471-2458-14-148

[20] Crawley, H. and Dodds, R. (2018). The UK Healthy Start scheme. What happened? What next?. First Steps Nutrition Trust, p56. Available at: https://static1.squarespace.com/static/59f75004f-09ca48694070f3b/t/5b8e2d0e575d1f6f1e5d2dcd/1536044307456/Healthy_Start_Report_for_web.pdf

[21] National Health Service. (2021). Healthy start uptake data: England uptake data. HMG. Available at: https://www.healthystart.nhs.uk/healthcare-professionals/

[22] McFadden, A. et al. (2014). Can food vouchers improve nutrition and reduce health inequalities in low-income mothers and young children: a multi-method evaluation of the experiences of beneficiaries and practitioners of the Healthy Start programme in England. BMC Public Health 14. Available at: https://bmcpublichealth.biomedcentral.com/articles/10.1186/1471-2458-14-148

[23] End Child Food Poverty campaign: https://endchildfoodpoverty.org/;

Healthy start uptake has risen: NFS Analysis based on: National Health Service. (2021). Healthy start uptake data: England uptake data. HMG. Available at: https://www.healthystart.nhs.uk/healthcare-professionals/

[24] NFS Analysis, based on population of 0–4 year olds on universal credit or equivalent 2019/20: Department for Work and Pensions. (2021). Family resources survey: financial year 2019 to 2020. HMG. Available at: https://www.gov.uk/government/statistics/family-resources-survey-financial-year-2019-to-2020/family-resources-survey-financial-year-2019-to-2020

[25] Griffith, R. et al. (2018). Getting a healthy start: The effectiveness of targeted benefits for improving dietary choices. Journal of Health Economics 58, 176–187. Available at: https://www.sciencedirect.com/science/article/pii/S0167629616302533

[26] Estimated uptake of 60–90% based on current take up rates of 58% and assumption that Government promotion can drive further uptake: National Health Service. (2021). Healthy start uptake data: England uptake data. HMG. Available at: https://www.healthystart.nhs.uk/healthcare-professionals/

Recommendation 7. Trial a "Community Eatwell" programme, supporting those on low incomes to improve their diets.

What is it?

The Government should trial a "Community Eatwell" programme to provide targeted healthy eating support for people on low incomes. If the pilot is a success, the programme should be rolled out across England.

Pilot projects should identify patients who need dietary support and refer them to a Link Worker – a non-clinical staff member with specialised training to support healthy eating – who would design a programme to suit their needs and help them engage with local services. Patients would receive an Eatwell Prescription for free fruit and vegetables, perhaps alongside access to local programmes that encourage healthy eating (e.g. cooking classes in community kitchens). They would also get advice and support from their Link Worker to motivate them to engage in their personal programme.

Up to seven Primary Care Networks (PCNs) should be invited to bid for the chance to set up their own pilot programmes, to run over three years.[1] These programmes would use social prescribing and other interventions to support healthy changes in behaviour, in particular increasing fruit and vegetable consumption.

The exact makeup of the programmes should be designed locally, to take advantage of existing facilities and initiatives, and make sure the programmes respond to local needs.

Following the three-year pilot, a detailed evaluation should be conducted to help decide if and how the programme should be rolled out across England.

Rationale

We know that preventing disease is much more cost-effective than treating it. One study found that the average return on investment for public health interventions is 14, meaning every pound spent delivers fourteen pounds of benefits.[2] Yet in 2018, the NHS spent only 5% of its budget on preventing disease.[3] The Government is currently attempting to address this issue through a new "Green Social Prescribing" programme, which is being trialled in seven PCNs around England.[4] This is intended to improve patients' mental and physical health before they become acutely unwell. It enables GPs to prescribe therapeutic activities such as walking clubs, community gardening and food-growing projects.

The CEP would complement these existing services by giving practical support to patients to change their dietary behaviour. Exercise alone is not sufficient for people to lose weight. The CEP would help break down the barriers of knowledge, confidence, accessibility and cost that can stop people improving their diets.

Low consumption of fruit and vegetables is linked to cardiovascular disease, diabetes and cancer.[5] In 2019, diets low in fruit accounted for 10,066 premature deaths and approximately 210,000 disability-adjusted life years (DALYs) in the UK.[6] Diets low in vegetables accounted for 5,935 premature deaths and just under 98,000 DALYs. While almost everyone in the UK eats too little fruit and vegetables, the problem is particularly acute among the most disadvantaged. The poorest 10% of British people eat on average 42% less fruit and vegetables than recommended, while the richest eat 13% less.[7] The bottom 20% of the population by income eat a full portion of fruit and vegetables less a day than the top 20%.

A major reason for this is affordability. Healthier food tends to be more expensive per calorie than less healthy food.[8] The healthiest products in the Nutrient Profile Model scoring system (such as potatoes or broccoli) cost over six times more per calorie than the least healthy products (such as chocolate bars or pepperoni).[9] The poorest 10% of people in Britain would have to spend almost three-quarters of their disposable income on food in order to eat in line with the Government's recommended Eatwell Guide.[10] But convenience and knowledge also play a role. People on low incomes are less likely to have access to a car and therefore less able to travel out of their area or transport food in bulk.[11] They may not have a fridge or freezer.[12] Finally, they may lack knowledge about the benefits of fruit and vegetables in preventing disease, or how to cook with them.[13]

For this reason, initiatives aiming to increase fruit and

vegetable intake have been shown to be effective in improving people's health. They can reduce the body mass index (BMI) of patients suffering from obesity, hypertension and diabetes, as well as of overweight and obese children.[14] Increasing fruit and vegetable consumption has been shown to be more effective at improving health than reducing consumption of foods high in fat and sugar.[15]

An effective way to increase consumption is to provide people with free fruit and vegetables, including through prescription programmes.[16] In Washington DC, for example, the Produce Prescription Programme allows doctors to prescribe vouchers for fresh fruit and vegetables and receive cooking lessons, nutritional education and guided tours of shops and supermarkets to help them shop well. Of 120 patients who received produce prescriptions between 2012 and 2017, half lost weight while on the prescription.[17]

Such programmes can be highly cost-effective. The NHS spent over half a billion pounds on anti-diabetes medication in 2018/19, at an average cost of more than £300 per patient.[18] By contrast, in one US study, a fruit and vegetable prescription programme cut diabetic patients' blood sugar levels by an average of 7.5% in 13 weeks, at a cost of $40 per patient.[19]

We recommend that the Government should trial such a programme in the UK. This should be led locally by PCNs, working with community organisations: such local, community-based approaches have been shown to be effective at changing people's eating habits.[20]

Costs and benefits

The pilot programme would cost £2m per year, or £6m over the three-year trial.[21] The Department of Health and Social Care should secure funding for this through a bid in the next Spending Review. If the programme is rolled out across the country, the cost would increase.

The programme should increase consumption of fruit and vegetables in the communities where it is piloted. These communities should be among the most deprived according to the Index of Multiple Deprivation.[22] Patients should be monitored to see whether they experience direct health benefits, including weight loss and reductions in blood sugar, and whether this eases pressure on local NHS services – in particular GP appointments and the cost of medication.

Endnotes

[1] NHS England defines PCNs as follows: "GP practices working together with community, mental health, social care, pharmacy, hospital and voluntary services in their local areas in groups of practices known as primary care networks (PCNs). PCNs build on existing primary care services and enable greater provision of proactive, personalised, coordinated and more integrated health and social care for people close to home." NHS England. Primary Care Networks. Available at: https://www.england.nhs.uk/primary-care/primary-care-networks/

[2] Masters, R. et al. (2017). Return on investment of public health interventions: a systematic review. Journal of Epidemiology and Community Health 71, 827–834. Available at: https://jech.bmj.com/content/jech/71/8/827.full.pdf

[3] Office for National Statistics (2020). Healthcare expenditure, UK health accounts. HMG. Available at: https://www.ons.gov.uk/peoplepopulationandcommunity/healthandsocialcare/healthcaresystem/bulletins/ukhealthaccounts/2018

[4] Expression of interest process: National Health Service. (2021). Green social prescribing. NHS. Available at: https://www.england.nhs.uk/personalisedcare/social-prescribing/green-social-prescribing/

5. Aune, D. et al. (2017). Fruit and vegetable intake and the risk of cardiovascular disease, total cancer and all-cause mortality—a systematic review and dose-response meta-analysis of prospective studies. International Journal of Epidemiology 46 (3), 1029–1056. Available at: https://academic.oup.com/ije/article/46/3/1029/3039477

[6] Diets low in fruit means diets with less than 200–300g of fruit per day. Diets low in vegetables means diets with less than 290–430g of vegetables per day. Global Burden of Disease 2017 Diet Collaborators (2019). Health effects of dietary risks in 195 countries, 1990–2017: a systematic analysis for the Global Burden of Disease Study 2017. The Lancet 393, 1958–1972. Available at: https://www.thelancet.com/article/S0140-6736(19)30041-8/fulltext;

Global Health Data Exchange. (2021). GBD Results Tool. Institute for Health Metrics and Evaluation. Accessed July 2021 Available at: http://ghdx.healthdata.org/gbd-results-tool

[7] Public Health England & Food Standards Agency. (2018). National Diet and Nutrition Survey Rolling Programme Years 7 to 8 (2014/2015 to 2015/2016). HMG. Available at: https://assets.publishing.service.gov.uk/government/uploads/system/uploads/attachment_data/file/699241/NDNS_results_years_7_and_8.pdf

[8] Public Health England. (2015). Sugar Reduction: The evidence for action. HMG. Available at: https://assets.publishing.service.gov.uk/government/uploads/system/uploads/attachment_data/file/470175/Annexe_4._Analysis_of_price_promotions.pdf

[9] Analysis for NFS of data from Kantar Worldpanel. See NFS Evidence Pack.

[10] Scott, C. et al. (2018). Affordability of the UK's Eatwell Guide. The Food Foundation. Available at: https://foodfoundation.org.uk/wp-content/uploads/2018/10/Affordability-of-the-Eatwell-Guide_Final_Web-Version.pdf

[11] Caraher, M. et al. (1998). Access to healthy foods: part I. Barriers to accessing healthy foods: differentials by gender, social class, income and mode of transport. Health Education Journal 57(3), 191–201. Available at: https://journals.sagepub.com/doi/10.1177/001789699805700302

[12] Turn2us. (2019). Living without: The scale and impact of appliance poverty. Turn2us. Available at: https://www.turn2us.org.uk/T2UWebsite/media/Documents/Communications documents/Living-Without-Report-Final-Web.pdf

[13] Caldwell, E. et al. (2009). Perceived access to fruits and vegetables associated with increased consumption. Public Health Nutrition 12 (10), 1743–1750. Available at: https://www.cambridge.org/core/journals/public-health-nutrition/article/perceived-access-to-fruits-and-vegetables-associated-with-increased-consumption/26832E21FAAE8C75C4BCDECFBD0DB613;

Smith, A. (2018). Food poverty in Camden and Islington, January 2018. Camden and Islington Public Health. Available at: https://opendata.camden.gov.uk/widgets/a6rj-bnun;

House of Lords. (2020). Hungry for change: fixing the failures in food. Authority of the House of Lords. Available at: https://committees.parliament.uk/publications/1762/documents/17092/default/;

Haynes-Maslow, L. et al. (2016). Low-income individuals' perceptions about fruit and vegetable access programs: A qualitative study. Journal of Nutrition Education and Behaviour 47(4), 317–324. Available at: https://www.ncbi.nlm.nih.gov/pmc/articles/PMC4500669/

[14] Hypertension and diabetes: Cavanagh, M. et al. (2017). Veggie Rx: an outcome evaluation of a healthy food incentive programme. Public Health Nutrition 20 (14), 2636–2641. Available at: https://www.ncbi.nlm.nih.gov/pmc/articles/PMC5743436/;

Overweight and obese children: Huang, J. et al. (2019). Impact of fruits and vegetables prescription program in wellness group visits. Pediatrics 144(706). Available at: https://pediatrics.aappublications.org/content/144/2_MeetingAbstract/706;

Overweight and obese children: Jones, L. J. et al. (2020). Impact of a fruit and vegetable prescription program on health outcomes and behaviors in young Navajo children. Current Developments in Nutrition 4(8). Available at: https://academic.oup.com/cdn/article/4/8/nzaa109/5874246

[15] Epstein, L. H. et al. (2001). Increasing fruit and vegetable intake and decreasing fat and sugar intake in families at risk for childhood obesity. Obesity Research 9(3), 171–178. Available at: https://europepmc.org/article/med/11323442

[16] Free fruit and vegetables: Olsho, L. E. W. et al. (2016). Financial incentives increase fruit and vegetable intake among Supplemental Nutrition Assistance Program participants: a randomized controlled trial of the USDA Healthy Incentives Pilot. The American Journal of Clinical Nutrition 104(2), 423–435. Available at: https://academic.oup.com/ajcn/article/104/2/423/4668540;

Free fruit and vegetables: Fitzgerald, K. (2015). Food Insecurity Nutrition Incentive Grant Program (FINI). Fair Food Network. Available at: https://fairfoodnetwork.org/wp-content/uploads/2017/03/Consolidated-2015-Report_finaldigital-.pdf;

Free fruit and vegetables: Olsho, L. E. W. et al. (2015). Impacts of a farmers' market incentive programme on fruit and vegetable access, purchase and consumption. Public Health Nutrition 18 (15), 2712–2721. Available at: https://www.cambridge.org/core/journals/public-health-nutrition/article/impacts-of-a-farmers-market-incentive-programme-on-fruit-and-vegetable-access-purchase-and-consumption/542F29A9EA3B515286E4A801909B3513;

Free fruit and vegetables: Lindsay, S. et al. (2013) Monetary matched incentives to encourage the purchase of fresh fruits and vegetables at farmers markets in underserved communities. Preventing Chronic Diseases 10, E188. Available at: https://www.ncbi.nlm.nih.gov/pmc/

articles/PMC3830923/;

Free fruit and vegetables: Young, C. R. et al. (2013). Improving fruit and vegetable consumption among low-income customers at farmers markets: Philly Food Bucks, Philadelphia, Pennsylvania, 2011. Preventing Chronic Diseases 10, E166. Available at: https://pubmed.ncbi.nlm.nih.gov/24135390/;

Free fruit and vegetables: Freedman, D. A. et al. (2013). A farmers' market at a federally qualified health center improves fruit and vegetable intake among low-income diabetics. Preventative Medicine 56(5), 288–292. Available at: https://pubmed.ncbi.nlm.nih.gov/23384473/;

Prescriptions: Trapl, E. S. et al. (2018). Dietary impact of produce prescriptions for patients with hypertension. Preventing chronic diseases 15(15). Available at: https://pubmed.ncbi.nlm.nih.gov/30447106/;

Overweight and obese children from low income households: Ridberg, R. A. et al. (2019). Effect of a fruit and vegetable prescription program on children's fruit and vegetable consumption. Preventing Chronic Disease 16. Available at: https://www.cdc.gov/pcd/issues/2019/18_0555.htm;

Prescriptions: Jones, L. J. et al. (2020). Impact of a fruit and vegetable prescription program on health outcomes and behaviors in young Navajo children. Current Developments in Nutrition 4(8). Available at: https://academic.oup.com/cdn/article/4/8/nzaa109/5874246

[17] DC Greens. (2021) Produce prescription program (Produce Rx). DC Greens. Available at: https://www.dcgreens.org/produce-rx

[18] NHS Digital. (2019). Prescribing for Diabetes in England 2008/09 - 2018/19. Available at: https://digital.nhs.uk/data-and-information/publications/statistical/prescribing-for-diabetes/2008-09---2018-19

[19] Bryce, R. et al. (2017). Participation in a farmers' market fruit and vegetable prescription program at a federally qualified health center improves hemoglobin A1C in low income uncontrolled diabetics. Preventive Medicine Reports 7, 176–179. Available at: https://www.sciencedirect.com/science/article/pii/S2211335517301079

[20] Atkins, L. and Michie, S. (2015). Designing interventions to change eating behaviours. Proceedings of the Nutrition Society 74(2). Available at: https://www.cambridge.org/core/journals/proceedings-of-the-nutrition-society/article/designing-interventions-to-change-eating-behaviours/0FB561F47C354DBAA80B01F5ADDA6546

[21] This is an estimate informed by a comparable scheme: NHS England. (2021) Green Social Prescribing. Available at: https://www.england.nhs.uk/personalisedcare/social-prescribing/green-social-prescribing/

[22] Index of multiple deprivation: Ministry of Housing, Communities and Local Government. (2019). The English Indices of Deprivation 2019. HMG. Available at: https://assets.publishing.service.gov.uk/government/uploads/system/uploads/attachment_data/file/835115/IoD2019_Statistical_Release.pdf

Recommendation 8. Guarantee the budget for agricultural payments until at least 2029 to help farmers transition to more sustainable land use.

What is it?

Defra should guarantee the budget for agricultural funding until 2029, maintaining it at its current level of £2.4bn (in real terms). It should ring-fence £500m–£700m of this money for natural carbon removal and restoring semi-natural habitats.

The Government made a manifesto commitment to maintain funding for agriculture at an average of £2.4bn per year until the end of this parliamentary term (2024). This budget was based on 2019 rates of subsidy payment for farmers, rather than on a calculation of the cost of delivering specified environmental outcomes. It should maintain at least this overall spending commitment through the remainder of this decade, progressively shifting around £2.2bn of agriculture spending from Direct Payments (the Common Agricultural Policy subsidies we have inherited from the EU) to Environmental Land Management schemes (ELMs). This leaves around £200m for improving farm productivity and innovation, in line with Defra's proposals.

The Government should ring-fence £500m–700m for schemes to encourage natural carbon removal and habitat restoration. These schemes would incentivise farmers to convert their less productive land into nature-rich, carbon-sequestering landscapes. Some of these landscapes would still produce food, albeit with lower yields. Some priority habitats, such as heath and species-rich grassland, are best managed with conservation grazing. Very extensive grazing is compatible with creating new woodlands. Livestock farmers seeking to diversify into woodland entirely could retain roughly 10% of a typical commercial flock or herd.[1] Other areas of land (notably peatlands, which can only recover under extremely low grazing pressure) would not produce food at all.[2]

Farmers would receive payments on the basis of carbon sequestered and nature restored – both of which can be monitored using techniques developed by the Joint Nature Conservation Committee.[3] Schemes for land use change should be designed in ways that are simple and easy for farmers to enter: it should be no more difficult than the Sustainable Farming Incentive (SFI) that is already being rolled out.

The initial payment rate would be 100% of costs, with an additional per hectare uplift to make sure farmers receive a fair return on land brought out of production.

Defra should ensure that it is easy for tenant farmers to enter the schemes, as well as farmers who own their land. Each scheme should be carefully proofed to ensure it does not inadvertently disadvantage tenants or commoners. The schemes should be designed with sufficient flexibility to allow innovative approaches to achieving their goals.

Rationale

In the UK, agriculture is responsible for about 10% of total greenhouse gas emissions, and 83% of ammonia emissions, mostly from livestock farming and fertiliser use.[4] This has barely changed over the past ten years. Morever, intensive agriculture has had a devastating effect on biodiversity. Since 1970, 41% of UK wildlife species have decreased, and in the last ten years we have failed to meet 14 of our 20 biodiversity targets.[5]

Farms must be supported and incentivised to reduce their total environmental impact, in order to help meet a range of national targets, the most notable of which are the "30x30" commitment to protect 30% of land in England for nature by 2030, the 25 year plan for nature, and the net zero target and carbon budgets.

Some progress can be made through improvements in practice (such as lowering pesticide and fertiliser use or managing animal waste better). But changing the way agricultural land is used will be central to restoring nature and achieving our net zero goals. We estimate, in line with the Climate Change Committee's (CCC) 6th carbon budget report, that roughly one tenth of agricultural land in England will need to transition to woodland, restored peat, other semi-natural habitats and energy crops by 2035, as part of the broader UK road to net zero.[6]

This is why the Government is reforming the agricultural support system in England. By 2027, the previous land area-based Basic Payment Scheme (BPS) will be fully phased out and replaced by payments for public goods. ELMs will pay for farmers and land managers to do things such as maintaining hedgerows, low-till farming and maintaining new woodlands.

We think that Defra is, broadly speaking, taking the right approach. They will use 30% of the ELMs budget for the Sustainable Farming Incentive and will ensure that all payments are for changes that go beyond the regulatory baseline.[7] Farmers have received subsidies based primarily on the amount of land they farm, or the quantities of food they produce, for over seventy years. They need time – and money – to adjust their business models.

Nearly 40% of farms currently depend on Basic Payments to make a profit. Cutting these subsidies before they have had time to adjust could be disastrous for their bottom line. Livestock farms are more likely to be affected by these changes than other farms, and in the longer term, their prospects could get even worse:[8] new trade deals are likely to make the market for meat more competitive, while reductions in meat eating and increases in the consumption of alternative proteins will make it smaller.[9]

Of course, the whole point of ELMs is to incentivise sustainable farming practices over unsustainable ones. But for farmers to adapt and plan for the future they need clarity. Many farmers have voiced concerns about the lack of clarity over what ELMs will mean in practice, particularly for small farms;[10] and about the industry becoming increasingly unappealing to the younger generation because of the low profit margins and the uncertain future. This response to our call for evidence captures the bind that some farmers find themselves in:

"I write this with a real dilemma on my hands that I imagine must be typical of many farmers. We have a small upland farm with permanent grassland & don't use artificial fertilisers. We produce ruminants (deer) which make this small farm viable. Should we continue as we are, or should we plant trees and thereby have no income and no value to our land? Economically it's a no-brainer. But ecologically?" – National Food Strategy Call for Evidence.

Land use change for natural carbon removal and semi-natural habitats

Simply removing Basic Payments by 2027 would see nearly 40% of farmers go bust, even if they retain existing payments for nature.[11] At the other end of the spectrum, removing Basic Payments would still leave the top quintile of farms making profits of £30 to £50 for every £100 of input.[12]

These differences in profit are not just the result of farmers' effort or skill. Every farmer knows that much of the difference lies in the land itself. But the challenge of farming unproductive land can now be turned into an advantage, for both the farmer and the common good. Some of this unproductive land is exceptionally well suited to creating environmentally friendly landscapes, ranging from species-rich wood pasture grazed by rare breed cows, all the way to new biodiverse forests and rewetted peat bogs. They are overwhelmingly upland farmers, though lowland grazing farms appear in this group too. The nation needs the carbon storage and natural habitats that their land – around 20% of English farmland – is exceptionally suited to provide.

Reducing food production on some of this land poses very little risk to our food security. Losing the least productive 20% of farmland would reduce the calories we produce by only 3%.[13]

We commissioned Forest Creation Partners (FCP) to assess the suitability of agricultural land in England for the planting of both broadleaf and commercial coniferous forest, based on a suitability assessment incorporating physical, regulatory, and economic constrains (see online supplementary material). Using a search area of the least productive land in England, which produces less than 3% of our calories, their analysis suggests around 420,000 hectares are likely to be suitable for forestry creation.[14] This is enough land to meet the Climate Change Committee's tree planting recommendation for England by 2030 and 2050.

This is, however, unlikely to happen without Government support. Mixed broadleaf forest is not a commercial enterprise, due to a lack of private markets for carbon credits and eco-system services. Coniferous forest can be profitable without public support, beyond an initial establishment grant, but it is less good for biodiversity than mixed broadleaf forest.[15] Peatland can never be profitable in the absence of markets for carbon sequestration or natural capital restoration. Even extremely extensive grazing to maintain certain priority habitats is uneconomic without payments for nature. Over time, as markets for these goods are developed, farmers should be able to contract with private entities to supply them.

In the meantime we, the public, should provide a fair return for nature and carbon removal, just as we should pay a fair price for the food that farmers grow. We calculate that £500m–£700m per year –around a third of the ELMs budget – would enable the Government to give farmers a fair return for managing roughly 400,000 hectares of species-rich broadleaf forests, 325,000 hectares of restored upland peat and around 200,000 hectares of farmland land dedicated mainly to nature. This would start the land use change necessary to meet the country's nature and net zero goals.

Any scheme to support land use change needs to be designed in a way that is simple and easy to access. Previous woodland creation schemes have had limited participation due to the complexity of Countryside Stewardship prescriptions, along with delays in payments and lack of clarity over funding.[16] It also needs to be easy for tenant farmers to participate. At present almost half of agricultural land is tenanted.[17] Many recent tenancy agreements are shorter than five years and do not permit tenants to plant trees.[18] Potential solutions include extending tenants' rights to object to landlords prohibiting reasonable environmental changes being made on their land, and discourage short-term tenancies by restricting inheritance tax relief to tenancy agreements of ten years or more.

A scheme to enable land use change needs to be scaled up rapidly, so it is available to farmers seeking to respond to the following policy deadlines:

- The halving of BPS by 2024 and its removal by 2027.
- The 2030 "30x30" nature commitment.
- The 2032 end of the 5th carbon budget, in line with the UK's 2050 net zero law.
- The 2042 end date for the 25-year plan for nature.

Without rapid introduction of Defra's other planned environmental schemes, marginal farms are likely to see the Sustainable Farming Incentive (SFI) as the only viable source of support. Indeed, farmers and land managers have already made requests for eligibility for SFI to be as broad as possible.[19] Without a ring-fenced budget for land use change, and a clear route through the agricultural transition period, marginal farmers have limited options. They can either: lobby to expand the SFI into a scheme that could end up paying all farmers without providing environmental goods; attempt to intensify production in ways that cause both environmental damage and lost opportunity for carbon capture;[20] or else go out of business and sell their land, causing a structural shift in land ownership away from traditional, small-scale ownership.

The public values farmers, and wants to see them fairly paid for the work that they do.[21] Land use change through ELMS should pay farmers a fair wage for the nationally important carbon and nature restoration work they will do. Our economic analysis shows that ELMS should expect to pay farmers around £775 per hectare for the multiple environmental benefits of broadleaf forest. Doing so will address the negative impact of current support schemes and farming methods on the health and wellbeing of farmers. (Roughly one in eight farmers never take holidays, despite the average working week exceeding 65 hours.[22]) It will also bolster rural incomes, supporting the economic viability of increasingly diversified rural economies.

Total funding for agriculture

To ensure that ELMs are successful in achieving their targets for the environment, Government will need to show the schemes are adequately funded, accessible, and guaranteed for the long term. Otherwise many farmers may seek to make up for lost income by increasing intensification. This would make it even harder to achieve our environmental goals.[23]

We have worked with the Wildlife and Countryside Link to estimate the costs of ELMs, working from models originally put together by the Royal Society for the Protection of Birds, The Wildlife Trusts and National Trust.[24] While far from complete, these calculations suggest that a budget of around £2.2bn per year is approximately what is needed to support the farming sector to contribute to environmental targets over the next ten years (Table 1). If we include Defra's 9–10% budget for measures improving farm productivity, this would suggest a total budget of £2.4bn–£2.5bn will continue to be needed for agriculture.[25] This would not, however, include provision to improve people's enjoyment of the natural environment, which is a target in the 25 year environment plan and a focus of public goods payments under the Agriculture Act 2020. So the total budget required is likely to be substantially greater. As an absolute minimum, therefore, the Government should commit to at least maintaining current agriculture spending until 2029.

Table 1

Annual cost to deliver Environmental Land Management outcomes over the next ten years (NFS updated RSPB model)

Land management practice	Cost (£m per year in England)
Priority habitats	£760
Boundary features	£333
Historic environment	£56
Arable land	£523
Grassland	£342
Organic	£17
Total land management	**£2,031**
Additional elements	
Environmental land management advice	£42
Securing vulnerable high nature value farming	£120
Business advice to vulnerable HNV farms	£3
Securing long term changes in land use	£10
Sub-total: Additional cost elements	**£175**
Total	**£2,206**

Costs and benefits

The benefits of the land use change component of ELMs should be consistent with the policy targets outlined above, and should include (by 2035 at the latest):

- The creation of at least 410,000 hectares of additional woodland in England, equivalent to 3% of the land area of England – bringing English woodland cover up to 13%.[26]
- The restoration of an additional 325,000 hectares (100%) of upland peat.
- An additional 200,000 hectares of agricultural land to be managed for nature that is not suited to living on a farm. This will involve allowing large areas to restore natural processes and rebuild ecosystems. Restorations may include lowland heath, large water bodies and marsh, reed beds, wet grassland habitats, and species-rich grassland. Specific actions will need to be tailored to local conditions.

Overall, this would enable an extra 7% of land in England to be protected for nature by 2035. This will contribute to the Government's "30x30" pledge, which requires 30% of the total land area of England to be protected for nature by 2030. Presently, 26% of land in England has some form of protection, meaning that at least 4% more land will be needed to meet the target.

In addition, much of the land that is already protected is in a poor ecological state: 75% of Sites of Special Scientific Interest (SSSIs) in English National Parks are in an "unfavourable condition", meaning they are not being protected sufficiently.[27] Alongside improvements to farmed land, ELMs could reverse the decline in English nature and help fulfil the 30x30 pledge.

Our calculations of the cost of land use change – which led to the recommendation of ringfencing £500m–700m – are based on forestry cost analysis from Forest Creation Partners (online supplementary material available on the National Food Strategy website), alongside analysis of the cost of restoring and maintaining peatland and other priority habitats. Based on these, we have calculated the annual costs required to support the creation and maintenance of these habitats. We made two assumptions that are relevant to the cost of this approach:

- Restoring forest, peat, or priority habitat must not be loss-making for the farmer. For forestry specifically, we adapted the FCP model, so that broadleaf woodland, which is loss-making without payments, would break even with a 0% rate of return over 40 years.
- The land manager must receive a fair and reliable income – the FCP's model assumes annual earnings of £28,000 for a 50-hectare plot. We have included similar labour costs in our assessments of peat and other priority habitats.

Assuming both of these requirements, and without carbon credits, total payments of £775 per hectare per year would be needed to support broadleaf woodland over a 40-year period. At a carbon price of £69/tCO_2e – below HMT's expected carbon price for 2030 – with carbon credits paid from year 15 of forest establishment, payments could drop to £250 per hectare per year.[28]

Currently, the least profitable 25% of upland farms receive ~£260/ha in annual subsidies, most of which are in BPS payments.[29] Despite this subsidy, the average upland farm relies on ~£28,000 in unpaid labour undertaken by farmers and their families.[30]

Without a carbon price, our broadleaf scenario is more expensive. This is because our forestry scenarios assume an annual salary, rather than expecting unpaid labour. If we assumed the same willingness to carry out unpaid labour for woodland management, the cost of broadleaf woodland, without income from carbon credits, would drop to £257/ha – demonstrating the comparative cost effectiveness of paying for woodland compared to our existing system.

In broad terms, peat restoration and maintenance of priority semi-natural habitat cost between £240–£600/ha before any carbon credits.

Each pound invested benefits the public several times over. Achieving net zero in the UK by 2050 would cost landowners a total of £1.6bn per year, and return £0.9bn per year in private revenues. It would return public benefits of £4bn per year, however, so public investment would provide value for money.[31] Nature restoration is estimated to yield benefits ranging from 2:1 (e.g. saltmarsh restoration) to 9:1 (inland wetlands restoration).[32]

Endnotes

[1] Chapman, P. (2017). Conservation grazing for semi-natural habitats. Scotland's Rural College. Available at: https://www.fas.scot/downloads/tn686-conservation-grazing-semi-natural-habitats/

[2] Lindsay, R. et al. (2014). IUCN UK Committee peatland programme briefing note no. 7. University of East London. Available at: https://www.iucn-uk-peatlandprogramme.org/sites/default/files/2019-05/7 Grazing and trampling final - 5th November 2014.pdf

[3] Joint Natural Capital Committee. Private correspondence.

[4] Greenhouse gas emissions: 55MtCO_2e/year in Climate Change Committee (2020). Sixth carbon budget. Available at: https://www.theccc.org.uk/wp-content/uploads/2020/12/The-Sixth-Carbon-Budget-The-UKs-path-to-Net-Zero.pdf;

Ammonia: Department for Environment, Food and Rural Affairs (2019) The future farming and environment evidence compendium. HMG. Available at: https://assets.publishing.service.gov.uk/government/uploads/system/uploads/attachment_data/file/834432/evidence-compendium-26sep19.pdf

[5] Emissions have barely changed: National Atmospheric Emissions Inventory (2021). Greenhouse gas inventories for England, Scotland, Wales & Northern Ireland: 1990–2019. Available at: https://naei.beis.gov.uk/reports/reports?report_id=1019;

Species decline: National Biodiversity Network. (2019). State of nature 2019 report. Available at: https://nbn.org.uk/wp-content/uploads/2019/09/State-of-Nature-2019-UK-summary.pdf;

Joint Nature Conservation Committee (2019). Sixth national report to the United Nations Convention on Biological Diversity. Available at: https://data.jncc.gov.uk/data/527ff89f-5f6b-4e06-bde6-b823e0d-dcb9a/UK-CBD-6NR-v2-web.pdf

[6] Around 19% of agricultural land in England: Climate Change Committee. (2020) Sixth Carbon Budget. Climate Change Committee. Available at: https://www.theccc.org.uk/publication/sixth-carbon-budget/

[7] Department for Environment, Farming and Rural Affairs (2021). Agricultural Transition Plan: June 2021 progress update. Available at: https://www.gov.uk/government/publications/agricultural-transition-plan-june-2021-progress-update/agricultural-transition-plan-june-2021-progress-update

[8] Department for Environment, Food and Rural Affairs. (2019). The future farming and environment evidence compendium. HMG. Available at: https://www.gov.uk/government/publications/the-future-farming-and-environment-evidence-compendium-latest-edition

[9] Increase in alternative proteins: Mintel. (2020). Plant-based push: UK sales of meat-free foods shoot up 40% between 2014–19. Mintel. Available at: https://www.mintel.com/press-centre/food-and-drink/plant-based-push-uk-sales-of-meat-free-foods-shoot-up-40-between-2014-19;

International competition, e.g., cost of production (lamb) in Wales compared with New Zealand: Meat Promotion Wales. (2018). Lamb production costs 2017/18. Meat Promotion Wales. Available at: https://meatpromotion.wales/images/resources/HCC_Lamb_production_costs_2017-18_-_ENG.pdf;

Meat & Livestock Australia. (2018). Market supplier snapshot sheepmeat, New Zealand. Meat & Livestock Australia. Available at: https://www.mla.com.au/globalassets/mla-corporate/prices--markets/documents/os-markets/red-meat-market-snapshots/mla-ms-nz-snapshot-2018.pdf

[10] Department for Environment, Food and Rural Affairs. (2021) Environmental Land Management: policy discussion document. HMG. Available at: https://assets.publishing.service.gov.uk/government/uploads/system/uploads/attachment_data/file/959727/elm-policy-discussion-document-analysis-responses.pdf

[11] Department for Environment, Food and Rural Affairs. (2019). The future farming and environment evidence compendium. HMG. Available at: https://www.gov.uk/government/publications/the-future-farming-and-environment-evidence-compendium-latest-edition

[12] Department for Environment, Food and Rural Affairs (2019) The future farming and environment evidence compendium. HMG. Available at: https://assets.publishing.service.gov.uk/government/uploads/system/uploads/attachment_data/file/834432/evidence-compendium-26sep19.pdf

[13] 3% of food production: NFS Analysis, based on data from Defra June Survey, see: Department for Environment, Food and Rural Affairs. (2021). June survey of agriculture and horticulture. HMG. Available at: https://www.gov.uk/agricultural-survey

[14] The suitability assessment accounted for regulatory restrictions, land quality and access, among other factors – see online supplementary material for detailed case study.

[15] Net Present Value and Rate of Return were estimated with and without land acquisition costs, and a range of 4.5–7% annual sale price growth of timber was assumed, based on Compound Annual Growth Rate in nominal timber price between 2000 and 2019 – see online supplementary material for detailed case study. Less biodiversity from coniferous forest: Burton, V. et al. (2021). Reviewing the evidence based for the effects of woodland expansion on biodiversity and ecosystem services in the United Kingdom. Forest Ecology and Management 430, 366–379. Available at: https://www.sciencedirect.com/science/article/pii/S0378112718306662

[16] Short, C. et al. (2018) Initial evaluation of the implementation of Countryside Stewardship in England in 2015/16. Fera Consortium. Countryside and Community Research Institute: Gloucester. Available at: http://sciencesearch.defra.gov.uk/Default.aspx?Menu=Menu&-Module=More&Location=None&Completed=0&ProjectID=19803

[17] Department for Environment, Food and Rural Affairs (2019) The future farming and environment evidence compendium. HMG. Available at: https://assets.publishing.service.gov.uk/government/uploads/system/uploads/attachment_data/file/834432/evidence-compendium-26sep19.pdf

[18] Tenant Farmers Association. Private correspondence.

[19] Blue Marble Research. (2021). Environmental Land Management Policy discussion document. HMG. Available at: https://assets.publishing.service.gov.uk/government/uploads/system/uploads/attachment_data/file/959727/elm-policy-discussion-document-analysis-responses.pdf

[20] Clark, C. and Scanlon, B. (2019). Less is more: Improving profitability and the natural environment in hill and other marginal farming systems. Royal Society for the Protection of Birds, The Wildlife Trusts and National Trust. Available at: https://www.wildlifetrusts.org/sites/default/files/2019-11/Hill farm profitability report - FINAL agreed 15 Nov 19.pdf

[21] Food Standards Agency. (2018). Food and You Survey. FSA. Available at: https://www.food.gov.uk/research/food-and-you

[22] University of Lincoln. (2019). Health and wellbeing research report. The Worshipful Company of Farmers. Available at: http://eprints.lin-

coln.ac.uk/id/eprint/41180/1/WCF-Health-and-Wellbeing-Research-Report-FINAL-April.pdf

[23] Clark, C. and Scanlon, B. (2019). Less is more: Improving profitability and the natural environment in hill and other marginal farming systems. Available at: https://www.wildlifetrusts.org/sites/default/files/2019-11/Hill farm profitability report - FINAL agreed 15 Nov 19.pdf

[24] Rayment, M. (2019). Paying for public goods from land management: How much will it cost and how might we pay? A report for the RSPB, the National Trust and The Wildlife Trusts. Rayment Consulting Services Ltd. Available at: https://www.wildlifetrusts.org/sites/default/files/2019-09/Paying for public goods final report.pdf

[25] 10% for farm prosperity: Department for Environment, Food and Rural Affairs. (2021). A path to sustainable farming: An agricultural transition plan 2021 to 2024. HMG Available at: https://www.gov.uk/government/publications/agricultural-transition-plan-2021-to-2024

[26] This is consistent with England's share of the Climate Change Committee's balanced pathway recommendation that requires at least 17% of all UK land to be forested by 2050. Climate Change Committee. (2020). Sixth carbon budget. CCC. Available at: https://www.theccc.org.uk/wp-content/uploads/2020/12/The-Sixth-Carbon-Budget-The-UKs-path-to-Net-Zero.pdf

[27] Campaign for National Parks. (2018). Raising the bar: improving nature in National Parks. Campaign for National Parks. Available at: https://www.cnp.org.uk/news/raising-the-bar

[28] Department for Business, Energy and Industrial Strategy. (2019). Updated short-term traded carbon values. HMG. Available at: https://assets.publishing.service.gov.uk/government/uploads/system/uploads/attachment_data/file/794186/2018-short-term-traded-carbon-values-for-appraisal-purposes.pdf;

Department for Business, Energy and Industrial Strategy. (2019). Valuation of energy use and greenhouse gas emissions for appraisal. HMG. Available at: https://assets.publishing.service.gov.uk/government/uploads/system/uploads/attachment_data/file/794737/valuation-of-energy-use-and-greenhouse-gas-emissions-for-appraisal-2018.pdf

[29] Least profitable 25% of Less Favoured Area grazing farms: Department for Environment, Food and Rural Affairs. (2021). Farm accounts in England results from the Farm Business Survey 2019/20. HMG. Available at: https://www.gov.uk/government/statistics/farm-accounts-in-england

[30] Department for Environment, Food and Rural Affairs. (2021). Farm accounts in England results from the Farm Business Survey 2019/20. HMG. Available at: https://assets.publishing.service.gov.uk/government/uploads/system/uploads/attachment_data/file/962279/fbs_farmaccountsengland_18feb21.pdf

[31] Vivid Economics. (2020). Economic iImpacts of net zero land use scenarios. CCC. Available at: https://www.theccc.org.uk/wp-content/uploads/2020/01/Economic-impacts-of-Net-Zero-land-use-scenarios-Vivid-Economics.pdf

[32] Greenpeace (2019). Government investment for a greener and fairer economy. Greenpeace. Available at: https://www.greenpeace.org.uk/wp-content/uploads/2019/08/Government-Investment-for-a-greener-and-fairer-economy-FINAL-30.08.19.pdf

Recommendation 9. Create a Rural Land Use Framework based on the Three Compartment Model.

What is it?

Defra should devise a Rural Land Use Framework, to be in place by 2022.

First, Defra should work with the Local Nature Recovery Networks to prepare a National Rural Land Map (as described in Recommendation 12). It should include:

- Data on the productivity of agricultural land derived from the June Farm Survey and the Agricultural Land Classification.[1]
- Priority areas for the environment (using, for example, existing data on Peaty Soils Location and Living England maps).[2]
- Areas where there are significant levels of pollution (with data from, for example, the UK Emissions map and the Together for Rivers map).[3]
- The England Tree Strategy, England peat action plan and Local Nature Recovery Strategies.[4]

Defra should then put together the Rural Land Use Framework and publish this as a report. This should provide detailed assessments of the best way to use any given area of land, and inform the many existing incentive schemes and land-based strategies in Defra. The framework should set out the best way to achieve a "three compartment model" for the country, including which land is most appropriate for semi-natural land, low-yield farmland and high-yield farmland, as well as land that is appropriate for economic development and housing. It should be clear how the model can help meet the Government's legal commitments to reach net zero by 2050, and protect 30% of land for nature by 2030 (the "30x30" target). The report would be updated annually.

Land changes cannot be imposed by central Government. Defra should make its National Rural Land Map freely available for land managers, to help them make decisions about the use of their land. The framework should also be used by central and local government in decision making – for example, to guide funding from Environmental Land Management schemes (ELMs) for Local Nature Recovery and Landscape recovery. There are currently at least eight different schemes that could influence land use– from the England Trees Action Plan to the ELMS – controlling funds ranging from £10m to £2.4bn per year. The Framework would help join these up. It would also be used to shape regulatory priorities (for example, to improve land management in Areas of National Beauty and National Parks), and to help planning officers take decisions on applications.

The data assembled for both the map and the framework should be shared across government, coordinated by the Geospatial Commission. In particular, Defra should work closely with the Ministry of Housing, Communities and Local Government in support of its housebuilding agenda and reforms to the planning system. The additional land needed for new housing is relatively small (approximately 2.2% of total UK land by 2060): sharing data across government can help make sure that the most appropriate land is used.

Rationale

Land is a scarce resource in England. In the past, we have used it for three main purposes: housing, recreation and food production. (This latter currently takes up 70% of English land.) We now need to do more with our land, using it for nature restoration as well as carbon reduction and sequestration.

The Climate Change Committee has estimated that approximately 21% of agricultural land in England will need to change function – to forestry, energy crops, peatland or agroforestry – in order to meet our net zero commitments.[5] This does not necessarily mean taking the land out of agricultural use entirely. Indeed, without using land for combined nature and carbon removals, or combined nature and food production, it may not be possible to meet all our targets. (At least, not without offshoring much of our environmental footprint and food production.)

Every piece of land is different. The kind of land that could deliver the greatest environmental benefits is often not very agriculturally productive. The most productive 33% of English land produces around 60% of the total output of the land, while the bottom 33% only produces 15%.[6] Similarly, making farming more environmentally sensitive in specific parts of the country could deliver disproportionate gains:

reducing runoff just from the 5% of agricultural land that produces the most water pollution could reduce phosphorus and sediment in our rivers by 25%, and their nitrogen load by 13%. Indeed, the only major area in England where our food, environmental and carbon reduction goals clash is the Fens. This is exceptionally good agricultural land, in large part because of its peaty soil, which would otherwise be a major carbon sink.[7]

This is why we need better data on how the land should be used. Unless we have a clear idea of which land should ideally be used for what, we could compromise our food security or make our environment even worse. Collating and publishing this information will help farmers and landowners to work together to improve conditions in local areas. It will also make the new ELMs much more likely to succeed. This was recognised by many stakeholders in the government's consultation on the ELM policy discussion document. They repeatedly highlighted the need for improved use of data and evidence to determine local priorities, including the use of land mapping data.[8]

In drawing together the recommendations in this report, we undertook an analysis which makes a start at doing just this. We identified land that is best used to protect both nature and carbon at the same time; showed that much of this land could be mainly used for nature and carbon at low risk to our food self-sufficiency; and analysed where within this low productivity land peat and woodland could be restored. Our results are summarised on four maps below (Figures 1, 2, 3, and 4). This underpins our recommendations for ELMs (Recommendation 8) and this land use framework.

Costs and benefits

A Rural Land Use Framework will outline the most effective means of achieving net zero by 2050 and 30% of land managed for nature by 2030. By using better data, we will be able to achieve these targets while reducing land used for farming by less than 1% of agricultural land per year up to 2050, maintaining food security, increasing forest coverage by 4% by 2050 and improving and increasing other land managed for nature.

Carbon nature food maps[9]

Figure 1

Priority regions for both carbon and biodiversity

It is possible to devise a combined carbon and biodiversity strategy by finding those areas that are high in both carbon and nature value and deprioritising areas that are high in carbon but very low in nature value.

Across Great Britain 90% of our highest priority carbon storage and 91% of our highest priority nature areas can be found in the same locations.

There doesn't need to be a conflict between protecting nature and reducing carbon.

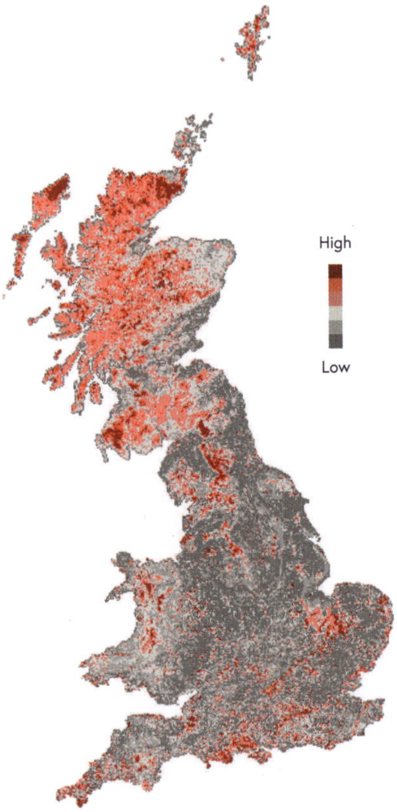

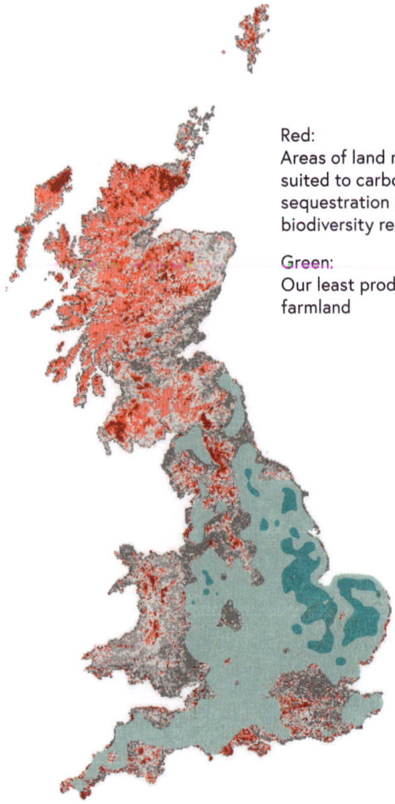

Figure 2

Much of the agricultural land that produces the least calories is high priority land for carbon and nature

The area in blue and green grows 75% of the total calories produced in England. The areas not covered in these two colours could – in theory – not be farmed at all if we reduced waste in the system. They contain many of the highest priority areas for nature and carbon protection - the Fens being the major exception.

Within this clear area, giving 10% of the least productive farmland to nature would mean producing 1% fewer calories. Doubling this to 20% would mean producing 3% fewer calories.

Figure 3

We can grow enough forest on our least productive agricultural land to reach our net zero goals

This map shows the share of the least productive 14% of farmland (across 2.4m hectares) that is suitable for forest creation. The underlying analysis takes place at farm scale.

The assessment excludes a large range of land due to physical suitability, planning constraints (all peat, protected habitats, and areas unlikely to receive planning permission are excluded), and future climate suitability.

Darker greens indicate a greater proportion of land is suitable.

In total, 424,456 ha (17%) within this area are plantable with the majority being suited to broadleaf woods. This is around the area which would need to become woodland to hit our net zero goals.

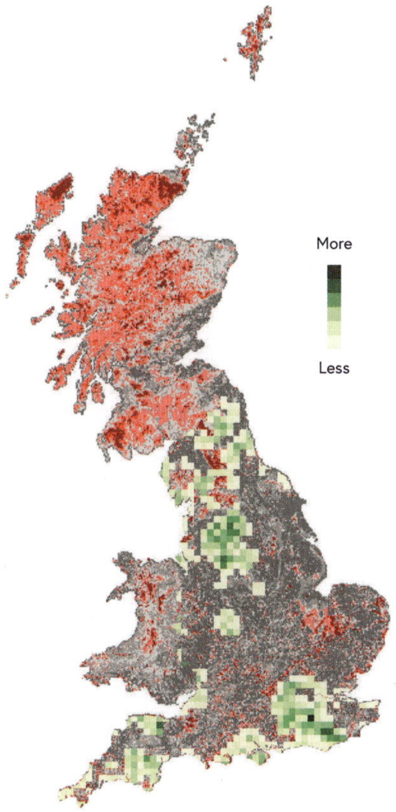

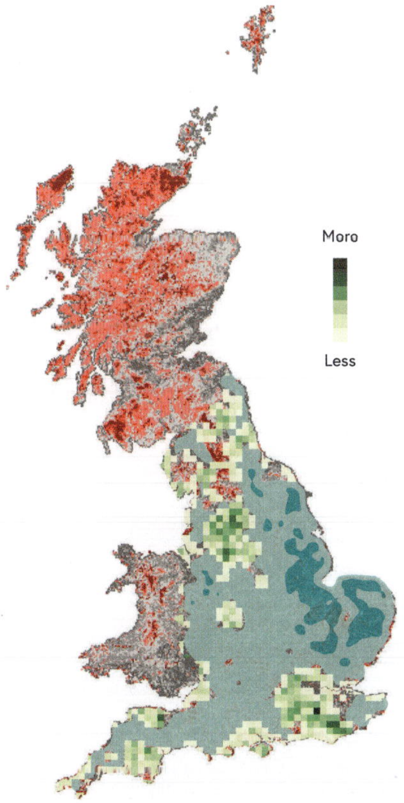

Figure 4

Priority land for nature and carbon, land suitable for forestry, and land that produces most of our food

Combining all these maps together shows, at a high level, areas in England where the land is most well suited to new woodland, restored peat, and other natural habitats (blank or green squares); those areas well suited to lower intensity farming (light blue), and higher intensity farming (dark blue).

A national map can only tell part of the story: farm productivity, habitat quality, and people's priorities vary at a local level, and this is ultimately where decisions on land use will be made.

Note: Calorie production and forest analysis conducted for England only.

Endnotes

[1] June Survey: Department for Food and Rural Affairs. (2021). June survey of agriculture and horticulture. HMG. Available at: https://www.gov.uk/agricultural-survey;

Agricultural Land Classification: MAGIC. (2019). Agricultural Land Classification – Provisional (England). HMG. Available at: https://magic.defra.gov.uk/StaticMaps/Agricultural Land Classification - Provisional (England).pdf

[2] Peaty Soils Location: Natural England. (2013). Peaty Soils Location. Natural England. Available at: https://data.gov.uk/dataset/c9eb1cd9-c254-4128-a18d-d368fbe6acf0/peaty-soils-location;

Joint Nature Conservation Committee. (2019). Habitat Extent. Joint Nature Conservation Committee. Available at: https://jncc.gov.uk/our-work/habitat-extent/

[3] Emissions: National Atmospheric Emissions Inventory. UK Emissions Interactive Map. Available at: https://naei.beis.gov.uk/emissionsapp/;

Pollution: The Rivers Trust. Together for rivers map. Available at: https://www.arcgis.com/apps/webappviewer/index.html?id=a6d-d42e3bc264fc28134c64c00db4a5b&extent=-401307.0872%2C6628364.5565%2C-130261.3849%2C6788576.5678%2C102100

[4] Peat action plan: Department for Food and Rural Affairs. (2021). England peat action plan. HMG. Available at: https://www.gov.uk/government/publications/england-peat-action-plan;

Trees action plan: Department for Food and Rural Affairs. (2021). England trees action plan. HMG. Available at: https://assets.publishing.service.gov.uk/government/uploads/system/uploads/attachment_data/file/987432/england-trees-action-plan.pdf;

Nature recovery network: Department for Food and Rural Affairs. (2020). The Nature Recovery Network. HMG. Available at: https://www.gov.uk/government/publications/nature-recovery-network/nature-recovery-network

[5] Climate Change Committee. (2020). Sixth carbon budget. CCC. Available at: https://www.theccc.org.uk/publication/sixth-carbon-budget/

[6] Department for Environment, Food and Rural Affairs. (2019). The future farming and environment evidence compendium. HMG. Available at: https://assets.publishing.service.gov.uk/government/uploads/system/uploads/attachment_data/file/834432/evidence-compendium-26sep19.pdf

[7] Evans, C. et al. (2017). Final report on project SP1210: Lowland peatland systems in England and Wales – evaluating greenhouse gas fluxes and carbon balances. Centre For Ecology and Hydrology, Rothamsted Research. Available at: http://oro.open.ac.uk/50635/

[8] Department for Environment, Food and Rural Affairs. (2021). Environmental Land Management policy discussion document – analysis of responses. HMG. Available at: https://assets.publishing.service.gov.uk/government/uploads/system/uploads/attachment_data/file/959727/elm-policy-discussion-document-analysis-responses.pdf

[9] See NFS Evidence Pack, pages 41, 45, and 48, available from: https://www.nationalfoodstrategy.org

Recommendation 10. Define minimum standards for trade, and a mechanism for protecting them.

What is it?

The Government should draw up a list of core minimum standards which it will defend in any future trade deals. These should cover animal welfare, environment and health protection, carbon emissions, antimicrobial resistance, and zoonotic disease risk. The Government must then set out which mechanisms it intends to use to protect these standards.

The UK has high standards of animal welfare and environmental protection. While many of these are important to our trading relationships, there are standards that are less relevant to international partners (for example, the way that we manage our grouse moors). There are also some standards that do not apply in the UK but are necessary to reduce serious harms overseas (for example, rules against deforestation of rainforests). The Government should set out a list of minimum standards which it expects imported food to meet in support of the objective of a healthy and sustainable food system.

The Government should also set out a mechanism which it proposes to use to defend these standards in trade deals. This means making sure trade deals do not force the UK to weaken its own standards, or open the UK market to imports that do not comply with those standards and thereby undermine them. One way to do this without breaking the WTO's anti-protectionism rules would be to make tariff reductions within free trade agreements (FTAs) contingent on products complying with UK core standards. Noncompliant products would incur the UK's full most-favoured-nation tariff, which is high enough to keep imports of such products at low levels. This is the mechanism we proposed in Part One of this strategy, and which was also suggested by the Trade and Agriculture Commission.[1] Whether the Government chooses this approach or another, it must have both the mechanism and the standards in place before taking any further steps towards trade agreements with countries such as the United States and Brazil.

Rationale

Signing free trade agreements with countries such as Australia, Brazil or the United States, who are able to produce food at a lower cost to the UK, is likely to cause our imports of food to rise. Many of the countries with which the Government is seeking to make free trade agreements can produce food at a lower cost than the UK. For example, the cost of producing beef in the UK is 2–4 times higher than in Australia (UK: ~ $480-780 per kg sold, Australia: $180-310 per kg sold).[2] Much of this difference is due to differences in landscape, weather conditions, scale of operations and other factors which have no connection with standards. Many Australian farm products would still be highly competitive on the UK market even if they complied fully with UK core standards.[3] There is even evidence to suggest that some overseas farmers can produce food at rather lower environmental cost than UK farmers can (for example, New Zealand lamb).[4]

But some countries do produce cheaper food through environmentally costly practices – such as ongoing deforestation for grazing land. Some have very low standards of animal welfare. If cheap food from these countries was allowed to flood the market, UK farmers would not be able to compete on price. Although UK consumers like the idea of locally produced food that is kind to animals and the planet, we are hugely influenced by price.[5] Cheap, low-standard food would quickly capture a greater proportion of the market than locally produced foods. This is particularly the case for ready meals, catering and processed foods, where provenance is less clear and which represent a large and growing fraction of our consumption.[6]

This risks seriously increasing our global impact on nature and the environment. The UK market for meat and dairy already takes up more land abroad than at home, and food that is imported has a total impact on species loss ten times greater than the food we produce domestically.[7] As the problems of the environment and nature are global ones it would be pointless – and hypocritical – to reduce the harms created by our own farming system while simply transferring those harms overseas.

Beyond carbon and the environment, there is the issue of animal welfare. The UK has some of the highest standards of animal health and welfare in the world.[8] For example, as part of the EU we banned growth hormones for cattle in 1981, while these are still in use in countries including Australia, Canada and the

US.[9] There are also examples where we have higher standards than the EU. The maximum stocking density for chickens is 39kg/m^2 in the UK, compared to 42kg/m^2 in the EU.[10] Access to the lucrative UK food market is a prized commodity: if we strike careful trade deals, which allow privileged access to our market only to producers with standards that match our own, we can incentivise positive change across the global food system. Conversely, if we accept goods with lower standards, we undermine our own values while disincentivising progress abroad.

The UK public feels strongly about maintaining our food standards as we enter trade deals. Numerous opinion polls have shown this to be the case, e.g. 82% would prefer to retain current standards;[11] 93% think food standards should be maintained after EU Exit;[12] 81% of respondents would be concerned if the UK Government relaxed laws on meat standards to secure trade deals with the USA and the rest of the world.[13] Red Wall swing voters have also said that they would not want our food standards to be undermined.[14]

This is why the Conservatives, in their 2019 manifesto, pledged that "in all of our trade negotiations, we will not compromise on our high environmental protection, animal welfare and food standards". In Part One of this strategy, we proposed a way to honour this pledge. We suggested that the Trade and Agriculture Commission should draw up a list of core standards, covering food safety, animal welfare, responsible antibiotic use and the prevention of severe environmental impacts (for example, the clearing of rainforest for beef grazing). In striking trade deals, it should offer to lower tariff barriers only on those products that comply with these standards. Our partner countries would be asked to set up verification systems, so that exporters wanting to benefit from reduced tariffs could prove that they were compliant with UK standards. These would be similar to those currently operated by the US Department of Agriculture, which verifies American beef producers wanting to export certified hormone-free beef to the UK and EU. A similar recommendation was made by the Trade and Agriculture Commission when it reported earlier this year.[15]

Despite these recommendations from two independent reports (both commissioned by the Government), the Government has still not said what standards it proposes to protect, or what mechanism it will use to defend them in trade negotiations. It has now agreed in principle a trade deal with Australia which contains no such mechanism. As things stand, this will eventually allow Australia to export unlimited quantities of meat to the UK, regardless of how it was produced. Australian standards are closer to the UK's than those of other countries, such as Brazil, and the volume of imports from Australia may not be large enough to seriously compromise the UK's attempts to protect the environment and animal welfare. But this deal sets a dangerous precedent.

If future trade agreements are made in the same way – with no core standards in place, and no way of enforcing them – it will make it much harder to carry through the recommendations in this strategy. Reducing the carbon footprint of meat consumption in the UK will be challenging enough as it is. But if we sign Australian-style deals with countries such as Brazil, it would mean allowing cheap beef with a much higher carbon footprint to undercut our own produce. Our true carbon footprint – including that from imports – would be worse than ever, and we would bankrupt our own farmers in the process. This would be both ethically and commercially absurd. That is why the Government must move quickly to implement its manifesto pledge.

Costs and benefits

We have not assessed the potential benefits of this recommendation. This is because it is intended to avoid worsening our position rather than to improve it.

Endnotes

[1] Trade and Agriculture Commission. (2021). Final report. TAC. Available at: https://assets.publishing.service.gov.uk/government/uploads/system/uploads/attachment_data/file/969045/Trade-and-Agriculture-Commission-final-report.pdf

[2] Behrendt, K. and Weeks, P. (2017). How are global and Australian beef producers performing? Meat & Livestock Australia. Available at: https://www.mla.com.au/globalassets/mla-corporate/prices--markets/documents/trends--analysis/agri-benchmark/revised_mla_agribenchmark-beef-results-report_jan-2017.pdf

[3] Menghi, A. et al. (2014). Assessing farmers' costs of compliance with EU legislation in the fields of environment, animal welfare and food safety. Centro Ricerche Produzioni Animali for the European Commission Directorate General for Agriculture and Rural Development. Available at: https://ec.europa.eu/info/sites/default/files/food-farming-fisheries/key_policies/documents/ext-study-farmer-costs-fulltext_2014_en.pdf

[4] Williams, A. G. et al. (2008) Comparative life cycle assessment of food commodities procured for UK consumption through a diversity of supply chains. Final report for Defra Project FO0103. HMG. Available at: http://randd.defra.gov.uk/Default.aspx?Module=More&Location=None&ProjectID=15001

[5] D'Angelo, C. et al. (2000). Food consumption in the UK: Trends, attitudes and drivers. RAND Corporation. Available at: https://www.rand.org/pubs/research_reports/RR4379.html

[6] Department for Environment, Food and Rural Affairs. (2020). Family food datasets. HMG. Available at: https://www.gov.uk/government/statistical-data-sets/family-food-datasets

[7] NFS analysis based on Poore, J. and Nemecek, T. (2018). Reducing food's environmental impacts through producers and consumers. Science 360(6392), 987–992. Available at: https://science.sciencemag.org/content/360/6392/987

[8] World Animal Protection. (2020). Animal protection index. Available at: https://api.worldanimalprotection.org/

[9] European Commission. (2021). Hormones in meat. European Commission. Available at: https://ec.europa.eu/food/food/chemical-safety/hormones-meat_en

[10] UK: Department for Environment, Food and Rural Affairs. (2019). Broiler (meat) chickens: welfare recommendations. HMG. Available at: https://www.gov.uk/government/publications/poultry-on-farm-welfare/broiler-meat-chickens-welfare-recommendations;

EU: European Commission. (2007). Animal welfare – protection of chickens kept for meat production. Available at: https://eur-lex.europa.eu/legal-content/EN/TXT/?uri=LEGISSUM%3Af82002

[11] The Progressive Policy Think Tank. (2018). Public willing to sacrifice US trade deal to protect food safety. The Progressive Policy Think Tank. Available at: https://www.ippr.org/news-and-media/press-releases/public-willing-to-sacrifice-us-trade-deal-to-protect-food-safety

[12] Which?. (2020). Ensuring trade deals work for consumers. Which?. Available at: https://campaigns.which.co.uk/trade-deals/wp-content/uploads/sites/31/2020/01/5e2f163d92b97-Trade-deals-v4-2.pdf

[13] UNISON. (2020). Public fears a lowering of meat standards in future US trade deals, says UNISON. UNISON. Available at: https://www.unison.org.uk/news/article/2020/02/public-fears-lowering-meat-standards-future-us-trade-deals-says-unison/

[14] Cracknell, J. and Rose, E. (2021). A view from the "Red Wall". Unchecked UK. Available at: http://redwall.unchecked.uk/wp-content/uploads/sites/2/2020/12/A-view-from-the-Red-Wall.pdf

[15] Trade and Agriculture Commission. (2021). Final report. TAC. Available at: https://assets.publishing.service.gov.uk/government/uploads/system/uploads/attachment_data/file/969045/Trade-and-Agriculture-Commission-final-report.pdf

Recommendation 11. Invest £1 billion in innovation to create a better food system.

What is it?

Under its new Innovation Strategy, the Government should invest in transforming the food system. This should include:

- Establishing a £500m fund, managed by UK Research and Innovation (UKRI), to invest in innovation for healthy and sustainable diets, including £75m for alternative proteins.
- Ensuring the £280m Defra has already earmarked for innovation through the Agricultural Transition Plan supports a full spectrum of "farmer-led" approaches, with priorities including agroecological farming, horticulture, and methods for reducing methane emissions from cows and sheep.
- £50m to help build, fund and support an innovation cluster where scientists and entrepreneurs can develop, test and scale up new alternative proteins.
- Setting up two What Works Centres, with a combined endowment of £200m, to strengthen the evidence for farming and food policies.

The Government should make creating a better food system one of the first "long-term missions" of its Innovation Strategy, due to be published very soon. All the Government departments and agencies with responsibilities for the food system should explicitly commit to this mission, including Defra, the Department for Health and Social Care (DHSC), the Department for Education (DfE) and the Food Standards Agency (FSA), coordinated by UKRI. The Government should pursue the mission through a package of innovation investment worth £1.03bn, of which £280m is already committed.

Challenge funding for healthy and sustainable diets

The mission should be backed by a new "challenge fund" of £500m, available over five years, targeted at practical innovation that supports a nationwide shift to sustainable and healthy eating. This fund should focus on achieving the changes in diet that we set out in Chapter 16. This might include accelerating work to reformulate processed foods, trying out new ways of helping customers change their habits, and boosting locally-led initiatives to improve diet and health. But it should also be used to help develop new ways of growing food, such as vertical farming and precision fermentation. In particular, and in addition to capital investment in the alternative protein cluster described below, the fund should allocate £75m to research on alternative proteins.

The fund should be managed by UKRI and open to applications from projects which are likely to have a practical impact. Projects of all sizes would be eligible for funding and could be commercial or non-commercial in nature. To ensure that support reaches a wide variety of fields, UKRI should invite people from businesses, community enterprises and government, as well as academia, to govern the fund and review project proposals. The funding should include innovative mechanisms for leveraging private investment, building on the experience of initiatives such as the Transforming Food Production Series A Investor Partnership Programme.[1] The challenge fund would be managed in coordination with complementary innovation funds across government.

Farmer-led innovation

Defra has already ring-fenced £280m to support innovation in its seven-year Agricultural Transition Plan. This funding focuses on "farmer-led" innovation, recognising that the driving force behind regenerative agriculture has usually been the people on the ground, trying out new ideas. This approach is designed to ensure investment goes not only on developing new tools and techniques, but also on making sure they are actually used in the field. It is crucial that Defra sees through this promise to take a farmer-led approach, and backs innovation across the full spectrum of regenerative farming: not just high-tech new ideas (important though these are), but also the agroecological methods that have been starved of investment up to now. It should draw on the experience of successful independent initiatives such as Innovative Farmers, the Yield Enhancement Network and Farmer Clusters.[2]

Fruit and vegetable production

One priority for Defra should be fruit and vegetable growing, with its innovation funding becoming a key component of an ambitious growth strategy for fresh produce, developed with the industry. This should be supported by a wider programme of investment to boost horticultural productivity sustainably, creating a less bureaucratic, more inclusive and better funded successor to the previous EU Fruit and Vegetable Regime.

Methane suppressants

Defra's £280m fund should also specifically include investment to develop new technologies to suppress methane emissions from cows and sheep, and to encourage their take-up by farmers. Defra should create a small team to scan the horizon for new methane-reduction products, develop a targeted research programme, and put together a timeline for integrating new products onto farms. At least initially, this is likely to require incentivising farmers to use the products or subsidising their cost, since the initial costs are likely to be high. Well-targeted investment could help bring new products to market and roll them out speedily.

Alternative proteins cluster

Defra should put an additional £50m towards a commercial innovation "cluster" to develop, test and scale up alternative proteins. This cluster should be based around an existing area of investment, such as the Centre for Process Innovation's novel food unit, or one of the Agri-Tech Centres. The funding would provide open-access facilities to allow emerging businesses to test and scale up new products. It would be complemented by commercial revenue.

What Works Centres

Finally, the Government should set up two What Works Centres to strengthen the evidence for policies and practices to improve the health impact and sustainability of farming and diets. The first, focused on effective policy and practical interventions to improve farming, has already been piloted by the Agriculture and Horticulture Development Board (AHDB), in the form of the Evidence for Farming Initiative (EFI). This could be expanded and formalised to play a pivotal part in improving the quality and coherence of advice on the practical implications for agriculture of goals such as net zero. Defra should ensure it has a long-term future by co-funding EFI through an endowment of £50m, alongside investment by AHDB and industry. As other centres affiliated to Government have already shown, an endowment fund will give the centre financial flexibility, as well as the ability to make longer-term plans and pursue a robust scientific strategy.[3] Defra should collaborate closely with EFI to inform future themes and priorities for its farmer-led Innovation fund.

The second What Works Centre should focus on improving policies and business practices to encourage a large-scale shift towards sustainable and healthy diets. It should take research already conducted by scientific institutions and governments around the world and translate it so that it becomes accessible to policymakers inside Government – for example through evidence briefings, data visualisations, summaries or guidance documents. It should also evaluate Government policies, conduct large-scale experimental studies, and assess small-scale pilots and experiments, to determine which new interventions are likely to be most effective. While the centre should remain independent of Government, it should maintain close links with relevant departments to ensure effectiveness. This centre should be established with an endowment of £150m, jointly funded by Defra and DHSC, to guarantee funding over 10 years. UKRI should work closely with the centre in developing priorities for the new challenge funding.

Rationale

Providing an abundance of healthy and sustainable food will require innovation. Many of the measures in this strategy will contribute to such innovation by helping businesses, government and academia direct their own research and development. For example, the legislation we propose (Recommendation 14) will set the direction for improving the health and sustainability of the food system, while the mandatory reporting (Recommendation 2) and the data programme (Recommendation 12) will help innovators and investors align with these goals. But direct innovation funding is also required.

Such innovation would have economic benefits, boosting the UK's involvement in emerging technologies such as gene editing, synthetic food production, nanotechnology, microalgae bioreactors, the internet of things (IoT), robotics and sensors, 3D food printing, and artificial intelligence. But it is also important that it should be directed in the public interest, which is why government investment is so important. The Government is expected to recognise this in its new Innovation Strategy, seeking to harness innovation to address social and environmental goals. The public want innovation to be a force for social change as well as economic growth.[4]

Innovation funding

The UK already produces world-class food science and invests a lot in agricultural research. Only scientists in the USA, where the Government spends seven times as much on agricultural research and development, are more frequently cited in research in agriculture and the biological sciences.[5] But the UK is less effective than comparable countries at innovation – the successful application of ideas. This has been a particular concern for businesses and policymakers concerned with food and agriculture.[6] A key innovation metric is change in total factor productivity (TFP).[7] From 2006 to 2016, TFP growth in the Netherlands was 2.6%, in Germany 1.8% and in Denmark 1.2%. In the UK it was only 0.6%.[8] The UK spends on agricultural research and development around as much as France and almost twice as much as New Zealand, but has seen slower productivity growth than either of those countries, relative to agricultural turnover.[9]

There are a number of reasons for this.[10] First, there has been an overall lack of funds for applied research: Defra's research budget has dropped dramatically over the past decade, from £225m in 2007 to £52m in 2017; over the same period, the Food Standards Agency's research budget fell from £17m to £2m a year.[11] Second, much of the public investment that has been made in innovation has been heavily focused on agriculture, particularly agricultural inputs, rather than the food system more generally. While the innovation funding Defra will provide under its Agricultural Transition Plan is extremely welcome, and rebalances agricultural funding towards the practicalities of farming, it will not correct the gap in public investment in food system innovation beyond the farm gate. Third, the current infrastructure for research and development is too centralised and does not offer sufficient involvement to the people who will actually have to apply new tools and technologies on the ground – farmers and agri-food businesses. Fourth, the Government's previous mechanisms for supporting farming and food innovation through Innovate UK have focused too narrowly on commercial innovation and have been inaccessible to non-commercial (e.g. policy or community) innovation projects, which are important for wider diet change.[12]

Fruit and vegetable production

Fresh produce is the sector of primary food production where growth most squarely aligns with the national interest. The link between what we grow and eat in this country is of course indirect, and the nation could eat 5-a-day without increasing production. Yet as Defra already promotes the case for Government investment to improve productivity, it makes sense to prioritise sectors where growth – through efficiencies and in volume – could directly benefit national health.[13]

Between 1985 and 2014 there was a 27% decline in the areas planted to fruit and vegetables.[14] Over the same period, our reliance on imports has increased sharply, only partly explained by seasonality and the increased demand for a wider range of products that cannot be grown in the UK. There are clear opportunities for UK growers to secure a greater share of the UK market.

Although the EU Fresh Fruit and Veg Regime has its flaws, notably the level of bureaucracy associated with the scheme, it has enabled the industry to co-invest and improve productivity. Defra should adapt the best elements of the EU scheme, to create a package of investment that aligns more closely with Government, consumer and grower requirements.

Methane suppressants

One area of innovation that urgently needs Government support is reducing emissions of greenhouse gases from cattle and sheep. Farmed ruminants (mainly cattle and sheep) emit methane equivalent to 22 MtCO2e/year, which is almost half of all UK agricultural emissions.[15]

Methane emissions can be reduced by:

- Rearing fewer ruminants, therefore eating less meat.
- Capturing the methane they emit, either by moving them inside or by attaching devices to them (both of which could harm their welfare).[16]
- Reducing the amount of methane each animal emits (methane inhibition).

There are a number of technologies for methane inhibition in development, but only one is so far commercially available: a feed additive called 3NOP. This has been found to have no impact on milk production or quality in dairy cattle, but its effects are short-lived so it needs to be given regularly in animal feed.[17] This makes it less practical for use in the kind of extensive grazing systems that are common in the UK. Other additives are currently in development, including a seaweed called Asparagopsis. Lab trials in Australia have found that adding 2% Asparagopsis cattle feed could reduce methane emissions by 99%.[18] In the longer term, selective breeding and "methane vaccines" may also provide a solution, particularly for sheep which are fed almost entirely on grass. Investing in these technologies offers our best hope of decarbonising livestock farming without massively reducing the number of farms in the sector and the amount of meat we can eat.

Alternative proteins cluster

Even if cows and sheep can be made to emit less methane, we would still be left with the high land-use footprint of ruminant production and the health risks of red meat.[19] We would still have to eat less meat than we do now. This is why an innovation cluster aimed at stimulating new alternative proteins would be so valuable.

> **Alternative Proteins**
>
> The umbrella term "alternative proteins" refers to a range of products that can serve as a substitute for conventional meats, from bean burgers to insect mince. These can broadly be separated into:
>
> 1. Plant-based proteins, which use existing vegetables and pulses. Many products of this kind are already available but come at a price premium and with varied flavour profiles and textures.
> 2. Insect-based proteins, which include some products for human consumption but are being developed more widely as animal feed.
> 3. Precision fermentation derived proteins, which use microbes such as yeast, algae or bacteria to replicate existing animal products (e.g. casein, egg proteins), create novel meat substitutes (e.g. Quorn), or create ingredients to flavour and enhance other foods.
> 4. Cell cultured meat, which involves growing animal tissue in vitro. This is currently a very expensive process and is unable to replicate the texture profile of meats, but is chemically identical to meat from animals.

Plant-based proteins produce 70 times less greenhouse gas emissions than an equivalent amount of beef, and use 150 times less land.[20]

Globally, per capita consumption of proteins has been growing over the past 50 years.[21] Coupled with population growth, this means our demand for proteins may outstrip production in the future.[22] While this problem is not one of need, as average global consumption of proteins currently far exceeds our biological necessity, the current trends will require new sources of protein.[23]

Even without any further advances in alternative proteins, 11% of global proteins could come from non-animal sources by 2035. But innovation could double that.[24] If we achieved that doubling in the UK, direct annual greenhouse gas emissions could fall by an additional 3MtCO2e / year, which is about 5% of total emissions from UK agriculture. Over 900,000 hectares – 5% of all the land used for farming in the UK – could be released for other uses, such as nature, carbon capture and extensification.[25]

Along with the environmental and other benefits, growing the alternative protein sector will benefit the UK economy. If the UK produces all of the new alternative protein it consumes, the industry could create an additional 10,000 good manufacturing jobs. In addition, 6,500 jobs would be retained in farming to produce inputs for the industry.[26] Without a strong domestic alternative protein sector, these factory and farming jobs could be lost to other countries.

The UK's competitors know this, which is why investment in the sector is growing globally. The US leads the global market in production of alternative proteins, with companies like Impossible Foods, Memphis Meats and Perfect Day last year raising $700m, $161m and $300m respectively in capital.[27] The Netherlands has developed one of the largest agribusiness regions in Europe – Food Valley – with universities, start-ups and multinationals working together to change the industry, by creating new vegan products and sustainable packaging alternatives.[28] Singapore and Israel have both proactively fostered alternative protein start-ups, and Singapore was the first country to give regulatory approval to a cultured meat product.[29] If we do not take action to support this sector, it is likely that start-ups will be more attracted to these other countries.

The UK has some existing advantages: our universities are leaders in alternative protein research, with an established research centre at Bath University directly linked to the production of alternative proteins, and projects at the universities of Cambridge, Newcastle, Manchester and Aston to improve production methods.[30] We also have nascent production centres for alternative proteins, for example at the Centre for Process Innovation (part of a Catapult), with links to farming through our Agri-Tech Centres. Establishing strong connections between academics, scientists, entrepreneurs and producers would give us a competitive advantage over other countries.

Some of the processes used to create alternative proteins are essentially the same as those used in the pharmaceutical and petrochemical industries, so the UK's strengths in these sectors means that skills and experience could be easily repurposed. Moreover, we have a large alternative protein market in which to sell new products. The UK has the largest market for meat alternatives in Europe, having grown by 40% from 2014 to 2019 and being projected to rise above £1.1bn by 2024.[31] This has led Tesco to set a target of 300% more alternative meat products by 2025 compared to 2018.[32]

In sum, our existing advantages and the scale of our domestic market could make England an attractive place for commercial investors in this new industry, but this needs to be supported by government investment. This would enable the UK to shape this new market in line with our standards and values, as well as building a new export industry to respond to protein shortages globally. If we do not act soon, we will end up as net importers of these products, losing out on new green jobs.[33]

What Works Centres

Finally, the two What Works Centres are intended to ensure that all this innovation actually gets the right results. The evidence currently available to farmers and agricultural policy-makers is fragmented, incoherent and confusing. The EFI, initially proposed by the Food & Drink Sector Council's Agricultural Productivity Working Group, was conceived by the farming industry to address this problem.[34] It has the potential to play a crucial part in translating the farmer-led research and development that Defra will be funding into quality-assured and widely relevant guidance for policy makers, farmers and their professional advisors. This will help to make the whole "knowledge and innovation ecosystem" that supports the transition in agriculture more effective. The initial evidence on net zero farming that EFI has collated during its pilot phase is testimony to its value.

There is currently no equivalent of the EFI collating evidence on how to change diets to increase the sustainability of our food system. The National Institute for Health Research, which gathers evidence and evaluates policy for DHSC, focuses exclusively on health. Moreover, there has been little focus to date on policies that can modify the economic and environmental factors that influence diet. The complexity and cost of testing and evaluating such approaches calls for dedicated resources.[35]

Experience suggests we need a new approach, as attempts to improve the national diet have so far had a very limited impact. Despite 14 Government strategies between 1992 and 2020 dedicated in whole or in part to reducing obesity in England, obesity prevalence has gone from 13% to 28%, and morbid obesity prevalence increased from less than 1% to more than 3%.[36] This is partly due to the tendency to focus on changing individual behaviour rather than making systemic interventions (with the exception of the Soft Drinks Industry Levy). But the failure to learn from previous mistakes is compounded by a lack of monitoring or evaluation.[37] We need more evidence and, in particular, more evidence which can be used to inform policy.[38]

The WWC model has been tried and tested across a range of complex areas of policy and public services. The nine existing WWCs have been effective in improving the impact of policy and services, in areas such as healthcare, education and policing.[39] It is a model that supports a flexible and pragmatic approach to evidence generation and policy design.[40] This includes the need for more trial and error for low-risk interventions, testing, learning and adapting.[41]

Costs and benefits

Establishing challenge funding for innovation to enable healthy and sustainable diets under its Innovation Strategy will cost the Government £500m over five years. This should be secured by Defra, DHSC and other Government departments, led by Defra, through their next Spending Review bids.

That funding should leverage an estimated £160m in private sector co-investment. This assumes 30% leverage for £200m for pre-commercial collaborative R&D projects with industry, and 200% for £50m in investor partnerships. The remaining £250m out of the total £500m funding is for non-commercial (e.g. public health) innovation projects.

This recommendation will deliver an estimated long-term net economic benefit to the UK of £3.5bn.[42]

Focusing Defra's existing innovation funding on methane reduction in ruminants will not involve additional costs to Government. If it succeeds, it could lead to total greenhouse gas savings of 50MtCO2e by 2050, or annual savings of approximately 7% of total agricultural emissions.[43]

Funding a new innovation cluster for alternative proteins will cost the Government £50m, which should all be delivered in year 1 (2022–23). Funding should be secured through a bid in the next Spending Review, coordinated by Defra and working with BEIS and UKRI.

This recommendation will deliver a long-term net economic benefit to the UK estimated to be £350m.[44]

Ensuring a long-term future for the Evidence for Farming Initiative will cost £50m in year 1 (2022-23) in the form of an endowment, to complement and underpin investment by AHDB. Funding for the endowment should be secured by Defra through a bid in the next Spending Review.

Setting up a What Works Centre for healthy and sustainable diets would cost the Government £150m in year 1 (2022-23). DHSC and Defra should collaborate to secure this funding in the next Spending Review.

Endnotes

[1] Innovate UK (2020). Transforming food production: series A investor partnership programme. HMG. Available at: https://apply-for-innovation-funding.service.gov.uk/competition/706/overview

[2] Innovative Farmers: www.innovativefarmers.org. Yield Enhancement Network: www.yen.adas.co.uk. Farmer Clusters: www.farmerclusters.com

[3] Bazalgette, L. (2020). A practical guide for establishing an evidence centre. Alliance for Useful Evidence. Available at: https://www.alliance4usefulevidence.org/assets/2020/06/Nesta-Evidence-Centre-FINAL-June2020-2.pdf.

[4] Nesta. (2020). Is the UK getting innovation right? Nesta. Available at: https://media.nesta.org.uk/documents/Is_the_UK_Getting_Innovation_Right.pdf

[5] Scimago Country Rank for Agricultural & Biological Sciences, 2018. Scimago Institutions Rankings. (2021). Scimago Journal & Country Rank. Scimago Institutions Rankings. Available at: https://www.scimagojr.com/countryrank.php?area=1100&order=ci&ord=desc;

Public agricultural R&D figures for 2013 (in 2011 US$): Heisey, P. and. Fuglie, K. (2018). Agricultural research investment and policy reform in high-income countries. United States Department of Agriculture. Available at: https://www.ers.usda.gov/webdocs/publications/89114/err-249.pdf?v=0. Table 3.1: USA = $4.30BN; UK = £0.59BN.

[6] Docherty, D. et al. (2015). Leading food 4.0: growing business-university collaboration for the UK's food economy. National Centre for Universities and Business. Available at: https://www.ncub.co.uk/index.php?option=com_docman&view=download&alias=214-leading-food-4-0&category_slug=reports&Itemid=2728

[7] Heisey, P. and. Fuglie, K. (2018). Agricultural research investment and policy reform in high-income countries. United States Department of Agriculture. Available at: https://www.ers.usda.gov/webdocs/publications/89114/err-249.pdf?v=0

[8] USDA Economic Research Service. (2020). International agricultural productivity. UDSA. Available at: https://www.ers.usda.gov/data-products/international-agricultural-productivity/

[9] Heisey, P. and. Fuglie, K. (2018). Agricultural research investment and policy reform in high-income countries. United States Department of Agriculture. Available at: https://www.ers.usda.gov/webdocs/publications/89114/err-249.pdf?v=0

[10] Agricultural Productivity Working Group. (2020). Report to the Food and Drink Sector Council. FDSC. Available at: http://www.fdsc.org.uk/fdsc/documents/APWG-report-feb20.pdf

[11] Constant 2017 prices. Data from Office for National Statistics. (2021). Research and development expenditure by the UK Government. ONS. Available at: https://www.ons.gov.uk/economy/governmentpublicsectorandtaxes/researchanddevelopmentexpenditure/datasets/scienceengineeringandtechnologystatisticsreferencetables

[12] UK Research and Innovation. (2021). Industrial Strategy Challenge Fund. UK Research and Innovation. Available at: https://www.ukri.org/our-work/our-main-funds/industrial-strategy-challenge-fund/

[13] Defra. (2020). The path to sustainable farming: an agricultural transition plan 2021 to 2024. Defra. Available at: https://assets.publishing.service.gov.uk/government/uploads/system/uploads/attachment_data/file/954283/agricultural-transition-plan.pdf

[14] Excluding potatoes. Schoenii, V. and Lang, T. (2016). Horticulture in the UK: potential for meeting dietary guideline demands. Food Research Collaboration Policy Brief. Available at: https://foodresearch.org.uk/wp-content/uploads/sites/8/2016/03/horticulture-briefing-final-24-March.pdf

[15] Centre for Innovation Excellence in Livestock. (2020). Net zero carbon & UK livestock. CIEL. Available at: https://www.cielivestock.co.uk/wp-content/uploads/2020/11/CIEL-Net-Zero-Carbon-UK-Livestock-FINAL-interactive-low-res-APP-revised-reference-Oct-2020.pdf

[16] James, A. (2020). Livestock wearables: cow mask to reduce methane emissions. Food and farming technology. Available at: https://www.foodandfarmingtechnology.com/news/weather-climate/livestock-wearables-cow-mask-to-reduce-methane-emissions.html

[17] Innovation Toronto. (2020). 3-NOP is a methane-inhibiting additive for cows if it can be made affordable and the public accepts it. Innovation Toronto. Available at: https://innovationtoronto.com/2020/07/3-nop-is-a-methane-inhibiting-additive-for-cows-if-it-can-be-made-affordable-and-the-public-accepts-it/

[18] Abbot, D.W. et al. (2020). Seaweed and seaweed bioactives for mitigation of enteric methane: challenges and opportunities. Animals 10(12), 2432. Available at: https://www.mdpi.com/2076-2615/10/12/2432

[19] Land use: Searchinger, T. D. et al. (2018). Assessing the efficiency of changes in land use for mitigating climate change. Nature 564, 249-253. Available at : https://www.nature.com/articles/s41586-018-0757-z;

Animal welfare: Rioja-Lang, F. C. et al. (2020). Prioritization of farm animal welfare issues using expert consensus. Frontiers in Veterinary Science 6, 495. Available at: https://www.frontiersin.org/articles/10.3389/fvets.2019.00495/full;

Health: Wolk, A. (2016). Potential health hazards of eating red meat. Journal of Internal Medicine 281(12). Available at: https://onlinelibrary.wiley.com/doi/pdf/10.1111/joim.12543.

[20] NFS analysis based on feed conversion ratios in: Good Food Institute. (2021). Anticipatory life cycle assessment and techno-economic assessment of commercial cultivated meat production. Available at: https://gfi.org/wp-content/uploads/2021/03/cultured-meat-LCA-TEA-technical.pdf. Type of product: https://www.meatless.nl/

[21] Henchion, M. et al. (2017). Future protein supply and demand: strategies and factors influencing a sustainable equilibrium. Foods 6(7). 53. Available at: https://www.ncbi.nlm.nih.gov/pmc/articles/PMC5532560/

[22] Shortage: Ismail, B. P. et al. (2020). Protein demand: review of plant and animal proteins used in alternative protein product development and production. Animal Frontiers 10(4), 53-63. Available at: https://academic.oup.com/af/article/10/4/53/5943509;

Henchion, M. et al. (2017). Future protein supply and demand: strategies and factors influencing a sustainable equilibrium. Foods 6(7), 53. Available at: https://www.ncbi.nlm.nih.gov/pmc/articles/PMC5532560/

[23] Food and Agriculture Organization of the United Nations. (2017). The future of food and agriculture. Trends and challenges. FAO, Rome. Available at: http://www.fao.org/3/i6583e/i6583e.pdf

[24] Boston Consulting Group. (2021). Food for thought. the protein transformation. Available at: https://web-assets.bcg.com/a0/28/4295860343c6a2a5b9f4e3436114/bcg-food-for-thought-the-protein-transformation-mar-2021.pdf

[25] NFS analysis. Based on proportion of different meats that are processed (and could be replaced). Greenhouse gas emissions and land use in: Poore, J. and Nemecek, T. (2018). Reducing food's environmental impacts through producers and consumers. Science 360(6392), 987-992. Available at: https://science.sciencemag.org/content/360/6392/987;

Life cycle analysis in: Delft, C.E. (2021). LCA of cultivated meat. Available at: https://cedelft.eu/wp-content/uploads/sites/2/2021/04/CE_Delft_190107_LCA_of_cultivated_meat_Def.pdf

[26] NFS analysis based on feed conversion ratios in: Good Food Institute (2021). Anticipatory life cycle assessment and techno-economic assessment of commercial cultivated meat production. Available at: https://gfi.org/wp-content/uploads/2021/03/cultured-meat-LCA-TEA-technical.pdf;

Tonnes per hectare of input in: Defra (2019). Farming statistics final crop areas, yields, livestock populations and agricultural workforce at June 2019 - United Kingdom. Available at: https://assets.publishing.service.gov.uk/government/uploads/system/uploads/attachment_data/file/865769/structure-jun2019final-uk-22jan20-rev_v2.pdf;

Agricultural workers per hectare in: NationMaster. Agricultural workers per hectare. Available at: https://www.nationmaster.com/country-info/stats/Agriculture/Workers-per-hectare

[27] Labiotech. (2021). Global funding for meat alternative companies tripled in 2020. Available at: https://www.labiotech.eu/trends-news/solar-foods-meat-alternatives/

[28] Live Kindly. (2020). How the Netherlands is leading the vegan food industry. Available at: https://www.livekindly.co/netherlands-leading-vegan-food-industry/

[29] Israel: Good Food Institute. (2021). Israel state of alternative protein innovation report 2021. Available at: https://gfi.org.il/resources/israel-state-of-alternative-protein-innovation-report-2021/?_ga=2.142138290.1497374895.1622640835-1621113986.1612276626;

Singapore: Singapore Food Agency. Safety of alternative protein. Available at: https://www.sfa.gov.sg/food-information/risk-at-a-glance/safety-of-alternative-protein

[30] Stephens, N. (2020). Cellular agriculture in the UK: a review. Wellcome open research 5. Available at: https://www.ncbi.nlm.nih.gov/pmc/articles/PMC7014924/

[31] ING Group. (2020). Growth of meat and dairy alternatives is stirring up the European food industry. Available at: https://think.ing.com/uploads/reports/ING_report_-_Growth_of_meat_and_dairy_alternatives_is_stirring_up_the_European_food_industry.pdf;

Mintel. (2020). Plant based push. UK sales of meat free foods shot up by 40% between 2014-2019 Available at: https://www.mintel.com/press-centre/food-and-drink/plant-based-push-uk-sales-of-meat-free-foods-shoot-up-40-between-2014-19

[32] Tesco. (2020). Tesco commits to 300% sales increase in meat alternatives. Available at: https://www.tescoplc.com/news/2020/tesco-commits-to-300-sales-increase-in-meat-alternatives/

[33] FAO. (2020). Food outlook. Biannual report on global food markets. Available at: http://www.fao.org/3/ca9509en/CA9509EN.pdf

[34] Agricultural Productivity Working Group. (2020). Report to the Food and Drink Sector Council. FDSC. Available at: http://www.fdsc.org.uk/fdsc/documents/APWG-report-feb20.pdf

[35] Ogilvie, D. et al. (2020). Using natural experimental studies to guide public health action: turning the evidence-based medicine paradigm on its head. Journal of Epidemiology and Community Health 74, 203-208. Available at: http://dx.doi.org/10.1136/jech-2019-213085

[36] NHS. (2013). Statistics on obesity, physical activity and diet, England, 2013. NHS Digital. Available at: https://digital.nhs.uk/data-and-information/publications/statistical/statistics-on-obesity-physical-activity-and-diet/statistics-on-obesity-physical-activity-and-diet-england-2013

[37] Theis, D.R.Z. and White, M. (2021). Is obesity policy in England fit for purpose? Analysis of government strategies and policies, 1992–2020. The Millbank Quarterly. Available at: https://pubmed.ncbi.nlm.nih.gov/33464689/

[38] Head, B. (2010). Reconsidering evidence-based policy: Key issues and challenges, Policy and Society 29(2), 77-94. Available at: https://www.tandfonline.com/doi/full/10.1016/j.polsoc.2010.03.001

[39] Gold, J. et al. (2018). The What Works Network five years on. The What Works Network. Available at: https://assets.publishing.service.gov.uk/government/uploads/system/uploads/attachment_data/file/677478/6.4154_What_works_report_Final.pdf

[40] Ogilvie, D. et al. (2020). Making sense of the evidence in population health intervention research: building a dry stone wall. BMJ Global Health 5. Available at: https://gh.bmj.com/content/5/12/e004017

[41] Prabhu, J. (2021). How should a government be? Bennett Institute of Public Policy, University of Cambridge. Available at: https://www.bennettinstitute.cam.ac.uk/blog/how-should-government-be/

[42] Based on evidence from UKRI that £1 public expenditure gives rise to £7 net-economic benefit to the UK. UK Research and Innovation. (2018). The UK's research and innovation infrastructure: opportunities to grow our capability. Available at: https://www.ukri.org/wp-content/uploads/2020/10/UKRI-201020-UKinfrastructure-opportunities-to-grow-our-capacity-FINAL.pdf

[43] NFS analysis. Methane reductions: Roque, B. M. et al. (2021). Red seaweed (Asparagopsis taxiformis) supplementation reduces enteric methane by over 80 percent in beef steers. PlOS One 16 (3). Available at: https://journals.plos.org/plosone/article?id=10.1371/journal.pone.0247820;

GHG emissions: Poore, J. and Nemecek, T. (2018). Reducing food's environmental impacts through producers and consumers. Science 360(6392), 987-992. Available at: https://science.sciencemag.org/content/360/6392/987

[44] Based on evidence from UKRI that £1 public expenditure gives rise to £7 net-economic benefit to the UK. UK Research and Innovation. (2018). The UK's research and innovation infrastructure: opportunities to grow our capability. Available at: https://www.ukri.org/wp-content/uploads/2020/10/UKRI-201020-UKinfrastructure-opportunities-to-grow-our-capacity-FINAL.pdf

Recommendation 12. Create a National Food System Data programme.

What is it?

The Government should create a National Food System Data Programme to collect and share data, so that the businesses and other organisations involved in the food system can track progress and plan ahead.

This programme should span and connect two main areas of evidence. The first is data about the land, to support the Rural Land Use Framework (Recommendation 9). This includes (among other things) the agricultural productivity of any given area of land, its potential for environmental restoration and carbon sequestration, and local pollution levels in air and water. Defra already holds much of this data, and is working with the Government's Geospatial Commission to pilot high-resolution interactive maps, with as many layers as possible available to the public. This will help the Government, landowners, developers and conservation groups make better decisions about how we use our land.

The second area of evidence comes from beyond the farm gate: data on food production, distribution and retail, and the environmental and health impacts of that food. These include data provided by companies under the mandatory reporting requirements we have proposed in Recommendation 2.

These two areas of evidence should be connected through a single programme, to create a clear, accessible and evolving picture of the impact our diet has on nature, climate and public health, to help guide decision making throughout the food system.

The Chief Scientific Adviser to the Government, alongside the Chief Scientific Advisers at Defra, the Department for Health and Social Care, the Department for Business, Energy and Industrial Strategy and at the Food Standards Agency, should work together to establish a specialist team of civil servants – including IT experts and strategists – to develop and manage the National Food System Data Programme. Working with the Geospatial Commission and the Office for National Statistics, this team should start by identifying the main "customers" for the data programme, and setting baseline data definitions, standards and hierarchies. The team should then identify gaps in the existing data, and broker agreements with third parties – such as retailers or unions – to fill in these gaps without breaching confidentiality.

The key data should be published using visualisation dashboards that make it easier for users to compare information, model future scenarios and assess the effectiveness of different policies or logistical models. These should include the National Rural Land Map (See Recommendation 9).

Some data will be commercially sensitive, and those supplying the data might be willing to share it with the Government but not with industry competitors. There would therefore need to be a "layered" permissions model, to control access to different levels of information. In some cases (such as electronic point of sale data), the Office for National Statistics already collects the data but is not permitted to share it with other parts of government and the wider food sector. Legislation should be introduced if necessary to allow data to be shared as far as commercial confidentiality permits.

Our initial recommendations for food system metrics against which data should be collected are set out in Table 1 below, alongside bodies that currently hold at least some of those data. In addition, the food system is closely connected to many other systems, both national and international. Over time, data on transport, energy, environment, healthcare and so forth should be added to the programme.

Table 1

Recommended food system performance metrics

Metric	Source of data
Environmental outcomes	
Agricultural land productivity (spatial)	Defra
Priority areas for biodiversity (spatial)	Defra
Priority areas for carbon recovery (spatial)	Defra
Air quality (spatial)	Defra
Water quality (spatial)	Catchment Sensitive Farming, Environment Agency / Defra
Species abundancy and diversity	England/UK Biodiversity Indicators, Joint Natural Capital Committee
Environmental footprint of food (domestic)	HESTIA, University of Oxford
Environmental footprint of food (imported)	HESTIA, University of Oxford
Total UK food system GHG emissions	BEIS, Committee on Climate Change (CCC), Waste Resources Action Programme (WRAP)
Percentage of food sourced from areas with sustainable water management	WRAP, World Wide Fund for Nature (WWF), World Resources Institute
Land used for agriculture	Farming Statistics, Defra
Healthy soils	25-Year Environment Plan, Defra (under development)
Food waste	Business reporting (Recommendation 2)
Health outcomes	
Childhood obesity	National Child Measurement Programme, National Health Service (NHS) Digital
Childhood obesity by deprivation	National Child Measurement Programme, NHS Digital
Diet-related healthy life expectancy	Metric to be developed based on Global Burden of Disease
Type 2 diabetes registrations	National Diabetes Audit, NHS Digital
Social outcomes	
Household food insecurity	Family Resources Survey, Department of Work and Pensions (DWP)
Social impact of food	Food & You Survey, FSA
Well-paid jobs	Annual Survey of Households and Earnings, ONS
Animal welfare	Royal Society for the Prevention of Cruelty to Animals (RSPCA) and Soil Association
System resilience	
Source of UK food	Defra
Trustworthiness of food	Food and You, Food Standards Agency (FSA)
Diet and food environment	
HFSS consumption	National Diet and Nutrition Survey (NDNS), Public Health England
Fibre consumption	NDNS, Public Health England
Meat consumption	NDNS, Public Health England
Fruit and vegetable consumption	NDNS, Public Health England
Fruit and vegetable consumption by income quintile	NDNS, Public Health England
Sales of HFSS food and drink	Business reporting (Recommendation 2)
Sales of fruit and vegetables	Business reporting (Recommendation 2)
Sales of protein by type and origin	Business reporting (Recommendation 2)
Sales of major nutrients including fibre, saturated fat, sugar and salt	Business reporting (Recommendation 2)

Metric	Source of data
Total food and drink sales	Business reporting (Recommendation 2)
Price and promotions by major food category (retail and out-of-home)	FoodDB, University of Oxford
Proportion of food outlets which are fast food	Office for National Statistics (ONS)
Exposure of children to junk food advertising	Based on method developed by INFORMAS (www.informas.org)

Rationale

There is global recognition that investment in accurate, up-to-date, geographically specific data is vital to solving many of our challenges.[1] Having the right information makes it possible to set the right goals, track progress and adjust course where necessary.[2]

Good data, cleverly organised, can help companies become cleaner and more efficient, and enable governments to devise and monitor effective policies.[3] We know that data dashboards, of the type that the National Food System Data Programme would produce, work. They are increasingly used across UK government departments and agencies to monitor performance and aid decision making, including Defra, FSA, BEIS, Department for Work and Pensions (DWP). Such platforms have been critical to the Government's efforts to address the COVID-19 pandemic, through the Joint Biosecurity Centre, and support the UK's EU Exit strategy.[4]

There are currently significant gaps in the data available for the food system. Even where data are made available by businesses, they are often difficult to understand and use because they are not presented consistently. For example, Sainsbury's, Marks & Spencer and Tesco have all committed to reporting health-related data.[5] But they publish different types of data in different formats. Standardising the collection and publication of data would make it vastly more usable. This is already recognised by the industry itself, which is asking for an open data framework.[6]

The Government is best placed to resolve this issue. It already collects much relevant data itself. It has the convening power needed to bring companies together and encourage them to share their data in a consistent way. It can also impose legal obligations on business to report consistently.

Improving data sharing in the food system complements the National Data Strategy and calls from the Council for Science and Technology to improve analytical capability and flow of information across government.[7] It will support international efforts to provide information on the food system, such as the Food Systems Dashboard, developed by the Global Alliance for Improved Nutrition (GAIN) and Johns Hopkins University.[8] There is a public desire for a more unified approach to food system governance, as we saw during the NFS Public dialogues. Participants in the dialogues discussed the need to "include more formal arrangements for bringing government departments together to plan strategically for food issues on, for example environment, health and social support measures".

Costs and benefits

The annual cost to Government to deliver this recommendation is £3.5m. Over three years the total is £10.5m.

Defra should bid to secure funding in the next Spending Review.

The improved data access it will provide will benefit the public and the Government by making it easier to set and track long-term health and sustainability goals for the food sector. But it will also help businesses themselves. Large businesses, which already collect extensive data, will see increases in its range, quality and reliability, while the benefit to the food sector's many small enterprises lies in providing credible data they can use for free.

Endnotes

[1] Annan, K. (2018). Data can help to end malnutrition across Africa. Nature 555(7). Available at: https://www.nature.com/articles/d41586-018-02386-3

[2] Vallance, P. (2020). Achieving net zero through a whole systems approach: Council for Science and Technology letter. Available at: https://www.gov.uk/government/publications/achieving-net-zero-carbon-emissions-through-a-whole-systems-approach

[3] Lloyd, L. (2020). Policy making in a digital world: How data and new technologies can help government make better policy. Institute for Government. Available at: https://www.instituteforgovernment.org.uk/sites/default/files/publications/policy-making-digital-world.pdf

[4] Lloyd, L. (2020). Policy making in a digital world: How data and new technologies can help government make better policy. Institute for Government. Available at: https://www.instituteforgovernment.org.uk/sites/default/files/publications/policy-making-digital-world.pdf;

Joint Biosecurity Centre: https://www.gov.uk/government/groups/joint-biosecurity-centre

[5] Sainsbury's. (2021). Healthy and sustainable diets. Sainsbury's. Available at: https://www.about.sainsburys.co.uk/sustainability/better-for-you/healthy-diets;

Marks and Spencer. (2018). Transformation Underway: M&S Plan A report 2018. Marks and Spencer. Available at: https://corporate.marksandspencer.com/annual-report-2018/mands_plan_a_2018.pdf;

Tesco. (2021). Tesco makes ambitious new commitments to support healthy, sustainable diets. Tesco. Available at: https://www.tescoplc.com/news/2021/tesco-makes-ambitious-new-commitments-to-support-healthy-sustainable-diets/

[6] O'Gorman, D. (2018). Transformative innovation across food supply chains to improve decision-making. Global Food Security Programme. Available at: https://www.foodsecurity.ac.uk/publications/transformative-innovation-across-food-supply-chains-to-improve-decision-making.pdf;

Food Standards Agency Science Council Working Group. (2020). Science Council Working Group on data usage and digital technology: final report to the Food Standards Agency. Available at: https://science-council.food.gov.uk/WorkingGroup4

[7] National Data Strategy: Department for Digital, Culture, Media & Sport. (2020). National Data Strategy. Available at: https://www.gov.uk/government/publications/uk-national-data-strategy/national-data-strategy;

Council for Science and Technology: Vallance, P. (2020). Achieving net zero through a whole systems approach: Council for Science and Technology letter. Available at: https://www.gov.uk/government/publications/achieving-net-zero-carbon-emissions-through-a-whole-systems-approach

[8] Global Alliance for Improved Nutrition (GAIN) and Johns Hopkins University. (2020). The Food Systems Dashboard. Available at: https://foodsystemsdashboard.org/;

Liebsch, T. (2019). Product Environmental Footprint (PEF) – a complete overview. Ecochain. Available at: https://ecochain.com/knowledge/product-environmental-footprint/

Recommendation 13. Strengthen government procurement rules to ensure that taxpayer money is spent on healthy and sustainable food.

What is it?

The Government should reform its Buying Standards for Food so that taxpayers' money goes on healthy and sustainable food. All public sector organisations should be required to apply these standards. The Government should aim to increase the role of small and local suppliers in public food procurement, including through the rollout of a web platform currently being trialled in the South West.

The Government should also introduce a mandatory accreditation scheme for caterers in schools, hospitals and prisons, working with existing certification bodies such as Food for Life, to support caterers to reach baseline standards and encourage them to aim higher still.

The Government already has Buying Standards for Food (GBSF), but they do not guarantee that the food is any good. Defra should redesign the GBSF to emphasise the importance of quality over cost. All tenders should be required to meet an achievable but high baseline standard for quality before cost is considered at all. In particular, all food supplied should be required to have been produced in compliance with UK standards. The current loophole allowing substandard food to be supplied where it is necessary to avoid a "significant increase in costs" should be removed. At the next stage of assessment, at least 60% of the marks available should be for quality rather than cost. This should be broken down into a weighting of 30% for public priorities (such as health, sustainability and social value) and 30% for customer service (such as menu variety, service style and customer satisfaction).

The redesigned GBSF should also meet the new Reference Diet that we recommend the Food Standards Agency develops with the Office of Health Promotion, the Scientific Advisory Committee on Nutrition, the Office of Environmental Protection and the Climate Change Committee (Recommendation 14). This diet is likely to recommend serving less meat and dairy and more wholegrains, fruit, vegetables and pulses, to maximise the health and sustainability of the food served. The GBSF should then be updated every five years, like the Reference Diet.

All public sector organisations should be required to apply the redesigned GBSF when procuring food, including those which are currently exempt (such as schools and local authorities). The Government should develop a monitoring and enforcement mechanism to make sure that the food served is healthy and sustainable. This could be achieved by introducing reporting requirements for organisations procuring food or by expanding the Food Standards Agency's remit (though this option would require the recruitment of more Environmental Health Officers and so would come at considerable cost).

The Government should also seek to increase the participation of small and local businesses in food procurement. As a first step, it should provide adequate funding for a pilot of a dynamic procurement system that is scheduled to launch in the South West of England from June 2022. This scheme, based on a web platform run by Bath and North East Somerset Council, should allow SMEs and local businesses to sell smaller quantities of fresh food and drink to public bodies.[1] If the pilot succeeds, the Government should roll out the system nationwide. The Government should also encourage the use of SME and local suppliers in the GBSF.

The Government should work with existing certifiers – such as Food For Life – to introduce a mandatory accreditation scheme for the food served in schools, hospitals and prisons.[2] This would provide training and support for leaders and staff. Institutions that complied fully with the obligations in the GBSF would be awarded a Bronze certificate. Taking further steps towards a good food culture would entitle an organisation to a Silver certificate, while a Gold certificate would be awarded to organisations that demonstrated a whole organisation approach to food.[3]

Rationale

The public sector is a colossal buyer of food. We estimate that it serves 1.9 billion meals a year – over 5% of the total UK food service turnover – at a cost of £2.4bn.[4] This makes public procurement the Government's most direct tool to shape the food system.

This tool is not being used as effectively as it could be. Much of the food served by public bodies is bad. Only 39% of primary school children who have to pay for school meals choose to eat them; while the main barrier for this is cost, another factor is that food is unappealing.[5] In hospitals, 42% of patients rated the food as either satisfactory, poor or very poor; 39% of staff rated the food as poor.[6] Over a third of the money hospitals spend on food goes on items that are thrown away uneaten.[7] Food served in prisons is rated even worse: only 29% of inmates describe the food they receive as "good" or "very good".[8] Some might say that criminals deserve what they get, but better prison food has surprising benefits: there is evidence that prisoners given higher-quality food are less likely to become violent and aggressive.[9]

The food served in Government institutions is often not just unappetising but also unhealthy. In many schools, breakfast consists of sugary cereals and white bread, as well as squash or milkshakes. In some cases, schools even serve chocolate-based cereals and croissants. Break time foods in secondary schools are dominated by unhealthy items, while at lunchtime children are served too much fat, salt and sugar, and too little fibre and vegetables.[10] Yet, even these meals are more nutritious than most packed lunches, which is why it is not only crucial to improve the quality of school food but also to increase access to free school meals (Recommendation 4).

In prisons, breakfast usually consists of breakfast packs, which contain cereal, milk, whitener, tea/coffee sachets, and in some cases some preserves. Prisoners complain about there not being enough fruit and vegetables and too much fat, carbohydrate, salt and processed food.[11]

These problems are in part due to a lack of competition among suppliers. The complexity of tendering processes has made it difficult for smaller businesses to compete. This has led to the market being dominated by a small number of suppliers: the top four contract caterers (Compass Group, Sodexo, Westbury Street Holding and Elior) have 61% of the contract catering market share.[12] The result is that there is often little competition for contracts. This limits procuring bodies' choice and their power to demand high quality. It also fails to encourage innovation.

The current Government Buying Standards for Food (GBSF) are clearly not working well, for a number of reasons.

- **First, the bodies that are required to apply them sometimes do not.** The NHS found in 2017 that only 52% of hospital caterers are fully compliant with the GBSF.[13] The Government does not consistently monitor or enforce the Standards, so there is no way of knowing what the compliance rates are in the wider public sector.
- **Second, even where they are applied, they do not guarantee quality food.** Public bodies are allowed to prioritise price over quality in their procurement decisions. With the challenging budgetary situation in recent years, many have assigned 50–80% of the marks available to price.[14] In practice, this means that the cheapest bid wins, leading to a race to the bottom among suppliers.
- **Third, they fail to take account of the wider impacts of food choices.** The standards do not require institutions to meet the Government's own nutrition guidelines (the Eatwell Guide) and do not consider the environmental impact of the food that is served. They do not reflect the public's clear preferences on issues such as animal welfare (for example, eggs from caged hens may be used). They even permit suppliers to provide imported food that was produced in ways that would not be legal for UK producers if to do otherwise would produce a "significant increase in costs".
- **Fourth, they do not promote a positive food culture in public institutions.** There is often no clear vision, leadership or training around healthy and sustainable food, and very little accountability for the quality of food or how funding is spent. Food is simply not a primary concern.[15]
- **Finally, they are not applied in all public bodies.** Only central Government, hospital food for patients, prisons and the armed forces are bound by them: local governments, schools, visitor and staff food in hospitals and care homes, for example, need not follow the standards.[16] So, even if the standards were effective, they would only improve a fraction of the food that the public sector serves.

Better Government procurement could have an enormous impact. In the first place, there would be a direct benefit to the diets of the 13 million people who eat those meals every year, many of whom are children, hospital patients, or otherwise vulnerable.[17] In particular, schoolchildren are much more dependent than adults on publicly procured food. Food eaten in schools could make up as much as half of a child's diet in term time, and for some children, a school lunch is their only substantial meal of the day.[18] The better school food is, the more likely it is that children will eat it rather than bringing in packed lunches, which are likely to be less healthy (see Recommendation 4 on free school meals for more on this point). One existing scheme aimed at improving the quality of school food, Food for Life, has been shown to increase consumption of fruit and vegetables by a third.[19] This is good for children's health and for their education.[20]

But there would also be wider gains: Government leadership influences business behaviour and can help nurture a better food culture, especially through its influence on children eating school meals.[21] It will signal to businesses that it is possible to transform menus at scale, demonstrate the Government's commitment to transformation in the food system to businesses, and incentivise innovation, investment and private sector efforts to the same end.

Such impacts have already been seen. When the GBSF were amended to require that all fish procured by the Government should be sustainable, there was change beyond the bodies that were directly bound by the standards.[22] At least 850 million sustainable seafood meals are now served every year across both private and public sectors.[23] Similarly, in Denmark, the introduction of a target that 60% of the food served by public caterers should be organic helped the Government achieve an increase of 57% in the share of agricultural land used for organic farming.[24]

The GBSF could make it more normal to serve and eat meals that contain less meat. Redesigning the GBSF to require more sustainable menus would lead to public institutions serving less meat and more vegetables, pulses and alternative proteins. This would have significant environmental benefits. If all public caterers moved to having even one meat-free day a week, this could reduce meat consumption by 9,000 tonnes a year, saving over 200,000 tonnes of greenhouse gas emissions.[25] Even without eliminating meat completely, many of the dishes typically served in institutional settings lend themselves to partial substitution of meat with vegetables – for example, including minced mushrooms in beef burgers, or beans as well as beef in a chilli.[26] A similar approach at the University of Cambridge saw carbon emissions per kilogram of food fall by a third, with similar reductions in land use per kilogram.[27] This also made the catering more profitable.

To make sure the benefits of higher standards are achieved in practice, proper monitoring and enforcement mechanisms are essential. At present, this is almost entirely lacking outside the NHS. Even in the NHS, it is incomplete: not all food standards are monitored, hospitals are not required to submit evidence and the process has become a "tickbox" exercise.[28] While the latest figures from the NHS's Patient Led Assessments of the Care Environment (PLACE) indicated that 90% of hospitals were compliant, the recent independent review of hospital food raised concerns that this number might not be accurate.[29] In contrast, in Scotland, the Scottish Government and local authorities have told us that inspection of schools has proved effective. Health and Nutrition Inspectors inspect schools to check they are complying with the School Food Standards. The inspectors work in a collaborative way with local authorities and, if a school is noncompliant, the inspectors work with the school to remedy the situation. This is a practical but relatively expensive option for driving compliance with the standards.

Beyond enforcing baseline standards, accreditation schemes are needed to raise the quality of food still higher. This is demonstrated by the Food for Life Served Here scheme. This framework for caterers monitors how food is sourced, cooked and promoted, with criteria covering health, nature, animal welfare and the climate. Institutions are rigorously inspected to make sure they deserve the Food for Life mark of quality. Over 2 million meals are served each day to Food for Life standards, including in roughly 50% of English primary schools, over 50 NHS hospitals and over 50 universities.[30] Some local authorities adopting this scheme are attracted by the incentives it creates for local sourcing: independent evaluation of the scheme has shown that for every £1 spent on local seasonal produce, £3 is generated in social, economic and environmental value in the local community.[31] Children in schools engaged with the Food for Life School Award – which incorporates menu accreditation, alongside food education and practical food activities – are twice as likely to eat their five-a-day and eat a third more fruit and vegetables overall, compared to children in other schools.[32] The quality of service has been recognised by the Scottish Government who fund Food for Life to support local authorities across Scotland. The majority of the 32 local authorities are working with Food for Life and to date 17 are accredited to at least bronze level.

Finally, increasing competition in the market through greater involvement of smaller, local businesses can also help drive up standards. Bath and North East Somerset Council succeeded in doing this via a dynamic purchasing system. They introduced a web platform that allowed 60 schools serving 30,000 meals per week to buy from more than 20 local SME food producers and suppliers. The council evaluation found that the carbon emissions of their supply chain had been reduced and costs had fallen by 6%.[33]

Costs and benefits

Over the next three years, the new expenditure required for the Government to deliver this recommendation is approximately £3m. The annual cost to the Government of delivering an accreditation scheme for public sector food in schools, hospitals and prisons would be approximately £750,000 with an initial support and set up fee of approximately £750,000. This is based on indicative costs given to us by Food for Life. Defra should bid to secure funding in the next Spending Review.

We are not able to determine the cost of ensuring all organisations follow new, redesigned GBSF because the Government does not know what it spends currently on food (the latest available data is from 2014). However, we do know that many organisations including Cambridge University, Chefs in Schools supported organisations and Bath and North East Somerset Council have managed to improve the health and sustainability of their menus without increasing costs by serving less meat and more vegetables, legumes and pulses, and by buying locally and seasonally.[34]

Endnotes

[1] House of Commons Environment Food and Rural Affairs Committee. (2021). Public sector procurement of food: sixth report of session 2019–21. HC469. House of Commons. Available at: https://committees.parliament.uk/publications/5509/documents/54917/default/

[2] Food for Life: https://www.foodforlife.org.uk/

[3] A whole organisation approach to food means integrating food into the life of the organisation: treating the dining hall or restaurant as the hub of the organisation, where everyone eats together; making food an integral part of the day; the cooks being as important other staff members; in schools, ensuring that food is part of a rounded education and, in hospitals, that food is considered as part of a patient's care and treatment: Dimbleby, H. and Vincent, J. (2013). The School Food Plan. Evidence pack. HMG. Available at: http://www.schoolfoodplan.com/wp-content/uploads/2013/10/School-Food-Plan-Evidence-Pack-July-2013-Final.pdf;

Shelley, P. (2020). The Report of the Independent Review of NHS Hospital Food. Available at: https://assets.publishing.service.gov.uk/government/uploads/system/uploads/attachment_data/file/929234/independent-review-of-nhs-hospital-food-report.pdf

[4] 1.9bn meals from NFS Analysis. Sources – Hospital patient meals: NHS Digital. (2021). Estates Returns Information Collection Summary page and dataset for ERIC 2018/19. Available at: https://digital.nhs.uk/data-and-information/publications/statistical/estates-returns-information-collection/england-2018-19;

Schools: Office for National Statistics. (2021). Schools, pupils and their characteristics, Academic year 2021/21. Available at: https://explore-education-statistics.service.gov.uk/find-statistics/school-pupils-and-their-characteristics;

Higher education: Higher Education Statistics Agency. (2021). Table 1 – HE student enrolments by HE provider 2014/15 to 2019/20. HESA. Available at: https://www.hesa.ac.uk/data-and-analysis/students/table-1;

Prisoners: Ministry of Justice. (2020). Prison population figures: 2020. HMG. Available at: https://www.gov.uk/government/statistics/prison-population-figures-2020;

Care homes: Office for National Statistics. (2020) Care home and non-care home populations used in the Deaths involving COVID-19 in the care sector article, England and Wales. ONS. Available at: https://www.ons.gov.uk/peoplepopulationandcommunity/birthsdeathsandmarriages/deaths/adhocs/12215carehomeandnoncarehomepopulationsusedinthedeathsinvolvingcovid19inthecaresectorarticleenglandandwales;

Ministry of Defence: Ministry of Defence. (2020). Quarterly Service Personnel Statistics 1 July 2020. HMG. Available at: https://assets.publishing.service.gov.uk/government/uploads/system/uploads/attachment_data/file/920074/1_July_2020_SPS.pdf;

Analysis does not include non-operational MOD staff nor NHS staff as data not available so is likely to be an under estimation.

£2.4bn: Department for Environment, Food & Rural Affairs. (2014). A plan for public procurement: food and catering. Defra. Available at: https://assets.publishing.service.gov.uk/government/uploads/system/uploads/attachment_data/file/332756/food-plan-july-2014.pdf

[5] Uptake: Dewberry Redpoint. (2019). School meal uptake research. Dewberry Redpoint Ltd. Available at: https://laca.co.uk/sites/default/files/attachment/news/SMU Research Report 2019.pdf;

Cost and quality are an issue: Dimbleby, H. and Vincent, J. (2013). The School Food Plan. Evidence pack. HMG. Available at: http://www.schoolfoodplan.com/wp-content/uploads/2013/10/School-Food-Plan-Evidence-Pack-July-2013-Final.pdf

[6] Patients: Care Quality Commission. (2020). NHS patient survey programme. 2019 adult inpatient survey. Care Quality Commission. Available at: https://www.cqc.org.uk/sites/default/files/20200702_ip19_statisticalrelease.pdf;

Staff: National Health Service England (2019). 2018 National NHS Staff Survey in England. NHS. Available at: https://www.england.nhs.uk/statistics/2019/02/26/2018-national-nhs-staff-survey-in-england/

[7] 52 of 227 trusts included, for data see: National Health Service. (2021). Estates Returns Information Collection (ERIC). NHS. Available at: https://www.england.nhs.uk/statistics/2019/02/26/2018-national-nhs-staff-survey-in-england/

[8] HM Inspectorate of Prisons (2016). Life in prison: Food. A findings paper by HM Inspectorate of Prisons. HM Inspectorate of prisons. Available at: https://www.justiceinspectorates.gov.uk/hmiprisons/wp-content/uploads/sites/4/2016/09/Life-in-prison-Food-Web-2016.pdf

[9] Smoyer, A. B. and Minke, L. K. (2015). Food systems in correctional settings. A literature review and case study. WHO. Available at: https://www.euro.who.int/en/health-topics/health-determinants/prisons-and-health/publications/2015/food-systems-in-correctional-settings.-a-literature-review-and-case-study-2015

[10] Guy's and St Thomas' Charity. (2020). Serving up children's health. Guy's and St Thomas' Charity. GSTT Charity. Available at: https://www.gsttcharity.org.uk/sites/default/files/30-GSTC- Schools-min.pdf;

Food for Life and Soil Association. (2019). State of the nation: Children's food in England, 2019. Food for Life. Available at: https://www.soilassociation.org/media/17422/state-of-the-nation-soil-association-report.pdf

[11] HM Inspectorate of Prisons (2016). Life in prison: Food. A findings paper by HM Inspectorate of Prisons. HM Inspectorate of prisons. Available at: https://www.justiceinspectorates.gov.uk/hmiprisons/wp-content/uploads/sites/4/2016/09/Life-in-prison-Food-Web-2016.pdf

[12] UK Parliament. (2021). Written evidence submitted by Dynamic Food Procurement National Advisory Board. UK Parliament. Available at: https://committees.parliament.uk/writtenevidence/9762/pdf/;

European Commission. (2015). Task 2: Market Analysis (draft) Working Document. European Commission. Available at: https://documents.pub/document/task-2-market-analysis-draft-working-2-food-service-activities-is-likely.html

[13] Department of Health. (2017). Compliance with hospital food standards in the NHS. HMG. Available at: https://assets.publishing.service.gov.uk/government/uploads/system/uploads/attachment_data/file/586490/HFSP_Report.pdf

[14] The Environment, Food and Rural Affairs Committee. (2021). Public sector procurement of food. House of Commons. Available at: https://committees.parliament.uk/publications/5509/documents/54917/default/;

UK Parliament. (2021). Written evidence submitted by The Soil Association. UK Parliament. Available at: https://committees.parliament.uk/writtenevidence/9028/pdf/;

UK Parliament. (2021). Written evidence submitted by Pelican Procurement Services. UK Parliament. Available at: https://committees.parliament.uk/writtenevidence/10183/pdf/;

Marshall, R. et al. (2020). Procuring food for the future. Food Futures. Available at: https://foodfutures.org.uk/wp-content/uploads/2020/11/FF-Procurement-Report-Final-November-2020.pdf

[15] Shelley, P. (2020). Report of the independent review of hospital food. Department of Health and Social Care. Available at: https://assets.publishing.service.gov.uk/government/uploads/system/uploads/attachment_data/file/929234/independent-review-of-nhs-hospital-food-report.pdf;

Impact on Urban Health. (upcoming). School food mapping: policy and funding review. The case for the introduction of a School Food Premium;

Impact on Urban Health; Dimbleby, H. and Vincent, J. (2013). The School Food Plan. HMG. Available at: https://assets.publishing.service.gov.uk/government/uploads/system/uploads/attachment_data/file/936238/The_School_Food_Plan.pdf;

Guy's and St Thomas' Charity. (2020). Serving up children's health: opportunities and barriers in the school food system to prioritise nutritious food for young people. GSTT Charity. Available at: https://www.gsttcharity.org.uk/sites/default/files/30-GSTC- Schools-min.pdf

[16] Although there are mandatory school food standards they cover nutrition only for all maintained schools and academies that were founded before 2010 and after June 2014. The Local Government Association estimates that two thirds of academies that are not required to follow them have taken up the standards voluntarily, see: Eichler, W. (2016). Nearly 2,500 academies not signed up to healthy school meal standards. Local Gov. Available at: https://www.localgov.co.uk/Nearly-2500-academies-not-signed-up-to-healthy-school-meal-standards/40554

[17] 13m people from NFS analysis. Sources – Hospital patient meals: NHS Digital. (2021). Estates Returns Information Collection Summary page and dataset for ERIC 2018/19. Available at: https://digital.nhs.uk/data-and-information/publications/statistical/estates-returns-information-collection/england-2018-19;

Schools: Office for National Statistics. (2021). Schools, pupils and their characteristics, Academic year 2020/21. Available at: https://explore-education-statistics.service.gov.uk/find-statistics/school-pupils-and-their-characteristics;

Higher education: Higher Education Statistics Agency. (2021). Table 1 – HE student enrolments by HE provider 2014/15 to 2019/20. HESA. Available at: https://www.hesa.ac.uk/data-and-analysis/students/table-1; Prisoners: Ministry of Justice. (2020). Prison population figures: 2020. HMG. Available at: https://www.gov.uk/government/statistics/prison-population-figures-2020;

Care homes: ONS. (2020) Care home and non-care home populations used in the Deaths involving COVID-19 in the care sector article, England and Wales. ONS. Available at: https://www.ons.gov.uk/peoplepopulationandcommunity/birthsdeathsandmarriages/deaths/adhocs/12215carehomeandnoncarehomepopulationsusedinthedeathsinvolvingcovid19inthecaresectorarticleenglandandwales;

Ministry of Defence: Ministry of Defence. (2020). Quarterly Service Personnel Statistics 1 July 2020. HMG. Available at: https://assets.publishing.service.gov.uk/government/uploads/system/uploads/attachment_data/file/920074/1_July_2020_SPS.pdf;

Analysis does not include NHS staff and visitors to hospitals as data not available, so is likely to be an underestimate.

[18] Breakfast, lunch and snacks at school = 2/3 of weekday food, therefore 0.47 over 7 days; Royston, S. et al. (2012). Fair and square: a policy report on the future of free school meals. The Children's Society, p12. Available at: https://d3hgrlq6yacptf.cloudfront.net/5f3ecf1e68cdc/content/pages/documents/1429471607.pdf

[19] Jones, M. et al. (2017). Association between Food for Life, a whole setting healthy and sustainable food programme, and primary school children's consumption of fruit and vegetables: a cross-sectional study in England. International Journal of Environmental Research and Public Health 14(639). Available at: http://www.mdpi.com/1660-4601/14/6/639

[20] Belot, M. and James, J. (2009). Healthy school meals and educational outcomes. ISER working paper series. 2009–01. Available at: https://www.iser.essex.ac.uk/research/publications/working-papers/iser/2009-01.pdf

[21] Bonsmann, S. S. G. et al. (2017). Public procurement: a policy tool to promote healthier food environments and choices. WHO Europe. Available at: https://apps.who.int/iris/bitstream/handle/10665/325204/php-3-4-649-654-eng.pdf?sequence=1&isAllowed=y

[22] Certified as sustainable by either the Marine Stewardship Council or the Marine Conservation Society.

[23] Sustain. (2012). Sustainable Fish Cities. Sustain. Available at: https://www.sustainweb.org/sustainablefishcity/

[24] Ministry of Food, Agriculture and Fisheries of Denmark. (2015). Denmark's organic action plan. Ministry of Food, Agriculture and Fisheries of Denmark. Available at: https://www.agroecology-pool.org/wp-content/uploads/2018/10/Denmark_final-1.pdf

[25] Public Sector Catering. (2021). 20 Percent Less Meat. Public Sector Catering. Available at: https://20percentlessmeat.co.uk/

[26] Friends of the Earth. (2020). Kale Yeah! Rebalanced menu guide for caterers. Friends of the Earth. Available at: https://campaigning.friendsoftheearth.uk/download/kale-yeah-rebalanced-menu-guide

[27] University of Cambridge. (2019). Removing beef and lamb from menu dramatically reduces food-related carbon emissions at Cambridge University. University of Cambridge. Available at: https://www.cam.ac.uk/news/removing-beef-and-lamb-from-menu-dramatically-reduces-food-related-carbon-emissions-at-cambridge;

The Cambridge Green Challenge. (2019). Our sustainable food journey. University of Cambridge. Available at: https://www.environment.admin.cam.ac.uk/files/uoc_sustainable_food_journey_report.pdf

[28] Shelley, P. (2020). Report of the independent review of hospital food. DHSC. Available at: https://assets.publishing.service.gov.uk/government/uploads/system/uploads/attachment_data/file/929234/independent-review-of-nhs-hospital-food-report.pdf

[29] PLACE: Hospital sites compliant with nutritional guidelines Data from the 53 Hospital sites, PLACE 2018. Data presented in: Shelley, P. (2020). Report of the independent review of hospital food. DHSC. Available at: https://assets.publishing.service.gov.uk/government/uploads/system/uploads/attachment_data/file/929234/independent-review-of-nhs-hospital-food-report.pdf;

[30] UK Parliament. (2021). Written evidence submitted by The Soil Association. UK Parliament. Available at: https://committees.parliament.uk/writtenevidence/9028/pdf/

[31] Kersley, H. and Knuutila, K. (2011). The benefits of procuring school meals through the food for life partnership. An economic analysis. NEF. Available at: https://www.foodforlife.org.uk/~/media/files/evaluation reports/fflp-nef----benefits-of-local-procurement.pdf

[32] The research design was a cross-sectional study in which schools engaged with Food for Life were compared with schools not engaged in the programme. Food for Life schools and Comparison schools were matched in the same local authority area by free school meal eligibility quintile and size: Jones, M. et al. (2017) Association between Food for Life, a whole setting healthy and sustainable food programme, and primary school children's consumption of fruit and vegetables: a cross-sectional study in England. International Journal of Environmental Research and Public Health 14(639). Available at: http://www.

mdpi.com/1660-4601/14/6/639

[33] Data provided to NFS by Bath and North East Somerset Council.

[34] Cambridge University: The University Catering Service. (2019). Our Sustainable Food Journey. University of Cambridge. Available at: https://www.environment.admin.cam.ac.uk/files/uoc_sustainable_food_journey_report.pdf;

Chefs In School: Improving the health of children through better school food & education. Chefs In School. Available at: https://www.chefsinschools.org.uk/; Bath and North East Somerset Council: Data provided directly to NFS by Bath and North East Somerset Council.

Recommendation 14. Set clear targets and bring in legislation for long-term change.

What is it?

The Government should set a long-term statutory target to improve diet-related health, and create a new governance structure for food policy, through a Good Food Bill.

The Good Food Bill's diet-related health target would complement the existing statutory target for carbon reduction, and proposed targets in the Environment Bill. The Bill would also require the government to prepare regular (five-yearly) Action Plans to make further progress beyond the initial steps we set out in this report. These Action Plans should set out interim targets, and measures to meet them, that are consistent with the food system's contribution to national health, nature and climate commitments.

In this, the Government would be assisted by the Food Standards Agency (FSA), whose remit would be formally extended. Its existing obligation to promote the consumer interest would be redefined in law to include our collective interest in tackling climate change, nature recovery and promoting health, in the resilience of our food supply, and in meeting the standards that the public expect.

The FSA would have powers and duties to advise the Government on the contents of its five-yearly Action Plans, and to provide an annual, independent progress report to Parliament. This is distinct from the food security reports that, under the Agriculture Act, the Government is now required to make at least every three years; the Government should produce these annually, with broad consultation, bringing in organisations responsible for nutrition, cybersecurity (our food system is concentrated and vulnerable to attack), infrastructure, climate change and the environment.

The FSA would have a statutory duty to consult with the Office for Environmental Protection (OEP), the Climate Change Committee (CCC) and the Office for Health Promotion (OHP) in drawing up its advice and reports, also liaising with the Food and Drink Sector Council.[1] The Bill should specify corresponding statutory functions for the OEP, CCC and OHP to advise the FSA on emerging issues within the remit of each body that are relevant to the scope of the FSA. The FSA would need sufficient resources to perform this expanded role effectively.

In addition, the Bill would put in place mechanisms to support a consistent approach to improving the health and sustainability of the food system across the whole public sector, and throughout the food industry in England. It would:

- Commit the Government to establish and periodically update a healthy and sustainable Reference Diet, to be used by all public bodies in food-related policy-making and procurement.
- Oblige all public sector organisations that spend public money on food to do so in line with specific procurement standards, consistent with the Reference Diet (supporting Recommendation 13).
- Commit the FSA to developing a harmonised and consistent food labelling system to describe the environmental impacts of food products, which we recommend it undertakes in collaboration with Defra and the Institute of Grocery Distribution.
- Require local authorities in England to develop food strategies, developed with reference to national targets and in partnership with the communities they serve.
- Facilitate the development of the National Food System Data Programme by requiring large businesses to publish data on the health and environmental impact of their product portfolios (supporting Recommendations 2 and 12).

Rationale

Targets

This strategy focuses on the three key issues affected by our food system: climate change, the environment and public health. We already have statutory targets with a robust monitoring mechanism for climate change: the Government is obliged by law to work towards achieving net zero carbon emissions by 2050, with the Climate Change Committee monitoring progress and providing advice.

The Environment Bill, which is currently proceeding through Parliament, will require the Government to define similar targets for protecting the environment and nature by the end of October 2022. It should be strengthened to include a legally binding target on the face of the Bill to halt biodiversity loss in England by 2030.

An equivalent mechanism is needed for diet-related health, where there are currently no long-term binding targets. The targets that do exist – a manifesto commitment to extend healthy life expectancy by five years by 2035, and references in policy to "reducing the number of adults living with obesity, halving childhood obesity by 2030 and reducing inequalities" – should be built upon and made binding.[2] The Government should develop a target to increase healthy life expectancy by reducing diet-related disease, comparable to the net zero target in the Climate Change Act. Healthy life expectancy should be defined and measured using available data on health outcomes (deaths, diseases and dietary risk factors). This is already feasible using data collected and models developed by the Global Burden of Disease Study.[3]

Governance

Maintaining the momentum and political focus necessary for large-scale change is hard. Previous efforts to correct the problems in the food system, such as the cross-Whitehall Food Strategy Task Force, have not lasted.[4]

The CCC reports to Parliament each year on progress towards the net zero target. The long-term environmental goals to be set under the Environment Bill will also be underpinned by interim targets and regular scrutiny by the OEP. A similar mechanism is needed to make sustained progress towards the new health target set under the Good Food Bill, while ensuring this is consistent with the other demands on the food system, including its major contributions to net zero and nature recovery.

The Government should have a duty to prepare and publish a Good Food Action Plan every five years, including legislative and non-legislative measures. The Minister responsible for the Action Plan should be required to consult the FSA in the course of preparing it. The FSA should have the authority and resources to monitor progress towards the current Action Plan and provide an independent report to Parliament, incentivising the Government to meet its commitments.

The FSA is ideally placed to support and scrutinise Government action on achieving the goals of the Good Food Action Plans, because it is an organisation with a clear and widely accepted statutory mandate to protect consumers' health and interests in relation to food, in preference to economic or political interest. As a non-ministerial government department, it is relatively shielded from changes in political leadership, and can hold successive governments to account. Its remit covers not just England but also Wales and Northern Ireland, and it has strong existing ties with Food Standards Scotland, which will enable a coherent UK-wide approach.

Reference Diet

A Reference Diet is an effective tool to ensure a consistent approach across Government policies. In the USA, the Federal Government applies the same set of dietary guidelines to all state-funded schemes, such as the National School Lunch Program and The School Breakfast Program.

Dietary guidance in the UK is based on evidence of the health effects of individual nutrients and foods rather than overall diet, and the different elements of this advice are not always consistent. Our current Eatwell guide, the closest we have to a reference diet, does not take sustainability into account.

In addition, the absence of mandatory dietary guidance for public procurement has been widely cited as a reason for the poor quality of food on offer in public settings (Recommendation 13). Placing the requirement to establish and periodically update a healthy and sustainable Reference Diet within the Good Food Bill ensures that it will stay current with scientific consensus and cultural shifts. This work should be led by the FSA, working closely with the OHP and Defra.

Creating a legal obligation for food procured by the public sector to comply with the Reference Diet will allow the Government to lead by example. It will also avoid inconsistencies undermining business and public confidence in the Government's food policy. The Government must not be seen to serve food that falls below the standards it recommends to everyone else.

Environmental impact labelling

There is currently no consistent in-store labelling to show the environmental impact of food. Evidence about the impact of environmental labelling on consumer choices is mixed, but simple systems like traffic lights can help us to make informed choices about what we buy.[5] Creating a simple and consistent method of labelling would ensure that all shops and manufacturers give us the same kind of information about our food. Having to record information about the environmental impact of food production could also influence the way that manufacturers make their products.

Local strategies

National strategies only work when they can be delivered on the ground, including locally. Local initiatives – designed to suit the communities they serve, and implemented with an understanding of local conditions and challenges – are therefore essential for the success of the National Food Strategy. Where local food strategies have already been developed, these have benefited communities and forged partnerships that increased their resilience in response to the COVID-19 pandemic.[6] The evidence from more than 50 cities, boroughs and counties that now have a local food strategy or partnership is that they can increase food security in the long as well as short term, support improvements in public health and wellbeing, and generate significant investment and innovation.[7] But whether you live in such a place is a lottery, and only a handful have the full backing of their local authority. Making this approach an obligation for local government provides an opportunity for these benefits to spread across the whole of England.

Costs and benefits

These measures will underpin the UK's long-term progress towards net zero, nature recovery and better health. They will provide continuity of ambition, enabling the Government – regardless of which party is in power – to lead the country through the difficult but necessary transition that is required in our food system.

The FSA needs sufficient resources to perform this additional role. We recommend it is allocated an additional budget of £5m per year for this, similar to the annual costs of the Climate Change Committee.[8] Over three years the total is £15m.

We do not recommend making specific funds available to local authorities to develop or implement their food strategies. Rather, these costs should be met through the funds Government is making available to support levelling up. These include the UK Shared Prosperity Fund, the Community Renewal Fund, the Community Ownership Fund and the Levelling Up Fund.[9]

Endnotes

[1] The OHP will take over the health promotion functions of Public Health England.

[2] Department of Health and Social Care. (2020). Tackling obesity: empowering adults and children to live healthier lives. Policy Paper. HMG. Available at: https://www.gov.uk/government/publications/tackling-obesity-government-strategy/tackling-obesity-empowering-adults-and-children-to-live-healthier-lives

[3] Available via Global Health Data Exchange at: http://ghdx.healthdata.org/gbd-results-tool

[4] The Strategy Unit. (2008). Food matters: towards a strategy for the 21st century. Cabinet Office. Available at: https://webarchive.nationalarchives.gov.uk/+/http:/www.cabinetoffice.gov.uk/media/cabinetoffice/strategy/assets/food/food_matters1.pdf

[5] Blythe, J. M. and Johnson, S. D. (2018). Rapid evidence assessment on labelling schemes and implications for consumer IoT security. PETRAS IoT Hub. Available at: https://assets.publishing.service.gov.uk/government/uploads/system/uploads/attachment_data/file/949614/Rapid_evidence_assessment_IoT_security_oct_2018_V2.pdf

[6] Sustainable Food Places. (2021). Supporting local food systems responses to Covid-19. Available at: https://www.sustainablefoodplaces.org/coronavirus/

[7] King, S. (2017). Making the case for a place based systems approach: public health professionals' assessment of Sustainable Food Cities. University of West England. Available at: https://www.sustainablefoodplaces.org/Portals/4/Documents/Making the case for a place based systems approach-pp.pdf;

Hills, S. and Jones, M. (2019). Sustainable Food Cities: phase 2 evaluation final report. University of West England. Available at: https://www.sustainablefoodplaces.org/resources/files/documents/Hills_and_Jones_2019_SFC_Final_Report.pdf

[8] Climate Change Committee. (2020). Annual report and accounts: 1 April 2019 to 31 March 2020. House of Commons. Available at: https://www.theccc.org.uk/publication/annual-report-and-accounts-2019-2020/

[9] Her Majesty's Treasury. (2021). Build Back Better: our plan for growth. HMG. Available at: https://assets.publishing.service.gov.uk/government/uploads/system/uploads/attachment_data/file/968403/PfG_Final_Web_Accessible_Version.pdf

Acknowledgements

So many people have helped with the creating of this strategy that it is impossible to do justice to them all here. But there are a few people to whom I must pay particular homage.

First and foremost, two women who dedicated time and energy far beyond what could be reasonably expected. My wife, the journalist Jemima Lewis, edited this report. She put in hundreds of hours of unpaid work, challenging assumptions, clarifying arguments and flushing out jargon. The end result, I hope, is a report that can be read and understood by anyone with a stake in the food system – which is to say, everyone.

Tamsin Cooper, leader of the National Food Strategy civil service team, is about as far removed from the obstructive Sir Humphrey of popular legend as it is possible to imagine. She has been astonishingly dedicated, driven and talented. For the past two years, she has explored the food system with me both literally and metaphorically: trudging around soilless vertical farms and peaty moorlands (always in the wrong shoes), interrogating, cajoling and enlisting experts, pulling together evidence, soothing exhausted team members, and – by the end – staying up long into the night double-checking every footnote. This report wouldn't be half the thing it is without her.

The civil service team Tamsin leads has done amazing work collating, analysing and testing the mountains of evidence that have gone into this report. I am so grateful for the professionalism and good temper of Joseph James, Jacques Launay, Eleanor Dowding, Jessica Heinemann, Simon Davies, Oliver Dye, Sarah Haley, Emma Quarterman, Grace Brocklehurst, Joanna Nixon, Tamas Borbely and Isabella Watney. I would particularly like to thank Daisy Lainoff, whose commitment and energy has been something extraordinary – almost supernatural – to behold.

I have leaned heavily on the expertise of several specialist advisors: Dustin Benton on climate and the environment, Tom MacMillan on land and farming, James Kane on trade, and Will Brett on communications. Their wisdom and generosity are hugely appreciated. My chief independent advisor, Anna Taylor, has been a rock throughout this two-year journey. As executive director of the Food Foundation, Anna brings deep knowledge to everything she does – as well as fantastic team spirit.

Elta Smith, Nils Indreiten, Shona Goudie, Victoria Jenneson, Jenny Sutherland and Brian Lainoff (Daisy's husband) have helped us as external consultants, with Brian giving his time for free right up to the wire. My assistant, Tracey Bade, has been (as always) calm, capable and humorous in a crisis.

Our Advisory Panel (see box) is made up of experts from right across the food system. They have done everything we asked of them: offered advice and illumination, introduced us to others in their field, reviewed our ongoing work, challenged and encouraged us. They haven't always agreed with us – or with each other – but their input has been invaluable.

Two of my fellow non-executives at Defra, Elizabeth Buchanan and Ben Goldsmith, have done a huge amount to help me understand, respectively, the concerns of farmers and those of environmentalists.

Many other experts have been generous with their time and wisdom. They include: Dave Lewis, former Tesco CEO and now WWF Chair of Board of Trustees; Professor Dame Rachel Griffith, Research Director, Institute for Fiscal Studies and Professor of Economics, University of Manchester; Sir Ian Boyd, Professor of Biology, University of St Andrews, former Chief Scientific Adviser, Defra; Professor Martin White, Professor of Population Health Research, Centre for Diet and Activity Research, MRC Epidemiology Unit, University of Cambridge; Dr Peter Scarborough, Nuffield Department of Population Health, University of Oxford; Dr Kevin Hall, Senior Investigator, Integrative Physiology Section, Laboratory of Biological Modelling, Intramural Research Programme, National Institutes of Health; Lazlo Barabási, Giulia Menichetti and Peter Ruppert, from the Barabási Lab; Dr Richie Harrington, senior researcher Big Data Institute, Nuffield Department of Population Health, University of Oxford; Professor Lord Krebs, Emeritus Professor of Zoology, University of Oxford; Sir Dieter Helm, Professor of Economic Policy at the University of Oxford; Dr David Nabarro, Professor of global health at Imperial College London, and curator of the UN's Food Systems Dialogues; Sir Charles Burrell, conservationist and founder of the Knepp Wildland; Stefano Agostini, CEO of Nestle UK & Ireland; Michael Dixon, Co-Chair, Social Prescribing Network; Sam Hall, Director of the Conservative Environment Network; Emily Miles, Chief Executive, Food Standards Agency; Professor

Dame Ottoline Leyser, Regius Professor of Botany at the University of Cambridge and Chief Executive Officer of UK Research and Innovation; Professor Tim Spector – epidemiologist, King's College London, and science writer; Professor Tim Lang, Emeritus Professor of Food Policy at City University ; Professor Guy Poppy, former Chief Scientific Adviser to the Food Standards Agency; Sue Pritchard, Chief Executive of the Food, Farming and Countryside Commission; Professor Corinna Hawkes, Professor of Food Policy, City University of London; Richard Benwell, Chief Executive of the Wildlife and Countryside Link; Mark Bridgman, President, Country Landowners Association; Martin Lines, UK Chair, Nature Friendly Farming Network; Gavin Lane, Farmer; David Fursdon, Chair of Beeswax Dyson Farming Ltd; Peter Brotherton, Director of Science, Natural England; Louise Davies, founder, Food Teachers Centre; Fiona Gatley, Royal Academy of Culinary Arts; Judith Batchelar, outgoing Director of corporate responsibility and sustainability at Sainsbury's; Sarah Bradbury, Group Quality Director, Tesco; Marie Polley, co-chair, Social Prescribing Network; James Rebanks, sheep farmer and author; Professor Herman Pontzer, Associate Professor in Evolutionary Anthropology, Duke University; Professor Alan Dangour, Professor in Food and Nutrition, London School of Hygiene and Tropical Medicine; Dr Rosemary Green, Associate Professor in Sustainability, Nutrition and Health, London School of Hygiene and Tropical Medicine; Dr Pauline Scheelbeek, Assistant Professor in Nutritional and Environmental Epidemiology, London School of Hygiene and Tropical Medicine; Iain Porter, Joseph Rowntree Foundation; Professor Jonathan Bradshaw, Emeritus Professor of Social Policy, York University; Dr Ben Richardson, Reader in International Political Economy, University of Warwick; and Dr Fiona Smith, Professor of International Economic Law, University of Leeds; Tamara Finkelstein, Permanent Secretary, Defra; Andrew Jarvis, Vice President, Public Policy Research and Evaluation, ICF; Professor Michael Lee, Deputy Vice Chancellor, Harper Adams University; Prof David Main, Professor of Production Animal Health & Welfare, Royal Agricultural University; Patricia Eustachio Colombo, Professor Michelle Morris, Leeds Institute for Data Analytics & School of Medicine, University of Leeds, Research Coordinator, Karolinska Institutet.

The work has been supported by the analysis and insight of Bain & Company, SystemIQ, Technopolis Group, Energy Systems Catapult, Policy Lab and Fleetwood Strategy. I thank you all.

This report and the Evidence Pack would not have been possible without the design expertise of all those at 10 Associates, particularly Michael Freemantle and Alex Finney, and Katie White at White Creative.

I am grateful to those people working in the Devolved Authorities who gave us their thoughts. They include: from Northern Ireland, Joy Alexander, Fiona Ferguson, Louise Brady, and Colette McMaster; from Scotland, George Burgess, David Gally, Ian McWatt, Gillian Provan, Garry Mournian, David Johnston; and from Wales, David Lloyd-Thomas and Nicholas Shilton.

Finally, there are things that government is not allowed to pay for in an Independent Review and we have been lucky for the support of a number of funders. Sustainable Healthy Food Systems consortium, funded by the Wellcome Trust, Esmée Fairbairn Foundation, and the Health Foundation together funded our youth engagement programme.

The Food People & Fix Our Food funded the Holiday Activities and Food programme we made with Marcus Rashford.

The Mark Leonard Trust, The Linbury Trust, The Ashden Trust,the European Climate Foundation and The Rothschild Foundation, all provided funding for communication.

We drew heavily on the work of Hannah Ritchie and Max Rosser at Our World in Data. They provide an extraordinary wealth of free and beautifully visualised data. Many people will have come across their work on COVID. Their work on the food system is just as rich and compelling.

Thanks to Naomi Duncan and Nicole Pisani, my colleagues at Chefs in Schools, for doing the work that really matters: educating the palates of the future.

Advisory Panel

Agriculture

Minette Batters, President, NFU

Helen Browning, Chief Executive, Soil Association

Craig Livingstone, Farmer of the Year, 2018

John Shropshire, CEO, G's Group

Rebecca Laughton, Campaign Coordinator, Landworkers' Alliance

Industry, Government and Non-Governmental Organisations

Denise Bentley, Co-Founder and CEO, First Love Association

Baroness Boycott, Member of the Food, Poverty, Health and the Environment Committee, House of Lords, former Chair of the London Food Board

Paul Clarke, Chief Technology Officer, Ocado

Tony Juniper, Chair, Natural England

Justin King, Former Chief Executive Sainsbury's, Non-Executive Director Marks & Spencer

Sarah Mukherjee, Chief Executive, Institute of Environmental Management and Assessment, former Chief Executive, Crop Protection Association

Sebastian Munden, Executive Vice President & General Manager, Unilever UK & Ireland

Andrew Selley, Chief Executive, Bidfood

Alastair Storey, Found and Chief Executive, Westbury Street Holdings (WSH)

Gerard van der Hut, Managing Director, Rijk Zwaan UK Ltd

Roger Whiteside, Chief Executive, Greggs

Academics and Experts

Dr Meredith Crowley, Reader in International Economics, University of Cambridge, specialising in international trade

Dr David Halpern, Chief Executive, Behavioural Insights Team

Professor Susan Jebb, Professor of Diet and Population Health, University of Oxford

Dr Tim Leunig, Economic Adviser to the Chancellor, Associate Professor of Economic History, London School of Economics

Professor Steve McCorriston, Professor of Agricultural Economics, University of Exeter

Professor Theresa Marteau, Director of Behaviour and Health Research Unit, University of Cambridge

Jeremy Oppenheim, Founder & Senior Partner, SYSTEMIQ

Professor Jonathan Valabhji, National Clinical Director for Diabetes and Obesity, NHS England

Daisy Stemple, our citizen member of the Advisory Panel, has advocated for those at the sharp end of the food system, giving a voice to those who are too often voiceless.

Citizen Dialogue

We would like to thank Henrietta Hopkins, Director, Hopkins van Mil and her team who masterfully ran our public dialogues process and the counsel of UKRI and Sciencewise. I would also like to thank all of the citizens that generously gave their time over 18 months. Their voices, which fundamentally informed my views, flow throughout this report. I am grateful for the advice of the members of the independent oversight group who helped oversee these dialogues with citizens:

Peter Jackson, Professor of Geography and Co-Director of the University of Sheffield Institute for Sustainable Food, University of Sheffield

Sue Davies, Head of Consumer Protection and Food Policy, Which? The Consumer Association

Matthew van Duyvenbode, Director of Strategy & Impact, the Trussell Trust

Ian Mace, Head of Public Affairs and Policy, Association of British Foods

Modi Mwatsama, Senior Science Lead (Food Systems, Nutrition and Health), Wellcome Trust

Toby Park, Principal Advisor, Energy, Environment & Sustainability, the Behavioural Insights Team

Paul Smith, Secretary General, Botanic Gardens Conservation International

Justin Varney, Director of Public Health, Birmingham City Council

Rachel Ward, Scientific Policy Director, Institute of Food Science & Technology

Laura Wellesley, Senior Research Fellow, Energy, Environment and Resources Programme at Chatham House

Ruth Edge, Chief Food Chain Adviser, National Farmers Union

Christine McDowell, Food Chain Adviser, National Farmers Union

Jack Watts, Agri-Food Policy Delivery Manager, National Farmers Union

Who we have met

Organisation	Sector
Agri-EPI centre	Academia / Research
Alan Turing Institute	Academia / Research
Barabasi Lab	Academia / Research
Blue Hat Man	Academia / Research
Bright Harbour	Academia / Research
Brunel University	Academia / Research
Centre for Innovation Excellence in Livestock	Academia / Research
Dasgupta Review	Academia / Research
Demos	Academia / Research
ECIU	Academia / Research
Education Policy Institute	Academia / Research
Food Climate Research Network	Academia / Research
Glasgow University	Academia / Research
Global Food Security	Academia / Research
Harper Adams University	Academia / Research
IDDRI	Academia / Research
Indigo Agriculture	Academia / Research
Institute for Fiscal Studies	Academia / Research
Institute for Innovation and Public Purpose	Academia / Research
Institute of Zoology, ZSL	Academia / Research
IPPR	Academia / Research
Meridian Institute	Academia / Research
National Physical Laboratory	Academia / Research
Newcastle University	Academia / Research
NIDDK	Academia / Research
Nottingham University	Academia / Research
Nuffield Department of Primary Care	Academia / Research
Oxford Risk Ltd	Academia / Research
QMUL	Academia / Research
Queens University Belfast	Academia / Research

Organisation	Sector
Reading University	Academia / Research
Royal Agricultural University	Academia / Research
RUG	Academia / Research
The Fitzwilliam Museum	Academia / Research
The Institute for Agriculture & Horticulture	Academia / Research
Turing Institute	Academia / Research
UCL Institute for Sustainable Resources	Academia / Research
Universiity of Herfordshire	Academia / Research
University College London	Academia / Research
University of Bath	Academia / Research
University of California Santa Barbara	Academia / Research
University of Cambridge	Academia / Research
University of Exeter	Academia / Research
University of Glasgow	Academia / Research
University of Leeds	Academia / Research
University of Nottingham	Academia / Research
University of Oxford	Academia / Research
University of St Andrews	Academia / Research
UWTSD	Academia / Research
City, University of London	Academia / Research
ICOSS, University of Sheffield	Academia / Research
AHBD	Government / Public sector
APPG on a Fit and Healthy Childhood	Government / Public sector
APPG on Longevity	Government / Public sector
Argyll and Bute Council	Government / Public sector
BBSRC	Government / Public sector

Organisation	Sector
Birmingham City Council	Government / Public sector
Cabinet Office	Government / Public sector
Carmarthenshire County Council	Government / Public sector
Centre for Digital Built Britain	Government / Public sector
Climate Change Committee	Government / Public sector
Crown Commercial Service	Government / Public sector
Department for Business, Energy and Industrial Strategy	Government / Public sector
Department for Digital, Culture, Media and Sport	Government / Public sector
Department for Education	Government / Public sector
Department for Environment, Food and Rural Affairs	Government / Public sector
Department of Health and Social Care	Government / Public sector
Digital Catapault	Government / Public sector
Education Scotland	Government / Public sector
Environment Agency	Government / Public sector
Food Standards Agency	Government / Public sector
Foreign, Commonwealth and Development Office	Government / Public sector
Global Resource Initiative	Government / Public sector
Greater Birmingham & Solihull Local Enterprise Partnership	Government / Public sector
Hackney Council	Government / Public sector
Health and Safety Executive	Government / Public sector
HM Prison and Probation Service	Government / Public sector

Organisation	Sector
HM Treasury	Government / Public sector
Hospital Food Review	Government / Public sector
House of Commons	Government / Public sector
House of Lords	Government / Public sector
Institue for Fiscal Studies	Government / Public sector
Kingsmead Primary School	Government / Public sector
Liverpool NHS Trust	Government / Public sector
Local Government Association	Government / Public sector
Ministry of Defence	Government / Public sector
Ministry of Justice	Government / Public sector
Natural England	Government / Public sector
NHS England	Government / Public sector
NHS Improvement	Government / Public sector
Office of National Statistics	Government / Public sector
Public Health England	Government / Public sector
Public Health Matters	Government / Public sector
Reach Academy	Government / Public sector
Scottish Government	Government / Public sector
The Prime Minister's Office	Government / Public sector
Trade and Agriculture Commission	Government / Public sector
UK COP presidency	Government / Public sector
UK High Level Climate Champion	Government / Public sector

Organisation	Sector
UKRI	Government / Public sector
UN COP26	Government / Public sector
Veterinary Medicines Directorate	Government / Public sector
Welsh Government	Government / Public sector
AI Council	Government / Public sector
Children's Commissioner	Government / Public sector
Climate Champions	Government / Public sector
Department for International Trade	Government / Public sector
Department for Work and Pensions	Government / Public sector
4SD	Industry
AB Foods	Industry
ABP Beef	Industry
ADAS	Industry
Agricultural Industries Confederation	Industry
Agrimetrics	Industry
AIC	Industry
Aldi	Industry
Aleph Foods	Industry
Alix & Partners	Industry
Allora	Industry
Arla	Industry
ASC	Industry
Asda	Industry
Association of Convenience Stores	Industry
Aviva Investors	Industry
Barfoots	Industry
Bartle Bogle Hegarty	Industry
Beeswax Dyson	Industry
Bidfood	Industry
Booths	Industry
British Retail Consortium	Industry
Capita	Industry
Catapult Energy Systems	Industry
Cellular Agriculture Limited	Industry
Cignpost Diagnostics	Industry
Classic Fresh Foods	Industry
Coca Cola	Industry
Compass Group UK	Industry
Competere	Industry
Co-Op	Industry
Covent Garden Market Authority	Industry
Daily Mail	Industry
Dawn Meats	Industry
Daylesford Organic	Industry
DPS	Industry
EatDrinkSleep	Industry
EFECA	Industry
Energy & Climate Intelligence Unit	Industry
Equilibrium Markets Ltd (FreshRange)	Industry
Erpingham House	Industry
FAIRR	Industry
Fidelity International	Industry
Food and Drink Federation	Industry
Greencore	Industry
Greensphere capital	Industry
Greggs	Industry
G's Fresh	Industry
Hall Farm	Industry
Hawksmoor	Industry
HSBC	Industry
Iceland	Industry
ICF	Industry
IDH Trade	Industry
IGD	Industry
Impact Investing Institute	Industry
Impossible Burger	Industry

Organisation	Sector
Industry Nutrition Strategy Group	Industry
Institute of Environmental Management & Assessment	Industry
International Meat Trade Association	Industry
ISS	Industry
Jamie Oliver	Industry
John Lewis / Waitrose	Industry
Kerry Foods	Industry
Knepp Estate	Industry
LACA	Industry
Lazard	Industry
Legendairy Foods	Industry
Leon	Industry
Lidl	Industry
Limewood Group	Industry
Local TV Network	Industry
Lockerley Estate	Industry
Lok'n'Store	Industry
Marks and Spencer	Industry
McCain	Industry
McColls	Industry
McDonald's UK & Ireland	Industry
McKinsey	Industry
Mondra	Industry
Morrisons	Industry
Mosa Meat	Industry
Mott McDonald	Industry
Moy Park	Industry
National Farmers' Union	Industry
Nestle	Industry
Ocado	Industry
Organic Research Centre	Industry
Ottolenghi	Industry
Pioneer Hospitality	Industry
Prestige Purchasing	Industry
Prezzo	Industry
Protein Industries Canada	Industry

Organisation	Sector
Public Sector Catering Magazine	Industry
Rathbones	Industry
Redefine Meat	Industry
Rijk Zwann	Industry
Riverford	Industry
Rubicon 3	Industry
Sainsbury's	Industry
Sean Rickard Limited	Industry
Severn Trent Water	Industry
Sodexo	Industry
Solar Foods	Industry
South West Water	Industry
Spar	Industry
SW Food Hub	Industry
Synthesis Capital	Industry
SystemIQ	Industry
Tenant Farmers Association	Industry
Tesco	Industry
The Mail on Sunday	Industry
The Rockefeller Institute	Industry
Thirty Percy	Industry
Triodos	Industry
TUCO	Industry
UK Flour Milling Industry	Industry
Unilever	Industry
Volac	Industry
Wahaca	Industry
Waitrose	Industry
Wall Street Journal	Industry
Westbury Street Holdings	Industry
Westminster Industry Group	Industry
Yeo Valley	Industry
Nature Friendly Farming Network	Industry
Institute for European Environmental Policy	INGO
OECD	INGO

Organisation	Sector
World Health Organisation (WHO)	INGO
A Greener World	Voluntary and charitable sector
Action on Salt and Sugar	Voluntary and charitable sector
AllFed Alliance	Voluntary and charitable sector
Behavioural Insights Team	Voluntary and charitable sector
Beyond GM	Voluntary and charitable sector
Big Society	Voluntary and charitable sector
BiteBack 2030	Voluntary and charitable sector
Blue Marine Foundation	Voluntary and charitable sector
Bremner Consulting	Voluntary and charitable sector
Broadway Initiative	Voluntary and charitable sector
Cambridge Sustainable Food	Voluntary and charitable sector
Canal & River Trust	Voluntary and charitable sector
Changing Food, the Copenhagen Food System Centre	Voluntary and charitable sector
Chatham House	Voluntary and charitable sector
Chefs in Schools	Voluntary and charitable sector
Children's Investment Fund Foundation	Voluntary and charitable sector
Citizen	Voluntary and charitable sector
Client Earth	Voluntary and charitable sector
Company Shop	Voluntary and charitable sector
Conservative Environment Network	Voluntary and charitable sector
Country Land and Business Association	Voluntary and charitable sector

Organisation	Sector
Country Trust	Voluntary and charitable sector
Danish Wholegrain Partnership	Voluntary and charitable sector
Dynamic Food Procurement National Advisory Board	Voluntary and charitable sector
Eating Better Alliance	Voluntary and charitable sector
Eden Project	Voluntary and charitable sector
Education Partnerships Group	Voluntary and charitable sector
Energy Systems Catapult	Voluntary and charitable sector
Environmental Funders Network	Voluntary and charitable sector
Esmee Fairbairn Foundation	Voluntary and charitable sector
FareShare	Voluntary and charitable sector
Fig Holding	Voluntary and charitable sector
First Love Foundation	Voluntary and charitable sector
Food Foundation	Voluntary and charitable sector
Food Frontier	Voluntary and charitable sector
Food, Farming & Countryside Commission	Voluntary and charitable sector
Foodome Project	Voluntary and charitable sector
Forest Creation Partners	Voluntary and charitable sector
Forward Institute	Voluntary and charitable sector
Freelance	Voluntary and charitable sector
Future Advocacy	Voluntary and charitable sector
Giki	Voluntary and charitable sector
Good Food Institute	Voluntary and charitable sector

Organisation	Sector
Green Alliance	Voluntary and charitable sector
Green Finance Institute	Voluntary and charitable sector
Greenpeace	Voluntary and charitable sector
Guy's & St Thomas' Hospital Charity	Voluntary and charitable sector
Humane Society International	Voluntary and charitable sector
Institute for Government	Voluntary and charitable sector
IUC Forest Programme	Voluntary and charitable sector
John Ellerman Foundation	Voluntary and charitable sector
Landworkers Alliance	Voluntary and charitable sector
Leading Edge Forum	Voluntary and charitable sector
Local Food Hubs	Voluntary and charitable sector
Longevity International	Voluntary and charitable sector
National Geographic Society	Voluntary and charitable sector
National Trust	Voluntary and charitable sector
Nesta	Voluntary and charitable sector
Nourish Scotland	Voluntary and charitable sector
Nourish UK	Voluntary and charitable sector
Nutrition Society	Voluntary and charitable sector
Onward	Voluntary and charitable sector
Oxford Farming Conference	Voluntary and charitable sector
Plantlife	Voluntary and charitable sector
ProVeg	Voluntary and charitable sector

Organisation	Sector
QC Foundation	Voluntary and charitable sector
RAND Europe	Voluntary and charitable sector
ResPublica	Voluntary and charitable sector
Rothschild Foundation	Voluntary and charitable sector
Royal Academy of Culinary Arts	Voluntary and charitable sector
Royal Society of Arts	Voluntary and charitable sector
RSPB	Voluntary and charitable sector
RSPCA	Voluntary and charitable sector
Sainsburys Family Charitable Trusts	Voluntary and charitable sector
Save British Farming	Voluntary and charitable sector
Save The Children	Voluntary and charitable sector
School Food Matters	Voluntary and charitable sector
School Food Teachers Centre	Voluntary and charitable sector
Scotland Food for Life	Voluntary and charitable sector
Seafish UK	Voluntary and charitable sector
Soil Association	Voluntary and charitable sector
Square Food Foundation	Voluntary and charitable sector
Street Games	Voluntary and charitable sector
Sustain	Voluntary and charitable sector
Sustainable Food Trust	Voluntary and charitable sector
TastEd	Voluntary and charitable sector
The Food Foundation	Voluntary and charitable sector

Organisation	Sector
The Food People	Voluntary and charitable sector
The Woodland Trust	Voluntary and charitable sector
Tony Blair Institute	Voluntary and charitable sector
UK Onward	Voluntary and charitable sector
Vegan Society	Voluntary and charitable sector
Ways to Wellness	Voluntary and charitable sector
Wellcome Trust	Voluntary and charitable sector
Which?	Voluntary and charitable sector
Wildlife and Countryside Link	Voluntary and charitable sector
Wildlife Trusts	Voluntary and charitable sector
World Wildlife Fund for Nature (WWF)	Voluntary and charitable sector
Worshipful Company of Farmers	Voluntary and charitable sector
WRAP	Voluntary and charitable sector

Additional reading list

The following is a list of key texts that we have drawn on in writing this report but are not specifically mentioned elsewhere:

Adams, W.M. (2003). Future Nature: A Vision for Conservation. New York, USA: Routledge

Banerjee, A.V. & Duflo, E. (2019). Good Economics for Hard Times: Better Answers to Our Biggest Problems. London, UK: Allen Lane

Barabási, A-L. (2003). Linked: The New Science of Networks. New York, USA: Perseus Books

Barber, M. (2021). Accomplishment: How to Achieve Ambitious and Challenging Things. London, UK: Allen Lane

Cocker, M. (2019). Our Place: Can We Save Britain's Wildlife Before It Is Too Late? London: Vintage Books

Coghill, I. (2021). Moorland Matters: The Battle for the Uplands against Authoritarian Conservation. Stroud, UK: Quiller Publishing Ltd

Cottam, H. (2018). Radical Help: How we can remake the relationships between us and revolutionise the welfare state. London, UK: Virago

Crisp, N. (2020). Health is made at home, hospitals are for repairs: Building a healthy and health-creating society. SALUS Global knowledge Exchange

Davis, A. et al. (2019). Understanding the Multi-functional Nature of the Countryside. Oxford, UK: Oxford University Press. Available at: https://blog.oup.com/2019/09/understanding-the-multi-functional-nature-of-the-countryside/

Deaton, A. (2015). The Great Escape: Health, Wealth, and the Origins of Inequality. Princeton, USA: Princeton University Press

Finkelstein, L. & Carson, E.R. (1985). Mathematical Modelling of Dynamic Biological Systems (2nd Edition). Totnes, UK: Research Studies Press

Food and Land Use Coalition. (2019). Growing Better: Ten Critical Transitions to Transform Food and Land Use. Available at: https://www.foodandlandusecoalition.org/global-report/

Kirkham, T.C. and Cooper, S.J. (eds). (2007). Appetite and Body Weight. Integrative Systems and the Development of Anti-Obesity Drugs. Amsterdam, Netherlands: Elsevier Ltd.

Lent, J. (2017). The Patterning Instinct: A Cultural History of Humanity's Search for Meaning. Buffalo, USA: Prometheus Books

Lobley, M. & Winter, M. (2009). What is Land For? The Food, Fuel and Climate Change Debate. London, UK: Routledge

Mazzucato, M. (2021). Mission Economy: A Moonshot Guide to Changing Capitalism. London, UK: Allen Lane

Mazzucato, M. (2018). The Entrepreneurial State: Debunking Public vs. Private Sector Myths. London, UK: Penguin Books

Monbiot, G. (2014). Feral: Rewilding the Land, Sea and Human Life. London, UK: Penguin Books

OECD. (2021). Making Better Policies for Food Systems. Available at: https://www.oecd-ilibrary.org/agriculture-and-food/making-better-policies-for-food-systems_ddfba4de-en

Parsons, K. et al. (2019). Rethinking food policy: A fresh approach to policy and practice. City University of London. Available at: https://nutritionconnect.org/resource-center/rethinking-food-policy-fresh-approach-policy-and-practice

Prabhu, J. (2021). How Should A Government Be? The New Levers of State Power. London, UK: Profile Books

Rebanks, J. (2015). The Shepherd's Life: A Tale of the Lake District. London, UK: Penguin Books.

Sandbu, M. (2020). The Economics of Belonging: A Radical Plan to Win Back the Left Behind and Achieve Prosperity for All. Princeton, USA: Princeton University Press

Snowdon, C. (2017). Killjoys: A Critique of Paternalism. London, UK: Institute of Economic Affairs

Spector, T. (2020). Spoon-Fed: Why almost everything we've been told about food is wrong. London, UK: Jonathan Cape Books

Stuart, T. (2009). Waste: Uncovering the Global Food Scandal. London, UK: Penguin Books

Tree, I. (2018). Wilding: The return of nature to a British farm. London, UK: Picador

Wallace, D.F. (2005). Consider the Lobster: And Other Essays. Boston, USA: Little, Brown & Company

Wilson, B. (2015). First Bite: How We Learn to Eat. London, UK: Fourth Estate.

Wilson, E.O. (2016). Half-Earth: Our Planet's Fight for Life. New York, USA: Liveright Books

Wilson, E.O. (2001). The Diversity of Life. London, UK: Penguin Books

Terms of Reference

Purpose

No part of our economy matters more than food. Food is vital to life and, for one in seven of us, it is the source of our livelihood. And no decisions have such a direct impact on our lives and wellbeing as the choices we make about what we eat.

Food shapes our sense of ourselves, too. Cooking and eating together is perhaps the defining communal act. The character of the English landscape and the culture of many rural communities are defined by the way farmers use the land. And although the vast majority of us now live in cities, growing food, seeing how it is grown, knowing that we can feed ourselves – these are all important to our sense of national belonging.

The free market performs a million daily miracles to present us with an abundant choice of safe and reasonably-priced food, creating millions of jobs and providing us with an ease of consumption unimaginable to our grandparents' generation.

But the way we produce, distribute, market and consume food raises a series of difficult policy questions which Government cannot shirk. The state already regulates in minute detail how food is grown, and livestock reared, in order to safeguard both human health and our natural environment. We subsidise food producers to an extent no other industry enjoys. We regulate the sale and marketing of food for health and other reasons. From the national curriculum to hospital meals, the availability of migrant labour to the public health impacts of obesity, Government is responsible for a myriad of actions which shape the nation's relationship with food.

And the need for Government to review and rethink its influence and role is only increasing. It's not just the case that we need to reconsider how food and drink, as our biggest manufacturing industry, fits into the Government's broader Industrial Strategy; there are other urgent and inescapable policy questions with which Government must grapple.

Globally, we are the first generation more likely to die as a result of lifestyle choices than infectious disease. Diabetes, cardiac disease and other obesity-related conditions are costing the NHS billions and drastically harming the lives of millions. Obesity is a particular issue for poorer communities and young people. Children from the most deprived areas are three times as likely to be obese as those from the least deprived.

Intensive farming, of the kind that has increased production so much since the Second World War, also generates environmental problems. The impact on soil health, air quality, river freshness, biodiversity and climate change has raised urgent questions about how we can make food production genuinely sustainable.

And we cannot afford to ignore new challenges to food security. With the world's population growing, a mass migration to cities, resource competition intensifying between nations, huge stress on water supplies, climate change altering what the land is capable of supplying, trade barriers re-emerging and new public health dangers growing, from antimicrobial resistance to viral mutations, it is critical to review how we secure the food of the future.

To address these growing problems, to ensure the security of our food supply and to maximise the benefits of the coming revolution in agricultural technology, the Government proposes to develop a new integrated National Food Strategy.

The purpose of the National Food Strategy is to build on the work underway in the Agriculture Bill, the Environment Bill, the Fisheries Bill, the Industrial Strategy and the Childhood Obesity Plan to create an overarching strategy for Government, designed to ensure our food system:

- Delivers safe, healthy, affordable food; regardless of where they live or how much they earn.
- Is robust in the face of future shocks.
- Restores and enhances the natural environment for the next generation in this country.
- Is built upon a resilient, sustainable and humane agriculture sector.
- Is a thriving contributor to our urban and rural economies, delivering well paid jobs and supporting innovative producers and manufacturers across the country.
- Does all of this in an efficient and cost-effective way.

We have a moral, as well as practical, responsibility to consider the role and impact of the food system. The purpose of the National Food Strategy is to set out a vision for the kind of food system we should be building for the future, and a plan for how to achieve that vision.

Scope

The scope will be England, but the strategy will consider our relationship with the devolved administrations, the European Union and our other trading partners.

The strategy will cover the entire food chain, from field to fork: the production, marketing, processing, sale and purchase of food (for consumption in the home and out of it), and the consumer practices, resources and institutions involved in these processes.

The strategy will consider the role of the central government departments, arm's-length bodies, local councils and city authorities. In doing so it will also consider the roles that individuals, the private sector, and social enterprises should play.

Reporting, activities, and timing

The purpose of the review is to consider how the UK's food sector operates currently, and to set out options (underpinned by detailed evidence, including in respect of the associated pros, cons, and trade-offs) for adjusting Government policies to better achieve the objectives for the Strategy set out above. Subsequently, the Government will develop a National Food Strategy White Paper informed, among other things, by this independent review. This is planned six months after the publication of the review.

The review will be led by Henry Dimbleby, co-founder of Leon restaurants, the lead non-executive director at Defra and co-author of The School Food Plan.

Henry will be supported by Defra officials. Henry will also consult stakeholders across the country and from all relevant government departments. An advisory group selected from across the food system will support him. The recently formed Food and Drink Sector Council will also be a source of close advice and counsel.

Henry will report to ministers on content which concerns their departments, as the review progresses.

The problems of BMI measurement in children

Eagle-eyed observers may notice that nowhere in this report do we use one of the most commonly quoted statistics on obesity in the UK: "One in ten children is obese when they start primary school, and one in five is obese by the time they leave, aged 11."

We have tried to be exacting in our use of data, and we believe the way this statistic is measured is problematic and probably worth rethinking.

The definition of obesity for adults is simple. If your body mass index (BMI) – your weight in kilograms divided by the square of your height in metres – is over 25, the NHS defines you as overweight; over 30, you are obese; and over 40, severely obese.†

This measure has its flaws even for adults – we all know the stories of lean, fit rugby players who are theoretically "obese" – but it is broadly fit for purpose at a population level.

For children, things are more complex. Because of the way young bodies naturally change shape as they grow – from chubby babies to stringy pre-teens and muscular adolescents – the BMI thresholds for children have to differ by age. To complicate things further, they also differ between boys and girls. To determine whether a child is underweight, overweight or obese, a doctor will consult one of two charts – one for each sex – that provide the BMI thresholds for every stage. A five-year-old boy, for example, would be defined as obese if his BMI exceeded 19.3. By age 11, it would have to exceed 25.1, and by 18 it would have to match the adult number of 30.††

Figure 1

Obesity prevalence in England across all age ranges†††

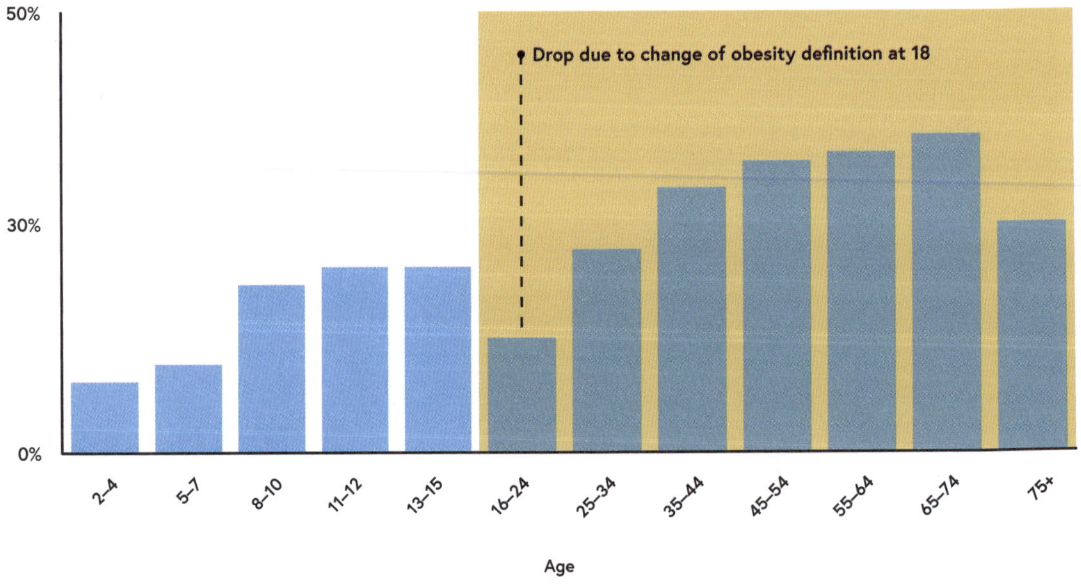

....

† NHS. (2019). *Obesity.* Available at: https://www.nhs.uk/conditions/obesity/

†† For age 5 and 11 see: NHS Great Ormond Street Hospital for Children. (no date). *Your BMI.* Available at: www.gosh.nhs.uk/children/general-health-advice/eat-smart/obesity-lowdown/your-bmi; for adult see: NHS. (2019). *What is the body mass index (BMI)?* Available at: https://www.nhs.uk/common-health-questions/lifestyle/what-is-the-body-mass-index-bmi/

††† NHS Digital. (2020.) *Healthy Survey for England 2019: Adult and child overweight and obesity.* Available at: http://digital.nhs.uk/pubs/hse2019

So far so good. But if we look at the overall statistics on obesity in the population, provided by the Royal College of Paediatrics and Child Health (Figure B1), we see something very strange. Obesity seems to rise steadily until the age of 15. Then, when we reach the 16-24 age category, obesity levels suddenly plummet by just under half, before rising again in adulthood.

How are our 16-year-olds performing this miraculous feat of weight loss? It doesn't make sense, either intuitively or scientifically: in a 2017 report, the same Royal College of Paediatrics and Child Health told us that "80% of overweight and obese children will become overweight and obese adults".[†]

The answer is, they don't lose the weight. It's just a quirk of data definition.

The guidelines for measuring BMI in children are based on 1990 measurements of the BMI of children of all ages – known as the UK90. For reasons that are very far from clear, it was decided that, from the ages of 0-15, the BMI threshold for obesity should be pegged to the BMI of the heaviest 5% of each age group in the UK90 data.[††]

Once children reach the age of 16, the way obesity is measured abruptly changes – to the adult definition of a BMI above 30. This is a much higher threshold: only around 2% of 16-year-olds had a BMI above 30 in the UK90 data. Overnight, therefore, a whole load of children who qualified as obese the day before their birthday become, statistically, merely overweight.

Because this abrupt change is built into the system for monitoring the weight of our population, it continues to distort the figures. Every year the chart appears to show the same inexplicable dip in obesity numbers at 16.

A threshold for measuring obesity is bound to be somewhat arbitrary - in the US in 1998, the definition of overweight changed from a BMI of 27 for women and 28 for men to 25 for everyone - which reclassified 29 million people as overweight overnight.[†††] But the data anomalies created by the childhood BMI thresholds in the UK, are troublesome enough to require rethinking.

....

† Royal College of Paediatrics and Child Health. (2017). *State of Child Health Report 2017.*

†† Public Health England. (2020). *Official Statistics: NCMP and Child Obesity Profile: short statistical commentary March 2020.* Available at: https://www.gov.uk/government/statistics/child-obesity-and-excess-weight-small-area-level-data-march-2020-update/ncmp-and-child-obesity-profile-short-statistical-commentary-march-2020

††† Squires, S. (1998). *Optimal weight threshold lowered.* The Washington Post.

Call for Evidence

In August 2019, Defra - on behalf of the National Food Strategy - conducted a Call for Evidence which lasted for ten weeks. Anyone with an interest in food was invited to contribute their ideas, whether big or small, on how the food system should be transformed. The opportunity to help shape the future of the food system in England was welcomed by many, with nearly 2,000 respondents submitting a total of over 5,000 suggestions. All of these were analysed and considered as part of this Independent Review.

A detailed summary of the issues raised and the solutions suggested is available on the gov.uk website. Every single response has been read, catalogued and considered carefully.

Who responded?

Responses came from all corners of society: from businesses, non-governmental organisations (NGOs) and academia. Members of the public who responded as individuals made up by far the largest proportion (see Figure 1). Five campaigns also organised a total of 84 responses: these came from Animal Rebellion, Four Paws, The Vegetarian Society, The Vegan Society and an unidentified campaign. These mostly focused on the links between livestock production, meat consumption and climate change.

A range of businesses with an interest in food responded, including farms, food processors, distributors, hospitality businesses, community interest companies, and manufacturers of agricultural or food technology equipment.

Respondents from academia included learned societies, think tanks, private-sector research firms and researchers from over 40 universities across the UK.

A large number of public sector organisations also submitted suggestions to the Call for Evidence, including local authorities, charities and trade bodies.

Figure 1

Number of respondents by sector

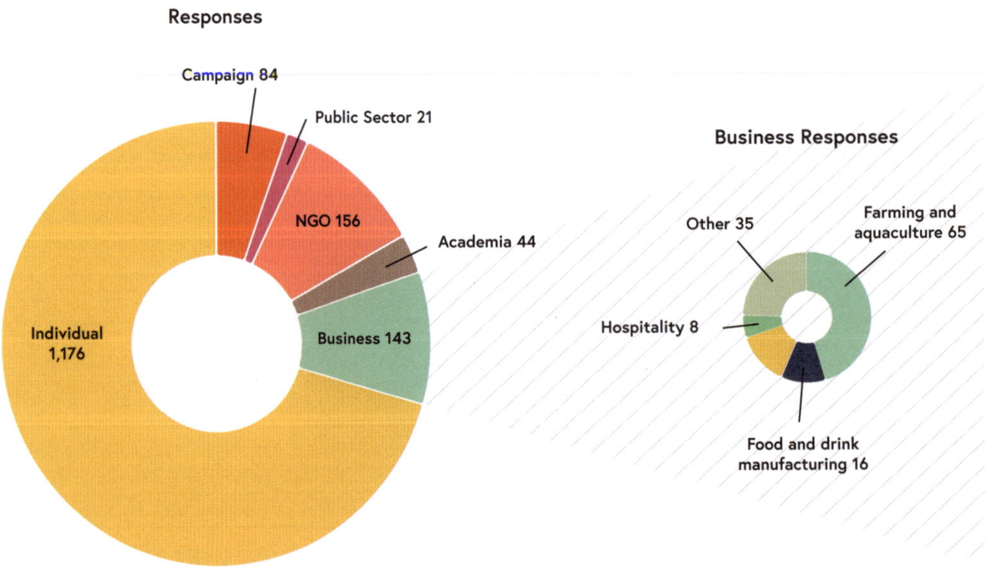

What did respondents most care about?

Each response was categorised into one of 40 topics which were then grouped into three overarching themes. Together these represent the outcomes that respondents most wanted to see:

- Food is produced and consumed in a responsible, environmentally sustainable way.
- Food is healthy, safe and valued by producers as well as consumers and their communities.
- The agri-food sector is robust, provides fair remuneration to workers, and is run sustainably.

All sectors cared about all three outcomes, with responses fairly evenly distributed across all outcomes. Businesses were mostly concerned with ensuring the agri-food sector is robust, and they provided ideas to achieve more sustainable business practices and improved consumer confidence. The primary concerns for individuals were animal welfare, climate change and reducing diet-related ill health. The suggestions submitted by public sector bodies were predominantly aimed at healthy and safe food. The responses of academics and NGOs were almost evenly split across the three themes (Figure 2).

What should the Government do to achieve these goals?

We were also interested to find out what role respondents saw for the Government in transforming the food system.

Figure 3 below shows a summary of the level of government intervention that respondents suggested. The ideas they proposed have been categorised according to an "intervention ladder" that ranges from least (e.g. education, information campaigns) to most (e.g. rules, bans) intrusive measures. Across all groups of respondents the most frequently suggested interventions were at either end of this ladder. Interventions such as incentives and taxes were much less frequently proposed.

Figure 2

Government interventions sought, by respondent type

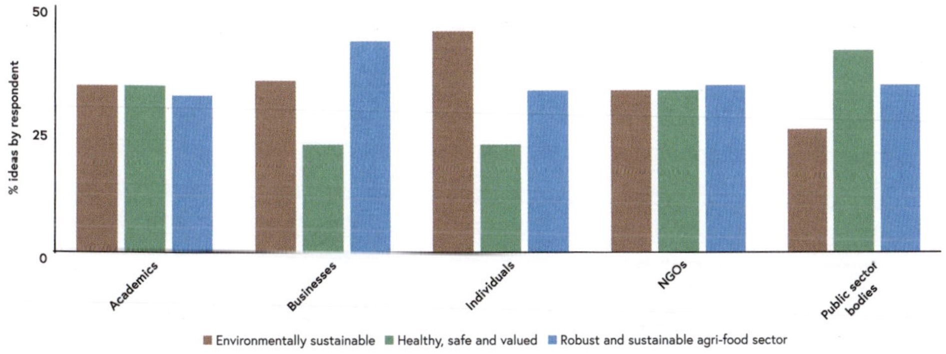

Figure 3

Outcomes sought, by respondent type

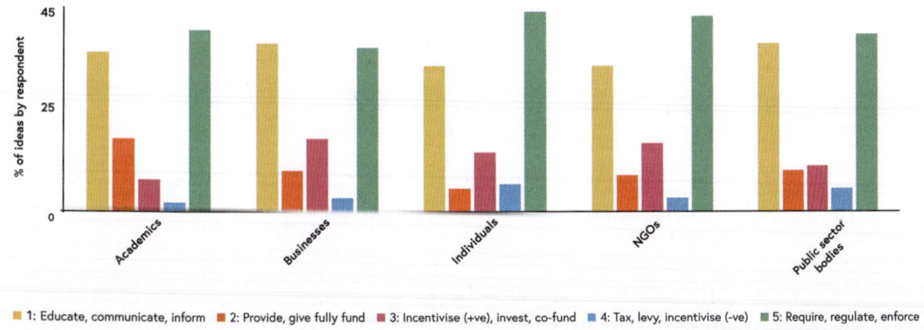

Glossary

Abiotic system

The set of non-living factors (such as sunlight, rain and temperature) affecting living things, i.e. plants and animals.

Agricultural Transition Period

Between 2021 and 2027, the Government will gradually phase out the current system of farm subsidies, moving from the Basic Payment Scheme to Environment Land Management, a new contract-based approach to paying farmers for producing public goods.

Agroecology

The application of principles from ecology (i.e. the study of relationships between living organisms) in farming, with the goal of achieving balanced growth and sustainable development.

Antimicrobial resistance

Antimicrobial resistance arises when microbes (such as bacteria and viruses) evolve and develop a resistance to antimicrobials (such as antibiotics) that used to be able to treat them. This is a natural phenomenon but can be accelerated by the misuse of medicines and other human practices.

Biodiversity

The variety of species and lifeforms in any ecosystem. It can refer to the whole world or to the life present in smaller areas.

Body mass index

Calculated as body mass (in kg) divided by the square of body height (in metres), BMI is a rule of thumb used to categorise a person as underweight (<18.5), normal weight, overweight (>25) or obese (>30).

Call for Evidence

Defra issued a Call for Evidence in August 2019, where it asked organisations and members of the public to respond by submitting ideas and comments on their priorities for the food system and how it could be improved.

Carbon capture and storage

The process of capturing carbon-dioxide emitted from industrial processes, before it enters the atmosphere, and storing it, for example in underground geological formations, instead of releasing it.

Carbon sequestration

The process of removing carbon dioxide from the atmosphere and storing ("sequestering") it. It happens through natural biological, chemical and physical processes, but can also be the result of human intervention, e.g. though carbon capture and storage

Challenge fund

The Industrial Strategy Challenge Fund is a form of Government grant available for projects that address the current, big societal challenges facing the UK, and address opportunities in areas such as clean growth and artificial intelligence.

Climate Assembly UK

Climate Assembly UK was the first UK-wide citizens' assembly, i.e. a body of randomly selected citizens to deliberate on an important issue. It was commissioned by six House of Commons Select Committees and published its final report on climate change in September 2020.

Climate Change Committee

The Climate Change Committee (CCC) is an independent, statutory body established under the Climate Change Act 2008. Its purpose is to advise the UK and devolved governments on emissions targets and to report to Parliament on progress made in reducing greenhouse gas emissions and preparing for and adapting to the impacts of climate change

Common Agricultural Policy

The European Union's flagship agricultural support programme. It is a complex set of income support, market regulation and rural development measures. Following the UK's Exit from the EU, farmers in England will no longer be eligible for payments under the CAP.

Diet-related health conditions

The effects of malnutrition and overnutrition include diseases associated with overeating, such as hight blood pressure, heart conditions, type II diabetes and certain types of cancers, as well as conditions caused by insufficient nutrition, such as stunted development in children, and shorter life expectancy

Environmental Land Management schemes

ELMs are schemes which will provide public money in exchange for public good. Following Brexit, the UK will no longer participate in the EU's Common Agricultural Policy (CAP). This will be replaced by ELMs, which will see a different set of land management outcomes newly incentivised by the Government

Eutrophication

The process of a body of water becoming enriched with minerals and nutrients. Without human interference, this is typically a very slow process, but the use of fertilisers and emission of untreated sewage into natural waterways leads to an accumulation of nitrogen and phosphorus which, in turn, stimulate the growth of algae and aquatic plants.

Feedback mechanism

When the outputs of a system also act as inputs into it, a feedback "loop" is created. A positive feedback loop is self-amplifying, for example when a microphone picks up its own inputs from a loudspeaker, leading to an ever-louder noise. A negative feedback loop is self-correcting, e.g. when high temperature leads to perspiration which, in turns, cools the skin.

Fixed-Term Parliaments Act 2011

This Act sets General Elections to take place every five years in May, unless in exceptional circumstances.

Food For Life

A lottery-funded programme run by the Soil Association charity, which aims to transform food culture in England by giving schools and communities access to seasonal, local food, and the skills needed to grow and cook fresh food themselves.

Food security

Having reliable access to sufficient food, both at the level of a nation and for an individual (or family). Despite advances in modern agriculture and global trade, food insecurity is an immediate concern for many, including in developed nations such as the UK.

Food system

The totality of the infrastructure, processes and people involved in the production, distribution and consumption of food as well as in the disposal of food waste.

Food, Farming and Countryside Commission

Set up in 2017 as an inquiry by the Royal Society of Arts, the FFCC became an independent charity in 2020. Its self-declared mission is to bring people together to find radical and practical ways to improve our climate, nature, health and economy.

Government Buying Standards for Food and Catering Services

The GBSF are defined by Defra, and constitute the minimum requirements for all food procured and distributed in the public sector. Its use is mandatory for central government and the NHS, and recommended for others.

Green Revolution

The advent of modern intensive farming, which became popular in the 1960s. The Green Revolution is particularly characterised by the use of pesticides and fertilisers, advanced farm machinery, and selectively bred crops.

Greenhouse gases

The three gases which account for the bulk of the warming associated with climate change: carbon dioxide (CO_2), methane (CH_4), and nitrous oxide (N_2O).

Holiday Activities and Food clubs

A Government-funded programme that ensures children from disadvantaged backgrounds have access to healthy food and enriching activities over the school holidays. In 2021, the Government adopted the recommendation made in the National Food Strategy – Part One, to extend the programme to the whole of England.

Holocene era

The Holocene is the name of the current geological epoch. It has been ongoing for approximately 11,700 years, having begun with the end of the preceding ice age.

Independent Review of Hospital Food

A "root and branch" review of the food served and sold in hospitals, launched by former Secretary of State for Health and Social Care, Matt Hancock, in 2019 following seven deaths caused by contaminated hospital food. Published in 2020, the Review made eight recommendations to improve quality, nutritional value and food safety.

Landscape Recovery payments

Landscape Recovery is one of the three constituent schemes of the ELMs, the other two being Sustainable Farming and Local Nature Recovery. Landscape Recovery payments will support land-use change projects that deliver ecosystem recovery, such as large-scale tree-planting and peatland restoration.

Loose products

Food products such as pick-and-mix and many bakery or deli items where the food is packaged very shortly before purchase or selected directly by the purchaser. Food in this category has lower requirements for showing nutritional content.

Low-intensity farming

Farming practices that prioritise environmental sustainability over maximising yield. This typically includes one or more of maintaining extensive grasslands and using little organic manure and manufactured fertiliser.

Malthusian catastrophe

The concept, described by Thomas Malthus in the 18th century, that when the population grows faster that agricultural production, the resulting scarcity of food will lead to famine and/or war which, in turn, will cause destitution and depopulation.

Manufactured food

A loosely defined term for foodstuffs that are treated in some way before consumption, rather than being eaten in the way they occur in nature. Depending on the nature of processing (e.g. extrusion, milling) and the type of additives used (e.g. acidifiers, colourings), they are categorised a processed, highly processed and ultra-processed foods. It is often not easy for consumers to tell which category a particular product falls into.

Mulesing

The controversial practice (common in some places, e.g. Australia) of removing skin from the buttocks of sheep so as to prevent the accumulation of faeces and urine in their wool, which would attract parasitic infestation by fly maggots.

National Dietary Nutrition Survey (NDNS)

The NDNS assesses on a rolling basis the diet, nutrient intake and nutritional status of the general population of the UK. It does so by looking at a representative sample of individuals over 1.5 years old.

Natural capital

The sum of the world's stock of natural resources, including water, air, soil and living beings. It is essential for human life, both directly (e.g. clean water and air) and indirectly (e.g. through pollination of plats by insects or water catchment to prevent floods).

Natural Capital Committee

The Natural Capital Committee (NCC) was an independent advisory committee which ran from 2012 to December 2020. It advised the Government on natural capital, including ecosystems, species, freshwaters, soils, minerals, the air and oceans, as well as natural processes and functions.

Net Environmental Gain

An approach for improving the condition of, and ecosystems that flow from, our natural assets in the context of development. Understanding local context and the relationship between communities and the natural environment in a given area is critical to an effective approach.

Net zero

"Net zero" means carbon neutrality, i.e. that an organisation or nation reduces its greenhouse gas emissions to zero or offsets any remaining emissions. The Climate Change Act of 2008 requires the Secretary of State to ensure that the UK has reached at least Net zero emissions by 2050.

Overweight and obesity

Excessive fat accumulation on a person that is associated with a range of health risks. In adults to be overweight is defined as having a BMI over 25, and for obesity, as over 30.

Paradigm

Paradigms are the intellectual frameworks consisting of interconnected theories, assumptions and viewpoints that shape how a particular aspect of the world is interpreted and discussed. By extension, false paradigms are mental models of complex systems that are, in fact, inaccurate.

Pigouvian Tax

A Pigouvian Tax is a tax on any market activity that causes an indirect cost to the individual. The tax is intended to correct an undesirable or inefficient market outcome.

Reformulation

Changing the composition of a manufactured food, typically to reduce its sugar, salt and calorie content. This can be done voluntarily by food and drink manufacturers, or in response to a Government-imposed levy on unhealthy products, such as the Sugary Drinks Industry Levy.

Regenerative farming

An approach to agricultural production that is characterised by using agroecological principles to promote conservation and rehabilitation, for example through topsoil regeneration, increase biodiversity and support biosequestration.

Rewilding

A form of ecological restoration, where humans' impact is deliberately reduced through efforts to return an area to its natural state, for example by re-introducing native species to increase biodiversity and create a self-sustaining ecosystem.

Satiety signals

Signals originating from the digestive system during eating, and relayed to the brain, which give a sensation of being full and suppress hunger. They are important to prevent overeating through excessive portion size or unhealthy snacking between meals.

School Food Plan

The School Food Plan was published by the Department for Education in 2013. It was written by Henry Dimbleby and John Vincent and pertains to improving the diets of schoolchildren in England.

Scientific Advisory Committee on Nutrition

The SACN advises Public Health England (PHE) and other UK Government organisations on nutrition and related health matters.

Social prescribing

Also known as "community referral", social prescribing involves non-clinical staff, usually link workers, working closely and holistically with individuals to support and improve their wellbeing by providing devoted time, emotional support, and by helping them access services and entitlements.

Soft Drinks Industry Levy

Also known as the "soft drinks tax", the Soft Drinks Industry Levy (SDIL) is sometimes referred to colloquially as the "sugar tax". It is a levy paid by manufacturers of certain types of soft drink on the basis of their sugar content. Since its introduction in 2018, many soft drinks have been reformulated to reduce their sugar content, including some which are exempt from the levy, such as milk-based drinks.

Soilless farming

An umbrella term for techniques for cultivating plants without soil, using water (hydroponics) or air (aeroponics) as a growing medium, for example. The main benefit of these techniques over traditional technologies is that they require less land area and water.

System dynamics

The area of study concerned with forms of interconnected movement, i.e. when one motion triggers a response in another part of the system. This relatively simple framework can help understand a broad range of vastly different systems, and makes it possible to understand how and where best to intervene in a given system to achieve a different set of results.

Trade and Agriculture Commission

The TAC was set up in 2020 to advise the Department of International Trade on agricultural standards and to make sure UK agriculture remains competitive in any new free trade agreement signed after the country's departure from the UK. Initially devised as a temporary body, the Commission was placed on a statutory footing in the Agriculture Act of 2020.

Ultra-processed food

Although no standard definition exists, this category includes foods containing additives that are foreign to a domestic kitchen, such as artificial colours and flavours or stabilisers, and substances extracted from foods, such as fats, starches, added sugars, and hydrogenated fats. Typical examples include crisps, sweetened breakfast cereals, and packaged soups.

Zoonotic diseases

Diseases that are caused by germs that spread between animals and people. Examples of zoonotic diseases include anthrax (from sheep), rabies (from rodents and other mammals) and Creutzfeldt-Jakob disease (from cattle).

Acronyms

30x30	30% of land protected for nature by 2030
3-NOP	3-Nitrooxypropanol
AHDB	Agriculture and Horticulture Development Board
AI	Artificial intelligence
APWG	Agricultural Productivity Working Group
ARI	Areas of Research Interest
ASA	Advertising Standards Agency
ATP	Agricultural Transition Plan
BBB	British Business Bank
BBC	British Broadcasting Corporation
BECCS	Bioenergy with carbon capture and storage
BEIS	Department for Business, Energy and Industrial Strategy
BMI	Body mass index
BOGOF	Buy one get one free
BPS	Basic Payment Scheme
BST	Bovine somatotropin
C4L	Change4Life
CAP	Common Agricultural Policy
CCC	The Climate Change Committee
CCS	Crown Commercial Service
CEPA	Comprehensive Economic Partnership Agreement
CH4	Methane
CHAP	Crop health and protection
CIEL	Centre for Innovation and Excellence in Livestock
CMO	Chief Medical Officer
CO_2	Carbon dioxide
COP26	Conference of the Parties (26th Conference)
COPD	Chronic Obstructive Pulmonary disease
CPI	Centre for Process Innovation
CQC	Care Quality Commission
CSR	Comprehensive Spending Review
CVD	Cardiovascular Disease
DAERA	Department of Agriculture, Environment and Rural Affairs (in Northern Ireland)
DALYs	Disability-adjusted life years
DEFRA	Department for Environment, Food and Rural Affairs
DfE	Department for Education
DHSC	Department of Health and Social Care
DPS	Dynamic Procurement System
DWP	Department for Work and Pensions
EEF	Education Endowment Foundation
EFI	Evidence for Farming Initiative
EHO	Environmental Health Officers
EID	Emerging Infectious Diseases
ELMs	Environmental Land Management schemes
EPOS	Electronic Point of Sales data
EU	European Union
EYFS	Early Years Foundation Stages
F&V	Fruit and vegetables
FAIR	Findable, assessable, interoperable and reusable
FAO	Food and Agriculture Organisation
FCP	Forest Creation Partners
FFCC	Food, Farming and Countryside Commission
FRS	Family Resources Survey
FSA	Food Standards Agency
FSM	Free School Meals
FTA	Free Trade Agreement

GAIN	Global Alliance for Improved Nutrition
GBSF	Government Buying Standards for Food and Catering
GCSE	General Certificate of Secondary Education
GDP	Gross Domestic Product
GERD	Gastroesophageal reflux disease
GFMC	Global Farm Metric coalition
GHG	Greenhouse gases
GDP	Gross Domestic Product
GWP	Global warming potential
HAF	Holiday Activities and Food programme
HbA1c	Haemoglobin A1c
HFSS	High fat, sugar and/or salt
HMG	Her Majesty's Government
HMRC	Her Majesty's Revenue and Customs
HMT	Her Majesty's Treasury
HPO	High potential opportunity
IFS	Institute for Fiscal Studies
IGD	Institute of Grocery Distribution
IMD	Index of Multiple Deprivation
IMF	International Monetary Fund
IoT	Internet of Things
JFC	The Junk Food Cycle
LACA	Local Authority Caterers Association
LDL	Low-Density Lipoprotein
LFA	Less Favoured Area
LSHTM	London School of Hygiene and Tropical Medicine
MHCLG	Ministry for Housing, Communities and Local Government
MPA	Marine Protected Areas
$MtCO_2e$	Megatonnes (i.e. million tonnes) of carbon dioxide equivalent
N_2O	Nitrous oxide
NCC	Natural Capital Committee
NCDs	Non-Communicable Diseases
NDNS	National Diet and Nutrition Survey
NFU	National Farmers Union
NGO	Non-Governmental Organisation
NHS	National Health Service
NHSx	National Health Service Joint Organisation for Digital, Data and Technology
NICE	The National Institute for Health and Care Excellence
NIHR	National Institute for Health Research
NOVA	A classification in 4 groups to highlight the degree of processing of foods
NRPF	No Recourse to Public Funds
NSBP	National School Breakfast Programme
NUPENS	Centre for Epidemiological Research on Nutrition and Health (University of Sao Paulo)
OBR	Office for Budget Responsibility
OECD	Organisation for Economic Co-operation and Development
OEP	Office for Environmental Protection
OH	Hydroxyl radicals
OHP	Office for Health Promotion
ONS	Office for National Statistics
OOH	Out of Home
PCN	Primary Care Network
PHE	Public Health England
PLACE	Patient Led Assessments of the Care Environment
PO	Producer organisation
QALYs	Quality-adjusted life years
R&D	Research and Development
R&I	Research and Innovation
RD	Responsibility Deal
RSPB	Royal Society for the Protection of Birds
SACN	Scientific Advisory Committee of Nutrition
SCC	Somatic cell count
SDIL	Sugary Drinks Industry Levy

SFI	Sustainable Farming Incentive
SFVS	School Fruit and Vegetable Scheme
SLCP	Short-lived climate pollutants
SME	Small and Medium sized Enterprises
SSSIs	Sites of Special Scientific Interest
TAC	Trade and Agriculture Commission
TFP	Total Factor Productivity
TRL	Technology Readiness Levels
UKRI	UK Research and Innovation
UN	United Nations
USDA	US Department of Agriculture
VAT	Value Added Tax
WHO	World Health Organization
WRAP	Waste Resources Action Programme
WTO	World Trade Organisation
WWC	What Works Centre
WWF	World Wide Fund for Nature

Notes

Designed by 10 Associates – Big Ideas Beautifully Executed

With sustainability in mind, the printed version of this report will use Carbon Balanced Paper.
The Carbon Balancing programme, delivered by the World Land Trust, offsets emissions through the purchase and preservation of high conservation value forest.